D0616879

APOLLO AND THE NINE

A HISTORY OF THE ODE

by

CAROL MADDISON

The Johns Hopkins Press
BALTIMORE, MARYLAND

First published in the U.S.A. 1960
by the Johns Hopkins Press

Made and printed in Great Britain

ACKNOWLEDGEMENTS

I should like to thank the Canadian Federation of University Women, the Johns Hopkins University, and the American Council of Learned Societies for the fellowships which made the research for this book possible and the Humanities Research Council of Canada for their grant in aid of publication.

Contents

Preface

IN this study I have tried to illustrate the steps by which the ode came into being as a modern genre in Italy, France, and England. After a brief survey of the classical lyric poetry that inspired it, I have made a detailed examination of the neolatin ode, the immediate background of the vernacular ode of the Renaissance. Then I have shown how the Italian and French odes were created under humanist impulse, how they reacted with one another, and how the English ode began in imitation of the French, but soon returned to the basic classical and humanist sources to find its inspiration.

My aim has been to show how a new poetic genre was created out of classical and medieval materials in each of these three related literatures. Therefore, in each of the literatures I have followed the early experiments in the ode up to the point where important poets have appeared who have definitively established the new form. With a detailed analysis of their odes I have left the particular literature. Thus I have ended my study of the Italian ode with Chiabrera and his followers, the French with Malherbe, and the English with Cowley.

Despite the fact that the period covered was one of considerable critical activity and despite the fact that many of the humanists were both critics and poets, there was very little criticism either of the contemporary ode or of the ode in general. Du Bellay's programme for the Pléiade was the exception. Before du Bellay only Minturno had commented on what he was attempting to do in his two odes. After du Bellay Scaliger discussed the various poetic genres and sub-genres, including the ode, and the subject matter and metres that were appropriate to each. The chief importance of his work on the ode lies in the encouragement that it gave to the metric experimentation which was to come to the fore in seventeenth-century England. Otherwise critics contented themselves with repeating Horace's familiar description of the ancient lyric, that its subjects were the gods, heroes, victorious athletes, youthful passions and careless drinking. They frequently added that the ode was like the *canzone*, *chanson*, song, or even ballad. Valuable criticism of the ode does not appear before the end of the seventeenth century. Critics needed to have the genre well established before they could judge it.

No studies of the ode exist in French or Italian apart from Carducci's brilliant essay "Dello Svolgimento dell' Ode in Italia," although there are, of course, in these languages, studies of individual poets who wrote odes. We have, however, two roughly complementary books on the English ode, Robert Shafer's *The English Ode to 1660* (Princeton and London, 1918) and George N. Shuster's *The English Ode from Milton to Keats* (New York, 1940). Although in my English chapter I am going over the same period as Shafer (which was also surveyed by Shuster), I am examining the ode from a different point of view. Both Shafer and Shuster take the continental tradition into account. Shafer, in particular, discusses some of the Italian poets and Ronsard. However, neither of these two scholars considers the English ode in the whole international humanist context, as a typical Renaissance creation. Neither do they make such detailed analyses of the English ode of the first half of the seventeenth century as I have done in this work, an analysis which has revealed the intimate relationship between meaning and metre in the irregular ode as perfected by Cowley.

Chapter 1

THE ODE

THE ode has had a long and important history. At different periods it has satisfied the Renaissance taste for the antique, the baroque for the flamboyant, the Augustan for the classical, and the romantic and Victorian for the sublime. To fifteenth-century Italians it brought back the days of Latin triumph, of universal empire, and of the pride and dignity of rational man. To sixteenth-century French poets it was the form that could liberate them from the oppressive rules of the "great" *rhetoriqueurs* and the crippling conventions of medieval poetry. Du Bellay and Ronsard made the vernacular ode great. Times changed. The Reformation bred the Counter-Reform. The ode, however, by being moral and hortatory, was able to avoid the post-Tridentine ban on frivolous poetry and flourish almost alone as the only lyric tolerated for the best part of two hundred years. But the ode was not only improving, it was also inspired—witness its now irregular baroque form and tone of rapturous enthusiasm. By the middle of the seventeenth century, Longinus' sublime Pindar was almost its sole patron. Thus the ode offered the eighteenth century a classical escape from its mechanical universe and the metronome tick of the heroic couplet, from stoicism and rationalism, to the imagined emotional abandon and freedom of expression of a more primitive age. Much of this eighteenth-century inspiration was imposture. Nevertheless, by the middle of the century the ode, through its belief in its own originality, had found new themes for lyric poetry, nature, and psychology. Thus the ode approached the age of revolution and romanticism with the aura of liberty and enthusiasm about it, with the result that some of the greatest poetic works of the nineteenth century were written in the ode form.

The story of the ode begins with Renaissance humanism and its adoption of the learned Greek word, "ᾠδή," ode, from "ἀείδειν," to sing, itself not a technical term, to supersede the more familiar Latin word *carmen*. Like *carmen* from *canere* it meant no more than song, but in the use of the Renaissance humanists it meant a song in the antique manner as distinguished from one in the medieval tradition. It meant a lyric poem written in the newly found classical tradition, under the influence of Horace, later of Pindar, and finally of Anacreon. Thus the humanists invented a new poetic genre, a poem celebrating contemporary experience in the ancient taste. The ode, then, became a poem of greater dignity than the *canzone* or *chanson*. At the same time it was trimmer in shape. In place of the long, sprawling strophes of the medieval poets there were the brief, agile stanzas that the ancients had used which were found to be well adapted to the quickening pace of mind and emotion. The ode was concentrated and packed with allusion to all branches of human experience. It was the poem that glorified man, his experience, and his works. It was learned, formal, and public, rather than private or personal. With its constant allusion in metre and turn of phrase to the glorious past which was now set up as the classic or norm, the ode became a completely new type of poem.

The ode invented by the humanists was adopted by vernacular poets when the necessity for writing in the language of the people again made itself felt. The vernacular ode was naturally several removes farther from the classical models; there were always strong native traditions to contend with and quite different demands of rhythm and expression. Thus the ancient poems and their neolatin progeny served more as sources of inspiration, as pointers to a new way to be found, rather than as patterns to be copied by Renaissance Italian, French, and English poets. This accounts for the great vitality and variety of the vernacular ode. The new genre, with its new form, its new outlook on life, its new themes, and its new attitudes towards them, was able to liberate French and Italian poets from the weight of tradition and offer them fresh inspiration without enslaving their imaginations to exacting rules. The vernacular ode was, however, roughly the same sort of poem as the humanist ode, from which it learned much. It was basically a formal, public or social poem, usually occasional, celebrating something. It was of moderate length, stanzaic, eulogistic, and philosophic or learned, reflecting on life by means of highly wrought imagery, mythology, and aphorism. And it was, as a true child of the Renaissance, always conscious of its classical tradition.[1]

The history of the ode is one of the longest ones among literary genres. Of forms of any scope only the epic and the hymn, closely related to the ode, have longer histories, and it is interesting to note that the earliest odes, those of Pindar, are both close to the epic in tone and intimately connected with religion.

Since any understanding of the modern ode is dependent upon a knowledge of its classical antecedents, the following chapter will examine the works of Pindar, Anacreon, and Horace.

[1] The term "ode" was also used in the Renaissance to describe the choral songs of Greek drama, a usage akin to that of the Orthodox Church which called certain hymns of the liturgy odes. Thus odes were written in the neolatin and vernacular classicizing dramas of the sixteenth century. These dramatic odes fall outside the scope of this work and will not be discussed here.

Chapter 2

PINDAR, ANACREON, AND HORACE

THE ode, from the time that it took form as a genre, has always had something of the priest-prophet about it. When a poet has chosen to write an ode he has always been to some extent conscious that he is addressing the group, that he is saying something of group importance, and that he has insight into the meaning of individual events that form part of a universal continuum. To put it the other way round, poets have chosen to write in this genre only when they felt that they had public reflections to make. These characteristics of the ode, though they were first acquired through Horace as intermediary, are ultimately traceable to the influence of Pindar, himself both poet, priest, and prophet, and to the choral lyric of the Dorians, which, however much it might be the creation of an individual, was also, literally, the voice of the community. A certain amount of formality, then, a presumed audience, a sense of responsibility on the part of the poet, and imagery that relates the immediate subject to a larger context and adds fitting dignity and weight to the poem are all characteristics that are intrinsic to the ode, and all characteristics that were acquired from Pindar.

Pindar was born in 518 B.C. at the time of a Pythian festival in a small village near Thebes. His father belonged to an aristocratic priestly family, to the most conservative society of archaic Greece. Thus it is not surprising that his musically gifted son was trained in music and poetry, both of them closely related to religion, first at Thebes, then at Athens, and that he devoted his life to celebrating the gods and the national festivals of the Dorians. At the age of twenty Pindar wrote his first commissioned ode to celebrate the victory of the boy Hippokleas at Delphi. Tradition has it that he lived until he was eighty. The last ode which can be dated certainly is the fourth *Olympian*, which was written in 452 B.C.[1] During his long life Pindar travelled widely over the mainland of Greece, to the islands, to Sicily, and to North Africa as spreading fame brought him commissions and invitations.[2] Everywhere his reputation reached such heights that myths grew up about him even in his own lifetime. The ode that Pindar wrote for Diagoras of Rhodes so delighted the citizens of Lindos that they had it inscribed in gold on the wall of the temple of Athena. Parts of another ode of Pindar's were inscribed on a column in the sanctuary of Zeus Ammon in Libya. Part of his ode to Hagesias has been found stamped on a brick in Syracuse.[3] The honours rendered to Pindar at Delphi approached those of a demi-god.[4]

The poetry that Pindar had written was classified by the great Alexandrian critic, Aristophanes of Byzantium (third century B.C.), into ten categories, nine of which were religious. They were ἐπινίκια (songs for victories in the great games),

[1] Basil L. Gildersleeve, *Pindar. The Olympian and the Pythian Odes* (London, 1892), p. xiv.

[2] Gildersleeve, pp. xii–xiii.

[3] Gilbert Norwood, *Pindar*, Sather Classical Lectures (Berkeley, California, 1945), p. 16.

[4] D. M. Robinson, *Pindar, A Poet of Eternal Ideas.* The Johns Hopkins University Studies in Archeology, #21 (Baltimore, 1936), pp. 19–20, fn. 25, lists Pindar's priestly connections and privileges: (1) There was an iron chair for him at Delphi when he came to sing his songs to Apollo. (2) He could eat with the priests; the priest of Apollo, before he closed the temple gates, invited Pindar to dine with the god. (3) The Pythian priestess bade the Delphians give Pindar equal share of all first fruits they offered to Apollo. (4) Pindar was buried in a tomb in the hippodrome. (5) His ghost was yearly invited to dine with Apollo. (6) He was a priest of Apollo and of Pan. (7) Pindar dedicated a shrine to Cybele in Thebes, a statue to Zeus Ammon in Lybia, and shrines to Apollo and Hermes in the Theban market-place.

See also Norwood, p. 15.

ὕμνοι (hymns), παιᾶνες (songs of thanksgiving or petition, addressed chiefly to Apollo), ὑπορχήματα (choral ballets with orchestral accompaniment, written for festivals), προσόδια (processional songs with flute accompaniment), παρθένια (songs in honour of the gods or great men, written for choruses of maidens, with flute accompaniment), ἐγκώμια (laudatory poems), παροίνια (drinking songs), διθύραμβοι (hymns to Bacchus), and θρῆνοι (laments). Only the epinicia have survived, possibly because they were less closely allied with paganism than most of Pindar's other works.[1]

Religious games were very ancient in Greece. Their institution goes back to the days when the myths were being formed, long before the time of the Trojan War and documented history. So Pindar was by no means the first Greek poet to write epinicia. By his time there were certain well-established conventions for the genre. The body of the epinician must be a myth related to the games or to the hero or to his city. There must be a certain amount of moral wisdom in the ode and it must be suitable for public performance by a chorus of dancer-singers. Naturally the ode must also say something about the victor, the contest, and the place where the victory was won. Pindar's immediate predecessor, Stesichorus (*c.* 640–*c.* 555 B.C.) had invented a rhythmical pattern that seemed admirably fitted to the exigencies both of choral performance and of the lengthy lyric.[2] He had built his odes up out of large, symmetrical units, each complete in itself, and each consisting of two like stanzas and a third different but complementary stanza which rounded the triad off, a structure that is common to poetry that is intended to be danced and sung, as the Italian *canzone a ballo* bears witness. Pindar inherited this form from Stesichorus, as he inherited the myth from his other predecessors.

However, there is evidence that Pindar was a great innovator in the genre that he had chosen. Certainly in his odes he often refers to the novelty of his method. In Norwood's view this novelty consisted in the invention of the dramatic lyric. While Stesichorus had treated the story of Orestes in two books, in the epic style inherited from Homer, Pindar treated it in twenty-

[1] Gildersleeve, pp. xvi–xvii. Norwood, pp. 23 ff.

[2] Guiseppe Fraccaroli, *Le Odi di Pindaro* (Verona, 1894), pp. 24–6.

four lines "speaking to the understanding."[1] That is, Pindar recounted only the high points of a myth, the parts that he felt relevant to his immediate purpose, while Stesichorus faithfully rehearsed the whole. Thus Pindar's allusions were brief and often followed swiftly on one another. A suggestion was enough, his auditors knew the stories, e.g.,

. . . a garland upon Kyrene, mistress of chariots—
Kyrene that once from the windy folds of Pelion Lato's son
    Apollo, he of the flowing hair,
carried away, a wild maiden, in his car of gold, to make her
dwell as queen in a country rich in flocks, in grain most rich,
flowering and desired, third branch of the mighty earth.

And Aphrodite, she whose feet are as silver, welcomed
her brother of Delos, laying a light hand
on the chariot built by skill of gods.
Over the delight of their bed she cast a spell of winsome shyness,
joining the close union of the god lying with the daughter of
    powerful Hypseus,
king in that time of the haughty Lapiths and a hero in the second
    generation
from Ocean; whom on a time in the storied valleys of Pindos
a naiad nymph, Kreousa, brought to birth, after her joy with
    Peneus;

Earth's daughter. And Hypseus reared a child,
Kyrene of the white arms. . . .

Pythia 9, first triad

This swift style, brief allusiveness, and emotional rather than logical arrangement have made Pindar's odes difficult for later ages to understand. As Pindar truly said, "most men need interpreters."[2]

The myth, then, was the core of the Pindaric ode, though it need not be placed in the dead centre of the poem. It was not necessarily an ὄμφαλος, as Westphal's theory of the Terpandrian νόμος would demand. The myth adorned the ode, yet expressed its inner meaning as an extended simile might, and, like the epic simile, it contained a certain amount of irrelevant detail, for its

[1] Norwood, pp. 169–70. The quotation is from *Olympia* 2, strophe 5. I have throughout this chapter used Richmond Lattimore's translation of *The Odes of Pindar* (Chicago, 1947).

[2] *Olympia* 2, strophe 5.

own sake. The myth was the most splendid part of the poem, indeed, that for which the ode existed. It was through the myth that the Greeks and their gods were glorified and the present event incorporated into the great national tradition. The myth was either externally or internally motivated. It either told something about the foundation of the games or about the hero's family or city, or it recalled a story that contained an analogy in it for the hero. In either case the myth assimilated the hero to the demi-gods, it idealized the present and transfigured the real, it made the temporal event timeless.

Apart from its myth the Pindaric ode was characterized by passages of gnomic wisdom and by what may seem strange at first, considering its public performance and semi-sacred character, by references to the poet's private feelings, to his inspiration, his artistic intent, his poetic rivals, and the jealousy he rouses. These personal references are not so strange, however, if we recollect the particular function of the epinician, which was to celebrate the glorious achievements of the Greek race recalled through this latest example of prowess, beauty, and divine grace. The poet, like the hero, was part of the glory of Greece. It was he who preserved the traditions, who gave life to those who otherwise would die. He, too, was god-inspired and as much a part of the great deed as the victorious athlete. Therefore it is not inappropriate that he should comment on his inspiration and how it is working, that he should celebrate his triumph too.

The ode regularly has a brilliant opening, often an image, or a piece of gnomic wisdom, sometimes a prayer or an invocation. This brilliant opening formed part of Pindar's aesthetic theory. "The forehead of every work begun must shine from afar."[1] The showman must catch his audience's attention. The following are a sampling of Pindar's openings:

Beloved brightness, loveliest of the cities of mortals,
house of Persephone, you who keep by the banks of Akragas
where the sheep wander, the templed hill. . . .

Pythia 12, strophe 1

Best of all things is water; but gold, like a gleaming fire
by night, outshines all pride of wealth beside.

[1] *Olympia* 6, strophe 1.

But, my heart, would you chant the glory of games,
look never beyond the sun
by day for any star shining brighter through the deserted air,
nor any contest than Olympia greater to sing.

Olympia 1, strophe 1

Mightiest driver of the weariless speed in the lightning's feet,
Zeus. . . .

Olympia 4, strophe 1

You who have your dwelling
in the place of splendid horses, founded beside the waters of
Kephisos:
O queens of song and queens of shining
Orchomenos: Graces: guardians of the primeval Minyai,
hear!

Olympia 14, strophe 1

Golden lyre, held of Apollo in common possession
with the violet-haired Muses: the dance steps, leaders of festival,
heed you;
the singers obey your measures
when, shaken with music, you cast the beat to lead choirs of
dancers.
You have power to quench the speared thunderbolt
of flowing fire. Zeus' eagle sleeps on his staff, folding
his quick wings both ways to quiet,

lord of birds; you shed a mist on his hooked head,
dark and gentle closure of eyes; dreaming, he ripples
his lithe back, bound in spell
of your waves. Violent Ares even, leaving aside the stern pride
of spears, makes gentle his heart in sleep.

Pythia 1, strophe 1—antistrophe 1

Immediately after the opening comes brief mention of the ode's occasion, e.g.,

. . Then take the Dorian lyre from its peg,
if any glory of Pisa or Pherenikos
slide with delight beneath your heart,
when by Alpheus waters he sped
his bulk, with the lash laid never on,
and mixed in the arms of victory his lord,

king of Syracuse, delighting in horses. . . .

Olympia 1, antistrophe 1—epode 1

> For the sake of a beloved city and these its citizens
> I embrace, in supplication, the hallowed knees of Aiakos, bearing
> this Lydian veil embroidered with clashing song,
> a thing to glorify Deinias for his two-length race at Nemea, and
> for Magas his father.
>
> *Nemea* 8, epode 1

The myth follows, often interspersed with brief, pithy reflections or comments on the poet's technique. Occasionally the poem ends with the myth. More often the myth is followed by praise of the victor, which brings us back to the beginning of the ode. The conclusion, then, is often a passage of philosophical reflection, sometimes of a general nature, sometimes admonishing or praying for the hero, sometimes referring to the poet's art.

It has been remarked that the Pindaric ode has a magnificent beginning and a flat conclusion, in fact that it has no conclusion at all, but just ends.[1] This is not true. One must imagine the occasion of the ode, on the day of the hero's return to his native city, after the triumphal procession of his whole family to the temple, after the thanksgiving and the burnt offering, at the joyous banquet that follows.[2] It is fitting that the ode, to suit the joyous occasion, should have the most magnificent opening that the poet can devise for it, that it should glorify the hero and relate him by myth to those apotheosized athletes, Pelops and Herakles, Castor and Pollux. Yet, *μηδὲν ἄγαν*. The victor must also be warned against the deadly sin of the Greeks, *ὕβρις*, pride. He must be reminded that he is a man with a man's imperfections and limitations, that he must not assume too much or the gods will destroy him, that he must guide his conduct by universally valid principles. Therefore the ode must conclude on a warning note, in a more sober mood. This is not to suggest that the conclusions of Pindar's odes were very profound or that Pindar was a great moralist. His moral code was one of a class, narrow and aristocratic. His precepts were familiar ones, but worded with the wonderful economy of phrase of the gnomic poets of his age:

[1] Norwood, pp. 78–9.

[2] Though there is some doubt as to exactly when the epinician was sung, Croiset, *La Poésie de Pindare* (Paris, 1880), pp. 108 ff., believes that it was at the banquet.

Best by nature is best; but many have striven before now
to win by talents acquired
through art the glory.
But the thing unblessed by God is none
the worse for silence, always. There are ways

that surpass others.
But no one discipline sustains
us all. And skills are steep things
to win. As you bring the games' prize,
be bold to cry aloud
this man that is blessed by nature,
strong of hand, nimble, with eyes of valor,
who at your feast, Aias, son of Oileus, has wreathed your altar in
victory.

Olympia 9, epode 4

. . . In brief space mortals'
delight is exalted, and thus again it drops to the ground,
shaken by a backward doom.

We are things of a day. What are we? What are we not? The
shadow of a dream
is man, no more. But when the brightness comes, and God gives it,
there is a shining of light on men, and their life is sweet.
Aigina, dear mother, bring this city to haven
in free guise, by Zeus' aid and strong Achilles;
Peleus and goodly Telamon aiding, and with Achilles.

Pythia 8, antistrophe 5—epode 5

The chorus gave such concluding passages additional emotional force and the semi-religious occasion made these admonitions more powerfully felt, so that the ode ended on the right note of reverence and reflection.

Theories of the principle of unity of Pindar's poems need not concern us here. Dissen's abstract idea, Boeckh's character of the hero, Hermann's poetic idea, Westphal's Terpandrian *νόμος*, Mezger's recurrent word, down to Norwood's symbol, are all theories which, when applied rigorously and universally, produce absurdities, and which, finally, are no more convincing than Erasmus Schmidt's neat rhetorical analyses which are more relevant to our period.[1] Schmidt divided the odes into

[1] *ΠΙΝΔΑΡΟΥ ΠΕΡΙΟΔΟΣ*, ed. E. Schmidt (n.p., 1616).

such parts as *exordium*, *propositio*, *digressio*, and *epilogus*, subdivided these parts, and found that the odes were constructed according to impeccable logic. The principle of order in Pindar appears to be in the eye of the beholder.

The complex controversy over metres maintained by a series of ingenious German scholars is also irrelevant to this study. Although it is important for the modern reader of Pindar to be able to read his poems in accordance with principles that he recognizes as musical[1]—hence J. H. H. Schmidt's cyclic dactyls, irrational longs, anacruses, etc.—nevertheless, for the purposes of this book only the Byzantine versification adapted in Renaissance texts is of importance. The author of the Byzantine text of Pindar believed that Pindar's strophes were made up of verses for the most part short. Therefore, in all the Renaissance editions, Pindar's strophes appear long and, for the most part, thin, although there are, occasionally, extraordinarily long verses. It is notable that Pindar's early imitators, Lampridio, Alamanni, and Ronsard, used only short verses in their Pindarics, *settenarî* in the case of Alamanni and *heptasyllables* or *octosyllables* in the case of Ronsard. Lampridio used a variety of short Latin lines. Since neither of the vernacular poets varied the length of line within the strophe as Pindar did, the effect in the modern languages of this imitation of Pindar is, at times, monotonous. None of Pindar's imitators in the modern languages sought to imitate his verse exactly, quantitatively, as they did Horace's. Therefore an adequate impression of Pindar's prosody for our purposes may be obtained from the quotation of a couple of his stanzas as they appeared in a Renaissance edition[2]:

''Αριστον μὲν ὕδωρ, ὁ δὲ
χρυσὸς, αἰθόμενον πῦρ
ἅ τε διαπρέπει νυ—
κτὶ, μεγάνορος ἔξοχα πλούτου·

[1] For this reason Norwood, despite his reservations, adopts Schmidt's scansion rather than Schroeder's. Here it is interesting to note Cicero's remark quoted by Croiset, p. 450, that the Pindaric ode separated from the music had no appreciable rhythm.

[2] *ΠΙΝΔΑΡΟΥ ΟΛΥΜΠΙΑ. ΠΥΘΙΑ. ΝΕΜΕΑ. ΙΣΘΜΙΑ*, ed. Zacharias Callierges (Romae, 1515). This was the first edition of Pindar to print the scholia. Note that here the strophe, antistrophe, and epode were clearly marked.

εἰ δε ἄεθλα γαρύεν
ἔλδεαι, θίλον ἦτορ,
μηκέθ' ἁλίου σκόπει
ἄλλο θαλπνότερον
ἐν ἁμέρᾳ θαεννὸν ἄστρον
ἐρήμας δι' αἰθέρος.
μήδ' ὀλυμπίας ἀγῶνα
θέρτερον αὐδάσομεν.
ὅθεν ὁ πολύθατος
ὕμνος ἀμθιβάλλεται
σοθῶν μητίεσσι, κελαδεῖν
κρόνου παῖδ' ἐς ἀφνεὰν ἱκομένους
μάκαιραν ἱέρωνος ἑστίαν—

Olympia 1, strophe 1

(this pattern was repeated, then the triad was completed by a different type of stanza)

συρακόσιον ἱπποχάρμαν
βασιλῆα· λάμπει
δέ οἱ κλέος παρ' οὐράνορι λυδοῦ
πέλοπος ἀποικίᾳ· τοῦ, μεγασθενὴς
ἐράσσατο γαιάοχος ποσειδῶν.
ἐπέι νιν καθαροῦ λέβητος ἔξελεν
κλωθώ. ἐλέφαντι φαίδιμον
ὦμον κεκαδμένον.
ἦ θαύματα πολλά·
καὶ που τι κὰι βροτῶν φρένα
ὑπὲρ τὸν ἀληθῆ λόγον,
δεδαιδαλμένοι ψεύδεσι ποικίλοις
ἐξαπατῶντι μῦθοι.

Olympia 1, epode 1

An analysis of a Pindaric ode may help to clarify the preceding remarks. Pindar's third *Olympian* was written for Theron, tyrant of Agrigentum, to celebrate his victory in the four-horse chariot race at Olympia in 476 B.C. It was composed to be sung at the Theoxenia, a banquet instituted by Castor and Pollux in commemoration of a feast at which they had entertained all the gods.[1] Thus "To the sons of Tyndareus," "τυνδαρίδαις," is the opening word of the poem, forming part of the poet's statement of his subject and his aims. The Tyndaridai appear again in the concluding third triad of the ode, in the third strophe as patrons, with Herakles, of the Olympic games and in the third antistrophe as the overseers of the games appointed

[1] See Gildersleeve's general notes on this ode and on the second *Olympian*, pp. 155–6 and 140–3.

by Herakles, as demi-gods particularly honoured by Theron's family, and as the source of their glory. It should be noted here that there was an altar to Castor and Pollux at the starting point of the hippodrome.[1] Thus Castor and Pollux, the presiding divinities of the present feast, are closely linked with the victorious Theron and with Herakles, the subject of the myth, like them a son of Zeus, a great athlete, and a patron of the Olympic games.

The introduction to the myth is simple. Theron is crowned with olive, the olive that Herakles first brought to Olympia from the land of the Hyperboreans. The myth, then, appears to be externally motivated, celebrating one aspect of the games at which Theron triumphed. But, in the moralizing in the final epode, we find that Theron has reached his pillars of Herakles. That is, the myth of Herakles is also, in some sense, internally motivated.[2] There are two unifying mythological threads in this ode, then, Castor and Pollux, for whose feast the ode was written, whom Theron and his family specially reverence, and who have rewarded him with his victory, and Herakles, the benefactor of Olympia, a man whose example Theron would do well to follow.

The ode opens with a brief prayer containing an evocative image, "to Helen of the beautiful hair," and ends with a reflective passage full of commonplaces.[3] The first strophe states the occasion of the ode, naming the victor, the contest, and the place. The first antistrophe discusses the poet's art and inspiration. Pindar's third *Olympian*, then, contains all the typical ingredients of the epinician.

The poet's method of arranging his materials is typical, too. Themes are not treated consecutively, but various ideas are interwoven, so that each thread runs throughout, but only

[1] Gildersleeve, p. 160, note to line 38.

[2] The terms externally and internally motivated are borrowed from Gildersleeve, pp. xlv–xlvi.

[3] L. Dissen, commentary on Pindar's odes, *Pindari Carmina*, ed. A. Boeckh, II (Gothae et Erefordiae, 1830), 49, notes that the proverbs about gold and water that Pindar also used in the first *Olympian* are from Thales. Dissen suggests that these proverbs about gold and water were probably recalled by the reference to Theron's celebration of the Theoxenia in the immediately preceding lines. Golden vessels and water were used for the rites.

occasionally appears on the surface. The four chief threads are the Tyndaridai, Theron, the poet, and Herakles, in order of occurrence. The Herakles thread, as the one which makes the myth, is the thickest and branches out in many directions. Thus in the first epode Herakles appears as the man who first commanded that the Olympian victor should be crowned with the olive which he brought back to Olympia from the Danube. In the second strophe we are told that he gained possession of the olive not by violence (as was his usual method) but by words. He wanted the olive to make a grove sacred to Zeus, a shady place for men, and a crown for their accomplishment. Previously, at the time when Zeus' altars were hallowed at the mid-month, the full moon had shone down on a bare and empty place. Here (second antistrophe), by Alpheus' river, Herakles had established the Olympic games, but the garden was bare of trees and must suffer from the fierce heat of the sun. So Herakles decided to go to the Danube where (second epode) he had been received by Artemis when he was hunting the hind with the golden horns, one of the twelve labours imposed by Eurystheus at the command of Zeus. There (third strophe), in the land of the Hyperboreans, he had seen the olive which he now wanted to plant at Olympia, whose festival he visits with Castor and Pollux, whom (third antistrophe) he left as presiding geniuses of the games. The myth, in its arrangement, preserves the original order of thought. Ideas are set down as they occurred to the poet's mind, not as logical principles of narration would rearrange them. This method of recounting the myth is both natural and intelligible. But it is different from that to which we had been accustomed up until the time of James Joyce.

For the modern reader this myth presents some problems, not in so far as it is externally motivated; for from that point of view its introduction is natural and obvious. But the reference in the last epode to Theron at his pillars of Herakles suggests that the myth is also internally motivated, that Theron should learn from Herakles. Even Herakles, the greatest hero of all, the man who stormed hell itself, recognized that there were limits to what he could do and he set up his pillars to make the boundaries of man's domain. Pindar says plainly that Theron has now gone as far as he can; he has achieved all that it is possible to achieve. To attempt anything further would be folly. We think of Theron's history. He has averted war with Syracuse, allied himself again by marriage with its ruling house, crushed rebellion, and exterminated his enemies. At this moment of triumph has come the news of the Olympic victory.[1] Theron must be warned against *ὕβρις*. He is in that very dangerous position, on the narrow pinnacle of worldly success.

But, were the pillars of Herakles introduced only because they are the most dramatic boundary marks, or were they brought in as a subtle suggestion to Theron that he learn a lesson from the story of Herakles, particularly the part alluded to in this ode? We notice first of all that Herakles got what he wanted in the instances cited here by persuasion, not by violence. And he got two things by persuasion, the olive, symbol of peace, which he used to adorn the cultural life of his people and to add to their comfort and well-being, and the hind with the golden horns which was sacred to Artemis. When Herakles had caught the hind after a year-long pursuit Artemis appeared to him and told him that it was sacred to her, but, when Herakles explained that he must present the hind to Eurystheus to fulfil the command of Zeus, Artemis yielded it up to him.

Is Theron to read a lesson in these two portions of the Herakles myth? Does he find himself flattered in the story of Herakles' getting the olive from the Hyperboreans? Is this an oblique reference to Theron's obtaining peace with Syracuse by negotiation when the two armies were already drawn up facing each other?[1] Does he then find this policy of *λόγῳ*, "reason," so strongly emphasized by its position as the first word of the second and central triad, recommended to him again in the account of the hunting of the hind with the golden horns? When Herakles the hunter found that the animal he had cornered belonged to someone else he did not try to take it by violence, but by persuasion. Is Pindar suggesting that Theron imitate Herakles in this sort of behaviour instead of decimating his opponents to get what he wants as he did in the case of Himera?[1] As Gilbert Norwood has pointed out in his commentary on the second *Olympian*, Theron and "hunter"

[1] See Gildersleeve's note on Theron, pp. 140–1.

were spelt exactly the same way and the difference in accent could not have made much difference in the pronunciation (θήρων and θηρῶν).[1] Theron's coin, too, which is reproduced in both Gildersleeve and Norwood shows an eagle with a hare in its talons.[2] Moreover the end of the second Olympian shows that Theron still had problems to face and opponents to reconcile.

So much for the Herakles thread and the myth. The interweaving of the Tyndaridai has been noted already. Theron himself appears by name in the first strophe, as the occasion for the ode, and in the final antistrophe and epode as the man who has gained glory, but who must avoid excess. Theron, the man for whom the ode was written, appears in the beginning and the end. The poet too appears in the beginning and the end, as the man helped by the Muse to find the Dorian dancing rhythm for the celebration, as the man god-inspired to mingle the lyre, the flutes, and the words (antistrophe 1) in a song for Theron, and as the man whom the victory makes speak (epode 1 and antistrophe 3—i.e., the reference to the poet in the third antistrophe picks up where the previous references to the poet had ended).[3] Finally, the poet appears again, somewhat mysteriously, in the last verse of the ode—he will not be guilty of ὕβρις. Gildersleeve quotes Dissen's comment which seems reasonable, "Suavius dicit de se quae Theroni dicere vult."[4]

The mechanism of construction is typical, too. The grammatical period usually does not end with the strophe, but there is a slight overlapping on the one side or the other, a kind of syntactical enjambement,[5] which makes a smooth transition between parts of the ode otherwise sharply separated by the changes in the music and the dance. Thus, a single word is carried over from the first strophe to the first antistrophe; a new subject begins at the end of the penultimate verse of the

[1] Norwood, pp. 130–1. Norwood, p. 252, note 44, points out that Verrall also believes that Theron was identified with the hunter.

[2] Norwood, plate facing p. 130. Gildersleeve, p. 154.

[3] See Norwood's chapter on Pindar as a literary critic, especially pp. 165–6.

[4] Gildersleeve, p. 161. The note appears in Dissen's volume of commentaries on Boeckh's edition of Pindar cited above, II, 49.

[5] This was noted by Croiset, pp. 356–7, and by J. B. Bury, *The Nemean Odes of Pindar* (London, 1890), pp. xxxvii–viii.

first antistrophe and is carried on into the first epode by a relative pronoun: a new subject begins in the last verse of the second antistrophe; a relative makes a link between the second epode and the third strophe; the third antistrophe begins with a relative; and the subject of the third antistrophe runs over one verse into the third and final epode. There are, however, stops at the end of each of the triads, although one subject spans the three triads. That is, the myth occupies the central part of the ode, beginning in the first epode and concluding in the third antistrophe, but at the end of each triad we also come to a pause in the development of the mythological material. This type of construction makes the ode a smooth-flowing whole.

One further remark about structure must be made. It has been noted above that the grammatical and prosodic periods do not coincide. However, as Fraccaroli has noted,[1] the prosodic and plastic periods do tend to coincide, so that, if a new subject begins in the last verse of a strophe, the imagery of that last verse will be harmonious with the imagery of the strophe in which it occurs, rather than with the imagery of the further treatment of the subject in the following antistrophe. For example, the single word ἀγλαόκωμον, "of splendid celebration," which is carried over from the first strophe to the first antistrophe contains the kernel of the imagery of the first antistrophe, splendour and revelry.

It remains to say something about Pindar's imagery. As will have been noted already, Pindar is the most visual and concrete of poets. Nothing is left to the vague, abstract word. Everything is clearly pictured. And Pindar's prevalent anthropomorphism carries this tendency extraordinarily far. Thus, in a statement of aesthetic theory, Pindar writes, "The forehead (πρόσωπον) of every work begun must shine from afar,"[2] in an historical reference he says, "when you stood her upon an upright ankle,"[3] referring to Thebes' help of Sparta. Norwood has noted that many of Pindar's most striking effects are secured by a blend of austerity and loveliness, by a background that is strongly differentiated from the foreground, usually

[1] Quoted by Norwood, p. 78. See also Fraccaroli, pp. 124–5.

[2] *Olympia* 6, strophe 1.

[3] *Isthmia* 1, lines 12 ff., noted by Norwood, p. 106.

brilliantly lit, e.g., "peace after wintry rain" (*Pythia* 5, line 10), "a radiant star in empty Heaven" (the sun, *Olympia* 1, line 6), "a far-shining star upon the dark-blue earth" (Delos, frag. 78), "malice requiting fair deeds" (*Pythia* 7, line 15), "In quest of the fleeting delight I walk softly into old age and the period of doom" (*Isthmia* 7, lines 45–7), "and Ino, the white goddess, keeper of the chambered sea" (*Pythia* 11, lines 2–3), "these also must drag their bright hair in the dust" (*Nemea* 1, line 77).[1]

Pindar's imagery, though brilliant, was as severely limited as his themes. Pindar was interested only in the heroic, aristocratic, and divine, in glory, happiness, and prosperity, in physical prowess, and in the dignity and decorum that befit both noble men and the gods.[2] So he drew his imagery almost solely from what was bright and shining and sharply defined. His images are those of form and light and sound; they are large and panoramic, not intimate and sensuous. Thus there are almost no colours in his poetry but gold, silver, bronze, white, and purple, but everywhere there is glowing light.

Pindar's legacy to posterity was a high seriousness in the lyric, the choice of themes of general importance and the treatment of them with confidence, the address of an audience, the illustration of the theme with myth and aphorism, and the conventional appearance of the poet in the ode as a personage of great importance with immortality in his gift.

However, all Greek lyric poetry was not written for the temple or the πόλις. In addition to the patriotic, religious poetry of the Dorians there were the soft enchantments of the Ionians. From the islands came the sirens' song and that Teian old man, Anacreon. No definition of the ode, however Procrustean, can be made to include both the choral poetry of Pindar and Anacreon's songs for a single voice; they are as different as the lyric can be. It can, however, include the modern Anacreontic; for, no matter how simple and song-like some of the ancient Greek poems may have been, modern poems written in imitation of them are, from the very fact that

[1] The idea is Norwood's, pp. 92–3, as are the first four examples. The other examples are mine.

[2] Pindar does not hesitate to reject or rewrite myths whose morality he abhors, see, e.g., *Olympia* 1, *Nemea* 5.

they are imitations, ceremonious and learned, and not the impulsive expression of individual emotion but the traditional expression of universal human experience. Thus, since the originals that they were imitating were never personal or intimate poems, however simple at times, the Anacreontic just falls inside our definition of the ode—which, we must remember, is a modern not ancient genre—and forms of it a legitimate if minor branch. The prototypes of the Anacreontics, then, the poems of Anacreon and of his early followers, must be subjected to a cursory examination.

The sixty-odd poems found in the middle of the sixteenth century under the name of Anacreon were probably written over a period of about one thousand years from somewhere around 500 B.C. to about A.D. 500. They are by various hands, in various styles, and of various sorts, but they are all pervaded by the same spirit, the spirit of the soft, easy Ionian, Anacreon. In the days of Ionian science, mathematics, materialism, and mutability, Anacreon knew with Heracleitus that *πάντα ῥεῖ*. Youth passes, beauty fades, and who can be sure of tomorrow? Then let us enjoy today:

> *τὸ σήμερον μέλει μοι*
> *τὸ δ' αὔριον τίς οἶδεν;*[1]
>
> Today is my concern
> Who knows about tomorrow?
>
> *ἱλαροὶ πίωμεν οἶνον*
> *ἀναμέλψομεν δὲ βάκχον*[2]
>
> Let us be merry and drink wine
> And strike up a song about Bacchus.

Bacchus can free us from cares:

> *Ὅταν πίνω τὸν οἶνον*
> *εὕδουσιν αἱ μέριμναι.*[3]
>
> When I drink wine
> My cares are put to sleep.

[1] Teubner Anacreon, ed. C. Preisendanz (Leipzig, 1912), p. 6. Henceforth all references to Anacreon will be to this edition.
[2] P. 31. [3] P. 36.

In a series of songs that remind us of the *Carmina Burana*—there is even a student's song:

> Τί με τοὺς νόμους διδάσκεις
> καὶ ῥητόρων ἀνάγκας;
> Τί δέ μοι λόγων τοσούτων
> τῶν μηδὲν ὠφελούντων;
> μᾶλλον δίδασκε πίνειν
> ἁπαλὸν πῶμα Λυαίου,
> μᾶλλον δίδασκε παίζειν
> μετὰ χρυσῆς Ἀφροδίτης.[1]

> Why do you teach me the laws
> And the necessities of the rhetoricians?
> Why so many reasons
> That are of no use?
> You would better teach me to drink
> The soft drink of the Releaser,
> You would better teach me to sport
> With golden Aphrodite.

Anacreon urges singing and dancing, wine, women, and roses. He is himself old—that is all the more reason to be gay.[2] Spring is described and, as in the medieval lyric, the *reverdie* is a call to love.[3]

In the post-mythological, semi-heroic age of archaic Greece, the Persian War period described by Herodotus, Anacreon, nevertheless, finds it impossible to write of noble deeds:

> Θέλω λέγειν Ἀτρείδας
> θέλω δὲ Κάδμον ᾄδειν
> ὁ βάρβιτος δὲ χορδαῖς
> Ἔρωτα μοῦνον ἠχεῖ.[4]

> I want to tell of the sons of Atreus
> I want to sing of Cadmus
> But my lyre on its strings
> Echoes only Love.

Even the loves of the gods are too lofty a theme for his

[1] P. 41.

[2] See the Teubner text pp. 2; 5–6; 6–7; 19; 25–6; 31–2; 32–3; 33–4; 34–5; 35–6; 36; 37–8; 38; 38–9; 39–40; 40–1; 42; 49–50.

[3] P. 33.

[4] P. 20. Stephanus chose this for his introductory poem in the *editio princeps* of Anacreon of 1554, although it was not the first poem in the manuscript.

lyre.[1] He can only write of his mistresses who are as numerous as the leaves of the trees and the waves of the sea.[2]

The aforementioned bacchics appear to be directly inspired by Anacreon, but other poems in this collection are clearly of Alexandrian inspiration. These are the *ἐκφρασεῖς*: elaborate descriptions of works of art, chased chalices, and drinking bowls, images of Eros, and paintings of Aphrodite, the boy Bathyllos, the poet's black-haired mistress, or the prosperous cities of men[3]; and the idylls: accounts of imagined, often allegorical adventures of Eros, and pretty elaborations of conceits about the love god.[4] Both these types of poems are highly artificial and elaborate and possess a kind of mannered charm, the source of their considerable popularity in the Renaissance.

Such were "Anacreon's" poems, the age-old drinking and love songs on the one hand, and the late Greek ecphrases and idylls on the other.

As to form, the Anacreontic is generally brief—although poems of the first general category are shorter than those of the second. It is written in short lines which are metrically simple, the iambic dimeter being a special favourite. It is sometimes strophic, and may have a refrain. It is monodic, not choral as was the Pindaric ode.

Pindar and Anacreon along with Sappho and Alcaeus, the two latter now largely lost, formed the Greek lyric which the Romans knew. It was from these sources that Horace drew his inspiration.

Horace's own claim to fame in the closing poem of the three books of odes which he published in 23 B.C. is that "princeps Aeolium carmen ad Italos deduxisse modos,"[5] that he "first adapted Aeolian song to Italian measures," and certainly his importance as the inventor of many new Latin metrical forms cannot be overrated. From the Aeolian poets, Sappho and Alcaeus, Horace borrowed two stanzas which became the most

[1] Pp. 50–2.

[2] Pp. 10–12; 17; 19–20; 21; 22; 22–3; 24; 24–5; 30–1. In Anacreon's love poems there are all the conventional conceits, the fires of love, the armies from the eyes, etc. The only particular love poems are those to or about the boy Bathyllos, pp. 8; 12–13; 17–18.

[3] Pp. 2–3; 3–4; 4–5; 8–9; 13–15; 15–16; 46–7.

[4] Pp. 3–4; 9–10; 18; 21–2; 23; 25; 26–7; 29.

[5] *Carminum* III, 30, lines 13–14.

important in Latin literature, from Asclepiades (third century B.C.) he adapted five choriambic metres, while from various other Greek sources he formed another twelve. In the process of naturalizing these Greek verse forms Horace carried through tendencies that were apparent in Hellenistic prosody and in Catullus. He made asclepiads, glyconics, pherecrateans, and usually alcaic hendecasyllables begin with a spondee, and he made the fourth syllable of the sapphic and the fifth syllable of the alcaic hendecasyllabic almost invariably long. He also introduced regular caesuras into various types of lines. Thus Horace eliminated any suggestions of iambic, trochaic, or dactylic rhythms from his Aeolian verse. Through these innovations he created metres that were particularly suitable for Latin. The lengthening of the doubtful syllables gave weight and dignity, while the caesuras, emphasizing the regular blocks of words that they divided, produced a monumental effect.[1] The lyric forms that Horace created for Latin poetry were never surpassed.

But Horace was more than a masterful prosodist. A poem is not just a pattern of syllables. It is the ideas and insights that the rhythmic pattern is made to express that are important, that make for the survival of the form and confer immortality upon the poet. Here, too, Horace made a permanent contribution to literature. In adapting Pindar and Anacreon and the Greek lyric to the needs of Imperial Rome, Horace truly wrote "carmina non prius audita,"[2] "songs never before heard." Pindar's lofty tone, the "mythological" exemplum, and the mantle of the priest were now assumed to exhort a decadent people, or at least their children, to old-fashioned moral virtue:

"Odi profanum volgus et arceo;
Favete linguis." Carmina non prius
Audita Musarum sacerdos
Virginibus puerisque canto.[2]

"I loathe the uninitiate horde and ward them off.
Please to keep silence." Songs not previously
Heard, I, the Muses' priest,
Sing for youths and maidens.

[1] These remarks on Horace's metrical innovations are borrowed from L. P. Wilkinson, *Horace and His Lyric Poetry* (Cambridge, 1945), pp. 10–11.

[2] *Carminum* III, 1, stanza 1.

The Pindaric age of useless heroism, of careless valour was past. Now there was need for steadiness, responsibility, reverence, and self-control. In the disorders and chaos of modern times the poet lauds the austerity, *pietas*, and sober fortitude of the old Romans—and he speaks for the government. But Horace has his Anacreontic as well as his Pindaric side. Here too he makes his peculiarly Roman contribution. Although he praises, but with a more philosophic melancholy, the Anacreontic pleasures of the passing day, Horace never forgets what is rational and decorous; to "θέλω θέλω μανῆναι," "How I want to throw off all restraint," "Dulce est desipere," he adds "in loco,"[1] "under the proper circumstances." He changes the careless Anacreontic into a statement of temperate epicureanism; he is ever mindful of his Roman *gravitas* and the Delphic "μηδὲν ἄγαν." In the ethical preoccupation which permeates all of his poetry and which has created a new type of poem lies Horace's greatest contribution to the ode tradition.

Unlike the Pindaric and the Anacreontic, the Horatian ode was almost never written to be sung.[2] Thus it has neither the orchestral magnificence of the epinician nor the song-like simplicity of most of the Anacreontics, but it is dignified, harmonious, and sonorous. Although it is full of allusions to mythology, it is never heroic in spirit. The exultant "Nunc est bibendum, nunc pede libero" on the fall of Cleopatra (I, 37) and the Regulus ode (III, 5) are almost the only exceptions. Horace, with his unfailing judgment and good sense, steers clear of the tempestuous sea of heroic action which is unsuited to his talent. Despite the enticements of Augustus and his generals, he usually limits himself to the ebb and flow of ordinary life. As the middle-aged moralist he philosophizes, not very profoundly, on the brevity of youth and beauty, on the uncertainty of life and the inevitability of death, on the vanity of human wishes and the futility of ambition, and on the unreasonableness of vice. He advocates a simplicity of life, rural retirement, an Epicurean ἀταραξία, and a more popular

[1] *Carminum* IV, 12, line 28. Cf. "Non ego sanius / Bacchabor Edonis: recepto / Dulce mihi furere est amico," *Carminum* II, 7, lines 26–8.

[2] The *Carmen Saeculare* is the only one known to have been sung, though "Mercuri, facunde nepos Atlantis," I, 10, and "Dianam tenerae dicite virgines," I, 21, as hymns, may have been sung.

Epicurean enjoyment of the pleasures of the flesh "dum res et aetas et sororum / Fila trium patiuntur atra," "while one's circumstances and age and the black threads of the three sisters permit." Throughout he sounds the strain of moderation, prudence, and sweet reasonableness. And his didacticism is made palatable by a ranging variety of illustration, by a good sense of situation,[1] by a sophisticated sense of humour,[2] by his own ironical self-revelation,[3] and by a "curiosa felicitas" of style which enables him to find the seemingly inevitable expression for his ideas. Horace has an unrivalled gift for the commonplace, for what has oft been thought but ne'er so well expressed.

Being moral and preaching the morality of the sane and civilized pagan, the Horatian ode is, naturally enough, largely concerned with other people. We are always aware of a social background. The poet is always a member of society addressing his fellow men. Almost every poem is directed to some particular person whom the poet mentions by name,[4] and very many of the poems refer to facts of universal social experience, to invitations and visits,[5] to separations, voyages,[6] and homecomings,[7] to infatuations[8] and bereavements.[9] They discuss other subjects of everyday interest, what one would talk about with one's friends: people and what they are doing,[10] the little accidents that make life individual,[11] the varied pursuits of man both for business and pleasure,[12] the changing seasons and their characteristic activities.[13] They reflect on Fate[14] and

[1] Wilkinson, p. 133.

[2] Wilkinson, pp. 148–9 and Tenney Frank, *Catullus and Horace* (New York, 1928), pp. 221–2, 230–1.

[3] Wilkinson, p. 175.

[4] For this convention see Tenney Frank, pp. 205–7 and 213.

[5] *Carm.* I, 17, 20; II, 7; III, 17, 19, 21, 29; IV, 11, 12.

[6] *Carm.* I, 3, 29; III, 27.

[7] *Carm.* I, 36; II, 7.

[8] *Carm.* I, 5, 8, 13, 19, 33; II, 4, 5, 8; III, 7, 9, 10, 11, 15, 20, 26; IV, 1, 10.

[9] *Carm.* I, 24; II, 9.

[10] *Carm.* I, 29; III, 7, 15, 20; IV, 13.

[11] *Carm.* I, 22; II, 13, 17; III, 8.

[12] *Carm.* I, 1, 8; II, 15, 18; III, 1, 25, 29; IV, 3.

[13] *Carm.* I, 4, 7; III, 17, 18.

[14] *Carm.* III, 1.

Fortune[1] without attempting any reconciliation between these two somewhat contradictory ideas; they speak of the various popular gods without any fervour of belief[2]—I am not convinced by "Paucus deorum cultor et infrequens"[3]—they express the popular reaction to various natural disasters,[4] the general alarm felt at repeated outbursts of civil commotion,[5] the anxiety at threats of frontier aggression,[6] and the joy at victory[7]; and, over and over again, they praise the policies of Augustus[8] and lend them their support with exhortations to the moral virtues of the antique Romans.[9] A small but important group of poems discusses the poet's calling.[10]

Most remarkable for such a social and moral poet is Horace's nature imagery. While he can describe nature very prettily in the conventional Greco-Roman mythological manner,

> Iam Cytherea choros ducit Venus imminente luna,
> Iunctaeque Nymphis Gratiae decentes
> Alterno terram quatiunt pedes, dum gravis Cyclopum
> Volcanus ardens visit officinas,[11]

> Now Venus, goddess of Cythera, leads the dancing beneath the hanging moon,
> And, hand in hand with the Nymphs, the lovely Graces
> Shake the earth with alternate foot, while fiery Vulcan
> Visits the heavy forges of the Cyclopes.

much of Horace's nature imagery is strikingly unconventional and reveals a patience and acuteness of observation and a degree of personal, particular sympathy that one does not find in his descriptions of urban life. He makes us experience the Italian countryside in its different seasons and moods. We see

[1] *Carm.* I, 34, 35; III, 29.
[2] *Carm.* I, 2, 3, 10, 12, 21, 30, 34; II, 19; III, 25.
[3] *Carm.* I, 34, line 1.
[4] *Carm.* I, 2.
[5] *Carm.* I, 14; II, 1.
[6] *Carm.* I, 26.
[7] *Carm.* I, 37; III, 5, 14; IV, 2, 4, 14.
[8] *Carm.* I, 2; IV, 5, 15.
[9] *Carm.* III, 1, 2, 3, 4, 5, 6, 24; IV, 9.
[10] *Carm.* II, 20; III, 4, 11, 30; IV, 3, 8, 9.
[11] *Carm.* I, 4, lines 5–8.

the thorn roughening in the breeze, the bramble stirred by the lizard, the fawn nervous and frightened:

Vitas hinnuleo me similis, Chloe
Quarenti pavidam montibus aviis
Matrem non sine vano
Aurarum et silvae metu.

Nam seu mobilibus vepris inhorruit
Ad ventos foliis, seu virides rubum
Dimovere lacertae
Et corde et genibus tremit.[1]

You flee from me, Chloe, like a fawn
Seeking her frightened mother on the trackless
Mountains, vainly fearing
The wind and the woods.

For when the moving leaves of the brier
Bristle in the breeze, or the bright green lizard
Darts the thorn aside,
Her heart and knees quiver.

We feel the force of the black wind on a moonless night[2]; we see the might of the storm: the yellow, swollen Tiber,[3] the leaves torn from the trees, the sea-weed strewn on the shore:

Cras foliis nemus
Multis et alga litus inutili
Demissa tempestas ab Euro
Sternet. . . . [4]

Tomorrow a storm
Sent down by the east wind will strew
The grove with leaves and the shore with
Useless sea-weed. . . .

[1] *Carm.* I, 23, lines 1–8.

[2] *Carm.* I, 25, lines 11–12. See also I, 5, lines 6–7, "aspera nigris aequora ventis."

[3] *Carm.* I, 2, lines 13–16 and III, 29, lines 34–41, where a real flood is described.

[4] *Carm.* III, 17, lines 9–13.

We feel the joyful release of spring,[1] the sultriness of summer,

Iam clarus occultum Andromedae pater
Ostendit ignem, iam Procyon furit
Et stella vesani Leonis
Sole dies referente siccos;

Iam pastor umbras cum grege languido
Rivomque fessus quaerit et horridi
Dumeta Silvani, caretque
Ripa vagis taciturna ventis.[2]

Already the bright father of Andromeda
Reveals his hidden fire, already Procyon rages,
And the star of the mad Lion,
While the sun brings back the days of drought.

Already the shepherd with his languid herd
In fatigue seeks the shade and the stream and the thorny
Hedges of shaggy Silvanus, and no wandering
Wind visits the silent river bank.

and the exhilaration of winter.[3] We feel the softness of the evening in the Apennines

Sol ubi montium
Mutaret umbras et iuga demeret
Bobus fatigatis, amicum
Tempus agens abeunte curru,[4]

when the sun was changing
The shadows on the mountains and unyoking
The tired oxen, bringing in
The friendly time with his departing chariot,

and the immortal freshness of the fountain of Bandusia, its bright, cold water tumbling from the hollow rocks beneath the ilex tree.[5] Even the poems to the country gods seem alive with feeling; Faunus becomes a real, if shadowy, power,[6] and the rustic offerings seem more than a formality.[7]

Horace's importance as a prosodist and his metrical debt to

[1] *Carm.* I, 4; IV, 7.
[2] *Carm.* III, 29, lines 17–24.
[3] *Carm.* I, 9.
[4] *Carm.* III, 6, lines 41–44.
[5] *Carm.* III, 13.
[6] *Carm.* III, 18. See also III, 22, "Montium custos nemorumque Virgo."
[7] *Carm* III, 23.

the Greeks have been mentioned already. An analysis of the principal verse forms appears at the foot of the page.[1] Suffice it to add that, of the one hundred and twenty *carmina* and *epodi*, seventy-eight, or about two-thirds, are written in quatrains, while thirty-four, or a little less than one-third, are written in couplets—and most of these are the epodes. Of the remaining eight poems, seven are monostrophic, and one is composed of tercets. The monostrophic poems are all homogeneous and composed of either the first or the fifth asclepiad lines or of the iambic trimeter.

Horace's sentence structure deserves some separate remarks; for it is one of the main contributing factors to the perfection of his poetry. Horace introduced the oratorical period into lyric poetry. His poetry was meant to be read aloud. Therefore the relationship between the words and the rhythms was of prime importance. Words were carefully placed in elaborately interwoven patterns, so that the poet could get the maximum effect from them, a technique that was rarely practised in Greek poetry. All devices of sound and rhythm that could reinforce

[1] Horace's favourite verse form was the alcaic stanza (37 / 120):

2 (⏓ | — ⏑ | — — ‖ — ⏑ ⏑ | — ⏑ | ⏓)
— | — ⏑ | — — | — ⏑ | — ⏑
— ⏑ ⏑ | — ⏑ ⏑ | — ⏑ | — ⏓

The sapphic stanza was almost as popular (25 / 120 and the long *Carmen Saeculare*):

3 (— ⏑ | — — | — ‖ ⏑ ⏑ | — ⏑ | — ⏓)
— ⏑ ⏑ | — ⏓

The five varieties of asclepiad metre were also exceedingly important (34 / 120):

1 — — | — ⏑ ⏑ — | — ⏑ ⏑ — | ⏑ ⏓

2 { — — | — ⏑ ⏑ — | ⏑ ⏓
— — | — ⏑ ⏑ — | — ⏑ ⏑ — | ⏑ ⏓

3 { 3 (— — | — ⏑ ⏑ — | — ⏑ ⏑ — | ⏑ ⏓)
— — | — ⏑ ⏑ — | ⏑ ⏓

4 { 2 (— — | — ⏑ ⏑ — | — ⏑ ⏑ — | ⏑ ⏓)
— — | — ⏑ ⏑ | ⏓
— — | — ⏑ ⏑ | ⏑ ⏓

5 — — | — ⏑ ⏑ — ‖ — ⏑ ⏑ — ‖ — ⏑ ⏑ — | ⏑ ⏓

the sense were used. "The elisions help to entwine the branches in the line, 'Umbram hospitalem consociare amant' (II, 3, 10). The relentless pounding of the sea is well represented by the reiterated quadrisyllables of, 'Quae nunc oppositis debilitat pumicibus mare' (I, 11, 5), the stamping of the feet by the repeated 'ter' in 'Gaudet inuisam pepulisse fossor *ter* pede *ter*ram' (III, 18, 15–16)."[1]

The characteristic development of the Horatian *carmen* is through image to aphorism. The thoughts that agglomerate about a particular idea are communicated concretely through specific illustrations; with the poet we repeat the experience and the observation; then we are led to the same general reflections.[2] In the place of propositions, there are pictures, in the place of arguments, illustrations. Even in didactic passages Horace prefers the specific example to the abstract generalization, e.g.:

Destrictus ensis cui super impia
Cervice pendet, non Siculae dapes
Dulcem elaborabunt saporem,
Non avium citharaeque cantus

Somnum reducent. Somnus agrestium
Lenis virorum non humilis domos
Fastidit umbrosamque ripam
Non zephyris agitata Tempe.

Desiderantem quod satis est neque
Tumultuosum sollicitat mare
Nec saevus Arcturi cadentis
Impetus aut orientis Haedi,

Non verberatae grandine vineae
Fundusque mendax, arbore nunc aquas
Culpante, nunc torrentia agros
Sidera, nunc hiemes iniquas.

[1] Wilkinson, p. 142. See also pp. 134 ff., 140, and 146 ff. On p. 4 Wilkinson quotes Nietzsche: "To this day I have got from no other poet the same artistic delight as from the very first a Horation ode gave me. In certain languages what is here achieved is not even to be thought of. This mosaic of words, in which every sound, by position and by meaning, diffuses its influence to right and left over the whole; the minimum in compass and number of symbols, the maximum achieved in the effectiveness of those symbols, all that is Roman, and, believe me, of excellence unsurpassed."

[2] See, e.g., "Otium divos rogat in patenti," II, 16.

Contracta pisces aequora sentiunt
Iactis in altum molibus: huc frequens
Caementa demittit redemptor
Cum famulis dominusque terrae

Fastidiosus. Sed Timor et Minae
Scandunt eodem quo dominus, neque
Decedit aerata triremi et
Post equitem sedet atra Cura.[1]

The man above whose impious neck the drawn
Sword hangs will not feel his saliva
Flow at the Sicilian feast.
Not the song of birds nor the harp

Will bring back sleep. Gentle slumber does not shrink
From the humble dwellings of country folk
On the shady bank of a stream
In a valley untossed by the west wind.

He who craves no more than he needs
Is not harassed by the stormy sea
Nor the cruel blast at the setting of Arcturus
Or on the rising of the Goat.

He knows not the worry of vines being whipped by hail
Nor of an estate that deceives his hopes, the trees now
Blaming the floods, now the stars that bake the fields,
Now the harsh winters.

The fish feel the seas getting smaller
As vast foundations are laid in the deep. Into it they sink
Cement, the hordes of contractors
And their household slaves and the lord who disdains

Dry land. But Fears and Threats
Climb to the same place as the lord.
He cannot draw away from them in his brass-fitted trireme and
Behind the knight dark Worry sits.

The aphorisms, too, tend to be specific and concrete. Instead of "Fate is not always against you" Horace says "neque semper arcum / Tendit Apollo,[2] "and Apollo does not always bend his bow."

[1] *Carm.* III, 1, lines 17–40.

[2] *Carm.* II, 10, lines 19–20.

Horace's example-images are drawn from mythology, everyday life, and nature. They are the accurate, clearly defined vignettes of the impartial observer. They are used to communicate ideas, not to create atmosphere. Horace is almost never suggestive; he almost never attempts to build up a mood or to persuade his readers emotionally; he seeks only to convince their intelligences. There are some few exceptions to this general rule: in a passage about the first mariner,

Quem mortis timuit gradum,
  Qui siccis oculis monstra natantia,
Qui vidit mare turbidum et
  Infamis scopulos, Acroceraunia?[1]

What manner of death's approach did he fear,
The man who with dry eyes looked at
The swimming monsters, the turbid sea,
And the ill-famed rocks of Thunder Cape?

"siccis oculis" may be not only a visual but also an emotional image, communicating some of the terror of the monsters of the deep; while the overwhelming sense of loneliness of the ageing courtesan whose shutters remain closed, who stands alone, weeping, in the doorway, is brought home by the final image of the north wind rioting through the streets on a moonless night, "Thracio bacchante magis sub interlunia vento."[2]

Horace's aphorisms and epigrams are well known and his mastery of the art of pithy statement is unquestioned. Suffice it to recollect a few examples:

Carpe diem, quam minimum credula postero.[3]

Enjoy today, with no trust in tomorrow.

Patriae quis exsul se quoque fugit?[4]

What exile from his native land escapes himself too?

Nihil est ab omni parte beatum.[5]

There is no unmitigated blessing.

Dulce et decorum est pro patria mori.[6]

Death for one's country is sweet and glorious.

[1] *Carm.* I, 3, lines 17–20.
[2] *Carm.* I, 25, lines 11–12.
[3] *Carm.* I, 11, line 8.
[4] *Carm.* II, 16, lines 19–20.
[5] *Carm.* II, 16, lines 27–8.
[6] *Carm.* III, 2, line 13.

The beginning of a Horatian ode frequently contains an address to the friend, occasionally deity, for whom the poem is nominally written. A few of the odes contain, in addition, an invocation to the muse or the poet's lyre. The middle of the ode is made up of a series of reflections pictorially expressed. The end is usually a picture which drives home the point of the poem. However, the development of the Horatian ode is linear rather than circular. We never return to the beginning. Although the addressee has occasionally inspired the subject of the ode, more generally it is as personal to him as a letter of Pliny's is to his correspondent. In sum, the Horatian ode is a relatively short poem usually written in quatrains, addressed to a friend, and containing moral or political reflections, communicated largely by means of images and aphorisms. As to his method of arranging his materials, Horace is fond of *tricola*, "the principle familiar in music by which the last of three related phrases is longer than the other two and sums them up."[1] This was a technique recognized by Demetrius in his remarks *On Style*.

In what he attempts to do, Horace is beyond compare. He is an exquisite miniaturist. But, like most miniaturists, his art is characterized by perfection rather than intimacy. He is always formal and, despite his particular pictures, always general. Even when he writes about himself, it is himself objectified, expressed through a literary or social tradition. His amorous discomforts are all conventional—the situations and the emotions they evoke. None of the young women—or men—assumes any personality; there is nowhere a Lesbia, a Cynthia, or a Corinna, and the feelings described never attain to any individuality. Even Horace's obscene epodes are genre pieces, not genuine personal outbursts. Horace's expression of his dedication to poetry is conventional, too, quite a different thing from Wordsworth's. The story of the doves covering the tired little boy with leaves and protecting him from the bears and snakes on Mount Vultur[2] is reminiscent of similar tales about Hesiod, Pindar, etc. This is Horace expressing himself through the tradition. Similarly, Horace's invitations to his friends are all written in the person of the urbane country gentleman, the *philosophe*.

[1] Wilkinson, p. 136. [2] *Carm.* III, 4, lines 9–20.

In speaking of his friends, too, Horace is never personal. Most of his friends were public figures, and we only meet their public personalities. What does Horace tell us of Tibullus, Vergil, or Maecenas? Only that Tibullus liked girls,[1] that Vergil went to Greece,[2] and that Maecenas had great wealth and power.[3] In Horace's poems these are only names, there are no idiosyncrasies to mark individuality, no nuances of feeling to differentiate relationships. Horace treats all his friends impartially in poetry.

Similarly, although Horace talks much about society in his lyrics, he leaves us with no vivid scenes of Roman life. It is Catullus who tells us about Asinius the napkin-stealer[4] and Arrius with his Cockney accent.[5] It is Ovid, not Horace, who describes the Roman siesta, the summer heat, the half-closed shutters, the twilit room, and the languid figure on the couch.[6] Both Horace and Propertius tell of Augustus' dedication of a new temple to Apollo, but it is Propertius who communicates the excitement and enthusiasm, it is Propertius who describes the temple and who makes the occasion real by telling us how the crowds made him late for a rendezvous with Cynthia.[7] To Horace the dedication of the temple is a fact referred to in a past participle, the occasion for a new statement of his philosophy.[8]

Horace says much about death but he never suggests the pathos and the depth of feeling of Vergil's "Sunt lacrimae rerum, et mentem mortalia tangunt."[9] Horace lost a father as Catullus a brother but he wrote no "Multas per gentes et multa per aequora vectus."[10] Horace never loved a girl enough to write:

Di magni, facite ut vere promittere possit
Atque id sincere dicat et ex animo
Ut liceat nobis tota perducere vita
Aeternum hoc sanctae foedus amicitiae,[11]

1 *Carm.* I, 33.
2 *Carm.* I, 2.
3 See, e.g., III, 29.
4 Catullus, *Carminum* 12.
5 Catullus, *Carminum* 84.
6 Ovid, *Amorum* I, 5.
7 Propertius, *Elegiarum* II, 31.
8 Horace, *Carm.* I, 31, "Quid dedicatum poscit Apollinem vates?"
9 Vergil, *Aeneid* I, 462.
10 Catullus, *Carm.* 99.
11 Catullus, *Carm.* 107.

Mighty gods, may she be able to give a true promise,
And may she ask it sincerely and from her heart,
That we may be permitted to maintain through the whole of our lives
This eternal bond of sacred friendship.

nor ever hated one enough to say:

Scribant de te alii, vel sis ignota, licebit,
Laudet qui sterili semina ponit humo.
Omnia, crede mihi, tecum uno munere lecto
Auferet extremi funeris atra dies.
Et tua transibit contemnens ossa viator
Nec dicet, cinis hic docta puella fuit.[1]

Let other people write about you, or be unknown, I don't care,
Let him praise you who sows his seed on barren ground.
All your gifts, believe me, will be carried away with you
On a single couch on the last, black, funeral day.
And the wayfarer will pass by, scorning your bones,
Nor will he say, "These ashes were once a learned girl."

Horace was not the delineator of the passionate soul nor of the warmth and bustle and variety of life; he was a moralist and a poet of ideas who used experience only as *exempla*—but with unsurpassed art and with a liveliness and wit that make his didacticism palatable and keep him from ever being dull.

It remains to say something about the epodes. The epodes, although conventionally placed after the *carmina* (since the Renaissance, "odes"), were written before them. Chronologically they come between the satires and the odes[2] and, in form, content, and treatment, they are transition pieces.

It was Archilochus of Paros (*c.* 700 B.C.) who made the iambic epode or refrain, the short iambic dimeter line following a trimeter, into a literary form for invective and lampoon, and Horace's seventeen epodes may, with reservations, be considered to be Archilochian in inspiration. All but five of the poems[3] are bitter or satirical in tone, and, while only the first ten are written in iambics, sixteen of the seventeen are written

[1] Propertius, *Eleg.* II, 11.

[2] Horace published his two volumes of satires in 35 and 30, his epodes in 29, and the first three books of odes in 23 B.C.

[3] The exceptions are 1, 9, 11, 13, 14.

in couplets which suggest the Greek form. The metres of the epodes were included in the general remarks on Horace's metres above.

The content of any one of the epodes might have been made up into an ode. Even the Canidia pieces (5 and 17), on analogy with the dialogue poem "Donec gratus eram tibi,"[1] might have been made into odes, although parallels in Theocritus and Vergil would suggest that they should be idylls or eclogues instead. The subject matter of many of the epodes[2] might also have found its way into the satires. What distinguishes these poems from the odes is their prevailingly iambic verse forms, their generally critical or abusive tone, and their greater looseness of construction. Their verse form equally distinguishes them from the satires,[3] as do the unity and simplicity of conception and the comparative compactness and brevity of expression. These latter characteristics make the epodes lyrical poems in the modern if not ancient sense. Indeed, in the epodes we can see Horace developing his lyric technique.

The polished art of Horace's odes is the result of years of the "labor limae," of painstaking practice and self-criticism, of training in economy until he has learnt to make the most of the least. In the odes Horace gives only the essentials but they are brought into sharp focus and clearly defined. In the epodes the style is more dilatory, there is more *overt* argumentation and more discussion, there are more generalized, abstract statements, more examples, and more details. The epodes are less compact, less tense, and less pictorial. They are also more emotional, more personal, and more romantic. In the epodes Horace alludes to his military experience with "Imbellis ac firmus parum,"[4] in the odes he is more specific, "Relicta non bene parmula."[5] In the epodes Horace takes ten long lines to say, with seven illustrations, "until the world is changed"[6]; in the odes he says, "put me anywhere in the world" in six short lines with two illustrations that cover all alternatives.[7] There is no description in the odes as long and rich and lingering as that

[1] *Carm.* III, 9.

[2] E.g., epodes 2, 3, 4, 5, 6, 7, 9, 10, 12, 15, 16, 17.

[3] Lucilius had made the hexameter the line for the satire.

[4] *Epodon* 1, line 16.

[5] *Carm.* II, 7, line 10.

[6] *Epodon* 16, lines 25–34.

[7] *Carm.* I, 22, lines 17–22.

of the Islands of the Blest in the sixteenth epode, in the section beginning "Vos, quibus est virtus, muliebrem tollite luctum,"[1] nor any passage anywhere in Horace's works so emotional and dramatic as the seventh epode:

> Quo, quo scelesti ruitis? Aut cur dexteris
> Aptantur enses conditi?
> Parumne campis atque Neptuno super
> Fusum est Latini sanguinis?
> Non ut superbas invidae Carthaginis
> Romanus arces ureret,
> Intactus aut Britannus ut descenderet
> Sacra catenatus Via,
> Sed ut secundum vota Parthorum sua
> Urbs haec periret dextera.
> Neque hic lupis mos nec fuit leonibus,
> Numquam nisi in dispar feris.
> Furorne caecus an rapit vis acrior
> An culpa? Responsum date!
> Tacent, et ora pallor albus inficit,
> Mentesque perculsae stupent.
> Sic est: acerba fata Romanos agunt
> Scelusque fraternae necis,
> Ut immerentis fluxit in terram Remi
> Sacer nepotibus cruor.[2]

> Where, where are you heading, guilty men? Why are swords
> That were sheathed arming right hands?
> In the fields and on the sea has not enough
> Latin blood poured forth?
> Not that the Roman might burn the proud
> Citadels of envious Carthage,
> Or that the unsubdued Briton might descend
> The Sacred Way in chains,
> But that, fulfilling the prayers of the Parthians,
> This city might perish by her own right hand.
> This has not been the way of the wolf, nor of the lion,
> Who are never beasts with their own kind.
> Is it blind madness or does a stronger force carry you away,
> Or is it guilt? Answer!
> They are silent, and their faces blanch,
> And their minds are aghast with shock.

[1] *Epodon* 16, line 39.

[2] *Epodon* 7.

So it is: harsh fates drive the Romans,
And the crime of a brother's death,
Ever since the blood of Remus sank into the ground,
A curse on undeserving posterity.

These, then, were the men, Pindar the poet-priest, Anacreon the *bon-vivant*, and Horace the pagan moralist, whose works served as models for the new ode genre developed by the Renaissance. In the following chapters we shall see how a new tradition was developed out of these raw materials and how individual writers adapted this tradition to their genius and times.

Chapter 3

THE HUMANIST ODE

IT was to be expected that the humanists should adopt classical lyric forms, that they should seek, by imitating the poetry of the ancients, to recapture the antique spirit and thereby revive, in some way, the glories and grandeur of Greece and Rome. Thus Filelfo's book of odes, of formal commentaries on contemporary affairs, written from authority, commanding respect, decorated with the mythological and sententious flourishes of a pedantic and imperious mind, and restoring the dignity and gravity of the ancient Latin language and prosody to public life, comes as no surprise. It is unfortunate that these odes, published posthumously in 1497 but written and circulated much earlier, are without literary merit. They are, however, of considerable historical importance, as marking the resumption of an old tradition and the establishment of a new.

It is to Filelfo as originator that we must ascribe the later convention of writing odes to great men; for it was he who first took the ancient type of lyric with its superior formality and dignity and adapted it to the flattery of princes. Admittedly there were examples of the use of the ode for the praise of great men in Pindar, whom Fifelfo knew,[1] and in Horace. But

[1] Francesco Filelfo (1398–1481) was in Constantinople from 1419–1427, as secretary to the Venetian consul general. There he studied Greek with John Chrysoloras, a relative of Manuel Chrysoloras already famous as a teacher of Greek in Italy, married John Chrysoloras' daughter, Theodora, and collected Greek manuscripts. One of the manuscripts that he brought

Pindar's great men were not usually princes, but popular heroes, while Horace's odes to Augustus and the Roman generals form a small part of the whole and are not, despite their political character, rigidly separated from his other odes to friends. Thus Filelfo was the first man in our western tradition to write numerous odes in the praise of men whose sole claim to greatness was power and from whom he expected no more than a generous remuneration.

Filelfo's original plan for ten books of odes dedicated to Apollo and the nine Muses and each containing ten similarly distributed odes was never completed. However, the five books that we have seem more than enough. Here there are odes to Charles, presumably the seventh, of France, Francesco Sforza of Milan and his general, Gaspar of the Insubres, Carlo and Ludovico Gonzaga of Mantua, Sigismundo Malatesta of Rimini, Alfonso, King of Naples, Pope Nicholas V, and various friends, generally referred to under pseudonyms. The odes discuss the recurrent wars, praise the successful *condottieri*, give thanks for generosity, solicit gifts, proffer advice, and make moralistic comments. A few of the poems arise out of crises in the lives of Filelfo's friends and offer consolation or advice, some are chatty epistles,[1] others epigrams[2] or invectives,[3] while two may be described as religious.[4] The two most interesting to read are the two epistles about the plague (III, 10, and IV, 5), and a rather comic description of the gout written to his friend, "Podargus" (I, 8).

Several poems are important, however, from the point of view of literary history. II, 1, although written in sapphic stanzas, seems to have been inspired by Pindar. Filelfo celebrates Carlo Gonzaga, first by telling the mythical history of Mantua, how it was founded by Bianor who named it after his mother Manto, then by recounting the history of the Gonzagas. This praise of a living man through myths of his city and family is Pindaric. Pindaric too is the method of recounting

back to Italy contained the odes of Pindar. However, this was not the first copy of Pindar to reach Italy. Aurispa had anticipated Filelfo by bringing back a Pindar manuscript in 1423, see J. E. Sandys, *A History of Classical Scholarship*. II (Cambridge, 1908), 36–7.

[1] Filelfo, *Odae* (Brixiae, 1497), II, 6; III, 3, 10; IV, 5, 6, 8.

[2] *Ibid.*, III, 7. [3] *Ibid.*, IV, 7. [4] *Ibid.*, I, 6, 9.

these myths and histories, the allusiveness and the confusion of temporal sequence. I, 3, with its internally motivated myth may also be Pindaric in inspiration. I, 1 appears to be the first Renaissance example of an ever-popular theme, the power of poetry. I, 9, with the two epistolary poems about the plague, is an example of the variety of content and treatment that Filelfo was willing to admit into his category of ode. This poem resembles a medieval *estrif*; Venus is summoned to Neptune's court to answer for the behaviour of her son who is driving the poet, now an old man, to a third marriage. Filelfo states the case against Venus: he already has sons and daughters old and young, he is over fifty, and he has not enough money to dower his girls. Venus replies about the comforts of having a wife and adds that it will give him more leisure for poetry. The poem ends with a prayer to Venus. The metre is second asclepiad, changing to iambic trimeter, a more conversational medium, for the court scene, then to various short lines, then back to second asclepiad.

This change of metre within the ode is a characteristic of Filelfo's found in nine out of fifty poems, distributed roughly two per book.[1] In some cases, as in the trial of Venus cited above (I, 9) and the account of the flight from the plague (IV, 5)—the death of the woman and their violent expulsion from Cremona are described in elegiac couplets, while the narrative beginning and ending of this poem are in first asclepiads—the metre has been changed the better to express the subject matter. In other cases, as in III, 8, where there are thirty-odd different metres, Filelfo seems merely to be working a sampler for display on the school-room wall:

Hunc flaminii fortiter armis
Pugnantem et flaminiis quisquis
Se stulticia socium iunxit
Violataeque obnoxia fidei.
Manus omnis populi omnes pariter
Experti stultitiae poenas
Ubi soluissent: Sphortia virtus
Generum sibi Francisce dicavit.[2]

[1] *Ibid.*, I, 9; II, 6, 10; III, 5, 8; IV, 1, 5; V, 4, 9.
[2] *Ibid.*, III, 8, sig. g iii r–iii v.

Here are patterns of almost every metre, Greek and Latin, stitched together without any governing rhythmical concept and decorated with a tasteless excess of alliteration and assonance.[1] Alliteration and assonance are common in Filelfo and almost always used without discrimination, e.g.,

Dum causam modulis in medium suis
Miranti referent mihi:
Quaenam tanta tentet nunc taciturnitas
Dicendi decus Andream.[2]

In addition to his Latin odes Filelfo wrote forty-four odes in Greek which he never corrected or published. Since it was his wish that no one should copy out any of these poems we will not follow Bandini in doing so.[3] However, if one can judge from the two odes that Bandini quotes, one in elegiacs to King Alfonso and one in sapphics to Cardinal Bessarion, these odes are at least more musical than the Latin ones. They are by no means of a high quality poetically, however. Apart from a few echoes of Pindar the odes are wholly taken up with hyperbolic eulogy of the illustrious persons to whom they are addressed.

Filelfo's poems, except for the few occasional notes passed to friends,[4] tend to be extraordinarily long and exceedingly dull. Apart from their metrical forms, a tendency to give mythological illustrations, and the two above-mentioned cases of possible Pindaric inspiration in the handling of the myth, Filelfo's odes bear little resemblance to Horace's and none at all to Pindar's. They are diffuse, verbose, and unimaginative, and they are lacking in music and poetry. They are the exercises of a great scholar and humanist, not the works of a poet. They are, however, important as pioneers in a new lyric form and in what is to prove a long-lasting association of the ode with the court and with the revival of antique attitudes in everyday life. They establish a new convention, that of the "laureate" ode, and they sketch in its terms, so that henceforth odes of this sort are from time to time expected from any poet

[1] *Ibid.*, III, 8, sig. g iii v, "Quid pluribus tempus terere verbis velim?"

[2] *Ibid.*, III, 5, sig. g r.

[3] Angelo Maria Bandini, *Catalogus Codicum Graecorum Bibliothecae Laurentianae*, II (Florentiae, 1768), 450–4.

[4] E.g., *Ibid.*, I, 2.

who wants patronage. Moreover, although he does not hand down a very precise notion of what the ode is, for Filelfo does not always distinguish carefully between odes, and poems written in classical Latin and classical metres which belong to other genres, ancient or medieval—"ode" is, at times, a general term used for poetry written under the new humanist impulse —nevertheless Filelfo's experiments in the expressive possibilities of different metres, in varying the metre within the poem, and his example of what was to become a common class-room exercise, the writing of all metres in one poem, were destined to be of primary importance in the development of the ode in the seventeenth century.

The history of the neolatin ode, as will become apparent in this survey of it, is an account of the struggle to adapt modern life and classical tradition to one another. Different adaptors put their emphases differently, but the most successful succeed in fusing the old with the new to create new kinds of poems. A man who hinted at the possibility of success in this synthesis was Cristoforo Landino (1424–1504), a member of Marsilio Ficino's Platonic Academy at Florence, a commentator on Horace, Vergil, and Dante,[1] the inspiration of Ugolino Verino, Naldo Naldi, and Alessandro Braccesi,[2] and the teacher of Angelo Poliziano.[3] His claim to poetic fame is a volume of poems, chiefly elegies, entitled *Xandra.* According to his modern editor, most of the poems about Xandra were written in 1443.[4] Three of these, with a dedication, were sent to Leon Battista Alberti for criticism in 1443–4 and three books were sent to Piero de Medici in 1458–9.[5] *Xandra* was not published until the beginning of the eighteenth century,[6] but thirty-six manuscripts attest to its contemporary popularity and wide circulation.

Two of the non-elegiac poems in this volume are written in

[1] Landino was editor of one of the earliest editions of Horace, Florence, 1482.

[2] Gino Bottiglione, *La Lirica Latina in Firenze nella 2a. Metà di Secolo XV* (Pisa, 1913), p. 25.

[3] *Ibid.*, pp. 70–1.

[4] *Ibid.*, p. 75.

[5] Christofori Landini, *Carmina Omnia*, ed. Alexander Perosa (Florentiae, 1939), pp. xxxvii–xxxviii.

[6] *Ibid.*, p. lii.

hendecasyllabics, although only one of these, the early dedication "Ad Leonem Battistam Albertum,"[1] belongs in the Catullan tradition. It claims that the book is the latest in the line from Catullus, "et te / Passeris illius querelis . . . extremum comitem dabis." The other hendecasyllabic poem, "Ad Ginevram,"[2] however, although it uses this metre for invective as Catullus often does, e.g., in *Carm.* 12, belongs rather in the Horatian, Propertian, Ovidian tradition of the poor poet's abuse of the beautiful girl who scorns him, and his warning picture of a frustrated old age when she will regret her pride. But it is more than classical; it unsuccessfully attempts a modern adaptation of the stock ancient theme. Ginevra is spoken of as a Roman courtesan, on whose doorstep the poet has lain for two nights, pleading, but who rejects him for the gold of Gabriele; but her appearance in the morning at the grated window is that of the medieval *donna*, while the decay of her beauty is imagined as coming about through continuous childbearing, the fate of the Italian matron, not that of the *fille de joie*.

In trying to adapt this classical invective to the modern situation Landino has only succeeded in emphasizing its artificiality and conventionality. The two concepts of woman are completely incompatible. We cannot imagine the Italian *mamma* with her numerous *bambini* as a foul, libidinous hag, maddened with desire, "equarum . . . furens libido." Landino's impulse, however, is good. If neolatin poetry is going to be anything other than merely academic it must come to terms with modern life. It must discover, in the classical inspiration, new insights into contemporary experience.

We see Landino trying to do this, again not quite successfully, in the sapphic "De Xandra."[3] This poem is Horatian in form and Petrarchan in conceit. There are some classical adornments and there is some Horatian imagery, dancing Naiads, Graces, and Satyrs reminiscent of *Carm.* I, 4, but there is also the eternal spring of medieval idealism, the everlasting *reverdie* with its budding greenery, bright-faced flowers, gentle breezes, musical nightingale, and happy peasants, and the poem is built on the exaggerated sentiments of the courtly love

[1] *Ibid.*, pp. 14–16. [2] *Ibid.*, pp. 33–5. [3] *Ibid.*, pp. 31–2.

tradition. Xandra has come to Fiesole and with her the spring; if Xandra leaves for Florence the trees will wither and the rivers go dry. There is no reason for the classical language, metre, and deities. The poem would be perfect without them, as are Shakespeare's and Dryden's versions of the same conceit.[1] The two traditions have not yet been amalgamated so that classicism adds a new depth of meaning, as it was to do later in the poetry of Pontano or of Ronsard at his best. Thus the imposition of this extraneous, bookish element only makes the poem seem strained and artificial. We miss the freshness of the vernacular models.

In the next sapphic, however, Landino has succeeded in mastering the ancient technique in order to celebrate a modern occasion. "Laudes Dianae"[2] is a hymn of thanksgiving on Xandra's survival of childbirth. It is a Horatian ode with an invocation to the Muse, "Candidae laudes, age, jam canamus / Musa, Dianae," and then to Diana, and an address to the newborn boy. The ode, like the majority of hymns, pagan and Christian, lists the deity's powers, parentage, and birth, alludes to several familiar "miracles," and then describes the present help for which thanks are given. However, its ending is distinctively Horatian, a pretty compliment to the mother and child.

The description of Diana's triple divinity and of her parentage and birth in stanzas one and two owes something to Catullus 34[3] where, it must be remembered, Diana is addressed as Lucina, the help of women in childbirth. However, the Catullan inspiration is not elsewhere evident. The poem is more massive and ornate than the Catullan poem and more like a hymn of Callimachus. Stanza three tells the story of Niobe, stanzas four and five, the story of Actaeon. Diana's previous fame was based on her powers of destruction. Henceforth she shall be known for her saving strength; for Diana mitigated the pain and happily took to her benign bosom

[1] See Shakespeare, sonnet 12, "How like a Winter hath my absence been," and Dryden, "Song to a Fair Young Lady, going out of the Town in the Spring," "Ask not the cause why sullen Spring."

[2] Landino, pp. 22–3.

[3] Cf. the second stanza beginning "O Jovis summi decus omne prolis / Virgo," with Catullus 15, stanza two, "O Latonia maximi / Magna progenies Jovis."

Xandra's newborn son. Now Landino addresses the boy, bids him be worthy of his mother, be her pride and joy, "Sis, precor, matris decus et voluptas / maxima matris," and, echoing Horace,[1] he prophesies that the boy will be as much more beautiful than other boys as his mother is more beautiful than other women.

This ode imitates Horace in form and treatment of subject but the subject itself and the emotional attitude towards it are modern. Here Landino is much more successful in his adaptation than in the previous poem we considered, but he is still far from being master of the ode, as a comparison of this poem with the preceding prayer in elegiac couplets will emphasize. The elegiac couplet was written throughout the middle ages and the Renaissance. It is a familiar metre and Landino is at home in it. Moreover the elegy has a long personal and emotional tradition whereas the ode tradition is formal and public. The elegy is under no compulsion to objectify and generalize. Thus the prayer "Ecce dies partus: properat Lucina puellae" is simple and anxious and full of feeling. The ode, in contrast, seems mechanical and heavy, an intellectual exercise. Landino has learnt the formula but he wants ease in filling it. The mythological material remains a little recalcitrant; classical culture is still not completely assimilated.

A third sapphic, the shortest, liveliest, and, at the same time, in its extreme simplicity, compression, and economy, the most classical, the most Horatian of all, seems again to have received its particular inspiration from Provençal poetry[2] and perhaps to have learnt something of expressing its emotion from Catullus.[3]

> Corve quid dextrum crepitante rostro
> mi latus stringis celerique penna
> cur feris nostros humeros sinistrum
> garrula cornix?

[1] Horace, *Carm.* I, 16, line 1, "O matre pulchra filia pulchrior."

[2] In the poetry of the troubadours the bird was often the consoler, confidant, or messenger of love. The *chanson* with the bird as the messenger of love was widespread from Belgium to the Pyrenees, from the Atlantic to the Alps during the twelfth and thirteenth centuries and this type of poem survived in popular songs into the sixteenth century, P. Laumonier, *Ronsard, Poète Lyrique* (Paris, 1923), pp. 450–3.

[3] Cf., e.g., "Sirmio," Catullus, *Carm.* 31.

Cernimus? Vel qui misere premuntur
semper a duro nimioque amore,
dum suis curis cupiunt mederi,
somnia fingunt?

Cernimus certe: redit ecce nobis
rure materno, mea magna cura,
Xandra. Nunc omnis timor atque tristis
luctus abito![1]

Raven, why do you caw and pluck at
My right side, and why are you beating
My left shoulder with your swift wings,
Garrulous crow?

Do I see her? Or do those who suffer torment
Constantly from a cruel and boundless passion,
In a desire to cure their own sufferings,
Create dreams?

Yes, I see her. Look, she is coming back to us
From her mother's home in the country, my dearest love,
Xandra. Now all fear, sadness, and
Grief away!

Here at last is a completely successful fusion of ancient and medieval inspiration that has enabled the poet to communicate his particular emotion, and incidentally create a new type of poem, the modern ode.

Landino's last sapphic[2] is addressed to one Giovanni Antonio of whose friendship he wants to be assured. It bases its structure on Horace I, 7, lines 19–21:

Plance . . . seu te fulgentia signis
Castra tenent seu densa tenebit
Tiburis umbra tui. . . .

Plancus, . . . if the gleaming standards
Of the camp detain you or if I shall find you
In the deep shade of Tivoli. . . .

"Giovanni Antonio, whether you are in the country hunting birds with nets or coursing after hares or in Florence enjoying

[1] Landino, *Carm.*, p. 35. [2] *Ibid.*, pp. 40–1.

the conversation of your friends and the beautiful face of sweet Orecta, . . . reassure Landino of your friendship." In its content this ode is more strictly classical than any other of Landino's; it shows how humanism was changing the poet's outlook on life and also how life in fifteenth-century Italy was adapting itself to humanism. Under the Horatian influence Landino does not write a sonnet analysing the nature of friendship and possessively demanding the love of his friend. Instead he pictures Giovanni Antonio's life in its entirety, he surveys objectively his public person, and then asks for reassurance of his own relationship to all this. The classical influence has brought a new formality and objectivity even to Landino's emotional poetry.

Landino had the gift of being able to convey his feelings and, as appears in the quotation above, an easy-flowing, harmonious Latin style. Thus, although his bulk was small, he did much more for the ode than Filelfo. A new form is more likely to become popular when propagated by a poet rather than by a pedant. Landino has brought music and emotion to the ode; he has tried, however clumsily at times, to wed classical and medieval tradition, both in outlook on life and in poetic convention, and he has used the revived ancient form to celebrate events in ordinary social and domestic life. With Landino we feel that the ode can live, that it can become a new mode of expression for modern times.

Giovanni Antonio Campano (1429–77), through his friendship with Pope Pius II, bishop of Cotrone, then of Teramo in the Abruzzi, furthers this impression. Among his six books of poems, largely elegies, are a few pieces of Catullan, occasional verse in hendecasyllabics celebrating dinner parties,[1] answering friends' questions,[2] etc., and five odes. In the first of these, "In Dominae suae laudes,"[3] he addresses his mistress, "O dulces animi mei," in the second asclepiad metre, and tells her what pleasure he feels when he summons the Muses, whose coming, with song, dance, flowers, and perfume, he describes. Why? Because they praise his lady more than the Morning Star, more than they praise her who, on the couch of Jupiter, midst the

[1] See, e.g., Joannis Antonius Campanus, *Epistolae et Poemata* (Lipsiae, 1707), p. 145.

[2] E.g., *Ibid.*, p. 97.

[3] *Ibid.*, p. 96.

sport of kisses, with a soft hand, snatched the sceptre. It is a pretty poem, like those of Landino, uniting the classical with the medieval. An even closer and more successful union of the ancient and medieval is found in the lovely lyric "Ad Dianam."[1] Here a medieval type of poem, a catalogue of the beautiful things that yield in beauty to the beauty of Diana, is written in a Horatian metre and its theme is treated in the Horatian manner:

Purpurae quicquid pelago natare
Et legi quicquid poterit rosarum
Compares frustra niveae labellis,
Lippe, Dianae.

Caucasi cedet niveum cacumen,
Cum gelu horrenti glacieque bruma
Contrahit coelum, leporemque sistit
Colle nivoso.

Lillii cedunt folia et ligustri
Candido collo gracilique mento,
Dentibus cedent Phanii coossi
Albaque cuncta.

Every crimson mollusc that swims in the sea
And every rose that can be gathered
You would vainly compare, Lippus, with the mouth
Of fair Diana.

The snowy summit of Caucasus will not compare with her,
When, with bristling frost and ice, winter
Lowers the heavens, and halts the hare
On the snowy pass.

The petals of the lily and of the privet blossom do not compare
With her white throat and her delicate chin,
The shimmering samite of Cos, and all that is white will not
compare
With her teeth.

We recognize the emotional and sensuous richness that Landino has introduced into the ode.

"Ad Pium II, Pontificem Maximum,"[2] is written in hendecasyllabics and, with the Catullan metre, comes the Catullan

[1] *Ibid.*, p. 103. [2] *Ibid.*, pp. 100–1.

joy,[1] as well as occasional reminiscences of Catullus.[2] The poem as a whole, is, however, Horatian. "Let all rejoice:

Parnassi gemini novem puellae
Quae Cyrrhae colitis jugum atque fontem,[3]
Nunc laurus hederaeque pertinaces
Cingant templa, fores, et alta tecta,
Rugas excutiant senes severi,
Et jucunda juventus, omnis aetas,
Flora tempora colligant corona.
Spargatur viola forum, atque acantho,
Parcat nemo rosisque liliisque,
Decantentque novos modos Poetae,
Quales auderit nec ipse Apollo. . . .

You nine maids of twin-peaked Parnassus
Who watch over the ridge and fountain of Cyrrha,
Now let the laurel and the clinging ivy
Bind the temples, the gates, and the roof-tops,
Let the stern elders smooth out their frowns,
And let joyous youth, and all ages,
Bind their brows with crowns of flowers.
Scatter the square with violets, and acanthus,
Let no one spare lilies and roses,
And let the Poets sing new measures
Which not Apollo himself has heard.

"It is a great day for Siena and Tuscany and the sacred Muses; Aeneas Pius is bringing the poets to Lazio. What good things have the gods given this year, a new Aeneas to Rome! Tuscany, who first brought the Aonian Muses to Italy, what fitting thanks can we give to you?" Here the classical wit, the typical Horatian cleverness, is perfectly adapted to the expression of the enthusiasm of the new generation of classicists at the elevation of a humanist pope.

Another ode, "Ad Musas de Pio II,"[4] was apparently written on the occasion of the Pope's passage through Campano's diocese on his way to make war against the Turks. Unfortu-

[1] As, e.g., in the Sirmio poem, Catullus, *Carm.* 31.

[2] Cf. "sidera clarius micarunt / Illuxit dies Senae beatus," Campanus, p. 101, and Catullus, *Carm.* 8, line 3, "Fulsere quondam candidi tibi soles."

[3] The text reads, "Quae Cyrrhae jugum colitis atque fontem." I have changed the position of "jugum," *metri causa*.

[4] Campanus, pp. 98–100.

nately the Pope and a large part of his army were carried off by the plague near Ancona and the expedition came to nought. The ode is written in sapphic stanzas in the Horatian pictorial style and is, at times, quite successful. The poet begins by bidding the crowd in the Forum to move aside, to make room for the Muses and the poets; for Pius is coming. He calls on the various song gods to celebrate the humanist Pope. Then in cleverly constructed lines, he describes the scene from the point of view of one watching the procession and he echoes the cheers of the crowds,

> Et Pium celsae geminent fenestrae
> Et Pium curvae resonent tabernae
> Et fori duplex aditus frementis
> Et loca cuncta.[1]

> And "Pius" the topmost windows will answer back,
> And "Pius" the curved shop fronts will echo,
> And both approaches of the roaring square,
> And every quarter.

It is a glorious day, the Pope comes with forces from all over Europe—forces which the poet carefully describes. We will beat the barbarians!

"De Miseria Poetarum,"[2] a sapphic ode, is Horatian in all but its expansiveness. Its beginning is an adaptation, not lacking in originality, of Horace's "Pone me pigris ubi nulla campis"[3]:

> Vade, qua semper populi vagantur
> Qua manu ramis capiunt ab altis
> Qua Notus spirat tenui susurro
> Vellera seres.[4]

> Vade per sylvas Arabum beatas. . . .

> Aut agros Nili madidos calentis,
> Fer gradum ad superos Zephyri volatus,
> Quare per totum studiosus orbem. . . .

> Tu genus nullum reperis sub ipso
> Siderum lapsu inferius Poetis. . . .

[1] *Ibid.*, p. 99. [2] *Ibid.*, pp. 210–12. [3] Horace, *Carm.* I, 22, line 17.

[4] It will be noted that the conceit, "Vellera seres," comes from Vergil, *Georg.* II, 121.

Go where the peoples ever wander,
Where the south wind breathes with a gentle whisper,
Where they gather flocks of silk by hand
From lofty branches.

Go through the blessed woods of Arabia. . . .

Or the oozy fields of the warm Nile,
Climb up to the flights of the Zephyr above,
Earnestly seek through the whole world. . . .

You can find no race beneath the
Sliding of the stars worse off than the Poets. . . .

There follows a series of examples of the sufferings and sacrifices that the man endures who becomes a poet:

Quid manum prodest ferulae minantis
Tot pati poenas teneris sub annis . . . ?

Quid juvat longas vigilare noctes
Igne secerni Borea furenti,
Ducere et moesta juvenilis aevi
Tempus in umbra?

What profits it to suffer the threatening cane on one's
Hand, so much punishment in tender years . . . ?

What use is it to stay up long nights,
To have seen the north with its raging fire,
And to pass the time of one's youthful age
In darkness and gloom?

The poet confers immortality, he gives pleasure, and he teaches morality. Without the poet the highest born, the most exemplary men are forgotten. But the poet receives little reward for this. Others wear gold and gems, the poet has only a threadbare cloak. All other artists feed on their art, the painter and the tuba player. Only to the poet is the Muse a loss. Let dukes, kings, emperors, famous knights, and good men weep over the "damnosam Heliconis . . . ruinam."

Campano has left us more odes than Landino. His work reveals the importance of the new form and the way it is responding to the need for the expression of modern experience.

Like Landino Campano tries to create poems that are genuine classical expressions of contemporary events and he has had considerable success in assimilating the ancient pattern of thought to the modern mood; for he combines a Horatian vividness of expression with an ability to bring contemporary events to life. There are occasional awkwardnesses in his style, for he is not a professional classical scholar, but these are more than compensated for by the obvious sincerity of what he is saying. His themes are both new and traditional ones for the ode.

By the time of Campano ode writing had become popular. It was much practised by the Medici circle at Florence,[1] who used it for what was virtually their polite correspondence. It was time for a great poet to appear.

Giovanni Gioviani Pontano was an Umbrian, born in Cerreto near Spoleto in 1426 and, after the death of his father in political strife, educated at Perugia. At the age of twenty-two, through Antonio Beccadelli, il Panormita, he met Alfonso the Magnanimous in the course of the latter's campaign in Tuscany. Alfonso, patron of humanists, invited the young scholar to Naples and placed him in the chancellery. Ferdinand I made him his secretary and the tutor of his son, Alfonso, Duke of Calabria. Pontano was sent on diplomatic missions; he was made chief political adviser to the monarch, military secretary, and chancellor. For ten troubled years he was prime minister. He advised Naples to prepare for war. His advice was disregarded. When Charles VIII entered Naples in 1495 it was Pontano who, in the name of the people, swore fealty to the French crown. When the Aragonese came back the same year Pontano was in disgrace. The French returned under Louis XII in 1501 and offered to reinstate Pontano in his former dignities, but he refused. He died two years later. Pontano had two wives, to both of whom he was deeply attached, one son, and three daughters. Apart from his political and poetic

[1] See, e.g., Bartolomaeus Scala, *Carmina Illustrium Poetarum Italorum*, ed. Giovanni Gaetano Bottari (Florentiae, 1719–26), VIII, 490–1; Peregrinus Allius, *ibid.*, I, 119–23; Joannis Colentius, *ibid.*, III, 415–19; Carlo Marsuppini, *ibid.*, VI, 267–87; "Leonardo di Piero Dati," Francesco Flamini, *Giornale della Storia della Letteratura Italiana*, XVI (Torino, 1890), 58; and Ugolino Verino, *Flametta*, ed. Lucianus Mencaraglia (Florentiae, 1940).

achievements Pontano is known as the founder of the Neapolitan Academy and the inspiration of a new circle of humanists.

Most of Pontano's poetry, the personal love lyrics, the apparently effortless occasional poems, and the epigrams, was written under the influence of Catullus[1] and does not belong to the ode tradition. The ode tradition, whether it derives from the festival chorales of Pindar, the convivial songs of Anacreon, or the moral and political odes of Horace, is always a tradition of public, of formal poetry, of lyric that is objectified to express the sentiments of society not just of the individual. Horace made even a note sent to a friend into an exquisitely engraved, although not necessarily ornate, invitation. Catullus, on the other hand, was primarily concerned with expressing himself, what he himself thought and felt on a particular occasion. He might write verses to circulate among his friends and be praised for their grace and wit, but he never struck the pose of the public orator, of the rhetor of republican Rome. Granted, he did produce a few Alexandrian showpieces, much as Shakespeare wrote *Venus and Adonis* and *The Rape of Lucrece*, as more serious bids for poetic fame, but these were epyllia or epithalamia rather than odes. On the other hand, much of Catullus' lyric poetry, certainly the finest part, was written to a woman whom he loved passionately and desperately and to whom he poured out, in ecstasy, scorn, and grief, his intense, sensitive, and intelligent heart. Catullus' more personal poetry may be easier for us to understand than Horace's intentionally

[1] See A. Sainati, *La Lirica Latina del Rinascimento* (Pisa, 1919), for a discussion of Catullus' influence on Pontano. Pontano himself says in "Ad Laurentium Miniatum," *Amorum I. Carminum quae quidem extant omnium IV* (Basileae, 1556), p. 3279,

> Sed certe meus hic libellus unum
> Doctum post sequitur suum Catullum
> Et Calvum, veteremque disciplinam . . .
> Hoc quod non sonuere mille ab annis
> Musarum citharae, et Lyaei puellae.

> But, to be sure, this little book of mine follows
> Only after its learned Catullus,
> And Calvus, and the ancient discipline . . .
> That which the lyres of the Muses and the Lyaean maids
> Have not sung for a thousand years.

general odes; for the heart changes little and, in human affairs, somehow, the particular is often more universal than the general. But it was not primarily for us but for Lesbia that he wrote. Similarly, although it is different in quality from Catullus', most of Pontano's poetry is too intimate to be odic. There are, however, some odes in the Horatian tradition scattered here and there throughout his works which we will examine, both because of their intrinsic merit and because of the enormous influence of their author.

The first book of *Amores*[1] contains several odes. In iambic couplets, the favourite metre of Horace's epodes, Pontano writes to Fanny to enjoy life and love before she grows old and ugly.[2] Here we have a poem that is not particularly personal and individual but which, in the name of Fanny, addresses all young women. The theme, familiar from Anacreon and Horace, to mention only two of the poets who have used it, owes much in its development to Ausonius' "De rosis nascentibus."

> Puella molli delicatior rosa,[3]
> Quam vernus aer parturit,
> Dulcique rore Memnonis nigri parens[4]
> Rigat suavi in hortulo:

[1] The *Amores* are dedicated to a husband and wife (pp. 3246–7) and make the novel claim of being pure and chaste and fit for all to read. Although some of Pontano's poems are far from being chaste, even by Renaissance standards, a large number of them are frankly sensuous without being pornographic in intent, which is something new. Pontano's most original contribution, however, was his celebration of married love, a theme previously virtually untouched by the poets—it occurs only in Statius (*Sylvarum* III, 5, and V, 1) and in Ausonius.

[2] Pontano, *Carm.*, pp. 3251–2.

[3] This line may have inspired the beginning of Poliziano's "In puellam suam,"

> Puella delicatior
> Lepusculo et cuniculo,

> Maiden more caressable
> Than the bunny and the leveret,

Prose Volgari E Poesie Latine E Greche . . . , ed. Isidoro del Lungo (Firenze, 1867), p. 268.

[4] I have taken "dulceque" of the text to be a typographical error for "dulcique."

Quae mane primo roscidis cinctos foliis,
Ornat nitenteis ramulos,
Ubi rubentem gemmeos scandens equos
Phoebus peragrat aethera.
Tunc languidi floris breve et moriens decus
Comas reflectit lassulas.
Mox prona nudo decidit cacumine,
Honorque tam brevis perit.

Maiden more caressable than the soft rose
Which the air of spring brings forth,
And which the mother of black Memnon waters
With her sweet dew in its perfumed plot,
Which at dawn adorns the twigs decked with
Shining, dewy leaves,
When, mounting his jewelled steeds, Phoebus
Traverses the reddening skies.
Then, the brief and dying beauty of the delicate flower
Unfolds its languid petals.
Soon it topples headlong from its naked pinnacle,
And so brief a glory perishes.

This proemium owes to Ausonius the spring, Aurora, the dew, and the rose blooming to die that day. The description of old age that follows is borrowed from Horace[1] and the Latin classics, though it is not as cruel as they can be. The "carpe florem" conclusion has been voiced by so many poets, ancient and medieval, that it would be foolish to attribute it to any particular source.

The epode metre is extraordinarily appropriate here; for the theme is a composite of elegy and invective, and the couplets of unequal lines suggest the elegy, while remaining the traditional form for the invective. When we go beyond the merely technical requirements for genres and consider the effect of this metre in itself, we find that it is eminently suited to its theme. The iambics suggest conversation and the vernacular poetry. They are fresher, lighter, and less pompous than the dactyls of the elegiac couplet and more suited to express the grace and ephemerality of the rose, the rapid onset of old age, and the importance of snatching today. A comparison of this poem

[1] E.g., Horace, *Carm.* IV, 10.

with the preceding elegy[1] whose theme is somewhat similar, praise of Fanny's beauties and a desire to enjoy them, will reveal the different expressive capacities of the two metres. The dactylic couplets give the poet a tough and long-tested fabric which can bear heavy embroidery and enable him to elaborate a rich, sensuous poem.[2] The lighter, swifter-moving iambic metres make for something more airy and lyrical. This "Ad Fannian" written by one of Ronsard's favourite neolatin poets is the earliest Renaissance ancestor of "Mignonne, allons voir si la rose."

As was noted in chapter 2, the epode as written by Horace is, in its treatment of themes, a looser, more familiar type of ode. Like the ode it generalizes and universalizes its emotion and is consciously literary, but, unlike the ode, it admits of a more leisurely development of theme and a freer expression of feeling. It is typical of Pontano that he should choose this more informal type of ode. There is another similar poem in the *Amores*, also an "Ad Fanniam."[3]

In the *Amores* most of the poems in hendecasyllabics are Catullan in inspiration and are too brief, intimate, and personal to be considered odes. For example, "Ad pueros de columba"[4] is governed by Catullus' "Passer deliciae meae puellae":

> Cui vestrum niveam meam columbam
> Donabo o pueri? tibi ne Iule?

> To which one of you shall I give my snowy white
> Dove, children? To you, Julius?

Various alternatives are rejected. I will give it to my girl. The poem concludes with a pretty, sensuous description of the girl

[1] Pontano, *Carm.*, pp. 3247–8.

[2] This is not inconsistent with my previous statement (supra, p. 46) that the elegy can be used for simpler, more personal, emotional expression than the ode. The unit of the elegy, the hexameter line, with its truncated form, the pentameter, the most familiar, most commonly used line in Latin poetry, has, through its long history, developed a very wide range of expression. It has been used for the very ornate and the very simple, so that it can, with greater ease than other lines, be incrusted with the most elaborate ornamentation or left absolutely plain. An English parallel is the iambic pentameter line of blank verse.

[3] Pontano, *Carm.*, pp. 3251–2.

[4] *Ibid.*, pp. 3252–3.

kissing the dove. This is a light, delicate, sportive lyric inspired by the popular song and Catullus. Other hendecasyllabics are full of Italianate diminutives and characterized by song-like repetition:

> Amabo mea chara Fanniella
> Ocellus Veneris, decusque Amoris,
> Iube isthaec tibi basiem labella
> Succiplena, tenella, mollicella—
> Amabo mea vita. . . .[1]
>
> I will love my dear Fanniella,
> Venus' darling, Love's glory.
> Bid me kiss you, little mouth
> Moist, tender, soft—
> I will love my sweetheart. . . .

Only once did Pontano give ode treatment to a poem in this metre. "Ad musas"[2] expresses Horatian ideas in a typical prayer form.[3] The poet calls upon the goddesses, citing their various cult centres, and prays to be spared the malignant criticism of the "vulgus" and to have his locks bound with laurel.

Another poem is an ode of a type virtually invented by Horace in his third book, a type later to become very popular with the neoclassicists, the ode to or on an abstraction. "De infelicitate generis hominum"[4] is written in iambic trimeter. It is almost a satire, yet it is lyric in brevity and it does not attack the foolishness of man with specific illustrations as does the satire,[5] but it reflects dully, hopelessly, on the meanness of life itself. Its examples of infelicity are few and general; in hell there are the standard mythological sufferers, Tantalus and Ixion—and all the rest of us. Like Marlowe's Mephistopheles the poet feels "Why this is hell, nor am I out of it."

[1] *Ibid.*, p. 3265.

[2] *Ibid.*, p. 3256.

[3] The Renaissance *votum* or *voeu* was derived from the *Greek Anthology* and owed much of its later popularity to Navagero. It was often considerably influenced by Horatian ideas and methods of expression.

[4] Pontano, p. 3293.

[5] Contrast Rochester's "On Nothing" for example.

Sumus hic tot Inferi, quot homines vivimus.
Suusque quisque dirus est erebus sibi.
Nobis amores, et libido pectoris,
Et una non unius obstetrix mali,
Humana facies, cuius ex oculis fluit
Amor, odium, pax, ira, spes, metus, simul,
Et quas gerit cruenta Tisiphone faces.[1]

There are as many Hells as men who live,
And each man is his own dread abyss,
Our loves and the passions of our breast,
And that single midwife of not a single evil,
The human face, from whose eyes flow
Love, hate, peace, anger, hope, fear together,
And the torches that bloody Tisiphone bears.

We feel the depression of the author in the metre.

Then there are two odes in sapphic stanzas, the "Hymnus in noctem"[2] and "Auram alloquitur."[3] The "Hymn to Night," hymn and prayer, is a tone poem. Although it adopts the structure of Horace's "Mercuri facunde nepos Atlantis" and has much of the Horatian compression, it is full of an emotion and sensuousness never found in Horace. The hushed tone and the musical lines suggest the stillness and sweetness of the night. Using the form and technique of the ancients Pontano has made a new type of poem, a poem whose main function is to create an atmosphere—here of voluptuousness—and induce an emotional state. This kind of poem is typically modern, the logical development of a Christian culture that has been secularized. The ancients were not introspective by religion and hence were less concerned with psychological states and their evocation than the Christians.[4]

[1] Pontano, p. 3293.

[2] *Ibid.*, pp. 3255–6.

[3] *Ibid.*, pp. 3265–7.

[4] This statement is too sweeping to be completely true. There were evocative passages in the drama, notably in Euripides and Seneca, in the *Aeneid*, and in Theocritus, but the elaboration of a mood and the lingering over a sensation is nevertheless, generally speaking, a modern, not ancient, characteristic.

Let us look at the poem more closely:

Nox amoris conscia, quae furenti
Ducis optatam iuveni puellam,
Grata diis magnis, et amica blandae
  Nox bona lunae.

Quam colunt unam Geniusque Hymenque,
Et suo gaudens Erycina nato,
Quum ferus diras acuit sagittas,
  Tendit et arcum.

O voluptatis comes et ministra
Quae bona ex te fert thalamus, torusque,
Quas sopor fert illecebras, iocosque,
  Deliciasque.

Quas simul iuncti faciunt amantes
Inter amplexus, trepidumque murmur
Inter et ludos, tenerasque rixas,
  Dum furit ardor.

. . . . . .

Tu quies rerumque hominumque sola,
Tu graveis curas, et amara fessae
Amoves menti, et refoves benigno
  Pectora somno.

Tu redis[1] mundo redimita frontem
Syderum sertis, reficisque grato
Rore perfundens violaria, agros
  Frugibus exples.

Da meis finem dea magna votis,
Et quod optamus liceat potiri,
Ne voret tristis penitus calentes
  Flamma medullas.

Night, privy to love, you who lead
The desired maid to the passionate youth,
Cherished by the mighty gods, and enamoured, sweet
    night,
Of the moon's caress.

[1] The text reads "reddis," but the metre demands "rĕdīs," and the fact that "reddis," a transitive verb, occurs without an object, suggests that it is a printer's error for "redis."

Whom alone both Genius and Hymen worship,
And Venus joying in her son,
When fiercely he sharpens his fatal darts,
And bends his bow.

O companion and handmaid of pleasure,
What joys in your bosom for the marriage bed
and the couch!
What temptations sleep brings, and merriment,
And delights

Which lovers find, plunged in one another's arms,
Midst embraces and hasty whispers,
Midst playfulness and yielding struggles,
When passion is flame!

. . . . .

You alone bring repose to the world and to men,
You lift heavy cares and bitterness
From the tired mind, and your refresh the breast
With kindly sleep.

You return to the world, your brow bound
With garlands of stars, and you restore the banks of
violets,
Drenching them with welcome dew. You load
The field with crops.

Grant my prayers, mighty goddess,
And what I desire may I be permitted to possess,
Lest the dark flame burning within
Devour my heart.

The ode is classical in its definition of its deity by the area of life in which she is potent, by her relationships with the other gods in the pantheon, by her benefactions to humanity, and by her special powers. It has the Horatian brevity and uses his characteristic word order. The last stanza in which the prayer is uttered is reminiscent of Catullus. Yet this poem develops the atmosphere of night and love as only the moderns have done.[1] It is a prayer for night and the consummation of love like Juliet's "Gallop apace, ye fiery-footed steeds," but it is less

[1] Note that this poem was translated by Ronsard in his third book of *Odes* (1550) under the title of "Hinne à la Nuit."

vigorous, more passive, less passionate, but more sensuous, like Spenser's "Behold, O man, that Toilsome paines doest take" or Tennyson's "Now falls the crimson petal, now the white," or much of Rossetti's *House of Life*. It is without ancient parallel.

"Auram alloquitur"[1] is a similar ode, a combined hymn to a nature deity and a love poem, written in the same incantatory style. By enchantment he summons the breeze from one of her retreats to come and fan him as he reclines on the bank burning with passion for Fanny. In the end we feel that Aura has come; the poet has enchanted his readers as well as the breeze and, in the act of expressing his passion, has cooled his fever.

"Auram alloquitur" is an excellent poem, another example of Pontano's ability to crystallize a mood. Although by comparison it is shallow and trivial, nevertheless we are already on the way towards Coleridge's "Dejection Ode." An ancient hymn-prayer like the briefer Homeric or Callimachan hymns has been suffused with personal and private emotion and made to serve the ends of the modern, Petrarchan erotic tradition, thus forming a new, romantic type of ode. Pontano has taken the major step in bridging the gap between the ancient and modern worlds. "Auram alloquitur" also has affinities with the Theocritean-Vergilian incantatory eclogue. The sorcerer summons, the enchanted comes.

In his *Versus Lyrici* Pontano carries the development of this type of ode further. In another incantatory sapphic, "Ad Antinianam Nympham Iovis et Nesidis filiam,"[2] written on the occasion of his departure from Umbria for the gulf of Naples, the poet asks the nymph Antiniana to come to him, along with the other musical nymphs, that they may sing together in the shady groves; he asks spring to come, too, with flowers. At the coming of spring, as at the approach of Lucretius' Venus, flowers and trees bloom, the breeze blows soft, the nymphs, dryads, and naiads come forth. Now the poet approaches the shore and warns the nymphs to beware of Proteus; it is better to haunt the gardens. He warns them, too, to avoid the impudent Pans of the groves, but rather to trust themselves to the Muses. Here we have an ode of the invitation-incantation type with the scene so fully realized, with such a complex situation

[1] Pontano, pp. 3265–7.

[2] *Ibid.*, pp. 3529–30.

described, with so many characters introduced, and with such a large society, the pleasure-loving holiday-makers of Baia,[1] depicted beneath the mythological conventions that the poem has reached the borderline between the ode and the pastoral eclogue.[2]

Another poem in this series has almost evolved to the piscatory eclogue which Sannazaro developed in the same setting. "Patulcidem et Antinianam Nymphas alloquitur,"[3] adapting the conventional shepherds and shepherdesses of the eclogue to the maritime situation, recreates the mood of a hot, dry, breezy, summer's day by the bay. Addressing the two nymphs in sapphic stanzas, Pontano bids them come

> Aura dum aestivos relevat calores,
> Et leves fluctus agitant cachinni,
> Dum sonant pulsae zephyris arenae,
> Antraque clamant[4];

> While the breeze relieves the summer's heat,
> And laughter shakes the light waves,
> While the sands sing at the zephyrs' stroke,
> And the caves call out.

For Meliseus sings, playing his pipe on a lofty rock, Menalcas too, and Mergillina[5] is preparing her toilet in a mirror—Let the young men come to see her beauty. Palaemon sings and the hills and the nymphs dance in accompaniment. Triton drives along the shore. The nymphs hurry to see him. The peasants stroll singing, the woods make music, and all rejoice. The stones echo the sound; the mountains, caves, gardens, citadels, and ocean echo the harmony. The glorious celebration

[1] See *Ibid.*, pp. 3449 ff. for Pontano's poems about Baia.

[2] Note that the invention of the pastoral ode in Latin by Pontano, Carbone, and Rota, all Neapolitan poets, is paralleled by the invention of the pastoral *canzone* in Italian by Sannazaro (*Arcadia*, 1504) and Gareth (*Endimione*, 1506), also Neapolitans, and by the invention of the pastoral sonnet by Gareth, Molza, Tolomei, Varchi, and Bernardo Tasso. The invasion of other lyrical forms by the pastoral led also to the development of the *lusus pastoralis* by Navagero, Flaminio, and Amalteo in Latin and by Molza in Italian.

[3] Pontano, pp. 3530–2.

[4] *Ibid.*, p. 3531.

[5] A beautiful inlet on the bay of Naples still so called.

of the summer day is like the finale of an opera. There is Renaissance exuberance in the rich use of mythology. There is also an extraordinary impression of veracity; for, far from seeming artificial, the conventional figures chosen are so freshly portrayed and so appropriate to the bay of Naples that their presence adds to the reality of the description of the day. They seem animistic not literary, part of a genuine inspiration, not the repetition of meaningless conventions; we hear their voices in the wind, and see their gleaming shapes in the shimmering light. These conventional figures are also the natives of the region, idealized. In both cases they are a real part of the bay and the summer's day.

This poem is close to one of Sannazaro's *Piscatoriae*. Yet it is as the masque is to the opera; it is too slight to be an eclogue; there is neither action nor discussion; it is solely descriptive and evocative. It is, however, even farther removed from the classical ode; for, although it, like the ode, proceeds from picture to picture, it lacks the ode's intensity and concentration and purposiveness; it has the looseness of structure and the panoramic view of the novel; it could easily be part of a Renaissance *Arcadia*.

Another eclogue-like ode, again written in sapphic stanzas, is "Ad charites."[1] The poet summons the Graces to a pastoral summer festival at the river Sebethos. There is the usual hymn-like praise of the goddesses, a flower passage, and a final compliment to Fanny.

Now we come to two proper eclogues, still written, however, in sapphic stanzas, and thus disguised as odes: "Polyphemus ad Galateam"[2] and "Polyphemus a Galateas conqueritur in spretu litore."[3] These poems are both dialogues and their content is quite conventional, "Cur fugis virgo Polyphemon?"[4] Equally anomalous is "De Orpheo Navigante, et post ad inferos pro uxore descendente."[5] This poem, like the eclogues, is written in sapphic stanzas and tells the story of a love relationship, but it is not addressed to any particular individual nor written on any particular occasion as are the odes. Moreover, whereas the two eclogues are all dialogue, the "Orpheus"

[1] Pontano, pp. 3537–9.
[2] *Ibid.*, pp. 3544–8.
[3] *Ibid.*, pp. 3550–3.
[4] *Ibid.*, p. 3544.
[5] *Ibid.*, pp. 3523–7.

is mostly narrative, with only a small amount of dialogue. The "Orpheus" is more a lay or an epyllion than anything else; yet it is not written in the epic metre, although Vergil and Ovid wrote their versions of the Orpheus-Eurydice story in hexameters. Perhaps Pontano wrote his epyllion in sapphics because Orpheus was a lyric poet and the lyric metre made possible a lighter, more delicate, and more operatic treatment of the theme.

We have seen how the ode-hymn, tone poem could develop to approximate the eclogue. However, there were other odes which remained of a more conventional type. "De amoris Dominatu,"[1] "On the power of love," is a psychotherapeutic sapphic addressed to Erato, the muse of erotic poetry. It has a gnomic Pindaric beginning,

> Et sitim sedat liquor, et relaxant
> Corda languentem latices Thyonei;
> Ocium fessos levat: ast amantum
> Pectora carmen.[2]

> A drink allays thirst, and Bacchus' juices
> Bring relaxation to him who languishes at heart.
> Rest relieves the weary—but the hearts of
> Lovers, song.

followed by a prayer to Erato to ease his sufferings and let him hear her song. Then the poet lists the powers of love and the benefits which he confers on mankind. The powers of love are expressed first in mythological, then in metaphysical terms: Jupiter rules heaven, the gods and demigods rule the earth, Neptune the sea, and Orcus, the underworld. But love rules them all, heaven and earth, hell and sea, and the gods. This world, the world above, and all living creatures obey him. Love is the cohesive force in the universe.[3] It holds society together and the nations. It is the author of peace, law, and justice. Love produces the harvest and the flowers of spring. It causes the birds to nest and the cattle to bring forth. It governs the wild beasts. It leads the maid to her husband, and it

[1] *Ibid.*, pp. 3527–8.

[2] *Ibid.*, p. 3527. See Petrarch, *Le Rime In Vita Di Madonna Laura*, 127.

[3] Here we see the influence of the neoPlatonic ideas revived by the Florentine Academy.

generates offspring. Pontano prays to Erato that love may be merciful to him. He prays to love to be kind. This ode is a hymn celebrating love with a modern philosophical rather than an ancient mythological bent. As Ronsard translated Pontano's "Hymn to Night," so du Bellay adapted his "Power of Love."

"Ad amorem,"[1] also written in sapphic stanzas, is a lighter ode. It lists love's powers to taunt the god because some women are too tough for his arrows. A similar ode, in sapphic stanzas, is addressed "Ad solem."[2] After describing the god in his different aspects and listing his powers, it prays the sun to favour lovers, to burn the girls who spurn their suitors, and to help him with Fanny. Another ode is a mock hymn to Venus. He summons her to her altar to accept the dedication of a lock of hair and a kiss.[3]

Two other odes are epinicia. "Laudes Alfonsi, ducis Calabriae, de victoria Hydruntina"[4] appears to have been written for the civic triumph, for the victory procession, presumably in Naples, after the defeat of the Turks. In sapphic stanzas it addresses first Mens, the daughter of Jupiter, then the crowd. It pictures the different aspects of the victory and, to suggest the whole battle scene, it uses a common movie camera technique—it shoots a scene here and a scene there; it picks out the leaders in action; it focuses on a sword, a spear, a horse, a shield, and a standard. Then, shifting swiftly from the imagined past to the present, Pontano addresses the crowd and bids them cheer at these various objects of war that appear before them. Shout "Io triumphe," here is Alfonso! Now, rejoice, decorate the churches, the squares, and the houses, and bring forth the wine. The poem ends in Pindaric fashion with a reference to the poet's self. This is the type of lively public poem, like Pintoricchio's great paintings of state occasions, that Bishop Campano had already written for Pope Pius II. It is a successful laureate ode, roughly in the Horatian tradition, but its method of celebrating the victory through the description of the triumphal procession is original.

The second epinician is more Pindaric. "Laudes Alfonsi Aragonei, Ducis Calabriae, Ferdinandis regis filii de clarissima

[1] Pontano, pp. 3542–3.
[2] *Ibid.*, pp. 3532–4.
[3] *Ibid.*, pp. 3549–50.
[4] *Ibid.*, pp. 3535–6.

eius victoria,"[1] likewise written in sapphic stanzas, opens, in Pindaric style, with a series of general statements: worship adorns the gods; the shore, gems, and the fleet adorn the sea; ... and praise adorns man. There follows reflections on the desire for praise, fame, and glory, then descriptions of the feats of Hercules, Bacchus, Alexander, Caesar, and Scipio. An impulse similar to theirs governs Alfonso; so now all praise him. This ode is Pontano's most classical.

"Antinianam Nympham invocat ad cantandas laudes urbis Neapolis,"[2] as its title implies, a sapphic ode addressed to Antiniana praising the city of Naples, belongs to the familiar medieval genre of the praise of a city, popular still in the Renaissance.[3] "Ad fidem,"[4] a Horatian moral ode, is a protest against modern irreligion and ecclesiastical corruption, and an attack on the pope, apparently Roderigo Borgia. Like all Pontano's other odes it is written in sapphic stanzas. "Ad amicam de eius pulchritudine, et amantis infelicitate"[5] is a conventional love lyric, sufficiently described by its title.

[1] *Ibid.*, pp. 3540–2. [2] *Ibid.*, 3534–5.

[3] See, e.g., Ausonius' descriptions of twenty famous cities in *Opuscula* (Teubner text, Lipsiae, 1886), pp. 144–54; the eighth-century praise of Milan in *Poeti Latini Aevi Carolingii* I, 24 ff.; the ninth-century praise of Verona, *ibid.*, I, 119 ff.; the tenth-century praise of Rome, F. J. E. Raby, *A History of Secular Latin Poetry in the Middle Ages* I (Oxford, 1934), 29; the late tenth-century English poem "The Ruin" in the *Exeter Book*; Giraldus Cambrensis' description of the ruins of Caerleon, *Itinerarium Cambriae* I, 5; Hildebert of Lavardin's elegies on Rome, Raby, *op cit.*, I, 324–5; the twelfth-century English "Durham Poem"; and William Dunbar's "London, thou art the flour of cities all." For other Renaissance examples see Ugolino Verino, *De illustratione urbis Florentiae*; F. Nausea Blancicampianus, "Encomium Patavii Urbis," *Carmina Illustrium Poetarum Italorum* VI (Florentiae, 1720), 303–5; Andrea Navagero, "De Patavio a militibus vastata," *Carmina quinque Illustrium Poetarum* (Bergomi, 1753), pp. 74–5; Giovanni Francesco Quinziano Stoa, *Cleopolis* [praise of Paris], *c.* 1514; Marc Antonio Flaminio, "De laudibus Mantuae," *Carmina* (Fano, 1515) [pp. 25–6] (there is no pagination in this volume); Germanius Audebertus Aurelius, eulogies, with a description of their art and culture, of Venice, Rome, and Naples, *Delitiae C Poetarum Gallorum* I (n.p., 1609), 91–252; Joachim Bellay Andinus, eulogy of Rome, *ibid.*, I, 391–400; Hippolytus Capilupus, two eulogies of Rome in *Capiluporum Carmina* (Romae, 1590); and Marullus, *Carmina*, ed. Alessandro Perosa (Zürich, 1951), "De Laudibus Senae," pp. 58–9, and "De Laudibus Rhacusae," pp. 89–91.

[4] Pontano, *Carm.*, pp. 3548–9. [5] *Ibid.*, pp. 3543–4.

The last of the odes, "Uxorem in Somnis alloquitur,"[1] is again something new. The subject is a dream which the poet had in which he saw his dead wife, Ariadne, and his joy at the dream. Pontano praises night because it gives rest and also sends dreams, and restores the dead to life. This poem is an offering to his wife's spirit; till love rejoins them in heaven he asks Ariadne to visit him at night. Of Pontano's predecessors Tibullus—he describes a dream in which Apollo told him that Neaera wanted to marry another man[2]—and Propertius—he tells how he dreamt that Cynthia was shipwrecked[3] and how, later, on the day of her funeral, her image appeared to him in his sleep, fresh from the funeral pyre and the waters of Lethe[4] —alone described personal dreams. Generally speaking, the ancients were interested in dreams only for their utility,[5] for their prophetic importance, while medieval people, more introverted, examined dreams for an allegorical meaning. Now, perhaps receiving a hint from Propertius, Pontano has enlarged the confines of poetic expression by writing a modern dream poem based on modern ideas of love. After Pontano Navagero wrote an "Ad Somnum" describing a dream in which he possessed the scornful Neaera.

In the three books *De amore conjugali* there are no odes. This work is more like the traditional book of elegies than the *Amores*, since it tells the history of a whole relationship, but it is completely new and modern in that its history is one of married love and domesticity. The two books of *Tumuli* also contain no odes; neither does the conventional, Christian *De Laudibus Divinis*.

As the introductory and concluding poems suggest, the two books of *Hendecasyllabi seu Baiae* are composed of a kind of *vers de société*, of lascivious occasional poems and epigrams on the love and lechery of the Riviera of pre-Tridentine Italy. However, the collection does contain an occasional Horatian ode. "Laetatur de reditu Francisci Aelii"[6] is a real song of

[1] *Ibid.*, pp. 3539–40. This ode, as was suggested above, is in sapphic stanzas.
[2] Tibullus, *Elegiarum* III, 4.
[3] Propertius, *Elegiarum* II, 26.
[4] *Ibid.*, IV, 7.
[5] Tibullus, *Elegiarum* III, 4, discusses this himself.
[6] Pontano, *Carm.*, pp. 3457–8.

joy on the return of a friend from Rome to Naples. Pontano invites his other friends to dinner and imagines the gay festivities. "Dulce est, ob reducem madere amicum" he says, echoing Horace's "recepto / Dulce mihi furere est amico."[1] This poem, with its mythological allusions, is Horatian in content and technique, but Catullan in its enthusiastic raptures. It is an ode because it gives a universalized treatment to a universal human theme, though it is full of particular names and particular feelings. Another ode, Horatian in inspiration, is "Ad Actium Syncerum Sannazarium,"[2] an invitation and an exhortation to his fellow poet to leave his work and come to Baiae and enjoy the pleasures and romances of a holiday resort. The poem, though trivial, seems to have taken its controlling ideas from Horace's similar invitation to Vergil (not the poet) in *Carminum* IV, 12.

Pontano was not, like some of the humanists, a virtuoso experimenter, a writer of poetic exercises. He was a true poet, completely at home in Latin, who used the learned language for all his great works, as his own; Latin was the language of his business, as well as being the language of his relaxation. Sometimes, for his most familiar works, he made his Latin more tender with the friendly diminutives of Italian, but generally the Latin that he used in his poetry was thoroughly classical. Conventional, too, were the forms of his lyrics. Pontano's contribution to the development of the modern ode lay in the variety of mood and experience that he showed could be expressed in that genre. There were poems of emotion, poems of mood, and poems of society. Moreover, while his pastoral, eclogue-odes were not destined to produce any neo-latin progeny, they revealed to vernacular writers the possible breadth and richness of the ode. They revealed how, still remaining within the extreme limits of the lyric, one could interpret an event in its cosmic meaning. They showed the way, however distantly, to Milton's "Ode on the Morning of Christ's Nativity."

Pontano is at least a highly respected name among those who are interested in Renaissance poetry. Nevertheless, like the rest of the humanists, he is far too little known even in his native

[1] Horace, *Carm.* II, 7, lines 27–8. [2] Pontano, *Carm.*, pp. 3458–60.

Italy. Marullus, however, despite the fact that he was Ronsard's favourite neolatin poet—and Ronsard's judgment is not to be despised—Marullus is hardly known at all. There has been almost nothing written about him in French, although the Pléiade scholars Nolhac, Chamard, and Laumonier have demanded a study of the humanists, and little in Italian, despite the impulse given by Benedetto Croce's interest in him.[1] In English Marullus has been neglected along with almost all the other humanists. Yet he was an interesting person as well as an extremely fine poet. A Byzantine Greek by origin—he was born in 1453 as his family fled from the fall of Byzantium—he grew up in the little, but beautiful republic of Ragusa in the days of its glory. He was educated in Italy, in Ancona, and perhaps also in Venice and Padua. Then he became a soldier of fortune and fought in the slavic countries and in Italy, for the various Italian states. Marullus became a member of the Neapolitan Academy with Pontano and Sannazaro, fled from Naples in the midst of the Franco-Aragonese troubles, and then won the favour of the Medici in Florence. There, the story goes, he defeated Poliziano in love, and although middle-aged and without means, married the young, beautiful, and scholarly Alessandra Scala.[2] In the year 1500 Marullus was drowned trying to cross a river in flood. His wife entered a convent and died of grief six years later, barely thirty years of age.

In 1493 and 1497 Marullus had already published two volumes of Latin poetry, *Epigrammata* and *Hymni*, which entitle him to a high place in the rank of Latin poets, whether ancient or modern. These volumes we will consider here.

The *Epigrammata* is a collection of poems, mostly occasional, written in various metres, elegiac couplets, iambic trimeters, first and second asclepiads, hendecasyllabics, etc. Many of these poems are what we usually consider epigrams in the broader, ancient sense, short poems written to celebrate a

[1] See Benedetto Croce, *Poeti e Scrittori del pieno e del tardo Rinascimento* II (Bari, 1945), 269–380.

[2] Vittorio Rossi, *Il Quattrocento* (Milano, 1953), pp. 385–6, thinks the story of the rivalry with Poliziano over Alessandra Scala apocryphal. However, whether its cause was personal or professional jealousy, there certainly was a bitter feud between the two poets.

particular occasion or event, often amorous, and quite without "point" or sting. All of the poems written in elegiac couplets are epigrams and many of those in hendecasyllabics and other metres. Only the poems which have the elaboration and the generalization of the ode will be considered here.

One of the most pleasant surprises in humanist poetry is Marullus' "Ad Manilium Rhallum"[1] on May Day. Written in sapphic stanzas to a friend who is grieving on May morning, this poem, like the poems of Landino and Pontano, reveals how the Renaissance, at its best, increased the technical means of expression of the poet without deadening his inspiration, thus enriching the poetic tradition. Here Marullus uses the lyric technique that he has learnt from the ancients to celebrate a wholly modern festival in a poem that is immediately reminiscent of Herrick's "Corinna's going a-maying." The metrical form is Horatian and so, perhaps, is the consistently pictorial method of expression, the introduction of Cupid in his saffron cloak in the place of more abstract remarks on romance, the contrast between smiling nature and a festive society and the grieving friend, and the remarks on the brevity of human life and the folly of not enjoying it. Vocabulary and syntax, too, are often suggestive of Horace. But this poem is far from being a stale repetition of a Horatian formula. Marullus has, like Herrick, the precious ability to recreate a scene and recapture its emotion. The ode is full of motion and gaiety and life and, like most modern poetry, it is more leisurely in its development and more generous in supplying transitions than the sparely-built, tightly-constructed Horatian ode. There is a little more suggestiveness in its descriptions too, they are a bit more impressionistic, a little less clearly-defined than Horace's sharp, bright, firmly-circumscribed pictures. It is worth quoting Marullus' ode on May Day almost in full:

Non vides verno variata flore[2]
Tecta, non postes viola revinctos?
Stat coronatis viridis iuventus
  Mixta puellis.

[1] *Michaelis Marulli Carmina*, ed. Alessandro Perosa (Zürich, 1951), pp. 28–9.

[2] The opening seems to have been suggested by Horace, *Carm.* I, 9, "Vides ut alta stet nive candidum."

Concinunt Maias pueri Kalendas,
Concinunt senes bene feriati:
Omnis exultat locus, omnis aetas
  Laeta renidet.

Ipse, reiectis humero capillis,
Candet in palla crocea Cupido,
Acer et plena iaculis pharetra,
  Acer et arcu.

Et modo huc circumvolitans et illuc,
Nectit optatas iuvenum choreas,
Artibus notis alimenta primo
  Dum parat igni;

Nunc puellaris medius catervae
Illius flavum caput illiusque
Comit et vultus oculisque laetum
  Addit honorem.

Mitte vaesanos, bone Rhalle, questus:
Iam sat indultum patriae ruinae est:
Nunc vocat lusus positisque curis
  Blanda voluptas.

Quid dies omneis miseri querendo
Perdimus dati breve tempus aevi? . . .

Do you not see the houses decked with spring
Flowers? The door-posts bound with violets?
Blooming youths mingle with
Garlanded girls.

The children sing of the first of May,
Their elders sing, happy of the holiday.
Every place dances, every age
Beams with joy.

Cupid himself, his hair flung back on his
Shoulders, gleams in a golden cloak;
And he is swift with the darts from his full quiver,
And he is swift with his bow.

And now, flitting about, this way and that,
He links the young people in the dances they desire,
While he prepares the fuel for love's first fire
With his notorious arts.

Now, midst the company of girls,
He adorns that one's golden head,
And that one's face, and he adds the beauty
Of joy to their eyes.

An end, my dear Rhallus, to your distracted
lamentation,
Now you have indulged enough in the ruin of your
native land,
Now amusement calls and, your cares laid aside,
Sweet pleasure.

Why do we, wretches, complaining every day,
Lose the brief expanse of life that is given us? . . .

Many of Marullus' poems "Ad amorem" are conventional short love lyrics, Catullan in inspiration. One[1] is Horatian in its theme, "Yet another love," in its pictorial technique, in its phraseology, and in its second asclepiad metre. However, in addition to these, there is a full-scale Horatian hymn-ode written in sapphic stanzas.[2] Here, in the best Horatian manner, love is defined by listing his cult centres—not the best known—then by his parentage, through his iconography,

Nobilem flammis, et habente certa
Tela pharetra,[3]

Renowned for your flames and for the quiver containing
Sure darts

and finally by his powers. His powers are illustrated by two myths, the first of Apollo and Admetus' bulls, the second, of the wandering Io, of Apis and Isis. The first myth is accompanied by four natural illustrations, of the power of love over the whale, the lions in the Lybian sands, the nightingale, and the serpent. It will be noted that all the illustrations of the power of love emphasize its cruelty.

[1] Marullus, pp. 63–4. [2] *Ibid.*, pp. 70–1. [3] *Ibid.*, p. 70.

"Ad Somnum,"[1] although it roughly follows the same structural pattern as the foregoing is more like a neoclassical than a classical ode. The neoclassical ode to a personified abstraction represented the highest imaginative achievement[2] of that age of would-be original geniuses, perhaps because the subjects were fresher and suggested fewer clichés and well-worn illustrations on the one hand and because, dealing generally with moral qualities, they demanded fidelity to human psychology on the other. So this poem with its analysis of sleep stands out among humanist odes as a new expression of human experience and also as a foretaste of what was to be.[3]

Somne pax animi quiesque lassi,
Curarum fuga, Somne, saevientum,
Unus qui recreas fovesque saecla,
Idem regibus et popello inerti,[4]

Sleep, the soul's peace and the rest of the tired
  spirit,
Sleep, the remedy for ravening cares,
You who alone recreate and nurture the world,
The same to kings and to dull clods,

"Why do you shun some men and come to others only with terrors that lead to desperation and suicide?" It will be noticed that this poem is much less conventional than Pontano's tone poem on night. It may have received part of its inspiration from Statius' "Ad Somnum."[5]

Another group of odes is written to friends. In the third asclepiad metre Marullus writes to his fellow exile, Manilius Rhallus.[6] The ode is Horatian in its treatment of its theme which is itself a kind of anti-Horatian. "The west wind does not always blow, neither is the Adriatic always safe for sailing. The nightingale does not sing every day, nor do roses, lilies and hyacinths always clothe the earth. We have had our share of good; we have been distinguished men in our native land.

[1] *Ibid.*, pp. 92–3.

[2] E. R. Wasserman, "The Inherent Values of Eighteenth-Century Personification," *PMLA*, LXV (1950), 435–63.

[3] See, e.g., Wordsworth's sonnets to sleep.

[4] Marullus, p. 92.

[5] Statius, *Silvarum* V, 4.

[6] Marullus, pp. 77–8.

What is surprising about our change of lot, that we must suffer all the hardships of exile? Consider the fate of Croesus, of Priam who had to go on embassy to Achilles. The shepherd and peasant of Lazio, ignorant of their ancestry, have destroyed many kings, soon to be destroyed themselves. If exile awaits us we must live where the gods will. I rely on the kindness of Caesar [Maximilianus Caesar] who may even save my home." Here we have the Horatian series of pictures, the specific examples, the analogies between nature and the vicissitudes of human life, the emphasis on the instability of fortune, and the concluding tribute to the poet's patron. There are even Horatian echoes, e.g., "grata Favonii."[1]

"Ad Baptistam Faeram,"[2] written in second asclepiads, is completely different. It is another example of a new poem being created from the union of modern ideas and the recently mastered technique of the ancients. Like Tennyson in *In Memoriam*, Marullus expresses the passage of time since he has seen Baptista through natural phenomena. For the third time Ceres has come back with her temples bound with golden grain like Autumn in Keats's famous ode:

> Iam aestas torrida tertium
>   Aestatisque parens flava redit Ceres,
> Cincta concava tempora
>   Foecundae segetis muneribus sacris,
> Ex quo perditus occidi.[3]

> Now for a third time the broiling summer,
>   And the golden-haired mother of summer, Ceres, returns,
> Her rounded temples ringed
>   With the sacred gifts of the fertile cornfield,
> Since I perished, broken-hearted.

Now the poet wanders like a lost soul, "Styge naufragus,"[4] through groves and woods, everywhere haunted by a face:

> Nam quaecunque oculis patent,
>   Illic continuo vultus, et aurei
> Occursat capitis decor,
>   Et quae nec fugere est lumina nec pati.

[1] *Ibid.*, p. 77, line 1.
[2] *Ibid.*, pp. 86–7.
[3] *Ibid.*, p. 86, lines 1–5.
[4] *Ibid.*, p. 86, line 7.

Ipsa robora habent genas
    Oris purpurei et pectora eburnea,
Ipsa sibila frondium
    Charum nomen, et agnosco sub amnibus
Responsantis herae sonum,
    Tam diversa locis quam regio tenet.[1]

For wherever I look,
    There, straightaway, her face, and the beauty
Of that golden head, rush to meet me,
    And those eyes that one cannot escape from, nor endure.

The very oaks have the cheeks
    Of her rosy face, and her ivory breast,
The very leaves whisper
    Her dear name, and I recognize, beneath the rivers'
Sound, my lady's answering,
    Where'er I turn in the district.

We are reminded of Petrarch, who saw the absent Laura in every manifestation of nature,[2] of Keats, of the face Endimion saw in the pond, of Shelley, and Alastor's vision of perfection, or of Rossetti and the Blessed Damozel appearing in the sights and sounds of sunset. Here we have the Horatian metre, the Horatian pictorial method, and the adapted allegorical figure used as a means of expressing a medieval, i.e., for Marullus, a modern, concept of love; while the whole is suffused with the glamour of the half-unknown, with the suggestion of some mysterious sympathy between man and nature, and a hint at a supernatural. This is what makes romantic poetry.

The next group of poems is political. These odes are almost all written in Horatian metres; they all develop their themes according to Horatian formulae, use the Horatian technique in expressing their ideas, and even borrow Horatian phrases. "Ad Maximilianum Caesarem"[3] uses the ship of state metaphor, "De Victoria Ferdinandi regis Hispaniarum"[4] celebrates the royal triumph with an old bottle of Falernian and roses strewn on the ground, "De Maximiliano Caesare,"[5] on the

[1] *Ibid.*, p. 87, lines 13–22.

[2] See Petrarch, *Le Rime In Vita Di Madonna Laura*, 227, "In quella parte dov' Amor mi sprona," and 129, "Di pensier in pensier, di monte in monte."

[3] Marullus, pp. 55–6. [4] *Ibid.*, p. 62. [5] *Ibid.*, p. 80.

emperor's survival of an attempt at assassination, comments on our vain efforts to avoid death when the fated hour has struck, "Ad Carolum Regem Franciae"[1] prays the king to oppose the Turks as did his ancestor, Charlemagne, etc.

Marullus' *Neniae* are equally unextraordinary. They resemble the Horatian odes in subject, metre, and mode of expression, but are distinguished from the odes in that they are all complaints and are consequently written in a less literary, more conversational style. "De Acerbitate Fortunae"[2] is a long-winded and repetitious version of a familiar theme. "Nenia"[3] is a complaint about the poet's exile with comments on the current political situation. "De Morte Ioannis Medicis"[4] indicates the magnitude of the loss through mythological comparisons. "Ad Carolum Regem Gallorum"[5] advises the king to stop hunting and look after the dangerous political situation.

The last group are the hymns, which, like the secular odes, have learnt new means of expression from the classics without losing the fervour, the enthusiasm, that we associate with the medieval hymn tradition. The first of these hymns, "Jovi Optimo Maximo,"[6] can make only the most slender claim to be lyrical; rather it is a doctrinal preface to the whole. It is a philosophical and rational rather than an emotional statement of belief. It outlines the recently Christianized, neoPlatonic cosmology with its system of divine government through delegated powers.[7] It is appropriately written in hexameters.

The next hymn, "Palladi,"[8] is written in iambic couplets and, while it follows the Horatian hymn pattern, it has the expansiveness of the epode. The poet invokes Pallas, praising her in exclamations and listing her powers. He summons her from alternative cult centres—or perhaps she is in heaven

Quo non metus, non inquies penetrat dolor,
Dubiisque senium gressibus,
Aut sydus anni noxium, aut Auster gravis
Morbis domesticis signum.

[1] *Ibid.*, pp. 98–100. [2] *Ibid.*, pp. 169–72. [3] *Ibid.*, 172–6.
[4] *Ibid.*, 176–8. [5] *Ibid.*, pp. 178–81. [6] *Ibid.*, pp. 105–8.
[7] See Marsilio Ficino's commentary on the *Timaeus*.
[8] Marullus, pp. 108–10.

Sed cuncta vere germinans semper novo,
  Vivis malignae nescia.
Et nunc fluentis irrigantur lacteis,
  Nunc melle passim Hymetio.
At ipsa curru flammeo septemiugo
  Ter auream quassans comam
Longum citatas huc et huc agis rotas
  Ausis tremenda masculis,
Subsidit aether ipse, contremit fretum,
  Emota respondent sola.

Where neither Fear nor restless Grief can penetrate
  Nor Age with tottering steps,
Nor the star that wrecks the harvest, nor the South Wind,
  Big with disease.
But all things are in perpetual bloom in a new spring
  Which knows no evil change,
And now all is watered by streams
  Of milk, now by Hymettus honey.
But you, yourself, in the flaming, seven-yoked chariot,
  Thrice shaking your golden locks,
Long drive your whirling wheels this way and that,
  Awesome in your masculine daring:
The air itself sinks down, the sea shudders,
  And the quaking earth replies.

Here we recognize something of the apocalyptic vision of Saint John along with the classical, Homeric, Horatian concept of Olympus and the Insulae Fortunatae. It will be noted that the dilation of this description suggests that in Horace's sixteenth epode rather than anything in the odes.

Now, the poet visualizes Pallas in heaven, and again we are struck by the Christianity of the concept. Pallas inevitably suggests the Virgin Mary[1] and the three hundred maidens with their lilies, the medieval symbol of virginity, or their roses, the symbol of martyrdom, call to mind many devotional paintings including the great mosaic running along the whole of the north wall of the nave of the church of Sant' Apollinare Nuovo in Ravenna, a church that Marullus certainly knew,

Atque trecentae virgines stipant latus
  Olea revinctae candida,

[1] Cf. Hippolytus Capilupus' ode to the Virgin Mary infra.

Pars haeret uno fixa in obtutu Deae,
Tam forti ab ore pendula.
Aliae aut recenti lilio, aut spargunt rosis,
Quod quaeque potis est conferens.

But three hundred maidens crowd your side,
Their brows bound with the shining olive.
Part cling, fixed on the gaze of the goddess alone,
Hanging from so strong a visage.
Others scatter fresh lilies or roses,
Each one giving what she is able.

Among the maidens Homer and Orpheus, the great ancient hymn writers, sing lofty praises to their harps of adamant. Like the three magi in the Ravenna mosaic they adore their God with their gifts.

Pallas herself is described in typically Christian antitheses suggestive of the creeds, particularly the Athanasian:

Eadem virgo, mas eadem, eadem furor,
Sapientiaque eadem, et quies.

The same a maid, the same a man, the same madness,
And the same wisdom and quiet.

The poet describes her acts and gifts to men, fixed homes, the citadel and fortifications, the arts, justice and the laws, and friendship. She translates men to heaven and she is the teacher of heavenly doctrine. He prays that she may come:

Animisque nostris ades, et atra nubila
Discute tua immensa face.

And come to our spirits and dispel the black
Clouds with your enormous torch.

This hymn is remarkable for its tone of religious devotion and for its intense emotion.

"Amori,"[1] written in sapphic stanzas, Horatian in technique and phraseology, and like the odes in its structural tightness and economy, is strangely suggestive, at times, of Spenser's *Hymne in Honour of Love*, perhaps because of common ancestry in Ficino's commentary on the *Symposium*. The poem begins

[1] Marullus, pp. 110–12.

with a definition of the deity by his powers, his iconography (wings), his parentage, and through a myth (lover of nymphs). The extent of his domains, north, east, south, and west, is expressed by specific references. His power in heaven is described. It was he who formed chaos into the great chain of being maintained by forces of attraction and repulsion,

> Quid, quod et novas Chaos in figuras
> Digeris primus, docilemque rerum
> Mutuis nectis seriem catenis
> Pace rebelli.

> And why are you the first to direct Chaos into
> New shapes and to bind together the docile chain
> Of things with mutual bonds
> In a rebellious peace?

Love is the ruler of the world, the giver of laws and rights, and the teacher of reproductive acts. The poet pictures Cupid in the lap of his beautiful mother with his companions, the graces and the fates. He hymns the god,

> O quies magnae reparatioque
> Grata Naturae, columemque rerum,

> O rest, and welcome refreshment of
> Mighty nature, and mainstay of the world,

expresses his personal devotion, and prays that Cupid may show pity and release his heart from cares.

The ancient characteristics are evident. More interesting are the general parallels with Spenser. Spenser, too, defines love by his powers, birth, and parentage. For him, too, love is the former of Chaos. Spenser, like Marullus, pictures love in beauty's lap and he, too, complains about his own sufferings as a lover.

"Veneri"[1] is Marullus' outstanding poetic achievement. Here the ancient and modern are in perfect balance, Christian philosophy and pagan mythology, spiritual fervour and flawless art. This ode bears the same general resemblance to Spenser's hymn on the same subject as the previous ode does. What is

[1] *Ibid.*, pp. 129–33.

particularly surprising is that both poets wrote poems to love and beauty which were to a considerable extent repetitious of each other. Thus, in the present poem, Venus has become the orderer of chaos and the civilizer of man:

Ante nec terrae facies inerti
Nec suus stellis honor et sine ullis
Aura torpebat zephyris, sine ullis
  Piscibus unda.

Prima de patris gremio Cythere
Caeca Naturae miserata membra,
Solvit antiquam minimum pigendo
  Foedere litem.

Illa supremis spatiis removit
Lucidum hunc ignem mediasque terras
Arte suspendit pelagusque molles
  Inter et auras:

Tunc et immenso micuere primum
Signa tot coelo et sua flamina aer
Cepit, admirans volucrum proterva
  Proelia fratrum.

Tunc repentinis freta visa monstris
Fervere et nova facie novoque
Flore diffusos aperire tellus
  Daedala vultus.

Iam greges passim varios boumque ar-
Menta, iam pictas volucres ferasque
Surgere emotis erat hic et illic
  Cernere glebis;

At virum, quamvis etiam labante
Aegra plebs genu, meditari et urbes
Tectaque et iam tum sociorum amicos
  Iungere coetus.

Before the inert earth possessed its aspect,
And the stars their glory, when without any
Zephyrs the air lay still, and without any
Fish the sea,

Cythera first from her father's bosom,
Pitying the unsightly members of Nature,
Resolved the ancient conflict by a contract
Acceptable to all.

To space on high she removed
This gleaming fire and by art she hung
The earth in the middle between the sea
And the gentle breezes.

Then for the first time these many constellations sparkled
In the infinite heavens, and the air began
Its blasts, gazing in wonder at the headlong clashes
Of the brother winds.

Then the seas seemed to boil with sudden
Monsters and, with a fresh form, and never-before-seen
Flowers, the cunning artificer, earth, revealed
Her widespread countenance.

Now the flocks in their kinds and the herds of cattle,
Now the painted birds and the wild beasts appeared
Everywhere, emerging, on this side and on that,
From the crumbling clods.

But man, although still a weak race with a faltering
Knee, was seen to be planning cities
And buildings and then, even, forming friendly
Bands of comrades.

Creation and civilization finished, Venus departs for Cyprus borne along by yoked doves. The earth smiles at the coming of the goddess, as do the sea and the air. With her head wreathed she leads the choral dances. Youth, Pleasure, and the Graces follow her, and Mars neglects war to watch. Venus' influence over nature and her distraction of Mars remind us of the beginning of the *De Rerum Natura*[1] while the description of the dance calls to mind Horace's fourth ode of the first book, although it echoes a line, 16, from III, 18. Now the poet prays the goddess to reveal herself, to dispel the darkness and allow us to see her blessed temple. The conclusion has Christian overtones.

[1] There is even a borrowing from Lucretius, "Aura Favoni," Marullus, line 64, p. 132, Lucretius, I. 11.

Of the remaining hymns the two most outstanding are the "Aeternitati"[1] and "Soli."[2] "Aeternitati" is a hexameter ode to Eternity, queen of unmeasured time, who dwells in the gleaming temple of ether. There are some memorable descriptions of allegorical figures, of Youth, like Apollo, with uncut golden hair, Virtue with her foot of bronze, bounteous Nature, a venerable old man with a curved sickle, and the Hours and Years coming and going. "Soli" like "Iovi" is a long, semi-philosophical poem in hexameters that can make small claim to the title of ode though it certainly is a hymn, of the sort later cultivated by Ronsard. It is notable as being one of the earliest, if not the earliest Renaissance poem, to make extravagant claims to divine inspiration, borrowing from Aeschylus' Cassandra, Vergil's Sibyl, and Horace's introduction to his third book of odes, "Procul, O, procul este profani." I will quote this passage since this kind of opening was a bane to later odes where the intensity of the simulated frenzy was in inverse proportion to the quality of the poetic inspiration:

> Quis novus hic animis furor incidat? unde repente
> Mens fremit? horrentique sonant praecordia motu?
> Quis tantus quatit ossa tremor? procul este profani
> Este: movent imis delubra excussa cavernis
> Adventante Deo, et mons circum immane remugit.

What new madness now falls upon our spirits? Why does the mind
Suddenly resound and the heart pound dreadfully?
Why does so great a trembling shake the bones? Afar, profane ones,
Afar! In the depths of the cavern the sanctuary quakes
At the close approach of the god, and the mountain roars frightfully round about.

The hymn-ode—there were other examples as well as those that we have cited: "Coelitibus," "Baccho," "Pani," "Coelo," "Stellis," "Saturno," "Iovi," "Marti," "Mercurio," "Aetheri,"

[1] Marullus, pp. 113–14. Marullus' "Aeternitati" inspired Ronsard in his hymn to Eternity, H. Chamard, *Origines de la Poésie Française de la Renaissance* (Paris, 1920), p. 302.

[2] Marullus, pp. 136–44.

"Iovi Fulgatori," "Iunoni," "Oceano," and "Terrae"[1]—was Marullus' most important contribution to the developing and expanding new genre of ode. In this he was followed by Crinito and Flaminio in Latin and, through the latter, by Bernardo Tasso in Italian. Pontano's "De amoris dominatu" was roughly contemporary. These poems of Marullus celebrating the gods resembled neither the epic Homeric, nor the elaborately mythological Callimachan, nor the briefer, simpler Orphic (or similar short Homeric) hymns. They were like the new ode in form and extent, in sensuousness and emotion, and contained as much reflection as mythology. They were not works of pagan devotion but loving, lingering examinations of what was become, especially under the auspices of neo-Platonism, part of our culture, the beauty of hellenism. The gods are not just gods but concepts, in which we all have some sort of belief. This philosophizing and universalizing of the Greek gods makes it very easy for Marullus also to hymn an abstraction or an idea, to slip over unnoticeably from a "Veneri" to an "Aeternitati."

Marullus has taken another step in another direction towards broadening the classical lyric into the modern ode. Now all sorts of subjects can be celebrated in this new kind of classical inspired lyric, a poem of some weight, of moderate length, formal, and ceremonious, full of interpretative imagery, reflective and philosophical, but whose formality need by no means be obtrusive, and which, far from being cold and artificial, may be sensuous, and emotional, and suggestive. This is not to imply, however, that these odes have been bloated out of shape by a nebulous emotionalism. Despite their reflectiveness they retain a typical ancient concreteness and pictorial vividness. Pontano with his eclogue-odes may have suggested in one way the possibility of the "Nativity Ode." Marullus' hymns go much farther, adding depth and emotion and religious feeling to Pontano's highly decorated mythological panorama.

[1] *Ibid.*, pp. 112–13; 115–16 ("Baccho" inspired Ronsard's hymn to Bacchus, Chamard, *Origines*, p. 302); 117–20; 120 ("Coelo" inspired Ronsard's hymn to heaven, Chamard, *loc. cit.*); 121–2 ("Stellis" inspired Ronsard's hymn to the stars, Chamard, *loc. cit.*); 122–4; 124–6 (another hymn to Jupiter, not the one previously mentioned); 126–9; 133–5; 148–50; 151–5; 156–60; 160–3; 163–5.

Marullus' other poems, like those of Landino and Pontano, show emotion and sentiment, in this case particularly Petrarchism, establishing themselves in the ode. Even the most pedestrian of them recommends itself by a never failing felicity of phrase. Marullus was one of the most considerable poets of fifteenth-century Europe.

Another member of Lorenzo de Medici's circle and a student of Poliziano's, was Pietro Del Riccio, whose name was latinized as Crinitus and then italianized as Crinito.[1] Crinito was born in Florence in 1465 and died in the early years of the sixteenth century. His main works were *De honesta disciplina* (Lugduni, 1585), *De Poetis Latinis* (Lugduni, 1585), a translation of Horace with a commentary and notes (Venezia, 1590), and some sixty lyrics, many of which were odes.[2] Most of Crinito's odes, apart from the translations from the Greek, were Horatian in form, treatment, and content. Some few, however, were more daring, adaptations of types that were developed during the middle ages and that had no real classical prototypes. Though practically unknown in the present day Crinito is a poet of no little interest and merit. The first group of Crinito's odes might be called poems about the poet. These poems stress the Renaissance concept of the poet as the god inspired cultivator and benefactor of mankind. They labour the "odi profanum vulgus et arceo" theme *ad nauseam*, and they never tire of affirming the poet's conviction of his own immortality. The first poem of the book is "Quod Musis dicatus sit, reiecta populi inscitia,"[3] written in a four line stanza composed of two alcaics and two glyconics. It announces his dedication to poetry.

Musis dicatus semoveo procul
Vulgus profanum

Dedicated to the Muses I shrink far from
The uninitiate horde

[1] There seems to be some question about Crinito's original Italian name. Both the Vatican Library Catalogue, presumably on good authority, and Benedetto Croce in *Poeti e Scrittori del Pieno e del Tardo Rinascimento* II (Bari, 1945), 284, refer to him as "del Riccio," while Curtius in his *European Literature and the Latin Middle Ages* (London, 1953), p. 549, note 10, calls him "Ricci." Crinito is not mentioned in either Rossi or Toffanin's volumes of the *Storia Letteraria d'Italia*.

[2] Pietro Crinito, *Opera Omnia* (Lugduni, 1559), pp. 525–85.

[3] *Ibid.*, pp. 525–6.

is the appropriate Horatian beginning of a poem that is neatly constructed according to Horatian principles. Stanza one tells of the poet's dedication to the Muses and his consequent separation from the crowd. Stanza two contains two concrete pictures, of the prince's coat ("decora . . . Chlamyde") and gemmy goblets. These are the things that Crinito does not have. Stanza three contains one concrete picture, of the golden cloak of the poet ("chelys aurea"), what he does possess, as one taught by the god, "insignis cithara." In stanza four Melpomene weaves the evergreen laurel crown to enrol him in the ranks of the bards ("vatum . . . choris"). Stanza five describes Crinito's poetry, again using a specific illustration: in sequestered valleys Faunus hears the poet singing of the white neck and coral lips of Naevia. Stanza six pictures the poet finding consolation with his lyre. Stanza seven refers back to the first stanza, to the isolation of the poet with his poetry ("doctis carminibus"). Stanza eight argues that it is worse to serve the crowd than to spurn them. Stanza nine states how gladly he accepts his poet's calling; stanza ten, that he may testify to Neaevia's loveliness. Here we have the typical Horatian conclusion, a small, even trivial, concrete illustration of a vast, serious theme, a deliberate anti-climax to pay a pretty compliment to a girl and to love. We are reminded of "Integer vitae."

"De sua aeternitate ex oraculo Apollinis"[1] is written in a rather unusual stanza

3 (– – ⏑ – – – ⏑ ⏑ – ⏑ ⏓)
– – ⏑ – – – ⏑ ⏑

which tends to divide in half. Its subject is just what the title suggests. The development and style are thoroughly Horatian. "Ad Faustum, de suis studiis, et iniquitate sui temporis,"[2] in the first pythiambic metre, discusses the affect of war on morality and particularly upon the life of a humanist and poet. Its philosophy is a kind of Epicureanism familiar from Horace, with the emphasis shifted from wine to learning:

Inque dies vitam veluti moriturus in horas
Carpo, et reservo me mihi.

[1] *Ibid.*, pp. 526–7.

[2] *Ibid.*, pp. 533–4.

And day after day, as though I were going to die in hours, I
seize hold of
Life, and save myself for myself.

The technique is the usual Horatian pictorial. The couplets resemble Dryden's in "Annus Mirabilis," the hexameter line makes a statement, the iambic dimeter varies it, explains it more fully, or interprets it. Sometimes, too, as in "Annus Mirabilis" the one idea is elaborated through several couplets, one couplet merely varying or illustrating the other without advancing the theme:

Additur et nostris haec aetas ferrea damnis,
Qua Mars repressit Pallada.
Officiumque togae periit: tantum arma supersunt,
Geruntur omnia viribus.
Iam video instructas acies in bella vocari.
Promuntur enses Martii.

And added to our injuries is this iron age
In which Mars crushes Pallas,
And the citizen's role has disappeared. To such an
extent are arms supreme.
Everything is done by force.
Now I see the troops in their array summoned to war,
And the martial swords are drawn.

This fulness is, of course, not Horatian, but more modern. The last of these poems about the poet, "Ad Avitum de innocentia Vatum,"[1] is written in greater alcaic lines. It is Horatian in theme, content, and technique.

The next group of odes may be labelled moral. Surprisingly enough, they are less consistently Horatian. "Ad Avitum, de quiete vivendi,"[2] in the choliambic line, is Horatian in spirit. It preaches the Epicurean ἀταραξία, Horatian retirement, and the golden mean. It is competent and commonplace. Horatian, too, is "De sua quiete post multas calamitates"[3] with its sapphic metre, its retirement theme, and its analogy between the life of man and a ship at sea. But this ode is Christian, too; it has adapted a pagan structure to the expression of Christian ideas; for the ἀταραξία is achieved through faith and the retirement is to a religious life where the poet will devote himself to the

[1] *Ibid.*, p. 537. [2] *Ibid.*, p. 531. [3] *Ibid.*, pp. 531–2.

sacred muse. "Monodia de Fortuna et eius viribus"[1] is an undistinguished discussion of Fortune in the greater alcaic line, argumentative rather than pictorial. Equally unHoratian is "Ad Avitum, exhortatio ad Virtutem."[2] In iambic dimeters the poet harangues his straw man, Avitus, about virtue. The moralizing is commonplace and unenlivened by illustrative examples. Here we find the characteristic Renaissance idea that individual worth creates true nobility and that rulers without it are illegitimate. "Ad Phosphorum contra insolentia principum"[3] in the iambic strophe, with its attack on court life and tyrannical princes, is an epode rather than an ode. So is "Ad Marullum Byzantium de improba mordacitate Zoili tardipedis,"[4] an invective in the iambic strophe.

By far the most interesting and certainly the most poetic of the non-Horatian moral odes is "Ad Faustum, de sylva Oricellaria,"[5] also written in the iambic strophe. Here Crinito describes the famous Orti Oricellari outside Florence. On the death of his cousin Lorenzo de Medici in 1492 Bernardo Ruccellai (1449–1514), humanist, historian, and diplomat, proclaimed himself protector of scholarship and the arts in Florence. He built a palazzo with magnificent gardens for the humanists. Here the remnants of the Platonic Academy met, here Machiavelli gave many of his discourses, here Trissino read his *Dialogo della Volgar Lingua*, and here the intellectually alive in Florence assembled for discussions.

In his ode on the Orti Oricellari Crinito is somewhat indebted to the Horatian concept of leisurely retirement. Otherwise the poem is a description of nature of the medieval sort, detailed and catalogue-like.[6] The wood is described tree by tree, that is, species by species:

Dum vernat alta populus
Et dum virenti sibilat pinus coma

lines 12–13

[1] *Ibid.*, pp. 544–5. [2] *Ibid.*, pp. 527–9.
[3] *Ibid.*, pp. 556–7. The title reads ". . . contra insolentium principum," another obvious printer's error through assimilation of endings.
[4] *Ibid.*, p. 561. [5] *Ibid.*, pp. 534–6.
[6] While description was becoming increasingly important in Alexandrian Greek and Imperial Latin and was furthered by the training of the rhetorical schools, despite the important example of Vergil's *Georgics*, it was

In astra surgens maximi quercus Iovis,
  Protendit alta brachia[1]

lines 15–16

Illic et alnus blandienti gratia
  Intexit umbris gramina
Philyraque mollis pervenustis frondibus
  Procrescit in sylvae decus.

lines 19–22

When the tall poplar feels the spring,
And when the pine whispers midst its green locks,

The oak of mightiest Jove, rising up between the stars,
  Stretches out its lofty arms.

And there the alder, with graceful fondling,
  Plaits the lawn with shadows,
And the gentle linden with its flowery branches
  Grows into the glory of the woods,

. . .

only at the end of the classical period that the descriptive poem emerged as a genre. With the descriptions of the Moselle by Ausonius and later Fortunatus we cross the bridge into the middle ages. Here we find descriptive poems in Latin (such as the descriptions of cities previously cited, supra p. 67) and poems in which description bulks large. In the first vernacular literature description is important. We think of the seascapes in *The Wanderer* and *The Seafarer*, the garden in the *Phoenix*, and, later, of the woods and meadows in *The Owl and the Nightingale*, the garden in the *Romance of the Rose*, the elaborate descriptions in the late French romances, in *Sir Gawain and the Green Knight*, *The Pearl*, *The Boke of the Duchesse*, *The Parliament of Foules*, *The Legende of Good Women*, etc. The middle ages delighted in elaborate descriptions of the catalogue type. The description here appears to be medieval in inspiration because of its technique—it describes each species of tree in the wood—and because it describes them in the spring, the favourite season of the medieval poet.

[1] Is "in astra" just a conventional expression, a figure of speech that, through common use, has weakened in meaning until it is just a synonym for "high" or is its visual content intact? Are we supposed to see the stars through the stretching branches of the oak? Do they reach up and grasp the stars? Is Crinito approaching the romantics' imaginative independence, sensitivity, and daring? Cf. Keats, *Endymion*:

As when, upon a trancèd summer night,
Those green-robed senators of mighty woods,
Tall oaks, branch-charmèd by the earnest stars,
Dream, and so dream all night without a stir.

Then come the plants and flowers, then the animals, again species by species:

Lupusque subsilit pavens.
Proludit antris et cuniculus salax,
Sylvaeque cultor hinnulus

lines 50–52

And the wolf starts up in fear,
And the playful rabbit hops in front of its burrow,
And the young stag keeps to the woods.

Finally there is the eighteenth-century type of morally innocent scholarly retirement, a considerable idealization of the atmosphere of Florentine academic circles:

Et o beatum, qui sub antiqua ilice
Liventis expers ambitus
Vel sacra vatum curat, aut doctum otium
Curis solutior fovet.
Sic ille nil miratur aestus principum,
Nec sceptra regum suscipit. . . .

lines 63–68

And how fortunate he is, who, beneath the ancient oak,
Knowing no leaden-faced ambition,
Either gives himself to the poet's sacred art or cherishes a learned
Leisure, free from cares.
Thus, he is not startled by the commotion of princes,
And he does not snatch up the sceptres of kings.

After this we are not surprised at the Horatian egotistical "adunco naso"[1] conclusion:

Sed in virenti detinetur gramine,
Et se reservat posteris.

lines 69–70

But he lingers on the greensward
And preserves himself for posterity.

The remaining non-Horatian ode, "Ad Marullum Byzantium de Imagine et portento Avaritiae"[2] is still more medieval in its content. The poet tells Marullus how he wandered over the ridges of Fiesole consoling himself with a sapphic song [i.e.,

[1] Horace, *Sermonum* I, 6, line 5.

[2] Crinito, *op. cit.*, pp. 553–4.

with love poetry]. Then, laying aside his lyre beneath a green myrtle [Venus' tree], he had started walking towards Florence, the city of Lorenzo de Medici, the father of the Muses and their glory, who entertains and rewards Marullus, when his meditations were interrupted by the appearance of a monster. There follows an allegorical description of Avarice. The structure of this poem is obviously medieval, as is the allegorical monster.

Another ode of a medieval type, yet also new, "Carmen Charisticon ad Eridanum Fluvium pro recepta salute cum in eum decidisset,"[1] is a song of thanksgiving and praise written in the choliambic metre arranged in stanzas of varying length. It belongs to the medieval genre of the praise of a river. It celebrates the Po as Ausonius and Fortunatus celebrated the Moselle and, with echoes and reminiscences, it suggests the germ of this genre in Vergil's *Georgics*, e.g.,

Tot nobilis urbes, tot arduos montes
Et tot perennes amnium simul Nymphas
lines 19–20

Ut vesperi laboris optimi munus
Distenta portet ubera ad pium quaestum.
lines 30–31

So many famous cities, so many steep mountains,
And, all together, the Nymphs of so many unfailing rivers . . .

That at evening it might bring swollen udders
To the faithful milking, the gift of the most rewarding toil.

The "Carmen Charisticon" is much like the seventeenth- and eighteenth-century topographical poem, like Denham's "Cooper's Hill" and Pope's "Windsor Forest." It describes the river in mythological, then physical terms, its course, its cities, mountains, and tributary streams, its green groves, its glades, fountains, flowery meadows, and fattening herds, its silver fish,

Argenteo pisces colore fulgentes
Per blandientis fluminis natant undas,
lines 32–

The fish, gleaming a silvery colour,
Swim through the caressing waves of the river,

the choice varieties, and then the rest of the "lubricum pecus"

[1] *Ibid.*, pp. 543–4.

(line 40), the sighing breezes, and the changing light. And now the Po, with flowers on her head, gleaming with the half-light from heaven, shines a star among the stars.[1]

On a similar occasion, on the escape of his friend, Bernardo Caraffa, from a storm at sea,[2] Crinito contented himself with commonplace Horatian remarks on man's temerity and the inevitability of fate. While a river flows through the cities of men and plays a part in daily life, the sea is still part of a hostile environment, a cruel and mighty enemy with which man must grapple at times to gain material advantages. Man's dominion stops with the shore—Columbus is just now raising his sail in Barcelona—and with it his sympathy. The age has not yet arrived when he can look at the ocean itself and respond to its awful beauty and be moved by its mysterious power. Crinito looks forward to Pope, but not to Byron.

Another group of odes are the "naeniae," laments on the deaths of Lorenzo de Medici,[3] Pico della Mirandola,[4] and Marullus.[5] The first two are commonplace and feelingless, perhaps because of the public position of the men honoured. The "Naenia de obitu Poetae Marulli Byzantii," however, is more interesting. Though not pastoral in form, this ode contains many of the elements of the traditional pastoral elegy,[6] a poet laments the death of a poet, death shocks man into realizing the vanity of human aspirations, the contrast is felt between Marullus' expectations and his fate. This is the first part of the ode, the expression of grief. The second part of the ode, as of the elegy, is concerned with the composition of grief. It begins with the practical statement, "Where can we find a successor?" This is the commencement of adjustment, of the reconciliation of man with fate. The conclusion remarks on the vanity of complaining about the inevitable,

> Sed frustra inerti lacrymans naenia
> Quod arripit fatum potens.

[1] Again we notice in Crinito something akin to the romantics' response to nature. It is not the dancing blue waves of noon that Crinito remembers, but the silvery sheen of the full, smooth surface of the river at her loveliest moments, at dawn and at twilight.

[2] Crinito, *op. cit.*, pp. 557–8, "Ad Bernardum Carapham Neapolitanum."

[3] *Ibid.*, pp. 529–30. [4] *Ibid.*, pp. 563–4. [5] *Ibid.*, pp. 540–1.

[6] See T. P. Harrison, *The Pastoral Elegy* (Austin, Texas, 1939).

But he weeps in vain, in unavailing lament,
For what mighty fate carries off.

It contains no comfort; it is non-Christian; it suggests Horace's

Durum: sed levius fit patientia
Quicquid corrigere est nefas.[1]

It is hard: but patience makes it easier to bear
What the gods do not permit us to change.

There is a coincidental parallel between this ode and *Lycidas* since, in both cases, the poet friends died by drowning.

Crinito's love poetry lacks individuality. "Ad seipsum, de perfidia Neaera"[2] in choliambics plagiarizes Catullus, especially, "Miser Catulle, desinas ineptire,"[3] but it is weak and moralistic. Others have taken Horace as their model.

The mythological poems show more originality. One of the best is "De Natali Musarum,"[4] a brief description in iambic dimeters of the birth of the Muses in the presence of the laughing Lucina, the golden haired musician Apollo, Love, and Beauty. Jupiter looks after them in the cradle, kisses them, and takes them to a grove; then Pegasus carries them to heaven where they are fed on nectar. But best of all is the "Monodia de Saltatio[ne] Bacchica,"[5] written in glyconics arranged in stanzas of varying lengths which conclude with a dactylic penthemim (—⏑⏑—⏑⏓). This is a hymn of the worshippers of Bacchus. It has the usual two parts of exorcism and invocation; it banishes the hostile elements, the sounds and symbols of Mars who is inimical to Bacchus, a god of agriculture and the country, it invokes the spirit of the bacchanal, and it

[1] Horace, *Carm.* I, 24, lines 19–20.

[2] Crinito, p. 550.

[3] Cf., e.g., "Amata nobis, ut nihil magis posset," Crinito, *loc. cit.*, line 3, and "Amata nobis, quantum amabitur nulla," Catullus 8, line 5; "Et quod perivit, perditum quidem ducas," Crinito, *loc. cit.*, line 5, and "Et quod vides periisse, perditum ducas," Catullus 8, line 2; "Tu perfer, obdura, obstinatam habe mentem," Crinito, *loc. cit.*, line 12, and "Sed obstinata mente perfer, obdura," Catullus 8, line 11.

[4] Crinito, p. 574. Note the different treatment of this theme in Ronsard's ode to Michel de l'Hospital.

[5] Crinito, pp. 577–9.

summons the *comitatus* and then the god himself whom the troop joyously welcomes:

Gradivus valeat pater
Et saevus galeae sonus
Huc adsint nemorissequae
Nymphae cum Satyris: leves
Adsint Nisigeni simul,
Adsint et cava cymbala
Et cornu grave mugiat,
Tollite quisque pedem.

lines 1–8

Farewell father Mars,
And the cruel ringing of helmets.
Your presence here, grove-haunting
Nymphs and Satyrs; your presence
At the same time, fleet tribe of Nysa.
And let the hollow cymbals be here,
And let the deep horn bellow,
And, each one of you, lift up your foot.

Come Charis, Chromys, Hamadryas, Mnasyllus, Lyas, Melite, Canace, Dryo:

Mnasyllusque rubens genas,
Et fortis temeto Lyas,
Et nudata lacertulos
Melite, et Canace soror,
Lascivique pedis Dryo,
Pronis in zephyros comis
Ad numerum canite.

lines 14–20

And red-cheeked Mnasyllus,
And Lyas, strong with mead,
And Melite with her small arms
Bare, and Canace, her sister,
And Dryo, of sportive foot,
With your locks streaming on the breeze,
Sing to the beat.

Now let us all, dancing and singing, praise you, Bacchus,

. . . bone Vitifer,
Thyrso et palmite nobilis
Tu victor Semeleius
Summi progenies Iovis[1]

[1] Notice the echo of Catullus," O Latonia maximi / Magna progenies Iovis," *Carm.* 34.

Incingens hedera caput,
Auratas agitas comas
Perpetuoque cales.
Tu rex Euhye Bassareu,
Tu Brysseus, Hyalysus,
Liber, Nyctileus, vagus,
Nyseus, Bromius, sacer. . . .

lines 23–33

. . . good Giver of the Vine,
Famed for the thyrsus and the palm,
You are the victorious son of Semele,
The offspring of mightiest Jove,
Binding your head with ivy,
You toss your golden locks.
And you are ever afire.
You, High-born King, Clothed in a Fox Skin,
You are the god worshipped at Brisa, at Hyala,
The Releaser, the Nocturnal One, the wanderer,
The Nysian, The Roarer, the holy . . .

There follows a list of the god's achievements. Then, "Hail Bacchus, we follow you, our leader, with the snake-bearing head and the thyrsus, you who carried the torn Orpheus, you the source of warmth, the enemy of inertia, the ruler of all."

The ode has captured the spirit as well as the structure of the ancient hymn. It is permeated with Dionysiac enthusiasm. The metre is a light, swift-moving, dancing measure. The content is almost entirely image. It is vividly pictorial with the greatest economy—each deity is pictured in a single epithet. An occasional auditory or tactile image greatly enriches the sensuous impression of the poem. An outstanding characteristic of the ode is the evocative use of proper nouns.

"De potestate amoris,"[1] in sapphic stanzas, seems to be another product of the Florentine neoPlatonic revival and perhaps owes something to Pontano's "De amoris Dominatu" and to Marullus' "Amori" and "Veneri." It also derives inspiration from the opening of Lucretius' *De Rerum Natura.* Love, a fire in the stars, descends to cherish all things on earth. It binds the gods above, the elements below. It softens the hearts of tigers, lions, snakes, bulls, wild boars, and soldiers. Love warms the fish and the zephyrs. Mars forgets war in

[1] Crinito, pp. 574–6.

Venus' arms. Generation and all living things are due to love, the animals, plants, and the spring.

The occasional poems are various and fall into two principal categories, the political and the private. There is a series of political odes, like Filelfo's, but decidedly more polished, on the struggle between the Italian princes and Charles VIII of France.[1] These odes, like Filelfo's, are interesting chiefly for the metric experimentation, in this case for the skilful mingling of alcaics with glyconics into new Latin stanzas of real practical value. Of only commonplace human interest are the private poems: to a friend about their friendship, a letter asking for news of the Venetian poets, an account of the victory of a Tuscan wrestler over a French one, two attacks on an old woman, to his lyre, on shunning the ungrateful, to a friend to abandon his unhappiness and anxiety, about his love for Glycera, his return to slavery to Naevia, about his studies, and on his illness and imminent death, the last poem in the volume.[2] They are in no way unusual. They belong to familiar types and are treated in a manner with which we are well acquainted.

Crinito is an interesting and important minor poet who deserves a lot more attention than he has so far received. His output was considerable and always creditable, and at times it rose well above the level of talented mediocrity. As an ode writer he was in many ways like a late-seventeenth-century English poet. He wrote a large number of extremely competent but commonplace odes, political, amorous, occasional, and about the poet, together with a few more significant and original odes, often also of the seventeenth-century sort, and he experimented in verse form. Like the seventeenth-century poet's, his amorous odes were addressed to young ladies with classical names and his poems about the poet were somewhat strained and bombastic. They also, again like the seventeenth-century poet's, discussed the problems of the poet in a time of disturbance and war, although with different conclusions. Crinito also wrote a topographical ode, occasional in origin, with neoclassical classifications of the items of scenery, several retirement odes including one large description of the joys of

[1] *Ibid.*, pp. 538–9, 558–9, 541–3, 546, 551–3, 554–6, 548, 560–1.

[2] Crinito, p. 562, 563, 539, 565 and 569, 565, 570, 570–1, 579–80, 580, 582–3, 584–5.

withdrawal into the worlds of nature and philosophy, and a dithyramb. His ode on a purely mythological subject, the birth of the Muses, suggests Ronsard's ode to Michel de L'Hospital; his allegorical poem, "De imagine avaritiae," illustrates the continuing attempt to assimilate medieval types of poetry to the new classical form, although here the adaptation is so slight, perhaps because of Crinito's didactic purpose, that the poem does not become a proper ode. Crinito's experiments in verse, because of their very moderation and conservatism and their regard for the accustomed harmonies of Latin, hold out practical possibilities of enriching the technical means of expression of the neolatin poet. Finally, Crinito continues the trend of his neolatin predecessors in adding a new imaginative stretch and a romantic suggestiveness to the ode.

There were many minor poets and men of letters who wrote odes in Florence in the second half of the fifteenth century under the influence of Lorenzo de Medici and his brilliant circle. Alessandro Braccesi wrote elegies about his love for Flora and about her cat which was stolen. He also wrote Horatian sapphics to his friends and a single, commonplace alcaic.[1] Francesco Bresciano wrote, in hendecasyllabics, a Catullan dedication of his book to Carlo Fortebraccio and praised the victorious general in iambic couplets. He complained about the impiety of the age to Lorenzo de Medici in second asclepiads and he uttered his prayers and good wishes for Florence in sapphic stanzas.[2] Cantalicio wrote many poems, generally in couplets, to Lorenzo de Medici and Poliziano. He also wrote a sapphic prayer to Jupiter to stop the rain and the storms and a sapphic ode to his doctor thanking him for curing the trouble in his chest, both Horatian in treatment. His sapphics to St. Nicholas and the Blessed Bartolus followed rather the pattern of medieval saints' lives.[3] Panfilo Sasso of Modena wrote elegies on the deaths of Poliziano and Pico and a single sapphic, "Loca amanti jucunda,"[4] a charming lyric,

[1] *Carmina*, ed. Alexander Perosa (Firenze, 1944), pp. 86–7, 100–1, 101, 101–2, 104, 105, 130, 94.

[2] *Carmina Illustrium Poetarum Italorum* II (Firenze, 1719), 483, 486, 490–1, 492–3.

[3] *Carmina Illustrium* III (Firenze, 1719), 130–1, 139, 153, 154–5.

[4] *Carm. Illustr.* VIII (Firenze, 1721), 481.

close to the popular song, with a refrain at the end of each of the first five stanzas, "mea lux, meum cor / Qua manet ora?" The poet puts this question to the fountain, the tree, the mountain, the meadows, and the breeze. But the fountain is black, the mountain gloomy, the meadows dried up, and the breeze fallen; for his love is not there.

The Neapolitan humanists, Sannazaro (1456–1530) and Carbone (d. 1528) wrote few odes. Sannazaro's output seems limited to six good but conventional sapphics in the Horatian tradition,[1] while Girolamo Carbone composed a number of popularly successful Latin odes in praise of Ercole I of Ferrara that were sung in Ariosto's youth,[2] and a sapphic ode notable for the new direction that it suggests. The ode begins with echoes of Anacreon and Horace: "Let others sing of heroes' triumphs, of Troy and Thebes . . . and the wars of the giants 'ac Jovis tandem jaculata summos / fulmina montes,' I like to sing of the loves of the fauns and dryads, idle in the country under a tree, by the wave of a fountain. This is my Helicon. Here amid flocks I play my pipe to the sylvan Muse. Here are Pales, Pan, the nymphs, and satyrs. Now from me in the woods expect only rustic poetry and 'sparsas sine lege nugas.' My Muse is rural, my Minerva, 'crassa.'"[3] We remember Pontano's pastoral odes and that Naples was the city of the new Arcadia—Sannazaro published his famous work in 1504. (Sannazaro also invented the *lusus pastoralis*, a light pastoral lyric.) Later we shall find other Neapolitan humanists cultivating this hybrid while in Italian the pastoral sonnet and *canzone* come into vogue.[4]

If the Neapolitans other than Pontano were chary with the ode, this was not true of the Venetian Navagero (1483–1529) who wrote several odes in lyric metres. The first of these, "Ad Somnum"[5] bears a striking resemblance to the lately popular

[1] *Carm. Illustr.* VIII, 427–8, 448–9, 457–8, 462–4, 465–6, 466, 467–8, 469–70.

[2] Giosuè Carducci, *La Gioventù di Ludovico Ariosto e La Poesia Latina a Ferrara, Opera* XV (Bologna, 1905), p. 131.

[3] Pierre de Montera, *L'Humaniste Napolitain Girolamo Carbone et Ses Poésies Inédites* (Napoli, 1935), pp. 23–5.

[4] As was mentioned above, the pastoral *canzone* was established by Sannazaro (1504) and Gareth (1506) and the pastoral sonnet by Gareth, Molza, Tolomei, Varchi, and Bernardo Tasso.

[5] *Carmina quinque illustrium poetarum* . . . (Bergomi, 1753), pp. 69–70.

song "Goodnight Irene." In iambic couplets the poet addresses "Beate Somne" who last night brought him so many joys; for he dreamt he was kissed by the scornful and proud Neaera. If this continues he will be happier than the gods. Let Neaera flee from him whenever she wants, let her refuse his embrace; he will have her in his sleep, even against her will. Let her be hard, be cruel; she will nevertheless be gentle and willing. In the conclusion there is perhaps an echo of Sappho's "*'Ες 'Αφροδίτη*."

> *καὶ γὰρ αἰ φεύγει, ταχέως διώξει,*
> *αἰ δὲ δῶρα μὴ δέκετ,' ἀλλὰ δώσει*
> *αἰ δὲ μὴ φίλει, τάχεως φιλήσει*
> *κωὔκι θέλοισα*[1]

> For if she runs away, she will speedily pursue you,
> And if she refuses your gifts, she will make presents herself,
> And if she does not love you, she will speedily do so,
> Even against her will.

Two other odes are outstanding for the sensitivity of their nature description. In hendecasyllabics Navagero writes "In Vancium Vicum Patavinum amoenissimum."[2] He describes Vancius in the springtime and prays for its continued beauty and prosperity. Navagero shows himself to be a close and unconventional observer of nature. He relies on no trite formulae; he sees clearly the structural lines of vegetation and with ample, but only essential, details he makes plants grow into their shapes before our eyes, and then he halts the growth and, lingering over their present form, perpetuates the picture of the day. We see the vines growing, as they still grow in that part of Italy, trained up the stubs of willow trees; they burgeon, and spread their shadow, and then wave and whisper in the breeze, *in saecula saeculorum*:

> En *scandentibus* hinc et hinc flagellis[3]
> Per flavas salicum comas pererrans
> Vitis pampineas ministrat umbras;
> Per quas sibila murmurantis aurae
> Jucundum tenero strepunt susurro.[4]

[1] E. Lobel, *ΣΑΠΦΟΥΣ ΜΕΛΗ* (Oxford, 1925), p. 15.

[2] *Carmina quinque*, pp. 71–2.

[3] Note the pregnant use of the present participles; we see the tendrils twining upwards and the buds unfolding in the sun.

[4] *Carmina quinque* (1753), p. 71.

See, its tendrils climbing here, and here,
Wandering through the golden heads of the willows,
The vine proffers its vine-leaf shade,
Through which the whispers of the murmuring breeze,
Gently rustling, make delightful music.

Like Collins in his "Ode To Evening" Navagero lingers over his description, drawing out his delicate sensuous delight by the repetition of simple words and, equally like Collins, he enriches his description with a use of a mythology that is closer to animism than to literary convention. In "In Vancium," for example, he addresses the Naiads of the river and Venus:

Hic *gemmantibus* hinc et hinc rosetis[1]
Cultas texere vos licet coronas. . . .

(there follows a series of descriptions of other flowers *blooming*)

Queis comptas pariter comas revinctae,
Queis sparsae teretes simul papillas,
Ductetis pariter choros licentes:
Ductetis hilares simul choreas.[2]

In this place the rose bushes, budding here, and here again,
Allow you to weave elegant wreaths. . . .
With these, all alike, bind back your locks,
With these, also, adorn your smooth, round breasts,
And dance alike without restraint,
And also lead the blithe choruses.

Navagero's other nature poem is the sapphic "In Auroram,"[3] a description of a summer dawn which shows the same close observation of and feeling for nature. The description moves from the mythological to the natural, with an insertion of human lovers to bring the scene close and make it real; then back to the mythological, through a whole god-peopled

[1] See footnote 3 on p. 99 on use of the present participles.

[2] Cf. Collins:

If aught of oaten stop, or pastoral song,
May hope, chaste Eve, to soothe thy modest ear,
Like thy own solemn springs,
Thy springs, and dying gales.

[3] *Carmina quinque*, pp. 75–6.

panorama like a Renaissance allegorical painting to the final picture, again natural, of the nightingale lamenting on the bough. This final picture, specific and clearly delineated, a symbol-summary of the whole poem, is typically Horatian. The nightingale is also singularly appropriate to this poem; for the metamorphosed Philomela is eminently suitable to act as a mediator between the mythological and the natural, making the final scene the keystone that locks the arch. The nightingale with its associations with love and cruelty is also appropriate to this ode to the summer dawn in which the poet already sees *in potentia* the destroying fire of the midday sun. It is appropriate, too, to a love poem that links love with nature; for it is both a part of nature and, by tradition, the bird of romance.

The beginning of the ode calls to mind Ausonius' "De rosis nascentibus" and the memories of Ausonius' poem strengthen and enrich the meaning of Navagero's.

Now let us look at the text itself:

Dia Tithoni senioris uxor,
Quae diem vultu radiante pandis:
Quum genas effers roseas rubenti
  Praevia soli:

Roscidos ut nunc per agros vagari
Sub tuo adventu juvat et recentes
Quae tuos semper comitantur axes,
  Excipere auras!

Sicca jam saevus calor uret arva:
Jam vagi aurarum levium silescent
Spiritus: jam sol rapidus furentes
  Exseret ignis.

Dum licet, laeti simul ite amantes:
Dum licet, molles pariter puellae
Ire flaventes vario capillos
  Nectite serto.

Shining bride of aged Tithonus,
Who with radiant countenance reveal the day
When you raise up your rosy cheeks, precursor of the
Reddening sun.

How pleasant it is now to wander through the dewy
Fields against your coming and to catch
The fresh breezes which ever accompany
Your chariot wheels!

Soon the cruel heat will burn the dry fields,
Soon the vagrant breaths of the light breezes will
Be stilled, soon the hasting sun will thrust out
His raging fires.

While it is possible, go together happy lovers,
While it is possible to go, all alike, gentle maidens,
Bind your golden hair with
Different wreaths.

Then appear the Loves, Venus, the Graces with baskets of flowers, and Diana who ranges the woods with her Nymphs, hunting the deer and the lynx. Now the nightingale complains from the ash grove and the wood echoes her song.

A completely different type of poem is the alcaic "De Patavio a militibus vastata."[1] This is an occasional political poem in the Horatian tradition. It tells the history of Padua, how it was founded by Antenor after the fall of Troy. It praises its beauty, its arts, its genius, and its university thronged by students from all over the world. But now Padua is devastated. In Navagero's usual style we see the war *approaching* the city,

Quid culta tot pomaria conquerer?
Tot pulchra flammis hausta suburbia?
Quid glande deturbata ahena
Moenia, praecipitemque saevi

Mavortis iram . . . ?

What complaint can I make for so many cultivated
orchards?
So many fair suburbs consumed by flame?
What for the fortifications overthrown by the ball
Of copper, and the headlong rage

Of cruel Mars . . . ?

Fighting breaks out. Padua is captured and razed to the ground.

[1] *Ibid.*, pp. 74–5.

The development of this poem is very skilful; the progress of the war is clearly and briefly described; but the poem as a whole is marred by an apparent lack of feeling.

Another ode, "Ad Bembum,"[1] is a variation on the old Anacreontic theme, "*θέλω λέγειν 'Ατρείδας*," with obvious reminiscences of Horace. The poet tells how he tried writing of wars, but love forbade. He must write of Lalage. Sappho and Alcaeus live as well as Homer.[2] Also Anacreontic in theme is the sapphic, "Ad Venerem, ut pertinacem Lalagen molliat."[3] "Venus, mistress of creation, does your power stop short at one? Make Lalage love me and I will worship you with the myrtle, roses, wine, and milk, with the choral dances of boys and girls. I will sing of you and Cupid. I will scatter violets and roses. I will sacrifice a dove." These two odes are well written, in pleasant verse, but they do not rise to the level of distinction of the other poems which, in the originality of their descriptive methods, bear the mark of poetic genius.

A poet with a greater reputation than Navagero, whose flirtation with the ode was even more casual, was Ludovico Ariosto (1474–1533). Unlike Navagero Ariosto was an Italian not a Latin poet and his Latin verses were no more than the exercises of his youth. Thus they are sometimes unsound of metre,[4] overloaded with elision,[5] and burdened with rhetoric.[6] At their best they are written in correct but unmusical lines, and usually in *gradus* idiom.[7] "Ad Phileroem" in alcaic stanzas, Horatian in technique, and commonplace enough in content—the poet cares nothing for wars; he likes to lie beneath a tree by a waterfall watching the labouring peasants with Phileroe beside him, singing to the lyre—is somewhat of an exception. This poem reveals an interest in language not found elsewhere

1 *Ibid.*, p. 75.

2 Cf. Horace, *Carm.* IV, 9, lines 9–12.

3 *Carmina quinque*, pp. 78–9.

4 See, e.g., *Jo. Baptistae Pignae Carminum Libri 4 . . . Caelii Calcagnini carm. lib. III. Ludovici Areosti Carm. Lib. II* (Venetiis, 1554), pp. 307–8, "De Nicolao Areosto."

5 E.g., "De Julia," *Carm. Illustr.* I (1719), 351–2.

6 E.g., in a single stanza Ariosto uses four words of the same root. "beatius," "beatum," "beate," and "beasti," see "Ad Albertum Pium," *Carm. Illustr.* I, 360–1.

7 For a rather different appreciation of Ariosto's Latin poetry, however see G. Carducci, *La Gioventù di Ludovico Ariosto*, pp. 146–251.

in Ariosto's Latin poetry. Like Horace the poet here exploits the power of juxtaposition, e.g.,

Dum segetes Corydona flavae
Durum fatigant, Phileroe, meum,[1]

While, Phileroe, the golden sheaves
Exhaust stout Corydon, my friend,

where the juxtaposition of "durum," which of course modifies "Corydona," with "fatigant" strengthens the word "tire" to "exhaust" and nicely contrasts the back-breaking labour of the peasant with the langour of the poet:

sub arbuto
Jacentem aquae ad murmur cadentis.[1]

beneath the arbutus tree
Lying by the murmur of falling water.

Here, again, we notice something of the pastoral influence so strong at the time. This ode is suggestive of Carbone's pastoral ode as well as of Sannazaro's *lusus pastorales*; although it may have preceded both of them in time.

In his other poems, in alcaics, asclepiads, and hendecasyllabics, Ariosto compares Julia's singing to that of Sappho, Melpomene, and the sirens,[2] he invites his returning friend to visit him,[3] he advises a boy already high in the emperor's favour that *noblesse oblige*: "At quantum honoris, tantum oneris datur,"[4] he describes the vicissitudes of the lover in an incantatory ode that finally softens his mistress,[5] and he contrasts his simple desire for rural retirement with the ambition of his friend Pandulphus who risks his life in his prince's service, seeking his fortune.[6] All in all Ariosto's judgment was sound when he decided to make Italian not Latin the language of his muse. His odes are no more than typical examples of the kind

[1] *Carm. Illustr.* I, 350.
[2] *Carm. Illustr.* I, 351–2.
[3] *Ibid.*, pp. 360–1.
[4] *Pignae Carminum*, pp. 300–1. Note the *annominatio*.
[5] *Ibid.*, p. 301.
[6] *Ibid.*, pp. 303–4.

of poetry written by those whose education included the politer learning. They are in no way distinguished.

Benedetto Lampridio (d. 1540), however, is of first importance as an experimenter in Latin versification and as the first man to write the triadic Pindaric ode. Lampridio was born at Cremona towards the end of the fifteenth century. He became professor at the Collegio dei Greci founded by Leo X in Rome and directed by John Lascaris. In this capacity he perhaps helped in the publication of the first Greek book in Rome, Callierges' edition of Pindar (1515). After the death of Leo in 1521 Lampridio went to the University of Padua, where he remained until his death in 1540. At Padua he counted Michel de L'Hospital among his pupils and perhaps through him had some influence on the Pléiade. Like Filelfo, but with a skill and ease born of a century of humanism, Lampridio experimented with Latin lyric metres, created new stanzas, and revealed the wealth and variety of poetic form that could be exploited by the imitator of the Greeks.[1]

The most successful of Lampridio's odes both as a poem and as an imitation of Pindar is "Ad Cremonam Patriam."[2] This is written in four identical triads of ten line strophes and antistrophes and twelve line epodes. The metrical pattern is important. It shows how daring Lampridio was as compared with such later writers of Pindarics as Ronsard, Jonson, and Cowley, how far his form approximated current ideas of Pindaric versification, and with how much skill and smoothness he was able to combine standard Latin metres into new stanzas. The pattern for the strophe and antistrophe is,

1 ⏑ – ⏑ – – – ⏑ ⏑ – ⏑ –
2 – – – ⏑ ⏑ – ⏑ ⏑
3 – – – ⏑ ⏑ – ⏑ – ⏑ – –
4 – ⏑ – – – ⏑ ⏑ – ⏑ – ⏑
5 – – ⏑ – ⏓ – ⏑ – ⏑ – ⏑ ⏓
6 – – ⏑ – – – ⏑ ⏓
7 – ⏑ ⏑ – ⏑ ⏑ – ⏑ – ⏑
8 – ⏑ ⏑ – – – ⏑ – ⏑ – –
9 – – – ⏑ ⏑ – ⏑
10 – ⏑ ⏑ – ⏑

[1] His immediate predecessor in metrical experimentation was Crinito.

[2] *Benedicti Lampridii Necnon Io. Bap. Amalthei Carmina* (Venetiis, 1550), pp. 3r–5r.

for the epode,

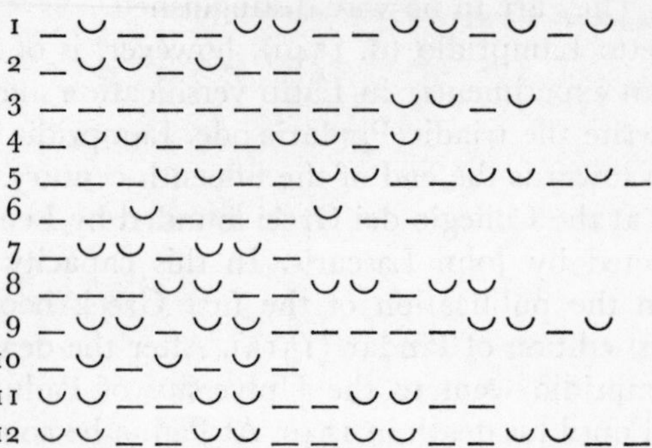

The triads themselves are functional; they no longer mark the movements of the dance but the movement of the thought. Each triad completes an idea and each stanza perfects a part of the thought of its triad. Thus, the first triad describes the games to be held annually at Cremona because her prayers have been answered. Within the triad, the strophe describes the games themselves, the antistrophe the beautiful brides who look on, and the epode the young man in love. The second triad, making the occasion more immediate, tells of the actual celebration of the games, of the festival day, and the occasion for rejoicing, the strophe describing the spectacle, the antistrophe the jollity in the citizens' houses at night when they drink to the return of the beloved Sforzas, and the epode the marriage, celebrated at Cremona, of the *condottiere* Francesco Sforza to Bianca the heiress of the Visconti who brought Cremona as part of her dowry. The third triad lauds Cremona and the Sforzas and rejoices that they are reunited. The strophe links this triad with the preceding one: Cremona is the city of the wedding of Francesco and Bianca, it is the first city of the Sforzas, famous for men of genius and for its arms, rich, eager for honour, and most beautiful. The antistrophe tells us that Cremona is also the poet's city, the epode, that this day of rejoicing comes after long suffering. The fourth triad tells how the Sforzas have been restored by force of arms and it warns the French and Italians that Cremona will fight if they try to interfere again. It is only in this last triad that the history of Cremona is completed and the occasion for rejoicing fully explained. It is only here that we discover that the triumphant hero is Francesco, grandson of the Francesco and Bianca whose marriage forms the central part of the poem.

The ode is Pindaric in its triadic form, in its subject, the celebration of a victory, in its mode of development, and in its device of praising the living through the dead. Like a Pindaric ode it begins describing games and ends with admonitions. However, it does not have the Pindaric intensity, the imagery, and the aphorisms. It is a looser, more narrative kind of poem. Moreover, we notice here the same uneasy sort of adjustment between ancient and modern ideas that we found in the poems of Landino. The games that Lampridio refers to are obviously a tournament—how else explain the beautiful young brides, the amorous youths, and the spirit of chivalry?—but his insistence on describing them in terminology appropriate to the ancient games marks the artificiality of his classicism. It is like seeing Louis XVI with his eighteenth-century powdered wig in the dress of a Roman general.

Despite its Pindaric prosody and rhetorical pattern the language of the ode is Horatian; in fact there are many borrowings from as well as echoes of Horace, e.g.,

> . . . humum alterno pede pulsant
> Astra quibus volucri contingit heros vertice.[1]

The other nine odes in proper triads[2] are roughly similar. The triads divide sections of the theme and the stanzas develop different aspects of the idea of the triad. The content tends to be Horatian rather than Pindaric. Yet the resemblance to Horace is due to borrowing, not to real artistic assimilation. The two odes on political themes, "Ad Franciscum Sfortium" and "Ad Ianum Ruffum," occasional poems addressed to important men, are, like Filelfo's odes, an augury of what is to come in the seventeenth and eighteenth centuries, pedestrian verses on contemporary events with Pindaric pretensions.

[1] *Ibid.*, p. 4v.

[2] *Ibid.*, pp. 5r–5v, "Ad Franciscum Sfortiam"; pp. 7r–8v, "Ad Ianum Ruffum"; pp. 27r–37v, "In Petri Melini Villam, Ubi Ille Poetas de More Familia Coena exceperat"; pp. 44v–45r, "Laurentio Bartholino" (monotriadic); pp. 40r–44v, "Scilicet superbiat"; pp. 45r–47v, "Petro Cursio"; pp. 47r–48v, "Lazaro Bonamico"; pp. 49r–51r, "Quid supremo nata Iove"; and pp. 52v–54r, "Petro Bembo."

Lampridio wrote other odes formally inspired by Pindar but technically more libertine. "Henrico Octavo"[1] is written in six line stanzas which group themselves into not exactly superimposable triads.[2] The metrical analysis of "In P. M. Villam"[3] yields much more complicated results, although it is roughly triadic. The content of the poem, incidentally, calls to mind a Chaucerian dream-vision like *The Boke of the Duchesse*; here we have the wood, the dream, descriptions of trees and flowers, mythological characters, and a contemporary event, the death of Leo X.

To another group belong the odes which are composed of irregular stanzas. In this group there are two types. The first type, represented by "Ad Olivetum Villam Laurentii Paccii Card. Sanctorum Quatuor.,"[4] is composed of stanzas which are all of the same length but which all follow different metrical patterns. The second type, of which there are five examples, is composed of stanzas which are all different lengths and follow different metrical patterns.[5]

The last and more conventional group of Lampridio's odes is composed of poems written in Horatian metres, iambics and asclepiads, on Horatian themes, the death of friends, the troubled times, the instability of fortune,[6] and in language that is borrowed from Horace, e.g.,

> pudor quis aut modus
> fiet dolori . .
> tam carum caput.[7]

There is a single Anacreontic in hendacasyllabics, "De Venere et Cupidine Fugitivo,"[8] and three hendecasyllabic imitations of Catullus, "Ad Puellas," "Ad Portiam Scortum," and "In Rosas, Quarum Spinis puella fuerat contacta."[9]

Lampridio's poetry, then, is chiefly important for the numerous and various attempts made to enlarge the expressive

[1] *Ibid.*, pp. 20v–22r.

[2] E.g., the first lines of epodes 1 and 2 differ metrically, but the last five lines correspond exactly.

[3] *Ibid.*, pp. 27r–37r.

[4] *Ibid.*, pp. 12v–14v.

[5] *Ibid.*, pp. 9r–v; 10v–11r; 11r–12v; 54r–57v; 57r–60r.

[6] *Ibid.*, pp. 9v–10v; 14r–v; 18r–v; 14r–15r; 57r–60r.

[7] "Antonio Tebal.," *ibid.*, p. 9v.

[8] *Ibid.*, pp. 22r–v.

[9] *Ibid.*, pp. 22v–23r; 23v–24r; 26v–27r.

capacities of Latin verse by finding it new forms, both by borrowing from the Greek and by treating conventional Latin prosody with revolutionary daring. Pindar's triads, adapted to Latin, are given new meaning. From marking the pattern of the choreography they now mark the movement of the thought. Moreover, perhaps inspired by his taste of Greek freedom, and remembering Filelfo and Crinito, Lampridio explored the possibility of inventing new Latin stanzas to free the poet from the tyranny of a rigid, repetitive pattern and to allow each poem to find its own form. Thus odes were written in strophes of equal length but different metrical pattern and then in completely dissimilar strophes, like the Cowleyan irregular ode. The "Henrico Octavo" in irregular triads perhaps marks a transitional stage.

It is unfortunate that Lampridio's metric inventiveness was not matched by a like fertility of mind, that his odes were so often a trite patchwork of Horatian ideas and phrases. However, perhaps that recommended them to some of his contemporaries—at least there was no difficulty of interpretation. At any rate there is reason to believe that Lampridio had an influence upon Ronsard and also upon the generations of schoolboys who prepared the Latin verse compositions that were so important in the formation of the seventeenth-century irregular vernacular ode.

Medieval in spirit though generally classical in metre were the odes of Giovanni Francesco Quinziano Stoa of Brescia (1484–1557). "Vitae humanae aerumna et instabilitas,"[1] a variation on the "Ubi sunt" theme, is interesting because of its archeological awareness. "Where are the baths, the acqueducts, the arches, porticoes . . . of Rome?"

Vivamus ergo conscii
Sortis labantis undique
Ne quando nos ex tempore
Mors imparatos occupet.[2]

Then let us enjoy life, conscious
Of fortune sinking on every side,
Lest sometime, suddenly, death
Should take us unprepared.

[1] *Carm. Illustr.* VIII, 2–4. [2] *Carm. Illustr.* VIII, 4.

The iambic dimeter of the concluding quatrain is admirably suited to the medieval sentiments it expresses. The rest of the ode is in first asclepiads.

Of some interest are the three funerary odes, "In Obitum Philippi Beroaldi, ad Geraldum Cadamustum," "Monodia in Annam Reginam Francorum," and "Margaretae Scotorum Reginae Monodiae,"[1] the last, the lament of Queen Margaret on the death of James IV. All these three poems are written in the same form, in glyconic strophes of irregular lengths which conclude with refrains which are slightly varied throughout the poems. Samples of the refrains are:

Philippus obiit
Ah Fatum Fatum!
Beroaldus obiit.

Abivit Anna
Proh dolor, dolor!
Recessit Anna.

Quid agam unica?
Hei mihi, mihi;
Quid sola faciam?

Philip has died,
Oh Fate, Fate!
Beroaldus has died.

Anne is gone,
Oh sorrow, sorrow!
Anne has departed.

What should I do alone?
Ah me, ah me!
What should I do alone?

Stoa was a humanist who spent some time in France and was known to the Pléiade and there are certain parallels between him and the French poets. His religious odes, exercises in putting Christian ideas into Horatian metre and phraseology, remind us of his slightly younger French contemporary, Salmon Macrin, the favourite of the mighty Cardinal du

[1] *Carm. Illustr.* VIII, 11–14, 24–5, 26–31.

Bellay and the Horace of France, while his "Vitae humanae aerumna et instabilitas" suggests Joachim du Bellay's *Ruins of Rome*. The conservative freedom with which he treated Latin metres in creating his long stanzas of short lines arranged in irregular lengths and concluded with refrains may have done something towards encouraging the Pléiade in their demand for an equally modest freedom for the French lyric.

Julius Caesar Scaliger was born in Padova in 1483 and died in Paris in 1558. He is chiefly known today for his Aristotelian, neoclassical critical theories. However, his *Art of Poetry*, which was published posthumously in 1561, is important to us for another reason. Here Scaliger illustrates every ancient metre, Greek or Latin, whose existence can even be assumed from fragments. He also illustrates some of the little known lyric types, the paen, a poem of a single strophe of medium length made up of short lines of unequal lengths, and the hyporchemata, a single strophe twenty-five lines in length composed of verses of very unequal lengths.[1] The number of syllables per line are 7, 7, 8, 8, 8, 11, 3, 3, 3, 8, 3, 8, 7, 4, 10, 12, 10, 10, 15, 11, 13, 17, 7, 13, 12. Words are broken at the ends of lines and one verse is composed of a single thirteen syllable word (line 21). Scaliger says that the dithyramb was very like the hyperchemata. The dithyramb was destined to become important at the beginning of the seventeenth century through the influence of Scaliger's *Poetics*, while the metrical experimentation so characteristic of the period owed much to his demonstration of possible verse forms.

Like most other humanists Scaliger wrote several volumes of Latin verse. His *Farrago* and *Arae Fracastoriae*, the latter with a eulogy in sapphic stanzas of the dead Fracastoro, both contain Horatian odes, while *Anacreontica ad Petrum Ronsardum* is composed of a large number of short poems in short lines on various subjects, supposedly inspired by Anacreon. In fact very few of them are what we normally consider to be Anacreontics. Towards the end of the book there are many poems addressed to Cupid which, in the Ovidian-medieval tradition, make much of the contradictions in love, but the rest of these "Anacreontics" are actually epigrams, jottings of the poet's thoughts on

[1] J. C. Scaliger, *Poetices libri septem* (n.p., 1581), pp. 124–5.

various subjects, witty remarks, puns, riddles, and paradoxes. As we might expect from the subjects, the language of these poems is usually familiar, conversational, and Italianate.[1] There are, however, many odd compound words which, along with Scaliger's tendency towards neoclassical periphrasis,[2] make the writing at times obscure. The term "Anacreontic" seems to apply only to the metrical form.

Scaliger also published a collection of *Poemata Sacra*[3] which contains two Pindarics which he calls *excessus*. Both these Pindarics are birthday odes, for Jesus and the Virgin Mary respectively. In the dedication to the "Natalia Domini nostri Iesu Christi filii Dei vivi"[4] Scaliger says that he is attempting the Pindaric, since there need be no moderation in holy things. The rather pedestrian content of the ode, the night, the birth, and the salvation of the virtuous, and the flat conclusion with its exercises in Christian paradox, seem not to justify this warning note. However, the poem is extravagant by Latin standards in its versification and it appears that it is in this sense that the term "Pindaric" is applied, just as "Anacreontic" was used. The "Natalia . . . Iesu Christi" is made up of two triads, the strophes and antistrophes of which are eleven lines long, the epodes twelve. The length of verse in the strophes and antistrophes varies from five to thirteen syllables, in the epodes from eight to eleven syllables, and the verses themselves are of mixed Latin and Greek types. In combining mixed Latin metres with Greek ones Scaliger is taking a big step in the direction of free verse. Another peculiarity of the verse is the internal off-rimes reminiscent of some early medieval Latin poetry. As to style, Scaliger trifles with wit[5] and indulges in puerile logical ingenuities. The result could not be called poetry. A sample of the second epode will serve as an illustration both of Scaliger's metrics and of his literary style:

[1] See, e.g., "Pelluciduli, turgiduli, / Rosculi, tumiduli," about the dew-drops, *Poemata* (n.p., 1574), p. 519. Cf. the diction of Pontano and Secundus.

[2] E.g., dewdrops are called "Soboles genitalis Aetheris," *loc. cit.*

[3] Coloniae, 1600.

[4] P. 101. The poem is on pp. 102–4.

[5] E.g., "necis nex venit improbae proba atrae," antistrophe 2.

Deus homo, et Homo Deus:
Unum fis, et nil mutaris:
Integer integro, toti totus,
Pius impio, ut fiam pius.
Tu, ut quod fueram, fierem:
Quod non eras, factus es:
Ut amitterem, quod eram.

God Man, and Man God,
You are one, and you change not,
Whole to the whole, all to all,
Faithful to the unfaithful, that I might
    become faithful.
That I might become what I had been,
What you were not, you have become,
That I should give up what I was.

The "Natalia semper Virginis Matris Mariae"[1] is the same sort of poem. It is made up of a single triad with a strophe and antistrophe of sixteen lines and an epode of thirteen. The strophe and antistrophe are composed of verses of seven and eight syllables, the epode of lines varying from five to twelve syllables. There is the same type of wit as in the previous ode and no beauty of thought or of sound.

Marc Antonio Flaminio (1498–1550),[2] the son of Giovanni Antonio Flaminio, poet[3] and schoolmaster, was born in Serravalle but spent his youth in Imola where his father migrated to teach. He was a delicate child but unusually precocious, so that, by the age of sixteen, he had written a sheaf of Latin odes that seemed to his father to merit a trip to Rome, to the court of Leo X. So the youth set out with two packets of poems, his own to present to the pope, his father's to present to a cardinal, and a series of parental admonitions and messages to distinguished men along the route. Flaminio's genius was recognized wherever he went and he was universally well received. From Rome he went to Naples, where he was kindly treated by

[1] Pp. 104–6.

[2] For information about Flaminio's life see Ercole Cuccoli, *M. Antonio Flaminio* (Bologna, 1897), pp. 27–147.

[3] For Giovanni Antonio Flaminio's poetry see *Carm. Illustr.* IV (1719), and *Marci Antonii, Joanis Antonii et Gabrielis Flaminiorum Forocorneliensium Carmina* (Patavii, 1743).

Sannazaro, whom he ever afterwards admired and who later influenced him, then to Urbino, where he was welcomed hospitably by Castiglione. The next year, 1515, with the help of Achille Bocchi, a Bolognese noble,[1] he published his early poetry, eighteen pieces in all, ten of which were odes, in a volume with some hitherto unpublished *neniae* and *epigrammata* of Marullus.[2] The same year he went to Bologna to study philosophy. Three months later Cardinal Sadoleto offered him a post in the office of the papal secretary, but his father refused to allow him to abandon his studies. His education completed, in 1523 Flaminio entered the service of Giovanni Matteo Giberti, bishop of Verona. Giberti felt strongly that the church needed reformation and he organized his household into a kind of Little Gidding community. The group met in the morning and evening for prayers. The day was spent in hard work and serious thought. The meals were frugal and were accompanied, refectory style, by pious readings. After the meals there was a discussion of the literature read. Little time was wasted with sleep. The bishop's library, to which friends like Fracastoro could come, was excellent and contained many unpublished Greek manuscripts. Here Flaminio studied philosophy and theology and lived an almost monastic life; indeed in 1532 he wanted to enter a religious community. Flaminio wrote a few more secular lyrics which he published with Sannazaro's *Odae* and Cotta's *Carmina* in 1529,[3] but generally he abandoned pagan poetry for the fifteen years that he spent in Giberti's household. Instead he translated part of Aristotle's *Metaphysics*,[4] paraphrased, first in prose,[5] then in verse,[6] some of the psalms, and explicated the psalter,[7] abandoning the traditional allegorical and anagogical methods of exegesis for a close examination of the text itself and its literal meaning. This,

[1] For Achille Bocchi's poetry see *Carmina Illustr.* II, 339–54.

[2] *Michaelis Tarchaniotae Marulli Neniae. Eiusdem Epigrammata nunquam alias impressa. M. Antonii Flaminii adulescentis Amoenissimi Carminum Libellus* (Fano, 1515).

[3] *Actii Synceri Sannazarii Odae. Eiusdem Elegia de Malo Punico. Ioannis Cottae Carmina. M. Antonii Flaminii Carmina* (Venetiis, 1529).

[4] The twelfth book.

[5] 32 psalms were published in 1538.

[6] 30 psalms were published in 1546.

[7] The exposition of the psalter was published in 1545.

his uncommon piety, and his part in the *Benificio di Cristo* which was later condemmed, have caused him to be suspected of Protestantism.[1]

In 1538, however, at the age of forty, Flaminio suddenly felt the need for freedom, while his delicate body longed for the gentleness of the southern winter. And so he left Bishop Giberti and his community and journeyed south to Caserta. Here, in the warmth and luxuriance of the south, the Flaminian lyric blossomed again after so many years of hard study, as sweet, mellifluous, sensuous, and pagan as it had been in the days of his youth. In 1542, however, he was back in ecclesiastical work, in the service of Cardinal Pole, at the Council of Trent. In 1545 Pole offered him the secretaryship of the council, but his failing health forbade. In 1548 three volumes of his poetry appeared, in Lyons, Paris, and Venice,[2] containing the new lyrics of the 1538–9 flowering, as well as those of the 1515 and 1529 volumes, and the poetical paraphrases of the psalms. In 1549, near death with a quartan fever, Flaminio, in great spiritual exaltation, wrote his last poems, to God. The fever recurred the following year and he died. On the order of Cardinal Pole he was buried in the English church at Rome, in St. Thomas of Canterbury's. The "sacred songs," dedicated to Marguerite de Valois, the sister of Henry II soon to become Duchess of Savoy, were published posthumously in Paris in 1551.[3] Flaminio's remaining poetry was published by his friends in 1552.[4]

Flaminio's early odes, published in 1515, are remarkable for their ease, their musicality, their poetic feeling, and their fidelity to the spirit of the ancients, but not for their originality. His admiration for Horace, particularly, and also Catullus, is

1 See P. Rossi, *Marc Antonio Flaminio* (Vittorio Veneto, 1931), G. Toffanin, *Il Cinquecento* (Milan, 1950), p. 71, and Croce, *Poeti e Scrittori*, I, 211–228.

2 *M. Antonii Flaminii Carminum Libri II . . . una cum Paraphrasi in 30 Psalmos versibus scripta* (Lugduni, 1548); *Doctissimorum nostra aetate Italorum Epigrammata: M. Antonii Flaminii libri duo. Marii Molsae liber unus. Andreae Naugerii liber unus. Io. Cottae, Lampridii, Sadoleti et aliorum. Miscellaneorum liber unus* (Lutetiae, n.d. [1548]). This book was edited by the Chancellor of the University of Paris; *Carmina quinque illustrium poetarum* [Bembo, Navagero, Castiglione, Cotta, and Flaminio] (Venetiis, 1548).

3 *M. Antonii Flaminii de rebus divinis Carmina ad Margaritam Henrici Gallorum Regis sororem* (Parisiis, 1551).

4 *M. Antonii Flaminii Carminum liber ultimus Eius amicorum cura* (Venetiis, 1552).

everywhere apparent. "Ad Litavium Sperantium,"[1] written in the third asclepiad metre, advises his friend that Cynthia does not always hunt, nor does Delius always bend his bow,[2] Calliope does not sing all day, nor does Cupid always burn with the fire of love. But he, Litavius, is spending more and more time on paling studies. Yet Socrates knew how to enjoy friends and wine and Scipio's Laelius used to read light poetry to forget public affairs. Let Litavius cease his philosophical inquiries. Let him indulge in leisure while he can and console himself with the poetry of Flaminio who is grieving over his break with his mistress Chloe and his new battles with Lygda. The ode is thoroughly Horatian, in metre, addressee, subject, treatment, and phraseology. Its development is exceedingly skilful and economical; its surprising concluding turn to the poet is quite in the Horatian manner.

A somewhat similar ode, structurally, is "Ad Guidum Posthumum."[3] "How all burn for the beautiful Ianthis . . .—she is described. How fortunate you, Postumus, are who love her and are loved. This is a greater joy than all wealth, all possessions. But how you will plead with the gods when fortune's wheel is turned. The heart of woman is lighter than cork and more cruel than the angry sea. It is unyielding. Once I too was as happy as you are, with Cynara. But now all is changed. The vision is fled as long-eared hares flee the swift hound."[4] The ode is Horatian in metre, subject, treatment, and phraseology and the conclusion, with a specific example, a vividly delineated picture, is typically Horatian. The metre, the second asclepiad, is well chosen as the vehicle for the elegiac theme; for the alternating asclepiad and glyconic lines, while lighter and more lyrical, suggest the elegiac couplet.

The other ode "Ad Guidum Posthumum"[5] is a more independent creation. Here the poet contrasts the spring without with the perpetual winter that reigns in his heart. The specific scenes illustrating the spring are Horatian, the conceits about the heart, Petrarchan:

[1] [P. 21] in the 1515 edition.
[2] Cf. Horace, "Neque semper arcum tendit Apollo," *Carm.* II, 10, line 20.
[3] *Carm.* (1515) [pp. 22–4].
[4] Cf. Horace, *Carm.* I, 5.
[5] Flaminio, *Carm.* (1515) [p. 30].

Sed curae heu miseri sunt animi dapes,
Sed cordis lachrymae pocula, sed quies
Confectum rigidae corpus humi iacens,
Sed carmen mihi flebilis

Questus, et dominae nomina, sic mihi
Nunquam veris eunt tempora, sic mihi
Soles non aliquo tempore candidi,
Sic mi perpetua est hyems.

But, alas, grief is the feast of my wretched soul,
But tears are the goblets of my heart, but a body
Worn-out, prostrate on the unyielding earth, is my rest,
But my song is tearful

Complaints, and my lady's name. So, for me
The springtime never comes, so, for me
There are no bright suns,
So, for me the winter is everlasting.

We recognize an echo of Catullus in the second last line.[1] The metre is Horatian, the third asclepiad.

Another ode, epigrammatic in its single sentence brevity, reveals a mastery of the convolutions of Latin syntax, a nice critical sense that makes for density of imagery without obscurity and achieves a perfect equilibrium between too much and too little, a Horatian pictorial imagination, and a thorough assimilation of ancient culture remarkable in one so young. His definition of Diana as the huntress goddess appears more appropriate to the theme of the poem, his friend Bocchi's dedication of an elm where he will hang the spoils of the chase, than the bachelor Horace's allusion to her as the protectress of women in childbirth in his dedication of a pine to Diana to win her tutelage over his home.[2] The value of the poem *per se* is unfortunately diminished by the very perfection of its imitation of the classics. We recognize particularly its debt to Catullus 34 and Horace I, 21, and III, 22. The poem merits quotation:

Casta Latonae soboles Jovisque
Quae pharetratis comitata Nymphis,
Cynthium collem peragras, nigrique
Silvam Erymanthi,

[1] Catullus 8. [2] See Horace, III, 22.

Bocchius, linguae decus utriusque,
Doctus errantes agitare cervos,
Hanc tibi villa media locatam
Dedicat ulmum;

Unde veloci domitae sagitta
Pendeant lynces, timidique damae,
Atque vivacis tibi consecrata
Cornua cervi.[1]

Chaste offspring of Latona and of Jove,
Who, in the company of the quivered Nymphs,
Range the Cynthian hill, and the forest
Of black Erymanthus,

Bocchius, the glory of the two tongues,
Skilled in rousing the wandering deer,
Dedicates to you this elm in the middle
Of his estate,

From which are to hang the lynxes brought down
By the swift arrow, and the timorous does,
And, consecrated to you, the antlers
Of the long-lived stag.

Here we notice, as in an inscription, the centring of the important facts, Bocchi's dedication of the elm, preceded by the name of the dedicee with her appropriate titles and followed by a statement of the function of the dedicated object.

The other early odes may be passed over more quickly. "Ad Cornelium Balbum"[2] is a rather serious *carpe diem* poem in second asclepiads. "De laudibus Mantuae,"[3] in hendecasyllabics praises a city, its streams, its palaces, its churches, its streets, . . . and its greatest living man, Castliglione. "Ad Philippum Beroaldum Iuniorem,"[4] in third asclepiads tells of the poet's disregard of wars and rumours of wars for love and poetry. It obviously leans heavily on Horace.[5] "Ad Lygdam,"[6] about his loss of his mistress, echoes, in second asclepiads, Catullus' "Si qua recordanti."[7] "Ad Achillem Philerotum

[1] Flaminio, *Carm.* (1515) [p. 22].
[2] *Ibid.* [p. 24].
[3] *Ibid.* [pp. 25–6]. For poems in praise of cities see supra, p. 67, fn. 3.
[4] *Carmina* (1515) [p. 26].
[5] See, e.g., *Carm.* I, 26.
[6] *Carm.* (1515) [p. 27].
[7] Catullus 76.

Bocchium,"[1] also in second asclepiads, offers consolation on the death of Achille's mother Julia. It will be noted that the poems listed here in second asclepiads are all inclined to be elegiac in theme. This tends to substantiate the suggestion made above that, in Flaminio's usage, there is a parallel between the second asclepiad metre and the elegiac couplet. A final ode, "Ad Bacchum,"[2] like Marullus' "Baccho" is written in Catullus' difficult galliambic metre.[3] It is dithyrambic in spirit but not particularly successful.

Flaminio's 1529 volume contains four hymns which Cuccoli thinks were inspired by Marullus with whom Flaminio published in 1515.[4] However, other humanists, notably Pontano and Crinito, had also published hymns even before that date, sometimes on the same subjects as Flaminio; so, since Flaminio is not specifically indebted to any one of these, it is rather hard to assign influence. At any rate, like Marullus and Crinito, Flaminio wrote an ode to Pan. His metre, the glyconic, was the same as Crinito's, but he closed his five line stanzas with a pherecratic (———⏓⏑—⏓). The "Hymnus in Pana"[5] is full of reminiscences of classical literature, notably Horace and Catullus, and, in the conclusion, of the nineteenth Homeric hymn. Its opening is a composite of Horatian and Pindaric commonplaces and it borrows a line from Catullus:

Jam satis cecini fera
Regum proelia: nunc age
Mater Pieri, quem deum,
Quem dulci Aeoliae fidis
Plectro rite canemus?

An te, lanigeri gregis
Silvarumque virentium[6]
Custos, cui nigra Maenali
Terga, cui gelidi placent
Summa templa Lycaei?

[1] Flaminio, *Carm.* (1515) [pp. 31–2].

[2] *Marci Antonii, Joannis Antonii et Gabrielis Flaminiorum Forocorneliensium Carmina* (Patavii, 1743), pp. 23–4.

[3] See Catullus 63. For Marullus' "Baccho" see Perosa's edition of his poems, pp. 115–16.

[4] Cuccoli, *Flaminio*, p. 188.

[5] Flaminio, *Carm.* (1743), pp. 6–9.

[6] This line is taken from Catullus 34, line 20.

Nymphae, semiferam Jovis
Prolem dicite, dicite
Pana capripedem, leves
Suetam cum Dryadis choros
Silvis ducere in altis.

Now I have sung enough of the fierce
Battles of kings. Come now,
Mother Pieris, what god,
Whom, shall we celebrate ritually with the
Sweet plectrum of the Aeolian lyre?

You, guardian of the woolly
Flock and the green
Forests, who delight in the black
Ranges of Maenalus, and the lofty
Temples of chill Lycaeus?

Nymphs, celebrate the half-animal
Son of Jove, celebrate
Goat-footed Pan, who is wont
To lead the light-footed dance
With the Dryads in the lofty woods.

There is a suggestion of Euripides' *Bacchi* in the description of the coming of the god:

En ut grata silentia
Cantu noctivago deus
Rumpit. cernite, io, venit,
En venit capitis feri
Serta pinea quassans.

Hear how the loved silences
Are broken by the song of the god
Wandering in the night. Look, "Io," he comes,
See, he comes, shaking the pine
Wreaths on his wild head.

The assembly of pure maids and youths that follows recalls Catullus, while the exorcism of the hostile forces reminds us of Horace[1]—and of the ancient religious rites from which Horace borrowed his phrase:

[1] Catullus 34 and Horace, *Carm.* III, 1. See also F. M. Cornford, *The Origin of Attic Comedy* (Cambridge, 1934).

Huc concurrite, virgines
Intactae, et pueri integri:
At quibus scelera impia
Mentem sollicitant, procul
Hinc abeste, profani.

Gather here, pure
Maidens and innocent youths,
But you whose minds are harassed
By impious crimes, afar,
Away from here, profane ones.

Now the god, again with an echo of Catullus, is described in his functions and powers, as the father of the Naiads, the driver of lynxes, the lord of the woodland, the good keeper of sheep:

Tu fontes liquidos gregi, et
Laeta pabula sufficis:
Tu custos ovium potens
Dictus, mollia candidis
Exples vellera lanis.

You supply the herds with fountains
Of water and joyful pasturage;
You are called the mighty guardian
Of sheep, you load their soft
Fleeces with snow-white wool.

The lambs that you have looked upon will not be carried off by the wolf nor die of disease. Happy are the leaves of the groves that have heard you singing your songs on your sweet pipe when dewy evening brought forth the wandering stars:

Felices nemorum comae,
Quae te, cum vaga roscidus
Vesper sidera protulit,
Dulci carmina fistula
Audivere canentem.

Tunc purae melius nitent
Noctis conscia sidera:
Tunc aurae Zephyri tacent:
Tunc laetas croceis humus
Spargit floribus herbas.

Non tam dulce sonat cadens
Udo in gramine cycnus, aut
Veris tempore floridi[1]
Ales sub siluae querens
Densis Daulias umbris.

Happy are the boughs of the groves
Which have heard you singing
Your songs, on your sweet pipe,
When dewy evening brought forth
The wandering stars.

Then, the stars shine more clearly,
Aware of the pure night,
Then, the breezes of the west wind are hushed,
Then, the earth pranks the joyful
Grasses with crocus flowers.

Not so sweetly sings the swan,
Dying in the water meadow, or
In flower-laden spring, the Daulian
Bird, complaining in the
Deep shadows of the wood.

Now Pan leads the hamadryads in dance and the grove echoes the sound:

Et cultrix nemorum gemit
Imis vallibus Echo.

And the denizen of the groves,
Echo, sighs from the depths of the valleys.

And, as they rest on a perfumed bank gathering the rosy apples or dipping their golden hair in the cool water, the nymphs sing of the birth of Pan, how Maia's son [Mercury] pastured flocks and preferred earth to heaven for the love of Dryope. But, when nine months were over and the child was born, the mother shrank in horror from the infant who smelt like a goat and had horns on his head. The father, however, wrapped it in

[1] The borrowing from the nineteenth Homeric hymn begins here, although it is only a borrowing, not a translation; much of the colour is Flaminio's own.

a fleece and took it to heaven and showed it to Jupiter, who laughed. All laughed but Venus, who took the baby and kissed him.

So hail Pan! Drive out disease and banish famine to the Arabs and Turks.[1]

This poem has the rich and luxurious beauty of Renaissance Arcadias and of nineteenth-century recreations of ancient Greek life and beliefs. Like Crinito's "Saltatio Bacchica," it is an exceedingly beautiful and highly suggestive evocation of pagan beliefs, the sort of thing that Keats would have liked to have achieved in *Endimion* or *Hyperion*.

The sapphic "Hymnus in Auroram,"[2] which, like the later "Hymnus in Dianam," clearly follows the conventional ode pattern, is deserving of attention not only for its intrinsic beauty but also because it inspired one of Bernardo Tasso's first efforts towards naturalizing the ode in Italian. It merits quotation almost in full:

Ecce ab extremo veniens Eoo
Roscidas Aurora refert quadrigas,
Et sinu lucem roseo nitentem
Candida portat.

Ite pallentes tenebrae, sub Orcum,
Ite, quae tota mihi nocte diros
Manium vultus, mihi dira semper
Somnium fertis.

Da lyram vati, puer; ipse flores
Sparge, dum canto. Bona diva, salve,
Quae tuo furvas radiante terras
Lumine lustras.

En tibi suaves violas, crocumque,
En odorati calathos amomi:
Surgit, et nostros tibi dulces aura
Portat odores.

Who can praise you, loveliest of goddesses?

Ut genas caelo roseas, comamque
Aurem profers, tibi fulva cedunt
Astra, decedit rutilante victa
Luna decore.

[1] Cf. Horace I, 21.

[2] Flaminio, *Carm.* (1743), pp. 11–12.

Te sine aeterna jaceant sepulti
Nocte mortales: sine te nec ullus
Sit color rebus, neque vita doctas
Culta per artes.

Tu gravem pigris oculis soporem
Excutis (leti sopor est imago)[1]
Evocans tectis sua quemque laetum ad
Munia mittis.

Exsilit stratis rapidus viator,
Ad jugum fortes redeunt juvenci,
Laetus in silvas properat citato
Cum grege pastor.

Ast amans carae thalamum puellae
Deserit flens, et tibi verba dicit
Aspera, amplexu tenerae cupito a-
vulsus amicae.[2]

Ipse amet noctis latebras dolosae,
Me juvet semper bona lux. nitentem
Da mihi lucem, dea magna, longos
Cernere in annos.

See from the farthest east Aurora
Comes, returning with her dewy team,
And, radiant, she bears gleaming light
In her rosy bosom.

Go, paling shadows, to the Underworld,
Go, you who bring me, all night through,
Dread visages of Hell, you who ever bring me
Dreadful dreams.

Give the poet his lyre, boy; and scatter
Flowers, too, while I sing. Good goddess, hail,
Who with your radiant light illuminate
The dusky lands.

[1] This half line is probably borrowed from Vergil, *Aeneid* VI, line 278, "consanguineus Leti Sopor."

[2] From "Evocans tectis" to "Cum grege pastor" seems to be an answer to Ovid, *Amorum* I, 13, while "Ast amans" to "amicae" appears to recognize the Ovidian point of view expressed in the first of "albas."

See, sweet violets for you, and the crocus,
See, baskets of aromatic herbs:
The breeze arises and carries our sweet
Perfumes to you.

When you put forth from heaven your rosy cheeks
And golden locks, the tawny stars give way
Before you, the moon withdraws, vanquished
By the blushing beauty.

Without you mortals would lie buried
In eternal night, without you there would be
No colour to things, nor a civilized life
Adorned by the arts.

You shake off heavy sleep from dull
Eyes—sleep is the image of death—
Calling from the roof-tops you send each man
Happily to his task.

The hurrying traveller springs out on to the road,
The sturdy bullocks return to the yoke,
Setting his herd in motion the carefree shepherd
Hastens into the woods.

But the lover in tears deserts the couch
Of the beloved maiden and utters harsh words
At you, torn from the desired embrace
Of his tender mistress.

Let him love the hiding-places of treacherous night,
May the good light ever please me. Grant, mighty
goddess,
That for long years I may see
The gleaming light.

Flaminio's other conventional hymn-ode, the "Hymnus in Dianam,"[1] in Catullan glyconic stanzas, identifies the goddess in the traditional fashion by recalling her cult centres and her iconography. In the list of her powers, her benefits to mankind are praised; she is the night light of heaven whom the stars follow; who nurtures the woods and the flowers with dew; she

[1] Flaminio, *Carm.* (1743), pp. 10–11.

is the ruler of the sea, of the south wind, and the rain. The "Hymnus in Dianam" is securely within the classical ode tradition yet, despite an inevitable echo of Catullus, it treats its subject with considerable originality. Quite another type of ode, the "Hymnus in bonam Valetudinem,"[1] written in sapphic stanzas, exorcises the hostile forces of ill-health and invokes the beneficent deity to cure the poet. It derives from Horace's odes to abstractions but, in its sustained personification of the abstraction and its mythological treatment of it, it is closer to the neoclassical odes of the eighteenth century.

Flaminio's "De Delia,"[2] in glyconics, is a translation, free in the Renaissance manner, of Petrarch's "Chiare, fresche, e dolci acque." It elaborates the conclusion in an almost Wordsworthian statement of the power that nature has gained over him because of his experiences in it.[3] Apart from its metre it has none of the characteristics of the ode.

Among Flaminio's later lyrics is another hymn, "De laudibus Lauri,"[4] in stanzas composed of four glyconics and one pherecratic. It praises the laurel and relates a myth. There is also a sapphic "Ad Gratias," a hendecasyllabic "Ad Bacchum," a sapphic "Ad Auram de Reginaldo Polo Cardinale," bidding the cool breeze go and fan the cardinal, and a sapphic "Ad Apollinem," which, in praying the god that he may always celebrate Alessandro Farnese in poetry, thanks the cardinal for his Maecenas-like gift of a farm.[5] This farm is the subject of three other odes, an "Ad Agellum suum" in iambic couplets which tells of his parents' joy in the farm, its loss at their death, its restitution to the poet by Cardinal Farnese, and the poet's Catullan-like excitement in visiting it; another in choliambics with a refrain,

Formosa silva, vosque lucidi fontes,
Et candidarum templa sancta Nympharum,

Fair wood, and you, bright fountains,
And the sacred temples of the radiant Nymphs,

[1] *Ibid.*, pp. 9–10.
[2] *Ibid.*, pp. 13–15.
[3] Flaminio says: "From *that* time the cooling fountain and the fresh meadows and the flowering tree have so bound my mind with love that whether night drives away day with his shadows or flees the swift sun I cannot ever rest anywhere else."
[4] Flaminio, *op. cit.*, pp. 22–3.
[5] *Ibid.*, pp. 37, 50, 43, 29–30.

which tells of his departure from the farm on foreign business and prays Diana, if he has sung her praises, to let him return to it; and another in hendecasyllabics which expresses his hope that he can return to the enumerated loved objects.[1] Two odes to Alessandro Farnese, the one in hendecasyllabics, the other in sapphics, beg the cardinal to take a rest from his strenuous diplomatic activities and come to the country, whose pleasures are described.[2] These odes are conventional humanist pieces ultimately derived from Horace's similar odes to Maecenas (III, 8 and 29), but their country scenes have a prettiness of their own. A similar ode in the first pythiambic couplet invites Antonio Mirandula[3] to leave Rome for pastoral pleasures. A magnificent "laureate" ode celebrates the anniversary of the creation of Paul III.[4] It describes the sun rising on the new Italy that the pope has made. Various occasional pieces tell of the onset of winter, congratulate Cardinal Farnese on his recovery from a serious illness, console a friend on his bereavement, and express the poet's longing for his dead mother and brothers and his thoughts on his father's death.[5] One of these odes laments the death of one who was young and beautiful[6] in phraseology that is rich with humanist associations:

Puella delicatior
Molli columba, pulchrior
Rosae rubentis flosculo,

Maiden more caressable,
Than the soft dove, more beautiful
Than the bud of the reddening rose,

why did the fates carry you off in your prime as the winds scatter the petals of a rose? We are reminded of Pontano's "Puella molli delicatior rosa"[7] and Poliziano's "Puella delicatior"[8] as well as all the rose-maiden poems ultimately derived from Ausonius' "De rosis nascentibus."

Most of the other poems in the first book, "Odas, Hymnos variique generis Carmina," of the definitive 1743 edition of

[1] *Ibid.*, pp. 26, 20, 24–5.
[2] *Ibid.*, pp. 18–19, 25–6.
[3] *Ibid.*, pp. 28–9.
[4] *Ibid.*, pp. 16–18.
[5] *Ibid.*, pp. 21, 49–50, 46–7, 27–8, 28.
[6] *Ibid.*, pp. 30–1.
[7] Pontano, *Carm.* (Basileae, 1556), pp. 3247–8.
[8] Angelo Poliziano, *Prose Volgari E Poesie Latine E Greche Edite E Inedite* . . . ed. Isidoro del Lungo (Firenze, 1867), pp. 268–71.

Flaminio, are urbane pieces of occasional verse, jokes with friends, and teasing, mock invectives.[1] They are not odes.

From the point of view of this study of the development of the ode Flaminio's poetical paraphrases of thirty of the psalms is important because it looks forward to the seventeenth- and eighteenth-century psalm-odes. In an introductory piece,[2] Flaminio portrays David as a shepherd playing his pipe and singing songs to God. The phraseology that he uses recalls the shepherd-poet of the classical, pastoral tradition, and hence points the way to the merging of the two traditions.[3] Moreover the paraphrase of the psalms itself, although reasonably close to the original, and restrained in taste, nevertheless incorporates interpretative material into the text (in this case commonplaces of Christian doctrine)[4] like Cowley's later translations of Pindar. Finally, Flaminio elaborates David's brief images into typical Horatian vignettes—thus reducing the dissimilarity between the Greco-Roman ode and the Hebrew psalm. For example, "As the hart panteth after the water brooks, so panteth my soul after thee, O God,"[5] becomes,

[1] Flaminio, *Carm.* (1743), pp. 21, 34 ff., 41, 42, 50 ff. [2] *Ibid.*, p. 206.

[3] This had already been done in the pastoral eclogue where the allegorical shepherd had been easily transformed into the Christian pastor by Radbertus in the tenth century. Petrarch had continued in Radbert's tradition writing ecclesiastical satire in pastoral eclogue form. See T. P. Harrison, *The Pastoral Elegy* (Austin, Texas, 1939).

[4] E.g., in his version of the 23rd psalm, *ibid.*, pp. 215–16, Flaminio says:

Uberrimis in pascuis,
Amoena propter flumina
Me spiritus sanctissimi
Aura beata recreat,
Dulcique mentem pabulo
Nutrit suae scientiae.

In the richest pastures,
Beside the fair rivers,
May the blessed breath of the most holy
Spirit restore me,
And nourish my mind with the sweet
Refreshment of its wisdom.

In "Ad Lectorem," *ibid.*, pp. 243–4, Flaminio says that he has not translated word for word but that he hopes that he has added nothing contrary to the sense of David. Basilio Zaucho, in a laudatory epigram, *ibid.*, p. 246, praises Flaminio for elucidating the obscurity of David.

[5] Authorized English Version, psalm, 42, verse 1.

Ut cerva fontem angela quaerit anxiae,
Quam vis canum sagacium
Vexavit, urit arva dum Sol igneus;
Sic te, pater dulcissime,
Desiderat anima mea.[1]

As the breathless hart, harassed by the
onslaught of keen-scented
Hounds, anxiously seeks the fountain,
While the fiery sun burns the fields,
So, sweetest father, my soul
Longs for you.

It is significant that the next poetical translator of David, who filled in the gaps left by Flaminio to make up a complete modern psalter in Latin verse, elaborates and embellishes far more than Flaminio and calls his psalms indifferently odes.[2] George Buchanan's roughly contemporary paraphrases of the psalms also use Horatian metres and with them some Horatian stylistic devices.

Flaminio's latest work, his *De rebus divinis Carmina*, dedicated to Marguerite de Valois,[3] is written in the medieval religious tradition. It also, in its religious fervour, in its revival of the mystical tradition with its extravagant conceits—this is the age of St. Theresa and St. John of the Cross—foreshadows baroque religious poetry. Like a sonnet sequence or a volume of baroque religious poetry such as Herbert's *The Temple*, it describes different aspects of the soul's relationship with God and it enumerates a series of spiritual exercises. Flaminio in his dedication says that he has abandoned his old way of writing and is imitating David here.[4] Yet the iambic dimeter, the metre of the Roman marching songs that St. Ambrose adopted for the Christian hymn, and the morning, noon, and evening prayers, recollections, perhaps, of the discipline of

[1] Flaminio, *Carm.* (1743), p. 219.

[2] See M. A. Flaminio and Francisco Spinula, *Davidis Regis et Vatis Inclvti Psalmi* (Basileae, 1558), argument to psalm 18, written by Spinula.

[3] The patroness of Bartolomeo Del Bene to whom Bernardo Tasso dedicated one book of *Rime* in 1554 and his *Salmi* in 1559. She also protected Joachim du Bellay, received dedications from Salmon Macrin, and was a friend of Ronsard's.

[4] *Georgii Fabricii Chemnicensis Odarum Libri Tres, Ad Deum Omnipotentem . . . M. A. Flaminii de rebus divinis Carmina* (Basileae, 1552), p. 136.

Bishop Giberti's household, suggest, rather, medieval sources of inspiration. I suspect that his statement about his imitation of David refers only to the fact that he is now writing religious rather than secular lyrics. Flaminio's language here is the language of the church and his style is simple and direct. But, in his new medium he reveals the same sense of music, the same exquisite discrimination in the choice of words that marked his pagan, classical poetry. Flaminio said that lyrics, like little gems, must be flawless and this aesthetic creed did not leave him when he turned to religious poetry.[1]

In the "Precatio matutina"[2] Lucifer, driving the shadows from the earth, warns Flaminio to rise and pray God to drive the shadows from his heart:

Iam noctis umbras Lucifer,
Almae diei nuncius,
Terra poloque dimovit.
Simulque nos cubilibus
Monet relictis pectore
Preces ab imo fundere.

Now Lucifer, the messenger of genial
Day, dispels the shades
Of night from earth and heaven,
And with it warns us
Leave our beds and pour forth
Prayer from our hearts' depths.

In his own religious poetry Flaminio returns to the allegorical habit of mind that he had rejected in his translations of the psalms. Thus, in the "Precatio meridiana"[3] he prays God to warm our cold hearts as the noonday sun warms the earth, to set them afire with a heat of love that will burn across the whole expanse of heaven and bind us to God with an unbreakable bond. In the "Precatio vespertina"[4] he prays that the shadows of night may not creep into his mind, that God's light may never leave our hearts. In other lyrics he asks Christ's aid because he is sick at heart, he affirms the blessedness of those

[1] See Cuccoli, pp. 146–7.

[2] *De Rebus Divinis* (Basileae, 1552), pp. 138–9.

[3] *Ibid.*, pp. 139–40.

[4] *Ibid.*, pp. 140–1.

who take up the cross and follow Christ, he praises Christ's benefits to man, he states what they must do who love Christ, he seeks to express the heat of his love for Christ, he lists the articles of his belief, he cries out to Christ, overcome with disease, he regrets that he is just beginning to serve God fully when he is old, he feels how sweet and salutary is perpetual meditation on the wounds and torments of Christ, he prays Christ to give him grace to live with piety and holiness, he thanks Christ for saving him, he predicts that without Christ he would fall into all kinds of evils, and, in the most medieval poem of all,

> Rector beate coelitum
> Qui sic amas mortalium,
>
> Blessed king of heaven
> Who so loves mortal man,

he finally commends his soul to God in the extremity of disease.[1] These poems are not odes; they are, rather, like a series of sacred sonnets done in Latin; but it was important to mention them because they stand at the beginning of a line of poetry that merged with the ode tradition in the early seventeenth century. It is the start of the literary Counter-Reformation.

Flaminio did not extend the scope of the ode. He just wrote exquisitely in the now familiar neolatin form. However he unwittingly broadened the province of the ode for the vernacular literatures by translating the psalms in the classical taste and by writing, for the first time since the middle ages, a collection of religious poetry.

This humanist accomplishment on the one hand and the living religious poetry on the other makes Flaminio fascinating both as a person and as a poet. He was, sincerely, the most delicious of pagans and yet the most fervent and exalted of Christians. It is as if George Herbert had been able from time to time to follow the inclination of his birth and spirit and take the way that takes the town.[2] How strange it is that, after some twenty years of philosophy and monastic devotion, Flaminio could pick up his pagan poetry almost exactly where he left off

[1] *Ibid.*, p. 161.
[2] George Herbert, *The Temple*, 18, "Affliction," lines 37–8.

at the age of seventeen and that, after this interlude of three warm, southern years, he was able again to return to the north and the church, bringing such abilities to the Council of Trent that in three years he was offered its secretaryship! Flaminio has attracted more attention than most of the neolatin poets mentioned here, except for the giants, Pontano and Sannazaro, because of his connection with reform and the suspicion of heresy. However he, too, like Marullo and Crinito, deserves, for his intrinsic merit, to be much better known than he is, especially outside Italy.

The Florentine, Giovanni della Casa (1503–56), like so many other minor humanists of the high Renaissance, wrote Horatian odes of outstanding competence and little originality. In della Casa we find the same stock situations, the same conventional occasions, the same mythological and geographical illustrations, and the same moral admonitions and philosophical platitudes that must have made even Horace's contemporaries feel at times that the world was growing old. One might say that della Casa differs from his fellow humanists and points to the future in his exclusive concern with moral and political themes, but then he had already written licentious poems in his youth. He also foreshadows the neoclassical ode in his preoccupation with his muse; he almost always mentions, addresses, or apostrophizes Thalia, Calliope, Melpomene, or just "Musa." One poem in its subtitle suggests the beginning of the Post-Tridentine debate, so important for aesthetics, on the value of lyric poetry, "De Horatiano Charactere. An qui lyrica scribunt, sint Poetis adnumerandi."[1] The poem itself says little, only that Horace did not write voluminously but polished a few lines.

Poets of some merit were the friends of Bernardo Tasso, the Capilupi of Mantua, Hippolytus, Laelius, Camillus, and Julius. Hippolytus wrote a number of religious odes, Tridentine in inspiration and sometimes baroque in image, but as thoroughly classical in content and technique as the secular Horatian odes to his friends. "Ad Beatam Virginem Mariam,"[2] e.g., opens with an invocation of the Virgin as of a pagan deity and in pagan terms describes her rites:

[1] *Carmina 5* (1753), pp. 134–5.

[2] *Capiluporum Carmina* (Romae, 1590), pp. 6–9.

Diva, seu caelo spatiaris alto,
Virginum sancto comitata coetu,
Sive qui totum regit unus Orbem
Carmine tollis,

Huc ades, dum te canimus; sacrasque
Supplices donis veneramur aras. . . .[1]

Goddess, whether you range the heavens on high,
Accompanied by your sacred band of maidens,
Or whether you extol in song him who, alone, rules
The whole world,

Be here present, while we sing of you and, suppliants,
Adore your sacred altars with gifts. . . .

Then she is pictured enthroned; her rays outshine the moon. The reference to the moon leads the poet into a Horatian digression, a particular picture of the moon. The Virgin surpasses Aurora too; she drives shadows from the mind and gives us heavenly light. She is incomparable; born of God, she is the mother of God, yet a virgin. She is crowned in heaven. The poet prays that she will help Italy threatened by the Turk. The array of forces is described, the emperor and the pope. The poem ends with another prayer for succour. "Ad Beatam Virginem Mariam" is like the Christian-pagan odes of Quinziano Stoa or Salmon Macrin. "Ad Lollius,"[2] in fourth asclepiads, gives moral advice. "Ad Bernardum Tassum,"[3] in the same metre begins with Horace's time-worn ship metaphor, a favourite of Tasso's. Hippolytus says that he would sing Caesar's deeds but his ship is too frail for the sea. But Tasso's is strong. Therefore let him tell of—there follows a rehearsal of Caesar's exploits as in Horace's ode with a similar disclaimer of such lofty abilities.[4] "Ad Ioannem Maricum,"[5] by no means original in theme, stands out because of its description of the attractions of contemporary Rome. It is also interesting in the history of taste. The poet asks his friend who has just returned

[1] *Ibid.*, p. 6.
[2] *Ibid.*, pp. 15–18.
[3] *Ibid.*, pp. 18–20.
[4] See Horace, *Carm.* IV, 2.
[5] *Capiluporum Carm.*, pp. 21–3.

from war why he wants to go back straight away. He gives specific examples of the terrors of war and contrasts them with the pleasures of comradeship at Rome where Caesar is celebrating his triumph over the East and his victory over Africa[1] and the poets are singing his praises and there are so many paintings and fountains. The other odes are mostly written to great men, dukes, princes of the church, popes.[2] They discuss contemporary events vaguely, in Horatian idiom. Exceptions to this are the two sapphic odes, "Ad Apollinem" and "De Pace inita inter Philippum et Henricum Reges,"[3] the one a lyrical description of the blessings of Apollo and a prayer that he will save the farmers from drought and famine and the people of Italy from the plague that is spreading with the war, the other a thankful vision of the joys of peace.

Laelius Capilupus shared Hippolytus' love for Rome. In the alcaic "Ad Julium Feltrium Urbinatem Cardinalem"[4] he urges the cardinal, since it is winter, to leave the country and come to the city and attend to business; Rome is a wonderful place! It is amusing to see Horace in reverse. Laelius' other ode[5] is a sapphic to Hercules Gonzaga from prison. The poet has no fear; for he is conscious of righteousness, but he asks Gonzaga's help and summarizes the political situation in Italy.

Camillus Capilupus' two odes make us regret that the author did not write, or at least publish, more. In "Ad Deum"[6] a completely assimilated Horace is made the medium for the expression of real Christian feeling. The poet is at sea and afraid; he is pursued by the monsters of the deep night and day; he is in darkness. He cries for light and peace; he asks God to receive him into his bosom:

Salve rerum opifex, salve hominum salus,
Qui coelum tonitru, qui pelagus cies
Nutu sedibus imis
Et mulces tumidum, ut libet.

Ad te confugio consilio indigens. . . .

[1] Charles V forced the Turks down the Danube in 1532 and conquered Tunis in 1535.

[2] See *Capiluporum Carm.*, pp. 26–9, 31–44.

[3] *Ibid.*, pp. 23–6, 29–31.

[4] *Carm. Illustr.* III, 195–6.

[5] *Ibid.*, III, 197–9.

[6] *Capiluporum Carm.*, pp. 243–4.

Tu lucem potes es luce carentibus
Et fessis requiem reddere mentibus
O spes certa, salutis
Me tandem excipias sinu.

Hail, creator of the world, hail, saviour of man,
You who move heaven with thunder, who summon the sea
By a nod from its depths,
And soothe it, when it swells, as you wish,

To you I flee for refuge, lacking counsel. . . .

You can restore light to those who lack light,
And give rest to weary minds,
O hope that will never fail, finally
Receive me in the bosom of salvation.

Here the Horatian technique and the Christian elements, allegory, "morality" battles with the passions, and Biblical imagery are perfectly united. It is the most successful of these classical-Christian odes. Camillus' other ode is a highly poetic hymn to night,[1] a favourite theme of the humanists, also in the fourth asclepiad metre.

Julius Capilupus' religious ode, "Ad Mariam Virginem quam Matrem Gratiarum Vocant,"[2] like those of Hippolytus merely inserts the name of the Christian divinity in the blank in the pagan form. Here we have Horatian language, Horatian imagery, and stock Horatian phrases about the gods only slightly adapted to their new functions. There is, too, the beginning baroque preoccupation with radiance and the favourite sun image[3]; we see the Virgin with her spikey halo:

Diva . . .
. . . radiis decora
Patris aeterni, magis ipsa puro
Sole renides.

Goddess . . .
. . . adorned with the rays
Of the eternal father, you shine brighter
Than the naked sun.

1 *Ibid.*, pp. 253–5.
2 *Ibid.*, pp. 260–2.
3 For the sun image see Salmon Macrin, Bernardo Tasso, and Bartolomeo Del Bene infra.

The poetry of the Capilupi, with its preoccupation with Christian themes, however treated, on the one hand, and its civilized Horatian odes exchanged with friends on the other, is characteristic of the age.

Characteristic, too, in a different way, are the poems of another of Bernardo Tasso's friends, the Neapolitan poet, Bernardino Rota (1509–75), who wrote pastoral odes in the Horatian tradition. His themes were Nisa and Lycidas,[1] and fountains,[2] breezes,[3] flowers, and plants.[4] He affirmed the superiority of the country over the city[5] and invited his friends to share his rural bliss; for "manet cras / flebilis urna."[6] The growth of the pastoral ode among the Neapolitan neolatin poets has already been touched on above in the discussion of the works of Pontano and Carbone. It is interesting to note that at this same period vernacular poets, e.g., Ludovico Paterno (also a friend of Bernardo Tasso's) in *Le Nuove Fiamme*,[7] were writing Italian pastoral sonnets and *canzoni*.

And now we are in the middle of the sixteenth century and the life has gone out of neolatin literature. University men with a facility in Latin verse continue the trite imitation of Horace; others, under the influence of Reformation and Counter-Reformation, seize upon the international language and the polite literary form to write religious polemics. They write purely didactic or dogmatic poems in Horatian metres and call them odes. A typical mid-century production is Georgius Fabricius Chemnicensis' *Odarum Libri Tres Ad Deum Omnipotentem* (Basileae, 1552). Let us list the titles of a few of the odes:

ode 1 "De excellentia fidei, et ad eam a Deo impetrandam, precatio";

ode 2 "Ne bonorum ignoratione petamus, quae sunt inutilia, vel noxia";

ode 3 "Pro Christianis Principibus, ut pie et iuste imperent."

[1] *Carm. Illustr.* VIII, 149–50.

[2] *Ibid.*, VIII, 150–1.

[3] *Ibid.*, VIII, 152–3.

[4] *Ibid.*, VIII, 156–8. There are no more odes in Dionigi Atanagi's edition of Rota's *Poemata* (Venetiis, 1557).

[5] *Carm. Illustr.* VIII, 156–8, 158–9.

[6] *Ibid.*, VIII, 158.

[7] Lyone, 1568.

A quotation from the last ode will indicate the quality of the poetry:

> Seu principe bono regamur, seu malo,
> Omnis potestas a Deo est.[1]

> Whether we are ruled by a good prince, or a bad one,
> All power is from God.

To complete the didacticism of the volume each of these unpoetical odes is preceded by a metrical analysis and a verbose technical description of the metre.

However, we must not leave the humanist ode for the clamorous vernacular with a bad impression of it. Although the second great floraison of Latin poetry has seen its day, the late rose lingers. Among the works of Torquato Tasso (1544–95) there is still to be found a poem that, in brief, sums up the greatness, the variety, and scope, that the neolatin ode achieved. "Ad Nubes" is Tasso's virtually unique exercise in the neolatin ode. It is essentially Horatian: it is written in the second asclepiad metre; it is an occasional poem whose occasion is universalized; it has an addressee; it evokes all that is traditionally associated with its subject in nature, mythology, literature, the Bible, and Catholic tradition to help to express its meaning; it substitutes picture for proposition; and it is brief and economically written. Yet it is a thing apart from the thousand Horatian odes written in the Renaissance; Tasso makes Horace serve him in the creation of an ode that is nearer Shelley's than anything ancient. It is a nature poem addressed to the clouds. It reveals the peculiarly Shelleyan combination of keen observation of nature, romantic emotion in its presence, and the reading of allegory into it. But there is something of Byron about this ode, too. Tasso feels with awe the powerlessness of man, of even the rulers of men, before the elemental forces of nature.

"Ad Nubes" is a prayer for rain, but subtle suggestions throughout the ode, culminating in the last two lines, transform the poem into a prayer for something more than physical rain, for rain as a sacrament, "The outward and visible sign of an inward and spiritual grace." It is a prayer for the refreshment

[1] This is the age of the divine right of kings, see the roughly contemporary *Mirror for Magistrates*, passim.

of the land and the refreshment of the spirit, for the rain that swells the grape and makes the sacramental wine, for the rain that makes the corn grow and gives us bread, and for the manna from heaven that prefigures the communion wafer that is both bread for the body and, symbolically, bread for the spirit. It is a prayer for a sign of God's mercy and the symbol of his promise to man; it is a prayer for grace.

"Ad Nubes" was written in 1570.[1] There had been a great drought in Italy and Pope Pius V had prayed for rain. Tasso asks that his prayers be answered:

> Neptuni genus humidae
> Nubes, quae volucri curritis agmine
> Qua caeci rapiunt Noti;
> E vestro gremio cum sonitu horrida
> Mittit fulmina Iuppiter,
> Si quando in superos gens fera verticem,
> Tollit, si veteres manu
> Lucos sacrilega polluit, hinc tonat
> Arx coeli, hinc micat ignibus
> Crebris. Vos placidae frugiferos agris
> Imbres mittitis et sata
> Laeta humore alitis. Vos sitientibus
> Succos vitibus additis,
> Mox libanda novis munera poculis;
> Vos largas pluviae nisi
> Effundatis opes, gramina non humus,
> Non flores dabit arida.
> Arescunt viduae frondibus arbores;
> Vestri languida corpora
> Ex desiderio, vix animas suo
> Languentes retinent sinu;
> Vos in pinifero vertice, seu tenet
> Atlas, seu Scythiae latus
> Seu vasto Oceani luditis aequore,
> Foetus imbriferos date;
> Rores in gremium spargite torridae
> Matris munera, roscidae
> Nubes, vestra Pio fundite Maximo;
> Quamquam gentibus imperat,

1 Antonius Martinius, ed., *Carmina Latina Torquati Taxi* (Romae, 1895), p. 29.

Non haec vestra Pius munera negliget;
Tandem o vos requiem date
Fessis irriguo rore animantibus.

Children of Neptune,
Moist clouds, who race in a fleet column
Wherever the sightless south wind snatches you,
From your bosom with dreadful din
Jupiter dispatches his thunderbolts,
Whenever a barbarian race raises its head against
The gods above. If it defiles ancient
Temple groves with sacrilegious hand, from hence the citadel
Of heaven thunders, from hence it flashes its flickering
Fires. You, when appeased, send fruitful showers
Upon the fields and you feed the
Flourishing crops with moisture. You give juices
To the thirsting vines,
Gifts soon to be offered as first fruits from new goblets.
Unless you pour forth a bountiful
Wealth of rain, the dry earth will not give us
Grain, nor flowers.
The trees bereft of foliage dry up.
Through a longing for you
Languid bodies scarcely keep their languishing
Souls in their own bosoms.
If Atlas holds you on its pine-clad crest,
Or the flank of Scythia,
Or if you sport on the vast plain of Ocean,
Give us your rain-bearing brood.
Scatter your dew on the lap of your parched
Mother, dewy clouds,
Pour out your gifts for mightiest Pius.
Although he rules the races of the world,
Pius may not neglect these gifts of yours.
At last, with your living dew,
Give rest to wearied creatures.

Since the ode was written in a time of drought, Tasso first introduces the clouds, themselves indifferent ("quae curritis *qua* rapiunt Noti"), as the agents of divine punishment for human pride and irreligion. The reference here (lines 4–10) to the gigantomachy is typically Horatian (see, e.g., I, 31, lines 37–40). But Tasso has skilfully chosen language that is both specific and indefinite, so that the flood, too, is included in this allusion.

However, the clouds are also God's agents of mercy, lines 10–14. They bring joy to the fields and they water the thirsting vines, whose wine in turn is poured forth as a thankoffering to God. Again, lines 15–21, we return to the destructive powers of the clouds. Without the rain there is death on the land and death in the souls of men. Therefore, in Horatian fashion, Tasso summons the clouds from wherever they may be, lines 22–4, and he prays for rain, lines 25–32, "Foetus imbriferos date," a prayer that is also for new life, for spiritual rest and refreshment. This other meaning of the ode, which has already been hinted at in the half-allusion to the flood and in the reference to sacramental wine, now comes to the fore in the vocabulary of the last seven lines, especially that of the last two lines where "requies" and "ros" with all their Christian connotations occur close to each other.

With Tasso we close this chapter on the neolatin ode in Italy. The ancient lyric, revived, perhaps under Greek influence—for Filelfo wrote his first ode after his sojourn in Byzantium—to make the court more august and to add lustre to the events of everyday life, has known widespread popularity and wide-ranging experiment both in form and in content. It has been written by men who were primarily scholars, like Filelfo, churchmen, like Campano, statesmen, like Pontano, soldiers, like Marullo, teachers, like Lampridio, or men of religion, like Flaminio. They have learnt how to write odes in all the classical metres and to create a wide variety of new forms, new lines, new stanzas, triads, and irregular verse. They have written on the ancient subjects and they have adopted the ancient form to express modern ideas. They have learnt the posture of the Pindaric poet-priest, the outlook of the Horatian philosopher, and how to make the classical language and form express the more highly developed sensibilities of modern times. They have explored the expressive possibilities of the ode; they have imbued it with an emotion that it never knew; they have used it to evoke a mood; and they have learnt, from the hymn and prayer, how to write the tone poem. They have broadened the ode to describe the panorama of nature, a modern festival, or the social scene. In Naples they have tried crossbreeding it with the popular pastoral producing a hybrid, eclogue-ode, unfortunately doomed because of the essential falsity of

Arcadia, but nevertheless revealing the potential bigness of the ode. They have made the ode into a hymn and the psalm into an ode, they have written didactic odes and delightful odes, and they have created a whole new body of Latin lyric poetry, classically inspired, but expressive of a new culture, greater in bulk, wider in scope than the ancient ode and not always inferior in poetic power. They have created poetry that opens the way both to the vernacular Renaissance and to neo-classicism. They have accomplished much, but now the enthusiastic creation in what is no longer a living language has died down. Tied to a vocabulary and mode of expression of what is realized to be a far-off, alien time, the best poets feel a dissatisfaction with neolatin poetry. Some, like Flaminio, turn back to the living Latin of the church to express their strongest feelings, others return to their mother tongues and, with the falling popularity of paganism after the Council of Trent and the new importance that writers should use the language of the people, the vernaculars have come into their own. Henceforth the great poetry is written in Italian, in French, and in English.

Chapter 4

THE ITALIAN ODE

ALTHOUGH neolatin poetry flourished all over Europe, as the great national collections of Jan Gruter reveal,[1] the neolatin lyric was incomparably at its best in Italy. It is for that reason that all the neolatin poets cited in the previous chapter on the humanist ode were Italians. Considering the number of Italian poets writing in Latin and the volume of verse that they produced, it is not at all surprising to find that the Italian ode was comparatively rare in the Renaissance. Classical inspiration, if sufficiently compelling to decree theme and form, tended to express itself in the ancient language. Of course, after a century of humanism and of classical revival, every sixteenth-century Italian poet knew how to adorn his work with a few fashionable ancient flourishes. Nevertheless, few who wrote in their own language broke with the familiar Petrarchan tradition before the beginning of the seventeenth century. It was not until the Pléiade put French on equal footing with Latin and firmly established the vernacular ode that the Italians began writing classically inspired lyric poetry in Italian Thus the first well-known Italian ode writer is Chiabrera. However, Chiabrera was not the first Italian poet who wrote odes and it will be the purpose of this chapter to rescue from comparative obscurity a predecessor of his who has been so unfortunate as to have his

[1] Janus Gruter, *Delitiae C poetarum gallorum* (n.p. [Frankfurt], 1609), 6 vol. *Delitiae poetarum germanorum* (Frankfurt, 1612), 16 vol. *Delitiae C poetarum belgicorum* (Francofurti, 1614), 7 vol.

name perpetually overshadowed by that of his greater son. I refer to Bernardo Tasso.

Bernardo Tasso, however, was not the first poet to write Italian odes. In the early days of the Renaissance, back in the first half of the fifteenth century, before Latin had become supreme, an Italian made an early attempt at naturalizing the new, admired, ancient poetry in his native language. It was the year 1441 and Florence was besieged by Filippo Maria Visconti of Milan. The people were worn with hardship and strain. There was need for distraction. It was in these circumstances that Leon Battista Alberti and Piero di Cosimo de Medici suggested that the Accademia Coronaria should hold a public debate on the nature of true friendship, in the church of Santa Maria del Fiore, on the twenty-second of October, after dinner. Various prelates and ambassadors were invited and the great cathedral was thronged with the people of Florence.[1]

Six scholars had already discussed friendship in *ottava rima*, Boccaccio's favourite verse form, or in *terza rima*, the metre of Dante, when Leonardo di Piero Dati (d. 1472) stepped up to the pulpit.

> I' son Mercurio, di tutto l'Olympico regno
> Nunzio, tra li omini varii iuntura salubre,
> Splendore de' saggi, porto al certamine vostro
> Si cose, si canto nuovo.

> I am Mercury, of the whole Olympian kingdom
> Herald, between all manner of men, the wholesome bond,
> Splendour of speaking I bring to your competition,
> Both subjects and songs that are new.

The speech is that of a character from a medieval mystery play but the metre is the classical, quantitative hexameter. After Mercury's speech announcing the experiment, Leonardo harangues his audience on the nature of friendship, still in quantitative hexameters. Then Amicizia speaks for herself:

> Eccomi, i' son qui Dea degli amici,
> Quella, qual tutti li omini solete
> Mordere, e falso fuggitiva dirli
> Or la volete.

[1] See Leon Battista Alberti, *Opere Volgari*, ed. Anicio Bonucci (Firenze, 1843), I, 167.

Here am I, I am here, the Goddess of Friends,
She whom all men are wont
To carp at and falsely call fugitive,
Then to desire.

Again the speech is that of a character in a medieval religious play, here a morality, but the metre is the Horatian sapphic, naturalized in Italian. Amicizia continues in the morality vein:

Eccomi; e gia dal soglio superno
Scesa, cercavo loco tra la gente,
Pront' a star con chi per amor volesse
Darne ricetto.[1]

Here I am; and I have already come down from the throne
Of the highest and have sought a place among the people,
Ready to stay with him who, for love, would be willing
To receive me.

The rest of the poem describes, in vivid allegorical language, the vicissitudes of friendship on earth among the various social classes. Apart from its classical metre, which is highly successful, this is in every sense a medieval poem, like the popular tirades of Folly.[2] It might, however, have been the beginning of the Italian ode had not Latin virtually obliterated Italian for the next two generations.

However, in the first quarter of the sixteenth century, Giovan Giorgio Trissino (1478–1550) of Vicenza, famed for *Sofonisba*, the first classical tragedy with the rules, wrote three triadic *canzoni* completely Petrarchan in spirit, but Pindaric in form,[3] and this second attempt to introduce a classical type lyric into Italian bore fruit. When Leonardo di Piero Dati wrote his "Amicizia" Horace was the only ode writer known, but now Pindar had been discovered and published and it was under the stimulus of the Aldine edition (1513) that Trissino, and Alamanni after him, wrote their Italian odes.

[1] G. Carducci, *La Poesia Barbara nei Secoli xv e xvi* (Bologna, 1881), pp. 12–21.

[2] Barbara Swain, *Fools and Folly during the Middle Ages and the Renaissance* (New York, 1932).

[3] The *canzoniere* was published in 1520.

Luigi Alamanni (1495–1556), went farther than Trissino in the introduction of the ode into Italian. He imitated both the Pindaric triad whose parts, unlike Trissino, he clearly labelled —*ballata*, *contraballata*, and *stanza* were the Italian terms he chose to represent strophe, antistrophe, and epode—and the Pindaric style, the myths, *sententiae*, digressions, and allusions, in a series of odes which he called hymns. Alamanni's Pindaric hymns are of particular importance because, through his long residence in France (1522–7 and 1531–8) and his laureate post at the court of Francis I, it seems likely that he influenced the Pléiade,[1] that he was one of the particular links between Italian humanism and French Renaissance poetry.

Alamanni's eight Pindaric hymns were published in the *Opere Toscane* in 1532–3 and dedicated to Francis I. In triads, with myths, celebrations of ancestors, allusive definitions of people or places, reflections on life, and the glorification of poetry, he praises Francis I, Marguerite of Navarre, and his own Petrarchan *donna*, Battista Larcara. The actual form of the stanzas, like Trissino's, is little different from that of the *canzone*.[2] The formal innovation, as with Trissino, consists in the existence of two stanza patterns for each poem. The stylistic innovations, however, are much more significant. Let us take the fourth hymn[3] as an example.

After the proud humanist boast that he is singing a new song perhaps never heard before in the Arno valley, a boast that also prefaces the first hymn, Alamanni exclaims how he is inspired by the beauty of his Pianta (Battista Larcara). Nowhere in the world (in Miltonic fashion the poet lists its geographical features: "riva," "monte," "seno," "due poli," . . .), beneath night or day, is such beauty seen.

[1] H. Hauvette, *Un Exilé florentin à la cour de France au XVIe siècle: Luigi Alamanni* (Paris, 1903), pp. 443 ff., discusses the possible influence of Alamanni on the Pléiade. He thinks it highly likely, although there is no conclusive evidence. However, du Bellay mentions Alamanni in his *Deffence* and Hauvette finds Ronsard's Pindaric odes much more suggestive of Alamanni than of Pindar.

[2] See, e.g., the metric pattern for the first hymn, *ballata* and *contraballata* abcbaccdeeddff, *stanza*, abcabccddee. The first hymn is representative of 7 out of 8 odes. All the lines are *settenarî*, a metre that, as the quotations on pp. 146 and 148 reveal, grows quickly monotonous.

[3] *Opere Toscane* II (Vineggia, 1533), 104r–105v.

Now, to praise Pianta, he is going to attempt a Pindaric flight:

Et s'io pur l'ali stendo
Con l'incerate piume
Per dare al Ponto nome[1] . . .

And, moreover, if I spread my wings
With feathers waxed together
To give the sea a name, . . .

Then, true to Pindar, he begins abruptly describing the site of Genoa:

Al mar Tyrrhen non lungo,
Non lungo al mar che bagnia
Il Provenzal confino;
Ove a Neptunno aggiunge
Et seco s'accompagna
L'alassimo Apennino,
Benignio ivi destino
De vicin colli e monti
Congiunsi tutto insieme
Il piu honorato seme
Di quei, ch'a viver pronti
Furon d'ingegnio e' d'arte
E' in piu nascosa parte
Da i suoi vicin sicuri
Si fer con fossi e muri.

Not far from the Tyrrhenian sea,
Not far from the sea that washes
The boundaries of Provence,
Where the highest soaring Apennine
Takes Neptune to companion
And goes along with him,
There the kindly destiny
Of neighbouring hills and mountains
Joined in one together
The most honoured seed
Of those who were ready
To live from ingenious art,
And, in the most hidden part,
Secure from their very neighbours,
They built their moats and walls.

[1] A translation of Horace, *Carm.* IV, 2, lines 2–4.

Alamanni praises the Genoese: first in counsel and in arms, dear to Neptune, they know the sea from the Arctic to Africa, from the Atlantic to the Ganges. Liguria is adorned with much glory and praise. One of her glories is Larcaro. Alamanni makes the briefest allusions to his piratical exploits, his enemy, and his services to commerce.[1] He praises Larcaro, the ancestor of his Pianta—May she ever live happily, "Viv' ella lieta e sempre." This praise of the living woman through her people and through her ancestor, the allusions to Larcaro's story as though it were familiar to everyone, the exact description of Genoa and the definition of the city through its physical setting, the specificity of every statement, the abruptness of transition, and the conclusion with its final prayer for the "heroine" following swiftly upon the conclusion of the "myth" are characteristics immediately recognized as inspired by Pindar. This is a completely different sort of poem in praise of a lady from the Petrarchan *canzone*. Alamanni is bringing a new learning and a new ceremonious dignity to the lyric. He is giving it a new kind of universality based upon knowledge rather than emotion. Like Pindar Alamanni attempts to celebrate each subject in its meaning for the whole group, not just for himself alone—and he chooses his subjects accordingly.

However, since Alamanni possibly had an influence upon the Pléiade, it is important to note the ways in which Alamanni differs from Pindar, the leisurely pace, the expansiveness, the absence of the metaphors and aphorisms which give Pindar's ode its characteristic concentration and intensity. Alamanni lacks the conciseness, the tightness of structure, and the pictorial vividness of Pindar, although he struggles to imitate the latter by iconographical, almost emblem book definitions of his heroes; for example, in the first hymn,[2] dedicated to the praise of Francis I, Odysseus is

[1] Hauvette, *Exilé*, p. 230, outlines the history of Megollo Larcaro. At Trebizond in 1381 Larcaro was slapped by a young favourite of the emperor, John Paleologus. Enraged at not being able to satisfy his honour he vowed revenge. He outfitted two galleys and as a pirate attacked Greek shipping and tortured his prisoners. The emperor sent four galleys against him but he defeated them all and again tortured his prisoners. Finally the emperor sent the young man. Larcaro did not torture him but demanded trade concessions for Genoa.

[2] Alamanni, *Opere Toscane* II, 97r–99v.

L'altro che' santo avviso
Del ingeniosa Dea
Per guida sempre havea,

The other who always had
As guide the holy counsel
Of the ingenious goddess,

Diomedes is

quel che di sangue tinto
Vide il suo ferro audace
Nella spietata piaga
Dell' honorata e vaga
Dea d'amorosa face;
Fuor d'ogni dolce e pace
Lontan dal patrio nido
Visse in dubbioso lido,

He, who stained with blood
Saw his daring sword
In the cruel wound
Of the honoured and lovely
Goddess of the torch of love,
Shut out from every sweetness
    and peace,
Far from his father's home,
Lived on a doubtful shore,

and Aeneas is

. . . il pio
Troian che 'l pio parente
Sopra le spalle tolse
Dall' impia fiamma ardente.

. . . the pious
Trojan who carried his pious
Parent on his shoulders
From the impious burning flame.

We will see later how these hymns compare with Ronsard's Pindarics.

The importance of Alamanni is not that of the interesting minor poet who is usually very bad but occasionally finds just the right words to express a real flash of insight, but rather that of the competent, pedestrian poet who never rises above or falls below the level of tame mediocrity but who, nevertheless, makes technical innovations of historical importance. Alamanni is important because he first wrote vernacular poetry in clearly marked triads. He thus stands at the beginning of one line of imitators of Pindar which survived until the end of the eighteenth century. But he is more important still because he was the first poet to introduce the fundamental characteristics of the Pindaric into Italian poetry, and hence, perhaps, into French and English. In the vernacular languages Alamanni was the inventor of a new kind of lyric, superior in grandeur and breadth, elevation and universality, to the traditional medieval poetry, a lyric that glorified man, his history, and his works with all the learning, dignity, and allusiveness of the new architecture which was already rebuilding his external world. If he gave courage to the Pléiade, it did not matter that Alamanni's poems were dull and his metres maddeningly monotonous.

Following Alamanni in his Pindaric innovations and improving slightly upon his imitation, Antonio Sebastiano Minturno (d. 1574) published in 1535 two long odes on Charles V's conquest of Tunis.[1] These are, like Alamanni's odes, written in triads whose parts are renamed in Italian *volta*, *rivolta*, and *stanza*, the source of Ben Jonson's "turn," "counter-turn," and "stand." In these odes the verse, though not musical, has been made a little less tiresome than Alamanni's by the mixture of *endecasillabi* with the *settenarî*, as was usual in the structure of the *canzone* strophe. The triads have now been given some meaning. Minturno, like Lampridio in Latin, uses his triads to mark the movement of the thought, and hence to aid in the development of the theme. These odes of Minturno's, however, are not much more readable than those of Alamanni. They are big, grand,

1 Minturno, *Rime et Prose*, ed. Girolamo Ruscelli (in Venetia, 1559), pp. 166–75 and 176–84. See Minturno's own comments on his odes in his *L'Arte Poetica* (Venezia, 1564).

Qual Semideo, anzi qual novo Dio
Tra gli huomini mortali,
Qual supremo valor, qual Giove in terra,
Qual Febo nel saver, qual Marte in guerra, . . . etc.[1]

What demigod, rather what new god
Among mortal men,
What supreme valour, what Jove on earth,
What Phoebus in wisdom, what Mars in war . . .

and dull, loaded with all the learning one would expect in the praise of the conqueror of Africa, and faithfully imitative of all the Pindaric superficialities, including the attack on the cock that crows against Jove's eagle, but they are unenlivened by inspiration, untransmuted by the poet's alchemy. Minturno's significant services to literature were done in the critical field.

However, as at the time of Pontano, the signs had appeared. There would soon be a true poet to write in the new style. In the same decade in which Alamanni and Minturno published their Italian Pindarics Bernardo Tasso[2] (1493–1569), the father of Torquato Tasso, published three volumes of classically inspired odes which show the poet, with gathering confidence and growing temerity, abandoning the Petrarchan tradition, at that moment supreme in the Italian lyric, for the newer, freer forms and techniques, for the fresher sentiments of the ancients. Two of Tasso's first three odes, published in the first book of *Amori* in 1531, and a third ode, published in the second book of *Amori* in 1534, are written in conventional *canzone* form[3] and can only claim the title of ode by virtue of their classical content, and, in the case of "A l'Aurora," because of humanist rather than *trecento* inspiration.[4] All the same, these three odes might equally well be termed classical *canzoni*[5] and

[1] Minturno, *Rime et Prose*, p. 166. The rhetorical gusto of this Pindaric, exclamatory, attention-catching beginning reminds us of John of Gaunt's speech in *King Richard III*. Unfortunately Minturno was unable to maintain the vigour of his bombast throughout and enjoy the life of the fustian Elizabethans.

[2] Bernardo Tasso's life is described fully in Edward Williamson, *Bernardo Tasso. Storia e Letteratura. Raccolta di Studi e Testi* (Roma, 1951). Therefore there will be only passing allusions to it here.

[3] Williamson, p. 84.

[4] "A l'Aurora" is deeply indebted to Flaminio's "Hymnus in Auroram," Carducci, "Dello Svolgimento dell'Ode in Italia," *Poesia e Storia, Opere*, XVI (Bologna, 1905), p. 378 and Williamson, p. 84.

[5] The term is Carducci's "Ode," pp. 373–4.

assimilated to the large group of such poems that appeared towards the middle of the century.[1] The third ode published in 1531, however, is written in a new verse form and henceforth, in the volumes of 1534 and 1537, except for the above mentioned exception, the *canzone* strophe is abandoned for shorter stanzas of *settenarî* and *endecasillabi*, five or six lines in length, that suggest the lyric stanzas of the ancients.

Tasso's classicism, like that of Ronsard and the Elizabethans, and like the hellenism of the English romantics, belongs to the fresh and new period of influence when the scope of poetry is dramatically enlarged and new possibilities are vividly realized, when men of imagination can transfigure their old, familiar poetry, quickening it into new life, without being driven by over education to an apeing accuracy in reproducing their models. It is the classicism of a Shakespeare, though one would not dream of comparing the quality of the two poets, not of a Ben Jonson. Thus in "A l'Aurora"[2] we find the well-worn *canzone* filled with new life by its classical theme. A different spirit has produced a different poem from the countless Petrarchan pieces of the period.[3] Yet there is little if anything here that we might not find in a *canzone* and it is extremely hard

1 Benedetto Gareth, called il Cariteo, born in Barcelona but naturalized as an Italian, first wrote these classical *sonetti* and *canzoni* in Naples under the influence of Pontano and Sannazaro. He published them in *Endimione* in 1506, Carducci, "Ode," pp. 373–4. His example was followed by large numbers of minor poets.

2 *Libro de gli Amori . . . Hinni et ode . . .* (Vinegia, 1534), pp. 75r–76v. The strophic pattern is abbAaCdDcC.

3 The difference of spirit could be attributed to the fact that Tasso is here imitating Flaminio's "Hymnus in Auroram," were it not that we find the same difference of spirit in Tasso's "A Diana" and "A Pan" which are not derivative from Flaminio's poems of the same name. That Tasso himself felt that a different spirit from that of the traditional poetry animated the classical lyric is apparent from the following extract from a letter to Girolamo della Rovere written the 25th of October, 1553:

> I walk sometimes through those paths of poetry which are marked by the tracks of the Greek and Latin writers and which, in my opinion, appear to be more beautiful and more lovely than those in which the old Tuscans were pleased to walk, for I consider, if I am not mistaken, that this poetry is more delightful and more full of spirit and vivacity than theirs, although I wonder whether it could be expected to please him who does not have a perfect knowledge of the best Greek and Latin literature.

to see any of the characteristics of the classics that Tasso later avowed imitating,

> drawn out and extended comparisons, ideas that can be pursued far beyond single clauses through several strophes, digressions into some well-found fable without a further return to the subject at hand.[1]

Perhaps the description of the dawn as a woman in stanza one may be considered to be a "comparazione protratta"; yet this is so conventional that one would hesitate to count it as an innovation. The reference to Aurora as Tithonus' wife in stanza seven may be considered to be a rudimentary myth, especially since it does not occur in the Latin poem on which Tasso's "Aurora" is based, but it is very rudimentary and was probably brought in to fill up the stanza, longer than the Latin one, rather than as something consciously new. There are no cases of run-on stanzas.

"A l'Aurora" is a work of Tasso's apprenticeship, when he was learning by adapting neolatin poems to the Italian *canzone* form how to write classical odes in the vernacular and so enlarge the scope of Italian lyric poetry beyond the confines of Petrarchism. "A l'Aurora" derives its motifs and general organization and many of its phrases and illustrations from Marc Antonio Flaminio's "Hymnus in Auroram." Yet it has, perforce, treated its source with some independence. The ode, with its brief stanzas, is much too tightly constructed for the *canzone* form, hence an adaptation must be also an expansion, and, in the course of this expansion Tasso has cut the cloth somewhat to the modern fashion, thus making "A l'Aurora" more a poem of the age than Flaminio's "Hymnus in Aurorem" which had appeared only five years before and so, by lessening the gap between learned and popular poetry, facilitating the adoption of the classical inspired lyric in Italian.

"A l'Aurora" begins echoing Flaminio's "Hymnus in Auroram," but it soon abandons its model for free, if unoriginal flights of fancy:

> Ecco, che 'n Oriente
> Incomincia a mostrarsi
> Co capei d'oro sparsi
> La madre di Memnon chiara, e lucente;

[1] Carducci, "Ode," p. 379.

Et gia nel cielo spente
L'accese faci, il mattutino raggio
Co begli occhi n'adduce,
Et con la vaga sua purpurea luce
Facendo a l'ombre oltraggio
Al sourano pianeta apre il viaggio.[1]

See, in the east
She begins to appear,
With scattered golden hair,
The mother of Memnon, bright and shining;
And already the lighted torches of
Heaven are spent when, with her beautiful eyes,
She brings us the morning's ray,
And, with her lovely, purple light
Outraging the darkness,
Opens the way for the sovereign planet.

There follows a classical invocation of Aurora, "Vieni candida Aurora," whose return all living creatures honour, then a stanza taken straight from Flaminio, supplemented by the familiar, medieval nightingale passage to make up the *canzone* strophe:

A te amaranthi, e rose;
Et amomo odorato
Con spirar dolce, e grato
Portano l'aure lievi, et amorose[2]:
Le sorelle dogliose
Ti salutan con lor soave canto
Tra piu frondosi rami,
Et par ch'ogn' una ti desiri, e chiami;
Accio che 'l lume santo
Tolga a la terra il tenebroso manto.[3]

To you amaranth and roses
And aromatic herbs,
The light and amorous breezes
Bring, with sweet and pleasant sighing.
The mournful sisters
Salute you, with their sweet song
Among the leafiest branches,
And all things appear to yearn for you and cry
For the holy light
To lift the shadowy mantle from the earth.

1 Bernardo Tasso, *Hinni et ode* (1534), p. 75r.
2 This is almost a translation of Flaminio's lines, see supra.
3 Tasso, *Hinni et ode*, (1534), p. 75r.

The moon is put to flight prettily in another stanza,[1] in another the coursers of the sun are yoked. A sixth stanza praises Tithonus' wife in all her beauty.[2] With the seventh stanza, as in Flaminio's hymn, we move from the description of dawn to her meaning to mortals; she drives away sleep, the companion of death[3]; she lights up the sailor's route[4]; she illuminates the pilgrim's path; and she gives the lover the promise of his lady's face. Soon the poet will look into the fond eyes of his *donna* who alone can compare in her beauty with the dawn. The surprising concluding compliment to the girl is securely within the Horatian tradition as we have seen it, but, although its nature is classical, its content, its spirit is medieval. From the third stanza with its nightingale to the eighth stanza with its pilgrim, in lieu of Flaminio's more classical wayfarer, to the ninth stanza with its idealized *donna*, we have seen Tasso working his compromise between the ancient and modern to produce a new type of poem potentially richer than either of them. Flaminio's conclusion blessing the light because it meant life and praying for length of days was centuries out of date. The humanist poet was nearer to the pagan philosopher than to the modern man. In the pagan tradition, too, was Flaminio's reference to love which was to accomplished adultery, a fact of no particular interest to him—for he was not the lover, nor was this an *alba*—and not the end of his poem.

However, we are still far from the ode here and very near to the *canzone*. If Tasso had not gone any farther than this, "A l'Aurora" would be merely an example of the classical *canzone*, showing how classicism was pervading the traditional Italian forms—one could adduce parallel examples from the sonnets—and giving them, with the new subject matter, a new lease on

[1] Tasso, *Hinni et ode*, pp. 75r–v. The moon goes in Flaminio, too, but with greater despatch.

[2] *Ibid.*, pp. 75v–76r. Flaminio, too, praises Aurora's beauty, but more briefly.

[3] *Ibid.*, p. 76r. This is again borrowed from Flaminio with the ultimate, Vergilian source in mind, cf. *Aeneid* VI, line 278. It is interesting to note that Tasso has omitted Flaminio's scientific appreciation of light as the source of colour.

[4] Tasso, *Hinni et ode*, p. 76r. Tasso has apparently recognized Flaminio's refutation of Ovid, *Amorum* I, 13, here and has expanded it by adding the sailor.

life. But the next ode shows progression, reveals a further step in the transformation of the Petrarchan *canzone* into the Italian ode.

"A Diana"[1] treats a classical theme, independent of any neolatin or ancient model. It is again written in the *canzone* form, but now in the briefest stanza, AbAbbcC, permissible. Petrarchan elements are still present, but the classical myth, barely hinted at before, now appears fully developed. "A Diana" begins its first stanza with a humanist commonplace and closes it with a Petrarchan conceit:

> Por freno Musa a quel si lungo pianto,
> Ch'Amor t'apre dal core;
> Et vestiti di ricco, e lieto manto
> Rendiamo a quella honore
> Che col vago splendore
> Facendo il cielo adorno
> Mostra quand' e piu oscuro un chiaro giorno.

> A rein, Muse, to that long complaint
> That Love opens in your heart,
> And, clad in a rich and joyful mantle,
> Let us honour her
> Who, with her fair radiance
> Adorning the heavens,
> Shows how much darker a bright day is.

Then, as in the preceding hymn, the deity's beauty and utility are described:

> O bella Luna, tu col bianco raggio
> Hor cornuta, hor rotonda . . .
> Questo nostro hemispero, e l'altro allumi;
> Et d'humor dolce, e grato
> L'herbette in ciascun lato
> Humida nutri; e rendi
> Fecondo, ovunque i tuoi bei raggi estendi,

> O beauteous Moon, you with your white beam,
> Now horned, now round . . .
> You light this hemisphere of ours and the other one,
> And, with moisture sweet and pleasant,
> You nourish the damp grasses
> Everywhere, and you bring
> Fertility wherever you shed your fair rays,

[1] *Hinni et ode*, pp. 78r–79v.

then her relationship with man:

Indi contempli de felici amanti
I cari furti, e senti
Lodar le donne lor con dolci canti;
Et le doglie, e i lamenti
Odi de piu dolenti,
Che parlan con gli augelli,
Con le fiere, co fior, co gli arbuscelli.

Thence you look down upon the dear thievery
Of happy lovers, and you hear
Them praise their ladies with sweet songs;
And you hear the griefs and the
Laments of the more sorrowful,
Who hold discourse with the birds,
With the wild beasts, with the flowers, and with the
shrubbery.

There follows the myth of Endimion, a picture of Diana the huntress with suggestions of Catullus 34, "Domina montium ut fores," and then, as in Catullus' poem,[1] a praise of Diana as Lucina, the help of women in childbirth.[2] This leads the poet to an invocation of the women to perform the rites of Diana[3]:

Spargete il ricco tempio o caste Donne
Di croco, e di viole
Il crin sciogliendo su le bianche gonne;
Et con dolci parole
La sorella del sole
Richiamate tre volte
Si, che dal cielo con pieta v'ascolte.

[1] Catullus, *Carm.* 34, "Tu Lucina dolentibus."

[2] *Hinni et ode*, p. 79r. Flaminio in his "Hymnus in Dianam" describes Diana as a huntress and also as the goddess of childbirth. However, I think these parallels are due to the intrinsic nature of the subject and also to the Catullan (34) and Horatian treatments of the subject rather than to any direct influence of Flaminio on Tasso.

[3] The idea of the religious rites may have been suggested by Flaminio's line "votaque virginum / Audi rite precantium," *Flaminiorum Carmina* (Patavii, 1743), p. 11. See supra.

Accendete cantando il puro foco
Sovra i sacrati altari;
Et spiri arabo odore in ogni loco;
Da i vestri dolci, e chiari
Accenti, ogniuno impari
Lodar la bella diva,
Et empia del suo nome Echo ogni riva.

Strew the rich temple, chaste damsels,
With the crocus and with violets,
With your hair unknotted upon your white gowns,
And with sweet words
Thrice summon
The sister of the sun
Mercifully to hear you from heaven.

Singing, light the pure fire
Upon the sacred altars.
And let the perfume of Arabia breathe everywhere.
From your sweet and ringing
Accents let everyone learn
To praise the beauteous goddess,
And let Echo fill every shore with her name.

Tasso's hymns to classical deities—there are a half dozen more—are much more romantic than Pontano's and much less philosophical than Marullo's, and yet he writes somewhat in the tradition of both of these and also of Crinito, and even of Landino. Nevertheless, in his imaginative recreation of ancient religious rites and in his fondness for fuming altars and garlanded devotees,[1] he reminds one rather of Keats.[2]

Tasso is not a poet of the first rank, of course, but nevertheless we can see from his earliest verse that he will be significant; for he has music in his soul, and can write up to the average standard of the Petrarchans in Italian, while still transforming the lyric less radically, but more surely, than Trissino, Ala-

[1] Besides "A Diana" see "A Pan," *Hinni et ode*, pp. 81v–82v; "Alma luce del Cielo," *Ibid.*, pp. 80v–81v; "O Gran Signor di Delo," *Rime II* (Bergamo, 1749), pp. 272–7; "Fumino i sacri altari," *Hinni et ode*, pp. 89v–90v; "Gli altar di gigli d'oro," *Ibid.*, pp. 85v–87r; "Dianzi il verno nevoso," Williamson, pp. 39–40; "Sovra la verde sponde," *Rime II*, pp. 267–72; *Ibid.*, pp. 224–7, etc.

[2] Cf. Keats, *Endymion*, *Hyperion*, and *Psyche*.

manni, or Minturno. Whereas his three predecessors attempted a slavish and mechanical imitation of Pindar Tasso followed more in the great neolatin tradition taking inspiration from the classics to create a new sort of poetry that would both anticipate and fulfil the demands of his age. It is notable that Tasso, along with all the other poets who have been successful in the ode, never imitated Pindar directly but always through Horace and his humanist successors, in the largest sense. Despite the fact that determined attempts have been made several times in several countries by poets of considerable worth to revive the Pindaric, Pindar has always proved too much rooted in an alien soil to survive the transplantation. The closer the imitation of the Pindaric, the more disastrous has been the failure of the ode. And yet somehow or other the Pindaric flight exercised a fatal fascination over European poets for some two hundred years and the literary panorama of the times is punctuated by the heels of so many disappearing Icari.

To return to the poetry of Bernardo Tasso: the only other early poem written in the *canzone* form, and, with a single exception,[1] the only other one that Tasso wrote, is "A Pan"[2] first published in the second book of *Amori* in 1534. Although written in the traditional Italian verse form—the stanza is aabAaccdD —"A Pan" is, in structure and content, more classical than the other two hymns. The poem has two addressees, first Pan, and later Syrinx. The poet announces that he will celebrate the rustic god, and, in the olive grove the winds listen and the birds cease their song. Then the poet tells two myths of Pan and hints that even Diana may have loved him in the moonlit groves. Now the bacchantes follow Pan. The poet would crown him. Again, as in the preceding hymn, the ancient deity is brought nearer to us through the imaginative recreation of his worship and the suggested participation in it. Here the poet is the intermediary, before it was the woman. The theme is a favourite humanist one but the technique of immediacy is Tasso's own.

The third of the 1531 odes, "Per li tre Abbati Cornelli,"[3] is written in a stanza form that is new, that can by no means be considered to be a part of a *canzone*, abacC, bdbeE, dfdgG, etc.

[1] Ode 23, *Rime II*, pp. 243–6.

[2] Tasso, *Hinni et ode*, pp. 81v–82v.

[3] *Ibid.*, pp. 76v–78r.

The poem is otherwise undistinguished except by the independent fantasy of the opening stanzas which suggest both the prettiness of Petrarch and the pagan visions of Collins, Keats, and Shelley:

> Cada dal puro Cielo
> Vaga pioggia di fiori
> Sovra 'l candido velo
> De la dotta Thalia
> Mentre cantando fa dolce armonia.
>
> I suoi soavi errori
> Fermino l'aure, e intente
> Odano i sacri honori
> De i tre Corneli, e i nomi,
> Che dal tempo non sien vinti, ne domi.
>
> May a lovely rain of flowers
> Fall from the pure sky
> Upon the shining veil
> Of the learned Thalia
> While she makes sweet melody, singing.
>
> May her sugared variations
> Halt the breezes, and, fixed,
> Let them hear the sacred honours
> Of the three Corneli, and the names
> That time may not overcome nor quell.

Three of Tasso's hymns to the Dawn, the Moon, and Pan, have already been discussed. A few others deserve mention. To Apollo, "Alma luce del Cielo,"[1] published in the 1534 volume, is a hymn and prayer. In a five line stanza, abAbB, the poet praises the sun and pictures the garlanded maidens and ploughmen with golden grain in their hair singing songs of thanksgiving to the sun for the harvest. But not at Salerno. Here the nymphs with dishevelled hair call on Apollo in voices low and grieving. Restore Salerno to her former happiness that you may see one thousand altars along the parapets of the sluggish Hiante and many bright fires burning arab leaves and hear "Phebo, Phebo" ringing over the waves. Again, by the vivid reconstitution of ancient rites, by the lively action scene in which we are made

[1] *Ibid.*, pp. 80v–81v.

to participate, the pagan deity is made a reality. This is a vital, meaningful classicism, the creation of a new imaginative world with a symbolic meaning for the present. Although it is written on the same sort of subject as Ronsard's "A Dieu pour la famine" (*Bocage*, 1550) or Torquato Tasso's "Ad Nubes" it has no suggestion of Christianity about it; it is more like one of Marullus' great pagan hymns in which the meaning of the gods for modern times is set forth.

Three later odes are prayers to Fortune for enslaved Italy, too long the scene of bloodshed, for his sick wife and daughter from whom he is forcibly separated, and for his motherless children in the time of his exile and ruin. In the first of these he prays Fortune to turn her wheel and then imagines the rejoicing chorus of her votaries:

> E tutti i colli sette
> Soneran del tuo nome,
> Ma in ogni parte con le sparse chiome
> Le vaghe fanciulette
> Inghirlandate in lunga schiera strette
>
> Le tue lodi o fortuna
> Con si soave accenti,
> Ch' acqueteranno il mar irato e i venti,
> Diranno ad una ad una
> Danzando al raggio della chiara luna.[1]

> And all the seven hills
> Will ring with your name,
> But everywhere, with scattered locks,
> The lovely little maids,
> Garlanded, and pressed close together in
> a long band,
>
> Will, one by one, tell
> Your praises, O Fortuna,
> With such sweet accents,
> Dancing by the bright moon's ray,
> That the angry sea and the winds will be
> charmed into silence.

1 Quoted in Williamson, pp. 39–40.

Here we notice the run-on stanza which Tasso tells us he adopted from the ancients. The other two prayers to Fortune are less classicizing and more emotional. They are interesting in showing how an Italian humanist could not only recreate their worship but also invest his resuscitated divinities with real religious feelings:

O Dea, senza la quale
Non e lieto, o contento
In questa vita umana uomo mortale:
Da cui ogni tormento
Fugge, qual nebbia da rabbioso vento . . .

O madre d'ogni bene,
Di tutto quel diletto,
Ch' allegri in questa vita ci mantiene:
Io pien di casto affetto
Chiamo il tuo aiuto, . . .

Non consentir, che morte
Spietata mieta e svella
Le mie speranze . . .[1]

O Goddess, without whom
Mortal man is not happy
Nor content in this human life,
From whom every torment
Flees, like cloud before the raving wind . . .

O mother of every good,
Of all that joy
That keeps us happy in this life,
I call upon your aid,
Overflowing with pure affection, . . .

Do not consent that ruthless
Death reap and uproot
My hopes, . . .

Very closely related to the hymns are the songs in praise of the living heroes, the great men and women of the day. "Enrico II

[1] Quoted in Williamson, pp. 53–4.

Re di Francia"[1] begins with a description of the chorus of pure youths and maidens who deck the altars of God with many-coloured flowers and who, like angels with their blond hair, glad eyes, and sweet voices, praise God for his government of the world and for the return of Henry in victory. Now the rivers of France can flow happy. Now the herds are safe and the shepherdess can sing her song of joy for the light with which she will see her shepherd safe. Thanks be to Henry. Long may he reign! The pastoral conclusion reminds us that Tasso comes from Sorrento and the kingdom of Naples, the birthplace of Arcadia.

Again close to the hymn is another political ode, "nel parto della Regina di Francia,"[2] on the parturition of Catherine de Medici. The freshness of this ode contrasts sharply with the frigidity of the countless seventeenth- and eighteenth-century essays at treating the same subject. It opens with the favourite picture of devotees and exotic rites but, perhaps because the setting is the Ile de la Cité with its flower-carpeted lawns, because the devotees are all high-born maidens, and because the flower is the rose, the effect is one of romantic medievalism rather than classicism:

Sovra la verde sponde
Di mille vari fior lieta ed adorna
Che con le torte corna
Sena tacita inonda,
Cento e piu Verginelle
Tutte di sangue illustre e tutte belle

Ornavan sacri altari
Di rose fresche tolte all' ora all' ora
Dal grembo dell' Aurora
E sovra i fochi chiari,
Accesi intorno intorno
Si spessi, che facean oltraggio al giorno

Versavan maschi incensi,
E quanti odor soavi anno i Sabei,
E gli Arabi, e i Panchei;

[1] Tasso, *Rime II*, pp. 191–3. Cf. "O Gran Signor di Delo," *ibid.*, pp. 272–7.
[2] *Ibid.*, pp. 267–72.

Tal che nembi condensi
Spargeano l'aria pura
D'ogni soave odor della natura.

On the green bank,
With a thousand different flowers gaily
 adorned,
Which, with its twisted horns,
The silent Seine waters,
A hundred and more little maidens,
All of noble blood and all fair,

Decorated the sacred altars
With fresh roses culled the very hour
In the bosom of Aurora,
And over the bright fires,
Lit on all sides, on all sides,
So close together that they outrage the day,

They poured noble frankincense,
And all the sweet perfumes of Sabea,
And of Arabia, and of Panchea,
So that thick clouds
Scatter upon the pure air
Every sweet odour of nature.

There follows a prayer to God, who is praised in the enumeration of his powers, to help the queen in childbirth:

O Sole,
Eterno Sole, che dai splendor e luce
Al Sol, che qui riluce,
Che la terrena mole
Sol col ciglio governi;
E fatt' hai de' Pianeti i moti eterni;

Ch' hai posta legge al mare;
I termini alla terra; il freno a i venti;
Che tempri gli Elementi;
Per cui si vago appare
Il Ciel di stelle cinto,
E 'l die di piu color vago e depinto.[1]

[1] Notice the influence of Renaissance neoPlatonism and the popular theory of correspondences in the sun images. See Marsilio Ficino's *Commentary on the Timaeus* and E. M. W. Tillyard's *The Elizabethan World Picture* (London, 1943).

O Sun
Eternal sun, you who give splendour and light
To the sun which shines here,
You who rule the terrestrial
Mass with no more than a glance,
And have made the eternal motions of the planets,

You who have laid down laws for the sea,
Boundaries for the earth, reins for the winds,
You who temper the elements,
By whom the heavens girt
With stars appear so enchanting,
And the day, more colourful, beautifully painted.

Then comes praise of the queen and a prayer for the royal infant.

A third group of odes might be termed personal; they are usually addressed to a friend and discuss the poet's affairs: since the year is already despoiled of flowers and the meadows of green grass, the poet on his birthday begs Apollo to lend him his laurel to decorate his altar; the servants will burn incense and he will sing of the learned Thalia and dedicate the day to Bacchus.[1] The poet pictures a Botticelli-like sequestered glade where the Muses, Loves, and Graces dance and sing. Here he could celebrate Amadis and Oreana, but, in the turmoil of political life, his prince must be content if he does his duty and makes him famous.[2] The poet on a shady bank on a summer's day considers various subjects of poetry, the twisted path of the sun, the cold moon wandering in the dark night, a lonely anchorite, Orion with his sword stirring up the mad sea, Aquilo shaking every mountain, every rock, with his swollen cheek. . . . He will write of none of these things but of great Henry's victories and of his queen Catherine.[3] From the land of the north wind and cloudy skies, from a miserable life among strangers [presumably from Paris], Tasso writes to his friend Lelio Capilupo of his longing for imperial Italy, land of glorious deeds and of all earthly goods.[4] He has sailed enough the stormy seas of wars and troubles; he needs rest, a pine that

[1] Tasso, *Rime II*, pp. 224–7.
[2] *Ibid.*, pp. 227–9.
[3] *Ibid.*, pp. 307–9.
[4] *Ibid.*, pp. 233–8.

gives shelter from the rain or a nightingale-haunted shade where he can hear the birds calling in April. He would walk at dawn on the hills gathering flowers for his lady; he would hear the sea chattering with the summer breezes and see the sea-gods gently playing in the crystal depths. But he needs Capeccie's help to bring his ship to shore. He will raise a votive tablet.[1] A later ode tells of his joy at returning to Italy,[2] a later one still complains of the slings and arrows of outrageous fortune.[3] Finally, from exile, he writes his wife a letter of despair; for "Il povero villan, ch' ha sparso il seme"[4] is a little nearer to one of Ovid's *Tristia ex Ponto* than to a Horatian ode. It is the cry of grief of a man who has borne up under many misfortunes sustained by the vision of his family and home, but whose frustration bursts forth when he finds even this consolation denied him: The peasant who sees his carefully tended harvest burnt by the enemy still has his wife and family to comfort him but the poet who saw his richly laden barque almost safe in port after long, stormy years of service at sea has been surprised by a sudden tempest which has foundered the ship and swept him away from his longed for refuge. The poet wonders who will close his eyes and give him the final kiss. Tasso was very fond of Horace's comparison of life to a ship at sea, a comparison also favoured by Ovid and Petrarch, and he used it over and over again, particularly when discussing his own life.[5]

The ship image recurs frequently in the closely related group of odes to his friends. Tasso advises Vincenzo Laureo to avoid Fortune's stormy seas that have been his [Tasso's] ruin and to seek the consolation of philosophy. Blessed are those who can spend their days in study.[6] Again, on Laureo's departure for France, Tasso laments the loss of his pilot.[7] He also likens Vittoria Colonna's spiritual calm in the midst of disaster to a rich merchant ship riding safely in harbour while the storm rages in the open sea,[8] and he seeks to cheer his own wife by reminding her, in perfect Horatian style, that the ocean is not always tempestuous nor Mars always bloody.[9]

1 *Ibid.*, pp. 230–3.
2 *Ibid.*, pp. 243–6.
3 *Ibid.*, pp. 299–301.
4 Quoted by Williamson, pp. 50–1.
5 See, e.g., "a Giov. Bat. Giraldi," *Rime II*, pp. 314–15.
6 Tasso, *Rime II*, pp. 312–13.
7 *Ibid.*, pp. 330–2.
8 *Ibid.*, pp. 247–50.
9 *Ibid.*, pp. 253–5.

Tasso's odes to his friends, apart from their inveterate tendency towards looseness and dilation, are surprisingly Horatian in structure and content, right from their first appearance in 1534. Perhaps this is because the reflective, moral ode to a friend is Horace's most typical and most imitable ode. It should be added, however, that these odes of Tasso's are, just because of the closeness of the imitation, also his least interesting. In the hymns, the political, and even personal odes, the classical authors gave him new ideas on how to handle themes that already were important to him. Here the classics have not only taught him how to write; they have also supplied him with his subjects and their development. Thus, in his odes to his friends, Tasso has produced a series of competent "neo-classical" odes that are indistinguishable from countless others written—not, it is true, in the vernacular—by scores of Italian humanists for the past sixty years. Thus, Tasso, advising Vittoria Colonna to compose the grief she has been nurturing for seven years and write, in her pure and perfect style, the history of her husband's exploits, merely adapts Horace II, 9:

> Non sempre il cielo irato
> Nasconde il bel sereno,
> Ne 'l mar d'Adria turbato
> Ogn' hora alzando l'onde. . . .
>
> Non sempre Appennin pieno
> Di fredde nevi, e bianche
> Mostra l'horrido seno;
> Ma talhor dilettoso
> Vagheggia il sol col crin verde
> e frondoso.[1]

> The angry heaven does not always
> Hide the fair blue sky,
> Nor does the Adriatic sea, in turbulence,
> Every hour raise its waves. . . .
>
> Not always does the Apennine, loaded
> With cold white snow,
> Reveal its awful bosom,
> But sometimes it courts
> The sun, delightful with its green and
> branchy locks.

[1] *Hinni et ode*, p. 79v.

Sometimes the winds make peace with the tired waves, sometimes the skies are cloudless. But you weep in the seventh year as in the first. The suns come and go, but your words are always sad:

Ma torni, o parte il Sole
Sente le meste vostre alte parole.

But the sun, rising or setting,
Ever hears your high, sad words.

Phaeton's sisters do not always lament him, neither does Thetis always weep over her son with the nymphs, the daughters of Ocean. Therefore, seal up the fountain of your tears, etc. Robert Herrick, perhaps following Bernardo Tasso, was to adapt this same ode later on to comfort an English lady on the death of her husband.[1]

Of the same Horatian stock are the other odes to friends, offering consolation on bereavement, praising a benefactor, cheering the ailing, celebrating a birthday, or urging a fellow poet to write.[2] Some, however, stand out from the crowd because of an unusual image or a delightful piece of description. "Why," he asks a friend, "do you grieve continuously over your brother's death although he was plucked in his spring, a beautiful flower. Cruel river gods,

Lo tiraste nel fondo
Del vostro gorgo allor alto e profondo
Per baciarli i coralli
E le brine del viso
Ne' liquidi cristalli
Contra 'l vostro voler l'avete ucciso.[3]

You drew him into the depths
Of your whirlpool, then deep and profound,
To kiss the coral of his lips
And the frost of his countenance.
In your crystalline waters,
Unwilling, you killed him.

[1] *The Poems of Robert Herrick*, ed. F. W. Moorman (Oxford Standard Authors, Oxford, 1947), p. 105.

[2] Tasso, *Rime II*, pp. 250–2, 325–7, 279–82, 277–9, 310–11, 219–21, 289–291.

[3] *Ibid.*, p. 250.

The baroque conceit is very effective. It reminds one of Sannazaro in his piscatory eclogues. Two of the other odes contain charming descriptions of the dawn ("nel Natale di Antiziana")[1] and of the spring ("a Lelio Capilupo").[2]

Tasso had a feeling for nature and a fondness for its description that reminds one of his greater contemporary Ronsard, although there is no possibility of influence; for nature was a part of Tasso's poetry long before his visit to France in 1552–3, when Ronsard's epoch making volume of odes had just appeared. Tasso's descriptions of nature, almost always idyllic, appear above all in his amorous, pastoral, or eclogue odes, in "Ombre fresche e secrete," e.g., which, with its bushes, birds, and stream, and lady whose name is carved on all the trees, recalls the forest scenes of *As You Like It*[3]; in "Crescete o vaghi fiori,"[4] which describes and blesses the flowers on which Antiniana walks; and in "O Pastori felici,"[5] which praises the shepherd's life through the different seasons of the year and contrasts it with the courtier's uneasy joys, all familiar types of poems. A more independent ode is "ad Austro,"[6] which upbraids the east wind for bringing back bad weather when already the winter was past and lovely spring was at hand:

> Perche con tanto orgoglio
> O nimico di giorni allegri e chiari
> Turbando l'aere e i mari
> Fai ch' ogni duro scoglio
> Piangia con alta voce il suo cordoglio?
>
> Gia il verno orrido e duro
> Co' tardo passo e giunto al suo confine;
> E le nevi, le brine,
> E i ghiacci al lento e puro
> Fiumicel freno raccogliendo, al scuro
> Suo antro fa ritorno.[7]

[1] *Ibid.*, pp. 219–21. [2] *Ibid.*, pp. 289–91.

[3] The Franco-Latin poet, Salmon Macrin, also carved his lady's name on trees, anticipating Tasso, see Macrin, *Carminum Libellus* (Paris, 1528), sig. a ii r–v. This carving of names on trees is a genuine pastoral as well as literary tradition. For the literary side, see Propertius, I, 18; Vergil, *Ecl.*, 10, 53–4; Ovid, *Heroid.*, IV, 12–30 and 139.

[4] Tasso, *Rime* (Bergamo, 1749), pp. 221–4.

[5] Tasso, *Hinni et ode* (Vinegia, 1534), pp. 87r–89r.

[6] Tasso, *Rime* (Bergamo, 1749), pp. 297–9. [7] *Ibid.*, p. 297.

Why so pridefully,
Enemy of cheerful, bright days,
Do you stir up the air and the sea,
And make every hard reef
With a deep voice lament its heart-ache?

Already winter, horrid and harsh,
With a slow step has reached its bourne,
And, gathering up the snows,
And the frosts, and the ice, the brake
On the brook which is slow and clear, it returns
To its gloomy cavern.

However, in "Mentre co caldi raggi"[1] Tasso reveals himself a true Neapolitan, if only by adoption. Like Pontano and Sannazaro, Tasso writes a piscatory eclogue: Battus complains about Galatea. "Cruel one, come from the sea to the verdant meadow. Are not these green and leafy tracts that spring has clothed with beautiful flowers more lovely than the deep and foamy waters that are usually angry and stormy? The wet, ugly seaweed is not worthy of the sojourn of your beauty, gentle nymph." There follows a picture of *primavera*, the flower carpet, white and yellow, the burgeoning shrubs, the woods, and hills, and cool, shady valleys.

Tasso, like the humanists before him, added David to Pindar, Anacreon, and Horace as exemplar for the ode. Unlike his predecessors,[2] however, he fused the inspiration from David with the Catholic, medieval tradition of penitence,[3] as well as with the classical ode style that he had already assimilated, thus going a step farther than Flaminio, who had introduced classicism into his translation of the psalms but who kept his devotional poems free of any suggestion of paganism. The result is a new poem that hints at the baroque religious poetry that is to come; religious emotion is expressed in shocking imagery, though not as shocking as in the baroque, and the allusions are classical rather than Christian. The Petrarchan

[1] *Hinni et ode*, pp. 83r–84r.

[2] Williamson, p. 66, lists some neolatin and Italian poets who had paraphrased or imitated the psalms. See also Cuccoli, *Flaminio*, p. 174.

[3] Williamson, p. 85.

sonnet sequence as well as church Lenten traditions, with perhaps a hint from Flaminio's recently published sacred songs, led Tasso to write a series of psalms, thirty in all, describing the changing relations of his soul with God. The whole calls to mind, though much inferior in power, Herbert's *The Temple* or Donne's *Holy Sonnets* on the one hand; on the other, in so far as it consists of a series of lyric variations on the theme of grief and final composition of it, it is like Tennyson's *In Memoriam.*

Tasso wrote his thirty *salmi* during Lent in 1557. These poems, personal lyrics in the intensity of their private emotion, as works of penitence must be, but odes in the objectification of that emotion and in the tough, rigid fabric of classical construction, express the poet's grief over sin, his longing for spiritual comfort, and the final gift of grace. In their conscious emphasis on doctrinal orthodoxy they reveal the influence of the Council of Trent. These late fruits of Tasso's genius not only savour of a changed moral and spiritual clime; they also, in their combination of a mystic tendency to express religious emotion in terms of physical pleasure—a characteristic, incidently, of much medieval Latin religious poetry[1]—with a profusion of extraordinary and extravagant conceits borrowed from a great variety of incongruous human experience, offer a foretaste of poetry fifty years hence. Classical influence is seen in the structure, which follows that of the other odes—in so far as generalizations can be made. There tends to be a statement of the subject, an elaboration of the theme with wide-ranging comparisons which form the body of the poem, and a return to the theme in the conclusion. This structural pattern is not characteristic of Horace whose odes have a linear rather than circular scheme of development—though there are many exceptions—but it is classical,[2] it is in accordance with the Aristotelian precepts that were having at that time such a powerful influence on remolding the Italian sonnet in the

[1] See, e.g., Remy de Gourmont, *Le Latin Mystique* (Paris, 1892).

[2] Pindar tends to return to his immediate subject in his last triad, though his and Tasso's odes may be considered to be circular in form only in the sense that a string of equal-sized beads is circular because it has a clasp at either end. They are not circular in any developmental sense like a necklace of graduated pearls.

hands of Angelo di Costanzo (1509–91).[1] Tasso's humanism is also revealed in his natural rather than spiritual comparisons and in his allusions to classical literature.

Now let us look at the psalms. In the first psalm Tasso laments his offences which are greater in number than the birds in the air, than the fish that Neptune hides in the waves; his heart grieves as the sun shines, as the night darkens the earth with her dark shadow. The poet grieves, but he cannot grieve enough for his sins. In the second psalm he recognizes his own depravity. But he will become God's; for God's help rescues him from the serpent, God gives him a shield and arms against the Enemy, though he be held like a lamb by the wolf.[2] Now he will hymn God the creator who made the heavens and the sun and the seasons; his praises will be numbered by the waves every minute and by the flowers that the earth brings forth. The third psalm recognizes his own unworthiness and God's worthiness of love. In the fourth psalm Tasso compares God's grace to a lamp that lights and warms. In the fifth psalm he compares himself to the nightingale:

Come vago augelleto,
Che i suoi dogliosi lai
Fra i rami d'arbuscel tenero e schieto
Chiuso di Febo a i rai
Sfoga piangendo, e non s'arresta mai.

Like the lovely little bird
With its mournful lays which
Among the branches of the bush, young
and straight,
Shut in from Phoebus' rays,
Flees lamenting, and never comes to rest.

So he laments his sins day and night. He asks pardon. He prays God to save his soul; he has not the strength for salvation alone.

[1] G. Toffanin, *Il Cinquevento*, 4th ed. (Milano, 1950), p. 342, says that in the course of the sixteenth century Petrarchism evolved into Aristotelianism. On p. 343 he describes how Angelo di Costanzo found a new form for the sonnet that emphasized beginning, middle, and end, and turned the sonnet into a clever epigram.

[2] Here is an example of Tasso's using Christian rather than classical imagery.

There is his enemy, the serpent, and there are the harpy-cares. Again he prays, psalm six, "Be my consoler, be my doctor, mightier than any ancient physician. Light up my foul heart, which I wash with grief, and drive away the night of sin. As the waves of the sea are my miseries which break with their strength the adamantine ice in my soul." There follow the usual statements about the Enemy, the usual comparisons of his grief to the number of twigs on a bush in spring, to the number of flowers in a grassy meadow; then comes the prayer with the mystic word, "piacer":

Scaccia l'interna sete
Col tuo torrente vivo
Del piacer, che fa liete
L'anime nostre; e non con fonte, o rive.

Quench the inner thirst
With your living flood
Of pleasure which makes our
Spirits joyful—and not with fountains or
rivers.

In the seventh psalm the common Christian metaphor of God as the source of light, which we have noted already in "Sovra la verde sponde" as well as in psalms four and six and which we will meet with later in psalms ten and thirteen, is developed into the image of the gleaming sun, derived presumably from the great chain of being and its table of correspondences, which became so popular in baroque art.[1] Psalm

[1] See A. O. Lovejoy, *The Great Chain of Being* (Cambridge, Mass., 1936) and Tillyard's *Elizabethan World Picture*. Cf. the prayer in "Sovra la verde sponde" quoted above.

Note the spikey gold rays emanating from a baroque cross or such a baroque religious poem as Herbert's "The Star":

Get me a standing there, and place
Among the beams which crown the face
Of him, who died to part
Sin and my heart:
That so among the rest I may
Glitter, and curl, and wind as they
That winding is their fashion
Of adoration.

eight, elaborating another aspect of the same metaphor, describes the fire of God's love. The poet would be "infiammato"; he would have his every desire turned towards God as the shaft of a good archer towards the target:

Fa ch'ogni mio desio
A te si volga, come a segno strale
Di bono arcier.

Make my every desire
Turn to you, as the good archer's
Shaft to the target.

In the ninth psalm as in the eleventh we return to Tasso's trite image of the sea of calamity and his shattered ship. In the former we also find the darts of Fortune and the fountain of living waters, a favourite metaphor of the psalms. In the tenth psalm we meet again not only the sun with his coursers and God's fountain of living waters but also the harpy-sins. The serpent is everywhere, in psalms ten and twenty-four, as well as in psalms two, five, six, seven, and eight previously mentioned.

Psalm twelve analyses the conflict between sense and reason. Psalms fourteen and eighteen ask God's mercy for suffering Italy and Europe respectively. With psalms fifteen and sixteen the emphasis shifts from Tasso's sense of sin to his love for God. He returns to God, he will praise him. Let him stretch out his hand and lift up the fallen heart. Psalm seventeen begins with "As pants the heart," psalm nineteen, perhaps borrowing from Horace I, 23, compares the poet's soul to a nursing doe, nervous of the Enemy. In psalm twenty Tasso returns to God in penitence. Psalms twenty-one, twenty-two, and twenty-three implore the grace that can alone bring salvation. In psalm twenty-five the poet is again overwhelmed by the sense of his sin as he thinks of God's benefactions to man, reason and an immortal soul, the moon, sun, light, rain, flowers, grass, the birds, winds, bushes, perfumes, plants, grains, fruits, flowers, animals, water, gold, pearls, purple—But man, he is a new Titan, an impious son of earth who makes war against heaven! After this final burst of despair Tasso turns again to God in psalm twenty-six. In the silence of the night he sings God's praises and now with a free and open heart he can give thanks for God's bounty.

Tasso is a poet of considerable merit, but he is also severely limited. He appears to much greater advantage in extracts and abstracts than in reality. He has few ideas and images and his vocabulary is small. The borrowed ship image appears over and over again as the core of a large number of the odes and psalms.[1] Similarly the same words are constantly recurring; for Tasso is not very precise. "Vago" can describe anything that is attractive, "reo" anything evil, "hair" is always "chiome," "locks," and the tiresome ship referred to above is alternately "palmata" and "spalmata."

Tasso was classically inspired and, of the ancient poets, he is most like Horace. He writes on similar themes, political events of the day and personal and private conduct, in a somewhat similar fashion, with natural metaphors and classical allusions. However his range is much narrower than Horace's; in particular, he is not concerned with such a wide variety of human conduct and he tends to draw his illustrations from the non-moral world. Moreover Tasso lacks Horace's flair for the *mot juste* and his ability to give the inevitable expression to commonplaces. Tasso creates his effects with a large sweep of lines, he does not polish and perfect details as does Horace and he is not given to epigrammatic philosophizing; he does not condense his whole thought into an unforgettable phrase. Thus Tasso lacks Horace's precision and concentration. On the other hand, in his hymn-odes he generally surpasses Horace in his suggestiveness, in his ability to create another world beyond our everyday reality. He does not merely decorate his poetry with classical baubles but he successfully adapts Greco-Roman mythology to sixteenth-century Italian poetry and, in finding the modern meaning in the ancient myth, he broadens our experience and increases the range of poetry. Moreover, in his introduction into Italian lyric poetry of the classical outlook on life and on personal experience, simultaneously with new,

[1] See, e.g., odes 20, 25, 28, 38, 48, 49, 51, 54, and psalms 9 and 11.

lighter, and freer metric forms[1] in which the thought runs on in brief, swift lines from strophe to strophe without a pause, he has taken a most important step in making the break with outworn Petrarchism and old, inherited clichés. He has shown the possibility of the existence of a new kind of poetry, with new subjects, a new style, and new forms. He has gone considerably farther than Flaminio did in Latin in trying to make a poetic reconciliation between the new humanist culture and the Catholic faith. He is one of the forbears of baroque religious poetry.

Contemporary with Bernardo Tasso was Claudio Tolomei, who tried, with his *Versi e regole de la nuova poesia toscana* (1539), to introduce quantitative verse, primarily the metres of Horace, into Italian. This effort, like similar French and English experiments, was doomed to failure.

In Bartolomeo Del Bene as in Luigi Alamanni we find another link between the Italian and French Renaissance odes. Although he was born in Val d'Elsa on the banks of the Arno, Del Bene was from the beginning headed towards a career in France; for his father had served Louis XII and Francis I. Thus, when he was little more than a boy, Bartolomeo Del Bene went to the French court which he served in various capacities for nearly twenty years. Then, about 1554, he became

[1] Except for the four previously mentioned *canzone* forms, Tasso's lyric stanzas were new if not always original with him. He created in the odes and psalms more than forty different five- or six-line strophes based on six different rime schemes and varying patterns of *settenarî* and *endecasillabi*. The rime schemes were:

(1) ABACC, BDBEE, DFDGG, etc.
(2) ABBAA
(3) ABABB
(4) ABABAA
(5) ABABA
(6) ABBACC.

Tasso's favourite rime schemes, ABBAA and ABABB, were also favourites with Bartolomeo del Bene with whom he disputes the laurels for having been the first to create *Italian* equivalents of the Horatian stanzas. Previous and contemporary poets only knew how to imitate the Latin metres in quantitative Italian verse. See, e.g., Claudio Tolomei, M. Antonio Renieri, Dionigi Atanagi, Annibal Caro, P. P. Gualterio, Alessandro Bovio, Benedetto Varchi, and Leonardo Orlandino Del Greco, in Carducci's anthology, *La Poesia Barbara nei Secoli XV e XVI* (Bologna, 1881).

part of the retinue of Marguerite of France, Duchess of Savoy. Except for occasional embassies for Catherine de Medici he stayed with Marguerite in Torino until her death in 1574. Then he returned to France and entered the employ of Henry III. He died sometime after 1587.

Del Bene left ninety-five odes in manuscript, two of which were inscribed to Ronsard. One of these was published in the 1604 edition of Ronsard's works and this ode with seventeen others was published "ora per la prima volta" in Livorno in 1799.[1] A few other odes were published for the biographical information that they contain by Camille Couderc in "Les Poésies d'un Florentin à la Cour de France au XVIe Siècle," *Giornale della Storia Letteraria Italiana*, XVII (1891).[2] It is these published odes that will be discussed here. Formally, they are all of the same type. They are written in four or five line stanzas based on four simple rime schemes: ABBA, ABBAA, ABAB, and ABABB, which are varied into seventeen different stanza forms by changing patterns of *settenarî* and *endecasillabi*, that is, these odes are written in Italian adaptations of the Horatian lyric strophe, which approach even closer to their models than do Tasso's; for Tasso was never able to create a stanza under five lines. Moreover, like Horace's, each of these odes is addressed to someone and written on some particular occasion, it contains reflections on life and pictorial descriptions. But Del Bene's odes are written in the Italian tradition as well as the classical. While, as in Bernardo Tasso, Horace's well-worn comparison of life to a ship at sea crops up regularly,[3] so do Petrarchan conceits about his lady's eyes[4] and, rather inevitably,[5] all the medieval "Marguerite" symbolism.[6] Del Bene undoubtedly finds it particularly hard, if not undesirable, being an Italian living abroad, to escape from the powerful influence of his day, Italy's great *trecento* tradition newly in

[1] In *Rime di Bartolomeo Del Bene*.

[2] Couderc's article, pp. 2–12, has been the source of the biographical statements made here.

[3] See, e.g., "A Madama," quoted by Couderc, *GSLI*, XVII, 35–6; "A Guiliano Del Bene," *ibid.*, pp. 36–7; "Alla Corte di Francia," *ibid.*, pp. 41–2.

[4] See, e.g., "A Madama," *loc. cit.*

[5] Since he was in the service of Marguerite of France.

[6] See, e.g., "A Giuliano Del Bene," *loc. cit.*; "A Caterina Tornabuoni Del Bene," *Rime di Bartolomeo Del Bene* (Livorno, 1799), pp. 43–5.

vogue. Especially would this be the case since now in France Petrarch was become a classic on a level with the ancients.

Del Bene, though not great, was, as a court poet, far from pedestrian. He could, midst reflections on the vanity of human grandeur, write lively descriptions of the wedding festivities of Francesco de Medici and Giovanna d'Austria,[1] he knew how to put a rousing speech into the mouth of the Venetian admiral at Lepanto,[2] and his compliments to princes were often pretty and always appropriate[3]—although he was strikingly forthright in addressing the Duke of Savoy on the Renaissance poet's favourite theme, the immortality that poetry alone confers.[4] In his treatment of another favourite Renaissance theme, the old man in love who, with his dyed beard and hair, his bright coloured clothes, and his myrtle wreath, cuts a comic figure[5] Del Bene was light and amusing with none of the scurrility of the humanists nor any of the cruelty that Shakespeare shows towards Malvolio. At the same time he was able to describe with tenderness and sensitivity the "castello et borgo d'Esperne,"[6] the village in Champagne where he spent happy years of his youth writing poetry:

> Antico borgo amato
> Che Marna bagna et cinge, hor pian, hor colle,
> Fecundo d'un liquor soave et molle,
> Da Cerere et Sylvan, da Flora ornato. . . .

> Beloved ancient village
> Which the Marne washes and embraces, now plain, now
> hill,
> Rich in a liquor sweet and soft,
> By Ceres and Sylvanus, by Flora adorned. . . .

Del Bene's poems to Ronsard,[7] on the other hand, are disappointingly empty, especially when one considers that he

[1] "A Giulio di Francesco Delbene . . . , *GSLI*, XVII, 33–4.

[2] "A Nettuno," *Rime*, pp. 55–8.

[3] See, e.g., "A Carlo Emmanuel Principe di Piedmonte Pel Giorno Della Sua Nascita," *ibid.*, pp. 47–50; "Enrico III. Re di Francia E Di Polonia. Per la sua subita partenza di Pollonia," *ibid.*, pp. 63–6.

[4] *Ibid.*, pp. 51–3. [5] *Ibid.*, pp. 71–4. [6] *GSLI*, XVII, 38–9.

[7] *In Rime*, pp. 116–19, and in Blanchemain's edition of Ronsard's works, II (Paris, 1857), 380.

was trying to do in Italian literature what his contemporary Ronsard was doing so successfully at the same time in French—and Ronsard recognized the kindred spirit and wrote in appreciation of Del Bene

> qui non seulement a surpassé en sa langue Italienne les plus estimez de ce temps, mais encores a faict la victoire douteuse entre luy e ceux qui escrivent auiourdhuy le plus purement et doctement an vieil langage Romain.[1]

However, although he attempted in his own slighter way a reformation of the Italian lyric on the lines of Ronsard's contemporary innovations in French and although, in imitation of Horace, he introduced the lyric quatrain into Italian poetry, the inferiority of his genius, the lack of a real vocation as a poet, his long separation from his own people, and the fact that he did not publish his works kept Del Bene from exerting any influence on his native literature. Thus, although Del Bene was admired by Ronsard[2] he was probably unknown to Bernardo Tasso and his works were not widely circulated or read in Italy.[3]

The new poetry of Trissino, Alamanni, Minturno, and Tasso had little effect on the Petrarchan and Provençal booms in Italy. Mid-century anthologies and volumes of poetry, even by avowed admirers of Bernardo Tasso, contain nothing new. Saccharine *sonetti* and musical *canzoni* expressing the tender sentiments that every Italian loves continued to be the standard production of the Italian poet until almost the beginning of the seventeenth century. Then, however, the triumph of the Pléiade coupled with France's political supremacy began having its effect. Italy's first great classical lyric poet turned to Ronsard and Belleau for the inspiration that was at last to liberate the Italian lyric from its subservience to Petrarch.

Gabriello Chiabrera was born in Savona in 1552. He died in 1638. He left Savona for Rome when he was nine years old. He was educated at the Collegio dei Padri Gesuiti and was a

[1] *Abbrégé De L'Art Poëtique François* (Paris, 1565), p. 3v. The *Abbrégé* is dedicated to Del Bene's son, the Abbé Alphonse Del Bene.

[2] P. de Nolhac, *Ronsard et ses Contemporains Italiens* (Paris, n.d. [1921]), p. 6, quotes Ronsard's poetic tribute, "Del-Bene, second Cygne apres le Florentin," in which he calls Del Bene a new Horace and a new Pindar.

[3] Carducci, "Ode," p. 379.

student of Muret, the author of a commentary on Ronsard's *Amours à Cassandre.*[1] He entered the service of a cardinal but an ill-advised duel forced him to leave Rome abruptly. He returned to Savona and studied the poets. It was then, as he himself says,[2] that he decided to imitate Pindar and the classics and wrote his first experimental poems in the manner of Anacreon, Sappho, Pindar, and Simonides.[3] Although his life was jarred by another duel, his course now was set, and, under the guidance of Tasso and the Pléiade, he became the acknowledged laureate of latter-day heroes (who were only too glad to buy the immortality of his praise) and the focal point of a new classicism in the vulgar tongue. Modern criticism of Chiabrera, as of his master, Ronsard, prefers his *canzonette*, his *odicine*, his "lesser odes"[4] inspired by Anacreontic and Horatian traditions to his typically baroque, epideiktic Pindarics, formal, external, grandiose, and frigid, with all the trappings of inspiration or "enthusiasm" that a calculating wit could devise, with all the lofty locutions, all the flowers of rhetoric that should characterize an elevated style, and with a richness of mythological illustration that on first sight might appear to rival Pindar's—until the irrelevance and vanity of the mythological decoration is perceived.

Chiabrera's lyrics are divided into *canzoni eroiche*, *lugubri*, *morali*, and *sacre* and *canzonette amorose* and *morale*. Roughly, the *canzoni* are the Pindarics and more solemn Horatians; the *canzonette* are the Anacreontics and social Horatians. It will be noted that Chiabrera like Mutio before him[5] prefers the familiar Italian to the more pompous foreign term, which he realizes denotes basically the same thing, and thus avoids rousing any possible animosity of the sort provoked by du

1 Nolhac, *op. cit.*, p. 5, thinks that this was the source of Chiabrera's interest in the Pléiade.

2 *Rime de Gabriello Chiabrera* I (Milano, 1807), pp. xix–xxxiii, "Vita di Gabriello Chiabrera Savonese da lui medesimo scritta." This autobiography, A. Belloni's section on Chiabrera in *Il Seicento* (Milano, 1943), and Carducci's remarks in "Ode" are the sources for my statements about Chiabrera's life.

3 Chiabrera, *Rime* (1807), p. xxii.

4 The term is borrowed from John Dennis, *The Grounds of Criticism in Poetry* (1704), quoted in *Critical Essays of the Eighteenth Century 1700–25*, ed. Wm. Higley Durham (New Haven, London, Oxford, 1915), p. 150.

5 Girolamo Mutio, *Rime e Diverse* (In Vinegia, 1551), p. 3.

Bellay's and Ronsard's insistence on the exotic word. However, while Mutio merely equated, with his terminology, the traditional Italian poetry with the classical, Chiabrera used the old words to denote something new, Italian poetry that disowned the native Petrarchan tradition both as to form and content and strove to revive the antique. In this his only predecessors were Trissino with his triadic *canzoni*, Alamanni (better known in France than in Italy) with his triadic hymns, Pindaric in development, Minturno with his two Pindaric odes to Charles V, a scattered group of humanists who did exercises in the translation or adaptation of Horace in Italian, reproducing, in varying degrees, both his form and content, and Bernardo Tasso and Bartolomeo Del Bene who created new poetic forms consistent with the Italian tradition with which to express their new interpretation of life based on the classics. Other predecessors in a collateral line had, since the beginning of the century, classicized the content without altering the form of the Petrarchan sonnet or *canzone*, thus breeding hybrids. Chiabrera's contribution to all this lay in the fixing of the vernacular classical tendencies by the final establishment of metrical modes of expression, more revolutionary than anything that Tasso or Del Bene had attempted, that offered real alternatives to the time-hallowed Petrarchan forms and that were intimately associated with a completely different set of ideas.

Thus, Chiabrera's *canzoni* abnegate the Petrarchan *canzone* structure for an adaptation, suited to the genius of the Italian language, of the Pindaric strophe as it was then understood.[1] He abandons the divided stanza[2] with its familiar patterns of *settenarî* and *endecasillabi*, whose monotony after nearly three centuries exasperates him,[3] for lighter, freer strophes of lines of varying lengths hastened in their flow by the occasional

[1] The Renaissance editors of Pindar, following the Byzantine, divided Pindar's poems up into long thin strophes composed of verses of varying length. Sometimes words were broken at the ends of lines or even at the ends of strophes. See chapt. 2, pp. 11–13 and chap. 5, p. 205, fn. 1.

[2] Belloni, *Seicento*, pp. 116–17. Later Chiabrera revived it in his triadic poems (Carducci, "Ode," pp. 389–90) but he had already taught the Italians a large number of alternatives.

[3] Carducci, "Ode," pp. 394–5.

omission of rime and by broken words that rush the reader on from line to line and from stanza to stanza. In this he was following the examples of Bernardo Tasso and Del Bene (he was probably not, however, familiar with the latter) on the one hand and of the French and Spanish poets on the other; for, although Tasso and Del Bene used shorter, svelter stanzas than the Petrarchans, they still did not question the sway of the seven and eleven syllable lines, but the poets of the other two romance languages, unhampered by such powerful national traditions, had experimented with metrical variety and had excited Chiabrera with the new possibilities of poetic expression that this revealed.[1] Moreover, Chiabrera thought of lyric poetry as written to be sung and the richness of the new music inspired him to seek similar effects in words by introducing a wide variation in the number of syllables per line.[2] Jacopo Peri who set many of Chiabrera's lyrics to music praised them especially for their diversity.[3]

Late in life, when he was already seventy years old, Chiabrera yielded to the persuasions of his old friend, Cardinal Barberini,[4] soon to become Urban VIII, and took the more revolutionary step, though it was a revolution to the right, both because it limited the poet's freedom by the necessity of complying with the formal procedure of the ancients and because, as Carducci has pointed out,[5] it was an unwitting return to the rigid structural pattern of the medieval *canzone a ballo* and hence of the divided stanza, of writing in triads, as Trissino, Alamanni, Minturno, and Ronsard had done in the vernacular before him. The triadic odes form a small proportion of Chiabrera's

[1] *Ibid.*, pp. 393–5.

[2] See Carducci, *ibid.*, p. 395: "the musicians, to the great delight of others and with little trouble to themselves, vary the notes to the verses, which are not always the same."

[3] Carducci, *ibid.*, p. 396.

[4] *Ibid.*, p. 399. Maffeo Barberini (1568–1644) wrote a certain amount of religious poetry in Latin and Italian. His three triadic Pindarics to the Virgin Mary, David, and the Contessa Matilda reveal Chiabrera's stylistic influence. His other odes derive from Chiabrera and from Ciampoli's Horatian inspired moral poems (Belloni, *Seicento*, p. 149).

[5] Carducci, *ibid.*, p. 401: "In the song for dancing with its two changes and its recapitulation, and thence in the divided stanza, the threefold strophic structure is the musical harmony of the Tuscan song."

lyric output.[1] They are more unsuccessful than the other odes because their peculiar structure is meaningless.

The heroic *canzoni*, what Chiabrera considered his most important contribution—for was he not the first to bestow upon the Italian nobility the immortal glory that they merited so much more than the Greek "jockeys"[2] whom Pindar had praised?[3]—were always dedicated to aristocrats and celebrated important events in their lives, either public, e.g., a naval victory with the consequent liberation of the Christian slaves and the enslavement of the Turks or the ascension of the first balloons, or personal, e.g., the horse ballet at the wedding of the Grand Duke Cosmo, a masked ball, the birth of an heir, or a noble illness. The *canzoni* open with addresses to the lyre, Muse, Apollo, etc., and references to appropriate mountains, vales, or springs. They praise their heroes, who lose all their personality and individuality in baroque hyperbole and become so many Achilles' and Hercules', and they recount a myth, sometimes tenuously related to the subject of the poem through supposed analogy or an imagined ancestry. There is, as in Bernardo Tasso's odes, a monotony of thought, illustration, and image. The metaphorical ship is still suffering the same maritime vicissitudes and inspiration always takes possession of the poet-medium like some form of seizure. The tone throughout the odes is tirelessly heroic. A few of the *canzoni eroiche*, e.g., one to his fellow Savonese, Christopher Columbus, and another to the women of Genoa have some poetic merit; for Chiabrera, although he lived in a most unheroic period in Italy and had nothing whatever in common with Pindar, had a seventeenth-century flair for the description of the picturesque.

Equally uninspired were the *canzoni sacre* written in triads and dedicated to various saints, the *canzoni morali* directed against Luther, Calvin, etc., and the *canzoni lugubri* on the deaths of distinguished people. The *canzonette*, however, written in shorter (six lines and under), slimmer stanzas, in lines that are sweet and musical, with rimes that follow close, uttering praises, that need no imposture, of the fleeting pleasures of this

[1] Appropriately, one of the best triadic odes was written to celebrate Urban VIII's birthday. See Chiabrera, *Rime*, I, 82–90.

[2] I have borrowed the expression from Dr. Johnson.

[3] Carducci, "Ode," pp. 386–7.

world, or voicing gravely, and with simple dignity, the gnomes that every moralist knows, still win the praise of critics,[1] though even here there is a disappointing triteness. The little odes are charming, but not quite fresh enough. Perhaps the flavour of Chiabrera as a courtly poet can best be suggested by adding that not only did he write pompous Pindarics for cavaliers, his stint of polemic and religious poetry for the church, and darling little odelettes with soothing worlds of worldly wisdom for the ladies, but also masques and scenarios for musical entertainments.[2] One must not forget, too, that in his aesthetic the function of poetry was to "far inarcare le ciglie."[3]

Chiabrera's own estimate of his own importance and that of his contemporaries may best be summarized in the words of his old school-friend, Cardinal Maffeo Barberini, newly elected Pope Urban VIII,[4]

> . . . for by your means lyric poetry, which spent itself before on wine and debauchery on the street corners, and consorted with sordid lust in the shadows, has now been ennobled by the riches of the Greeks, has been led both up to the Campidoglio to ornament the triumphs of virtue, and into the Church to sing the praises of the saints . . . and you have taught the peoples that poetic genius can rage without a mixture of madness and the filth of sin.[5]

Critics today, however, while acknowledging, perforce, his historical importance as the man who definitely established classicism in the Italian lyric, consider his most valuable contribution to have been the enlargement of the means of metrical expression in Italian through the introduction of new stanzas, new lines, and new types of rime.[6]

[1] See, e.g., Belloni, *Seicento*, pp. 114, 117, 119, 120; Carducci, "Ode," pp. 394–6; and the *Enciclopedia Italiana*.

[2] Carducci, "Ode," pp. 397–8.

[3] Graf, "Il Fenomeno del Secentismo," *Nuova Antologia*, CXIX (1905), 367.

[4] In 1623. He was pope until 1644. He composed Chiabrera's epitaph on his death in 1638 proclaiming him a second Columbus, the discoverer of new worlds of poetry, E. Donadoni, *Breve Storia della Letteratura Italiana* . . . , 3rd ed. (Milano, 1951), p. 192.

[5] Appended to Chiabrera's "Vita," *Rime*, I, p. xxix.

[6] Carducci, "Ode," pp. 395–6; Belloni, *Seicento*, pp. 120–1; *Enciclopedia Italiana*.

Now before leaving the Italian ode let us take a brief glance at its later history in the seventeenth century.

Maffeo Barberini (1568–1644), later Urban VIII, wrote a certain amount of religious poetry in Latin and Italian. His three triadic Pindarics to the Virgin Mary, David, and the Contessa Matilda reveal Chiabrera's stylistic influence. His other odes derive from Chiabrera and from Ciampoli's Horatian-inspired moral poems.[1]

Guido Casoni (d. 1640) wrote a successful if ephemeral book of odes in five to seven line stanzas of mixed *endecasillabi* and *settenarî*, like those of Bernardo Tasso, in a neo-Petrarchan, conceited style that reminds one that this is also the age of Marino. The baroque love for the striking phrase, for oxymoron, hyperbole, and lavish ornamentation is as apparent in the dogmatic religious odes as in the stale Petrarchan trifles about his mistress's eyes. Thus, in a poem about God, he writes,

Con regolati errori
Gira il Ciel. . . .

In divisa unione
Principio egli e senza principio eterno
Una, e sola Cagion senza cagione
Primo Motore senza moto interno
Fine infinito, e spiritoso foco
Ch' arde beando, e senza loco ha loco.[2]

The heavens turn
In regulated aberration. . . .

In divided union,
He is the beginning and without beginning
eternal,
The one and only cause without cause,
The prime mover without internal motion,
The endless end, and the mystical fire
Which burns, blessing, and without place has
place.

One can well imagine how this goes on, page after page. Another subject that readily lent itself to such paradoxical

[1] Belloni, *Seicento*, p. 149.
[2] Guido Casoni, *Ode* (In Venetia, 1605), pp. 1–2.

treatment, the Virgin Mary, is exhausted in six similar, idiotically ingenious pages.[1] Another long, paradox-ridden ode, to the rose, develops a series of conceits: the spines are her warriors, jealous lovers armed in the flower's defence, etc.[2] A splendid example of baroque gingerbread is the ode to the moon; a glance will suffice:

> E le faci lucenti
> De l'ingemmata, e trepidante sfera,
> I purissimi argenti
> Liete spargendo a l'aria ombrosa, e nera,
> A te fanno d'intorno
> Ricca corona; onde n'ha invidia il giorno.[3]

> And the gleaming lights
> Of the gem-studded and trembling sphere,
> Joyfully scattering
> Purest silver on the air shadowy and black,
> Create a rich crown
> Round about you, the envy of the day.

There are odes on Venus and Vulcan[4] and themes borrowed from the *Gerusalemme Liberata*.[5] There are Alexandrian descriptions of mythological paintings[6] and samples of the stock occasional poems; for our poet can write equally well—and in exactly the same style—of a victory or a dance, of a wedding or a funeral.[7] There are also the time-worn Petrarchan love poems on Chloris' mouth, or the heaven of her fair countenance.[8] It is typical of the time that each of the odes should be preceded by a long-winded summary.

Another contemporary, Gabriel Fiamma (1533–85), bishop of Chioggia, writes pretentious post-tridentine paraphrases of the psalms, pompous hymns to the cardinal and Christian virtues, and frigid little poems on Catholic subjects, like the

[1] *Ibid.*, pp. 5–10.
[2] *Ibid.*, pp. 11–16.
[3] *Ibid.*, p. 18. This last line was perhaps inspired by line 7 of B. Tasso's "A Diana." See supra, p. 155.
[4] *Ibid.*, pp. 21–2.
[5] *Ibid.*, pp. 60–9.
[6] *Ibid.*, pp. 41–3.
[7] *Ibid.*, pp. 81–2, 50–2, 57–60, and 61–5.
[8] *Ibid.*, pp. 27–35, 23–6.

crown of the Virgin. The psalms, except for one in *terza rima*, psalm 132, are written in the new four to six line stanzas, most of them borrowed from Bernardo Tasso (the *settenarî* and *endecasillabi* still hold unquestioned sway). The simple titles taken from the Vulgate emphasize the falsity of the new versions. Let us take the beginning of the twenty-third psalm as a sample:

L'eterno alto motore
Pasce la vita mia
Qual dunque ha il mondo ben, che mio non sia!
Ei qual saggio pastore,
Mi adduce, ove il terreno
Di varii fiori, e di ver' herba e pieno.[1]

The eternal mover on high
Feeds my life;
Therefore what wordly good may not be mine!
He, like the good shepherd,
Leads me where the earth
Is full of variegated flowers and of green grass.

The hymns or odes are written in traditional *canzone* form but reveal the stylistic influence of Horace in their invocations, in the definitions of the virtues by their powers and effects, in the clearly delineated settings, in the specific examples, precisely defined, and in the illustrations from classical mythology as well as from Bible story. Of course the precedent for odes celebrating the moral virtues was also set by Horace. Introductory notes explicate the virtues in Thomastic style. The interpretation of the cardinal virtues is, as one would expect, Aristotelian.[2]

Ansaldo Cebà (1565–1623) studied with the neoAristotelians, Sperone Speroni and Giason de Nores.[3] Hence he was impressed with the supreme importance of morality in poetry.[4] He felt great admiration for Chiabrera whom he praises in a sonnet in his *Rime* (Roma, 1611), for opening up new paths for

[1] Fiamma, *Rime Spirituali* (In Venetia, 1606), p. 168.

[2] See, e.g., the prefatory note to "Inno, overo Oda alla Fortezza," *ibid.*, p. 187.

[3] Belloni, p. 150.

[4] *Ibid.*, p. 151.

poetry "tra la via greca e 'l bel camino francese."[1] However, he decided to follow Chiabrera's theory rather than his practice.[2] The Pindaric praise of noble effort attracted him, but only in so far as it inspired him to render "immortali i sudori piu venerandi e le virtù piu eccelse."[3] The so-called Pindaric flights seemed to him the result of too little favour of the Muses rather than of great violence of passion and he scrupulously eschewed them.[4] Thus Cebà's poetry is a sober and austere celebration of the civic virtues.[5]

Ottavio Rinuccini, a less independent follower of Chiabrera's, wrote odes including rimed sapphics.[6] Giuseppe Favoni wrote Horatian moral odes in stanzas of four hendecasyllabic lines as Bartolomeo Del Bene had done.[7] Giovanni Ciampoli (1590–1643) was a bombastic follower of the Pindaric Chiabrera. Before Ciampoli wrote his more important *canzoni* he spent one month thinking of the material and reading up the ancients; then he wrote in a declamatory tone at the rate of fifty or sixty heavily decorated lines per day, ornamenting his work with large numbers of *sententiae*.[8] The result is secentistic obscurity. Like many of the moral poets of his day he was strongly opposed to erotic or frivolous poetry.[9]

The most important and influential of the poets influenced by Chiabrera was Fulvio Testi (1593–1646). Testi had both praise and blame for Chiabrera.[10] His metrical innovations he praised highly and followed.[11] He was less enthusiastic about his master's "Pindaric" characteristics.[10] He felt that Horace was right in calling Pindar inimitable. At the same time he felt that Horace was Pindar's greatest imitator and therefore determined to follow Pindar through him.[11] Like Horace he preferred the moral to the heroic virtues and many of his themes were Horatian, developed in the Horatian manner with the typical *sententiae*.[12] The influence of Pindar appeared, however, in his use of myth which is fuller and more elaborate than Horace's,

1 Carducci, "Ode," p. 394.
2 Belloni, p. 154.
3 *Ibid.*, p. 151.
4 *Ibid.*, p. 151.
5 Belloni, p. 154.
6 *Ibid.*, pp. 123–4.
7 Carducci, "Ode," pp. 392–3.
8 Belloni, p. 147.
9 *Ibid.*, p. 148.
10 Carducci, "Ode," p. 408.
11 Belloni, p. 135 and Carducci, *op. cit.*, p. 410.
12 Carducci, pp. 408–9 and Belloni, pp. 135–8.

although not such a large proportion of his poetry is mythological as Chiabrera's and he never uses myth as the subject of a poem as does Chiabrera.[1] Also Testi was not such a rigid classicist. He was fond of drawing his illustrations from the newer treasury of the Renaissance epic.[2] Unlike many of his moral contemporaries Testi also wrote love poetry. Abandoning the trite metaphysical and idealistic conceits long characteristic of Italian love poetry, he followed in the footsteps of Ovid, Tibullus, and Propertius, treating the subject more intimately.[3] The other principal category of his poetry was the occasional poem honouring contemporary events.[4]

Testi's earliest poetry was written in "versi sciolti," i.e., in "endecasillabi misti a settenarî, rimati senza legge e formanti de' brevi componimenti che hanno l'aria di quelli, molti piu lunghi, che il Marino chiamo idilli." [5] Later he wrote in the four line strophe of Rinuccini and Del Bene, in various six line stanzas invented by Chiabrera, and in longer stanzas that resembled those of the *canzone*.[5] He never tried the triadic form. Testi's odes were less ornamented than Chiabrera's and less elegant. They expressed more feeling; they were better developed, more massive and vigorous.[6] Leopardi felt that had he lived in a better age Testi might have been Italy's Horace, and a warmer, more intense, and more sublime poet than the Roman.[7]

Virginio Cesarini (1595–1624) followed Testi writing odes to promote virtue and to combat vice.[8] Like Ciampoli he was opposed to love poetry. Another follower of Testi, Ciro di Pers (1599–1663), flayed the moral degeneracy of contemporary Italians in *Italia Dissoluta* and preached a pessimistic philosophy in *Della miseria e vanità umana*.[9] A third follower of Testi, Carlo di Dottori (1624–86), wrote moral odes.[10]

1 Belloni, pp. 135–6.
2 *Ibid.*, p. 136 and Carducci, *op. cit.*, p. 410.
3 Carducci, *op. cit.*, pp. 409–10.
4 *Ibid.*, p. 410.
5 Belloni, p. 137.
6 Belloni, p. 48 and Carducci, "Ode," p. 411.
7 Belloni, p. 141.
8 *Ibid.*, p. 143.
9 *Ibid.*, p. 142.
10 Carducci, *op. cit.*, p. 412.

Benedetto Menzini (1646–1704) wrote Horatian odes in the metre and manner of Testi and Pindarics in the style of Chiabrera.[1] One triadic ode treats a moral argument in the Pindaric style,[2] i.e., in the manner of Cebà, it treats the favourite Horatian theme, mutability, with its lesson of Stoic ἀπαθεία, in a style inspired by Pindar. In Menzini's case that is a lax and florid style in which all the well known Horatian commonplaces on the subject are expanded in a wealth of illustration or "myth." Menzini's writing, however, is relatively restrained—and also flat. Criticism is his métier, and satire, as one would expect at that date, and his five book *Art of Poetry* is interesting both for its praise of Petrarch and the traditional Italian poetry and for its description of the current Pindaric writers and its satire on *secentismo*.

Vincenzo da Filicaia (1632–1707), a Florentine who lived at Rome at the court of Queen Christina of Sweden, wrote sacred and heroic odes cumbered with Old Testament religion. He introduced a Hebraic quality into the Italian ode, strove to achieve the sublime, and was notable for his descriptions of the picturesque.[3] His contemporary and fellow denizen of the Swedish court at Rome, Alessandro Guidi (1650–1712) of Pavia, notable also for his descriptions of the picturesque, wrote very irregular Pindaric *canzoni* with quite arbitrary rimes. Carducci believes that Guidi's metric aberrations are traceable to the influence of Cowley and Dryden transmitted through the court of the exiled James II.[4]

Now that we are at the end of the seventeenth century let us see what Benedetto Menzini has to say about the current state of the ode in Italy. As Horace attacked the melodramas in his *Ars Poetica*, Menzini attacks the Pindaric ode in his; for it is the Pindaric that has produced the most monstrous compositions. But Menzini's prescriptions, like Horace's, cover the whole range of his genre, the ode, and in themselves serve both as a description of the best practice of the period and as an

[1] *Ibid.*, pp. 412–13.

[2] "Trattasi Un Morale Argomento; Et e di stile all'imitazione di Pindaro," B. Menzini, *Arte Poetica con alcune Canzoni . . .* (Roma, 1690).

[3] Carducci, "Ode," pp. 414–19 and 431.

[4] *Ibid.*, pp. 421–4 and 431.

expression of its ideals. First, speaking of the bombastic Pindaric poetry, he says:

> O what fine phrase-making! O what gallant
> Thoughts! I am still expecting the stars
> To be tops rotating to the lash of harmony.
>
> Where did you ever learn such charming and beautiful
> Manners? And you reply, It's Pindaric
> The style: they are alike, these and those.

Did Pindar speak thus?

> What presumption, and what pride is this?
> With an absurd and insane speech
> To want to raise your head with Pindar?[1]

Pindar writes in the grand style, but it is the style that comes naturally to him without straining, and he remains always its master:

> For if he takes a turn and over an immense tract
> Drives his chariot, he knows, nevertheless, what point
> He has chosen as a kind of centre to his discourse.
>
> . . . .
>
> And if his expressions are too fiery,
> Know that the rich Grecian tongue
> Willingly makes itself a Proteus and a Vertumnus.
>
> Moreover Pindar had in his stable
> Certain noble steeds, and strong,
> Which did not shrink from the steep height's ascent.[2]

But the modern Pindaric horde knows only how to posture and pose:

> But you, earth-bent brains, little men . . .
>
> You, drink dissolved dawns,
> Pulverized stars, and the liquified
> Heavens which taste of ambrosia!
>
> Poor spirits![3]

[1] *Arte Poetica*, 2nd ed. (Roma, 1690), p. 93.

[2] *Ibid.*, pp. 93–4.

[3] *Ibid.*, p. 94.

Now that he has chastised them roundly, Menzini goes on to teach his contemporaries how odes should be written. First, as to style:

> I am quite aware that a grand harmonic concert
> Befits the ode and that it sometimes delights in
> An impetuous and violent style,
>
> And that there is one who always takes
> This precipitous path, and makes men marvel
> That he does not fall among the precipices.[1]
>
> But these noble and inspired feats
> Are not for all, and not to all is given the ability
> To create unusual and new forms.
>
> . . . .
>
> Sometimes Pindar's harp feeds
> Proud, high thoughts, then suddenly
> It appears to humble itself and to go slowly and to come
> to rest.
>
> . . . .
>
> But let it always be fixed in your mind
> That though you make a departure, your digressive songs
> Must return to that place from which they first set out.[2]

Then he discusses the verse. It must not imitate the monotonous beat of the metronome but it should be varied:

> Show that you are master of yourself, and do not
> Always advance by equal hops, but now make
> Your sentences longer, now shorter.[3]

And the conclusion of each strophe should not be a surprise but it should express some noble and lofty thought.[4]

Menzini ends his section on the ode with advice to youthful poets who seem to feel compelled to treat only life and death, war and peace, to avoid the Pindaric strain and to write on

1 From the "argomento" it appears that this refers to Chiabrera and also to Ciampoli.

2 *Op. cit.*, pp. 95–6.

3 *Ibid.*, p. 96.

4 Here Menzini seems to imply that Angelo di Costanzo's sonnet technique has influenced the ode. See Toffanin, *Cinquecento*, p. 343.

subjects more congenial to their years and more consistent with their experience, subjects, "aequam viribus,"[1] the joys, fears, and hopes of lovers, anger, and youthful boldness, audacious refusals, the arrogant quarrel, and the gnawing pangs of jealousy.[2]

[1] Horace, *Ars Poetica*, lines 38–9.
[2] Menzini, *op. cit.*, p. 97.

Chapter 5

THE FRENCH ODE

THE first important Frenchman in the history of the classical lyric of the Renaissance was a neolatin poet, Salmon Macrin. Although beginning their Renaissance a century later, the French started by following exactly in the footsteps of the Italians. However, the submission to Italy once made, more modern Italian influences swept the French swiftly down the current of time,[1] telescoping the history of the French Renaissance lyric. Thus only about twenty years separated Macrin's first *Carminum Libellus* from Peletier's *Oeuvres Poetiques*, du Bellay's *Deffence* and illustrative *Vers Lyriques*, and Ronsard's five books of *Odes*. The French, responding to the stimulus of humanist ideas a century later than the Italians, turned quickly to the creation of a vernacular ode

[1] Some general works on the cultural relationships between France and Italy in the Renaissance are:

Émile Picot, *Les Italiens en France aux xvie siècle* (Bordeaux, 1901–18).
— — *Les Français à l'Université de Ferrare au xve et au xvie siècles* (Paris, 1902).
— — *Les Français Italianisants au xvie siècle* (Paris, 1906–7).
— — *Des Français qui ont écrit en italien au xvie siècle* (Paris, 1907).
— — *Les Professeurs et les étudiants de langue française à l'Université de Pavie au xve et au xvie siècles* (Paris, 1916).
Henri Chamard, *Origines de la Poésie Française de la Renaissance* (Paris, 1920)
Pierre de Nolhac, *Ronsard et ses Contemporains Italiens* (Paris, n.d. [1921]).
Francesco Flamini, *Studi di Storia Letteraria Italiana e Straniera* (Livorno, 1895).
Antero Meozzi, *Axione e Diffusione della Letteratura Italiana in Europa* (Pisa, 1932).

with a freshness, enthusiasm, and inspiration that the Italians could no longer feel. Thus, although the great Renaissance odes in Italy were written in Latin, the great Renaissance odes in France were written in French.

Despite the fact that Franco-Latin poetry was relatively undistinguished, the single gifted representative of the earlier phase of the French poetic Renaissance deserves some consideration here. The man who was hailed in France as the modern Horace was Salmon Macrin of Loudun, protégé of the powerful cardinal, Jean du Bellay, a relative of the poet. Macrin published a book of Latin lyrics in Paris in 1528. They were not very original, but neither were Flaminio's odes of 1515. Moreover, while they lacked the latter's exquisite sense of music, his sweet sensuousness, and his unfailing flair for the *mot juste*, they had other qualities which seemed to hold forth great promise. Despite the fact that he was obviously imbued with the humanist tradition and had gone far towards mastering its idiom, Macrin was still capable of independence. He could describe nature as he saw it with a sincerity and enthusiasm that were readily communicable and he wrote of his young bride, Gelonis, in startlingly intimate erotic odes that recalled Pontano. There seemed to be prospects of the early emergence of a poet of real power. Unfortunately, Macrin's force was soon spent and, although he remained a well-mannered, tame genius for the rest of his life, his first volume was incomparably his best.

This first volume contains Catullan hendecasyllabics or Horatian alcaics, sapphics, and asclepiads written on the stock subjects and in the standard idiom of his Italian predecessors. It also contains poems about nature which describe recognizably French scenes with manifest emotion. These poems are, of course, indebted to Horace and Vergil, to the humanist Latin pastoral ode and the *lusus pastoralis*, and to their Italian counterparts, the pastoral *canzoni* and *sonetti*. But they are also independent of them. Here, often within the frame of a retirement ode, we have detailed pictures of the countryside which the poet loves and longs to return to, the banks of the Loire and the Vienne, with their vines, roses, fruits, warm fogs, fertile soil, healthy waters, woods, and birds. There he would sing and share his frugal board with like-minded friends who, at his death, would close his eyes and make his modest grave.[1] The theme is Horatian, as is the linear development of the poem with its final specific picture, but the description is of France. In another ode, the poet wants to leave the tedious court and wander again over his native fields in the springtime, listening to the rushing water and the mating birds and carving his bride's name on every tree trunk.[2] In other more learned odes the whole classical tradition of nymphs of fountains, of fauns, and satyrs, of piping poets, and of propitiatory offerings, the whole august pastoral tradition going back to Theocritus, is brought to bear, with lightness and grace, upon the description of a homely country stream that pursues its unromantic way through fields and pastures, a stream where his wife bathes on the hot days of summer and where the pigs sometimes wallow and the heifers frisk!

The first of these odes to the fountain Brissa[3] prays its nymph to ward off the satyrs and fauns when Gelonis goes bathing and promises in return the sacrifice of a kid and wine and flowers:

Brissa, quae custos trepide fluentum
Fontium, regnas per aprica prata,
Et foves rivi gelidi virenteis
  Potibus herbas.

Valle cui late dominanti opaca
Aesculi parent, salicesque glaucae, et[4]
Quae via fessis patet hospitali
  Populus umbra.

. . . . .

Neve subrepat latitans propinque
  Faunus ab antro.

[1] "Ad Egidium," *Salmonis Macrini Iuliodunensis Carminum Libellus* (Parisiis, 1528), sig. a viii v–b ii r. Cf. du Bellay, *Recueils Lyriques*, ed. Chamard (Paris, 1912–), III, 4–8.

[2] "Ad Petrum Borsalum," *Carm.* (1528), sig. a ii r–v. Admittedly the carving of names on trees is a literary as well as rustic tradition (see, e.g., Vergil, *Ecl.* 10, lines 53–4, and Propertius, *Eleg.*, I, 18, lines 21–2), but here Macrin seems to be writing from life rather than from the humanist's handbook.

[3] Macrin, "Ad Brissam Nympham Iuliodunensem," *Carm.* (1528), sig. a ii v–a iii r.

[4] The text reads "et sculi." The emended reading was suggested to me by Professor Leo Spitzer of The Johns Hopkins University.

Cespite exstructam viridi quotannis
Hoedus intinget tibi caesus aram,
Nec merum deerit, neque textae odoro
    Flore coronae.

Brissa, you who reign in the sunny meadows
As guardian of the trembling fountains,
And keep the grass fresh and green
    With draughts of your cool stream,

Mistress far and wide in the shady valley,
Whom the oaks obey, and the grey-green willows, and
The poplar which, by the roadside, extends its hospitable
    Shade to the wearied.

. . . .

If you do not let lurking Faunus creep up
    From his neighbouring cave,

A kid sacrificed to you will stain the altar
Annually constructed of green sods,
And there will be full-bodied wine and crowns
Woven from perfumed flowers.

The final *voeu*, popularized by Navagero in his *Lusus Pastorales*, traces its ancestry back through Horace's *vota* (*Carm.* II, 18 and 22, and the somewhat similar "O fons Bandusiae," III, 13), to the ἀναθήματα of the *Greek Anthology*. It was, for some reason, destined to become a particular favourite with the Pléiade, especially Ronsard.

The second Brissa ode,[1] a more elaborate poem in praise of Brissa herself, is replete with mythological comparisons. It ends, like Ronsard's "O bel aubepin," with a prayer that the fountain may always remain beautiful:

Sic glaucam tremula semper arundine
Incingare comam, perspicuas neque
Sus obturbet aquas, pratave proterat
    Lascivo pede bucula.[2]

So may you ever bind your grey-green locks
With the trembling reed, and may the pig not
Muddy your transparent waters, nor the heifer trample
The meadows with lascivious foot.

[1] *Ibid.*, sig. a iii v–iiii v.

[2] Cf. M. A. Flaminio, *Carmina* (Florentiae, 1552), p. 267.

In 1530 Macrin was ready with a second volume. A typical humanist's book, it contained odes to many of the important political, literary, and scholarly figures of the day, Henry VIII; the du Bellays, the soldier, Guillaume, and the cardinal, Jean; Lazare de Baïf; Erasmus; and John Lascaris; a few moral Horatian odes to friends; some hendecasyllabics and sapphics to his wife; a complaint on the recurrent wars in Italy; and three versions of Anacreon. An ode similar to the first "Ad Brissam" of the first volume, "Ad Faunum,"[1] exudes a country freshness amid these products of the study. Again we note an imaginative excitement in the presence of nature. And here there is something verging on belief in the shadowy presences of pagan animism. The moderns too know panic in lonely places:

> Faune sylvarum specuumque cultor,
> Saeve maiestas et opacus horror
> Quos inaccessos facit, et prophanis
>   Gressibus arcet,

> Faunus, dweller in forests and caves,
> Cruel majesty and shadowy dread,
> You who make them inaccessible and guard them against
>   The approach of the profane,

"protect my wife and me in the forest. Do not frighten us. Keep off the beasts and serpents. So may the nymphs and dryads not flee from you and the *nones* of December be ever sacred to you with the sacrifice of a lamb."[2] As can be seen from the outline, this ode, the least derivative of the volume, is still far from being independent. It follows the same Horatian formula as the first Brissa ode mentioned above and is, like it and Horace's ode to Faunus, a *votum* or *voeu*. Another ode to a pagan deity, "Ad Bacchum,"[3] handles a mass of mythology with skill but lacks the vigour of the hymns on the same subject by Marullo and Flaminio.

[1] Macrin, *Carminum libri IV* (Parisiis, 1530), pp. 18v–19r.

[2] See Horace's ode, *Carm.* III, 18, in which Faunus is referred to as "Nympharum fugientum amator" and the *nones* of December are given as his feast day. Elsewhere in classical literature it is February 13, the Lupercalia.

[3] Macrin, *Carm.* (1530), pp. 33r–34r.

These odes to pagan gods are balanced by a few typically French lyrics to the Virgin Mary; for medieval piety lingered in France, and most volumes of Franco-Latin poetry written in the first half of the sixteenth century contain a large proportion of religious pieces, as do Macrin's own later volumes. Indeed their religious themes together with a comparative barbarity of style, a lack of ease in the difficult lyric forms, and a stiff pedantry are the chief differences between contemporary French and Italian neolatin volumes. Macrin's first book, wholly secular and pagan in content, was the exception. In his second volume, however, we see Macrin, despite his earlier promise, turning into a fluent, facile, and assiduous Horatian, repetitious and derivative, suffering from a poverty of imagination coupled with a fatal facility in the writing of verses. Macrin very rarely achieves that perfect harmony between matter and metre, between words and word music that Latin poetry in the Horatian vein demands.

Macrin published another volume of poetry in 1531. These new odes fall into three main groups: there are laureate or patronage odes addressed to the great, chiefly Francis I, Marguerite of Navarre, and Cardinal du Bellay; there are religious odes, a growing proportion of Macrin's production, written for various feasts of the church; and there are personal odes written to his wife, Gelonis. A similar group offers trite Horatian advice to friends. Macrin, like Bernardo Tasso, labours the Horatian comparison of life to a ship at sea. The first ode of the first book addressed to Francis I [1] contains seven stanzas of seafaring illustrations before the real subject of the poem heaves into sight, Francis' own tempest-tossed bark. The poem follows the Horatian formulary but is excessively tedious. Indeed, of these laureate odes, only the two poems written to celebrate the return of the two ransomed princes from captivity in Spain [2] and the dedication of the second book to Francis I [3] with its discussion of the healing power of poetry are at all readable. The others are only too competent, but quite devoid of individuality. Most of the religious odes may be dismissed in

[1] Macrin, *Carminum Liber Primus, ad Franciscum Valesium Franciae Regem Huius Nominis Primum* (n.p., n.d. [Paris, 1531]), sig. A ii r–A iii r.

[2] Macrin, *Carm.* [1531], sig. A viii v–B r and B ii v–B iv v.

[3] *Ibid.*, B viii v–C ii v.

a similar fashion: the "Hymnus Divo Laurentio"[1] which abandons St. Lawrence for Hercules and Deianira, on the slimmest Pindaric pretext; the "Hymnus in Divae Ceciliae Laudem,"[2] which concerns itself with the parallel myth of the chaste Lucretia; the sapphic to his friends on St. Stephen's day,[3] which describes the early persecutions under Paul; and the odes to St. Margaret[4] and the Virgin Mary. "De Natali Christi,"[5] however, expresses the joy of Christmas in a series of exclamations that sound sincere, while "In Natali Virginis Mariae,"[6] despite the heavily ornate beginning with its descriptive catalogue of the heroes of *other* poetry, is redeemed by the poet's continuing delight in the description of nature. After the conception of the Christ child, the sun walls the Virgin's head with its gleaming rays, making her more beautiful than any star, and all nature breathes and works to serve her:

Lividas palmes tibi flexus uvas
Nutrit, umbrosas nemus omne frondes,
Pingue rus fruges, onerata baccas
  Palladis arbor.

Rete qui caeco, aut capiatur hamo
Piscis assuetis vagus errat undis,
Et suos voluunt tibi beluosa
  Aequora fluctus.

For you the pliant palm nurtures its dark
Fruits, the whole wood its shadowy branches,
The rich countryside its crops, and Pallas' fruitful tree
Its olives.

For you every fish that may be hooked or caught
In the unseen net wanders, roaming its wonted waters,
And the seas full of beasts roll their waves
For you.

Here the epithets are not conventional and borrowed, but derive from clearly defined images vividly present in the poet's imagination. "Flexus" is exactly the right word for the stem of the palm tree, and "lividas" for its shiny fruits. "Caeco," again, suggests the treachery and surprise of the net from the

1 *Ibid.*, sig. A vii v–viii v.
2 *Ibid.*, sig. B iiii v–v v.
3 *Ibid.*, sig. B vi r–v.
4 *Ibid.*, sig. C iv r–v v.
5 *Ibid.*, sig. C vi r–vii r.
6 *Ibid.*, sig. A iii r–v r.

point of view of the trapped fish, and the whole vision of a rich and exotic semi-tropical nature teeming with a life that actively worships its creator is clinched by the final two verses,

> Et suos voluunt tibi beluosa
> Aequora fluctus,

"and the sea full of beasts rolls its waves for you."

Movement, activity, had already been given to vegetable nature in the first line by a skilful choice and placing of words, by the juxtaposition of "flexus," "bend*ing*," with "uvas" which suggests that not only the stem of the palm but also its clusters of fruit are moving rather than immobile, that they are *active in worship*, "*tibi* flexus." But the conclusion of the passage with the great sea full of all kinds of animals rolling harmoniously in honour of the mother of god, awakens our consciousness to the implied music in the earlier lines. The swelling sound, the "o" 's and "u" 's reinforcing the meaning, brings out the unheard music of the swaying palms, the shadowy forests, the rippling grain, and the fruitful olive. The crescendo gives sound to the quiet beginning, turning the whole description of nature into a great hymn of creation.

Between 1531 and 1537 Macrin published no poetry, but in the latter year he compensated for his six years' silence by publishing both six books of odes and six books of hymns.[1] These volumes are indistinguishable. They both contain large numbers of faithfully Horatian religious poems and private or public occasional odes. Some of these poems were already published in earlier volumes, but a distressingly large proportion of them are new.

However we cannot follow Macrin's decline farther. Suffice it to add that these odes and those in the 1538 *Septem Psalmi . . . Paeanum libri quatuor* and the 1540 *Hymnorum selectorum libri tres* are all hack work whose shallow and frivolous fluency and unabashed pilfering from Horace make the treatment of their religious themes almost blasphemous and the reading of them intolerable.[2]

[1] Macrin, *Odarum libri VI* (Lugduni, 1537) and *Hymnorum libri VI* (Parisiis, 1537).

[2] For a brief account of the Christianizing of Horace, mostly later than Macrin, see Wilkinson, *Horace and His Lyric Poetry*, pp. 63–4.

The other Franco-Latin poets may be passed over briefly. Nicholas Bourbon's three editions of *Nugae*, 1533, 1538, and 1540 make no contribution to the lyric tradition. The poems are mostly epigrams or Catullan occasional verses. The dozen or so odes are stale and trivial. Many are on the familiar religious subjects, others are addressed to lawyers and laud their knowledge of canon law. Despite the Horatian trimmings these odes are the frail offspring of the moribund medieval muse. Etienne Dolet's *Carminum Libri Quatuor* (Lugduni, 1538) contains a large number of little occasional poems dedicated to different people, a few alcaics and sapphics to Bembo, Sadoleto, Rabelais, Marot, Budé, Macrin, and Bourbon, other odes to Francis I, Charles V, Paul III, and Marguerite of Navarre, a couple of medieval lyrics on the vanity of this world and the desirability of death, and, surprisingly enough, considering Dolet's later history, two hymns to the Virgin. None of these poems merits a pause. The Protestant poet, Theodore de Bèze, published a volume of Latin poetry in 1548. It is composed of *sylvae*, elegies, epigrams, and epitaphs. Jean Dorat of Limoges (1508–88), the distinguished teacher of the Pléiade, waited until after his pupils had made a success of poetry in the classical tradition before going into print himself. His first published ode was prefixed to the 1550 edition of Ronsard's odes. None of Dorat's odes is very distinguished. Although he generally writes in the idiom of Horace, his schoolmaster's learning makes him borrow an occasional abstruse image from Lucan or Statius, e.g., in "Ad Fontem Arculii, sive Herculei paga,"[1] he writes:

> Fons tu nobilium gloria fontium . . .
> Nec te vincat honos famaque gurgitis
> Quem pendentis equi protulit ungula,

> You are the glory of famous fountains . . .
> Nor may the glory and fame of the stream which the hoof
> Of the flying horse brought forth surpass you,

echoing Statius' "pendentis . . . ungulae liquorem."[2] Dorat's only unusual neolatin odes are two Pindarics, one to Ronsard[3]

1 *Ioannis Aurati . . . Poematia . . .* (Lutetiae Parisior., 1586), pp. 194–7.
2 Statius, *Sylv.* II, 7, line 4.
3 Dorat, *Poematia*, pp. 176–81.

"in the poet's own style" which is curious for its slight irregularities in the triadic form,[1] and another to the Cardinal of Lorraine,[2] in regular triads, which describes the development of the poet's function and then praises the house of Guise. The ode to Ronsard is a sorry Pindaric pastiche. Marc Antoine Muret (1526–85) also writing after the Pléiade had risen to fame wrote some creditable Latin verses including a fine version of Phaedra's temptation of Hippolitus:

Cur editorum per iuga montium
Antris latentes persequeris feras?
Tibi absque telis, retibusque
Praeda domi melior parata est.

Accede, neu te poeniteat mei
Fructus pudoris carpere primulos:
Non me ore natura indecoro
Protulit, immeritamve amari.

Quid vana legum vincula te movent?
Natura nullos concubitus vetat;
Sed compedes vanissima istas
Cura hominum sibi fabricata est.[3]

Why over the ridges of the lofty mountains
Do you pursue the wild beasts hiding in their lairs?
A better prey, without weapons or nets
Is waiting for you at home.

Approach, do not scruple to pluck
The first fruits of my modesty:
Nature did not bear me with an ugly
Face, or unworthy to be loved.

Why do you care for meaningless bonds
made by the law?
Nature forbids no unions,
But those chains of yours, man's
Vainest solicitude has manufactured for itself.

But after 1550 there is little point in exploring the backwater of Franco-Latin poetry.

[1] Rhanutius Gherus [Jan Gruter], *Delitiae C. Poetarum Gallorum* (n.p [Frankfurt], 1609), I, 358–62.

[2] Dorat, *Poematia*, pp. 209–18.

[3] Gruter, *Delitiae Poet. Gall.*, IV, 788.

The age before any great outburst of creativity always seems a particularly dark one. Yet poetry written in the French language immediately before the efflorescence of the Pléiade did in fact show some promise of the splendour that was to come. The court poet, Mellin de Sainct-Gelays (1491–1558), adapted the Petrarchan sonnet to French, imitated a Horatian ode in a new short strophe that was a complete departure from medieval metrics,[1] and did French versions of Secundus. His verse is musical[2] and varied, its content trivial. Sainct-Gelays' predecessor, Clement Marot (1496–1544), the protégé of Marguerite of Navarre, revealed in his elegance and wit, his urbanity and worldliness, in the ease of his lines and the music of his verse, and in a new sensibility to nature,[3] the refreshing influence of the southern Renaissance. Marot also did translations from Ovid, Vergil, and Musaeus (*Hero and Leander*) and wrote the Protestant psalter. Before either Ronsard or du Bellay took pen in hand French poetry was clearly trying to work itself free from the chains and fetters devised for it by the "great" *rhetoriqueurs* of the fifteenth century with their decadent summation of the medieval tradition, with their heavy authority wielded in favour of fixed stanza forms and strophic systems, complicated and difficult rime schemes, copious ornamentation, puns, and such exercises in ingenuity as acrostics, anagrams, and, above all, allegory, with its political, religious, or moral didacticism.[4]

The Pléiade generally claimed for themselves the honour of having introduced both the word and the thing "ode" into the French language and literature. In its literal sense this is manifestly false. The word "ode" is recorded as early as 1511

[1] For the poem, an imitation of Horace IV, 7, "Diffugere nives," see Mellin de Sainct-Gelays, *Oeuvres Complètes*, ed. Prosper Blanchemain (Paris, 1873), I, 81–2.

[2] Chamard, *Origines*, p. 191, says that Sainct-Gelays wrote his own music and sang his lyrics, accompanying himself. P. Laumonier, *Ronsard Poète Lyrique* (Paris, 1923), pp. 715–16, says that Marot, Sainct-Gelays, and Marguerite of Navarre sang their poetry. It was only with Malherbe that the lyre or lute became a metaphor.

[3] See Henri Chamard, "Introduction à l'Histoire de la Pléiade," *Extrait du Bulletin de l'Université de Lille*, 2e serie (janv. 1899).

[4] See Chamard, *Origines*, pp. 133–49 and Laumonier, *Rons. Poète*, pp. 665–9.

and was used by Rabelais.[1] Moreover, despite du Bellay's "Chante moy ces odes, incognues encor' de la Muse francoyse"[2] and Ronsard's boastful

> Premier j'ai dit la façon
> D'acorder le luc aus Odes,[3]

poems indistinguishable from many Pléiade odes had already appeared among the works of Marot, Sainct-Gelays, and Bonaventure Despériers,[4] while the genre had even been described and defined in a schoolbook that came out the year before du Bellay's *Deffence*, *L'Art Poetique Françoys*, commonly ascribed to Thomas Sébilet.[5] Nevertheless anyone but the

[1] According to: Chamard, ed. du Bellay's *Deffence* (Paris, 1904), notes, pp. 208–9, and "L'Invention de L'Ode," *RHLF*, VI (Paris, 1899), 31; Laumonier, *Rons. Poète*, p. xxxi; Godefroy, *Dictionnaire de L'Ancienne Langue Françoise. Complement*, X (Paris, 1902), "ode" occurs in the *Temple de Venus* of Jean Lemaire de Belges, 1511; in Jean Bouchet's *Epistre familière*, c. 1520; in G. Michel's *Oeuvres de Virgile*, 1529; in Jean Martin's transl. of Sannazaro's *Arcadia*, 1541; in Barthélemy Aneau's *Lyon Marchant*, *Satyre Françoise*, 1541; and in Rabelais, 1546.

[2] du Bellay, *La Deffence et Illustration de la Langue Françoise*, ed. H. Chamard (Paris, 1904), p. 208.

[3] Paul Laumonier, *Pierre de Ronsard, Oeuvres Complètes*, Édition Critique, I (Paris, 1924), 130. This edition is referred to henceforth as Laum., *Ed. Crit.*
Ronsard also claimed having introduced the ode in the "Preface Au Lecteur" of the 1550 ed. of the odes: "et osai le premier des nostres enricher ma langue de ce nom Ode"; in "A sa Lire," Laum., *Ed. Crit.*, I, 162–6, and in "A Caliope," *ibid.*, I, 174–9, both poems appearing in the 1550 ed. of the odes; in "Elegie a J. de la Peruse" in the 5th book of *Odes* of 1553, *ibid.*, V (Paris, 1928), 259–65 (see Chamard, "L'Invention de L'Ode," pp. 22–3); in "Au Fleuve du Loir," Laum., *Ed. Crit.*, II (Paris, 1924), 104–7, VI, 124–5, a poem first published in 1555. Moreover Peletier said in his *L'Art Poètique* (Lyon, 1555), "ce nom d'ode a esté introduit de nostre temps par Pierre de Ronsard."

[4] Laumonier, *Rons. Poète*, p. xxv, and Chamard, "L'Invention de L'Ode," pp. 27–9. The 1540's also saw the beginning of the translation of Horace into French, Laum., *Rons. Poète*, p. 20, fn. a.

[5] Sébilet had a section called "Du Cantique, Chant Lyrique ou Ode, et Chanson" where he compared and contrasted these three related forms of lyric poetry. He found that the subject matter of the *cantique* is sacred, that of the other two secular, usually amorous or bacchic, although the ode may take Pindar as well as Horace as model; that they are all composed of long and short lines, but that the smallest number of short lines is found in the *cantique*, the largest number in the *chanson*; and that ode and *chanson* have identical subject matter and style and are distinguished from one another only by the greater length of the former and by the greater variety of form and style of the latter.

narrowest of pedants would admit the virtual truth of the Pléiade contention; for they publicized a term and a brand of poetry little known in French before, and theirs has been the lasting contribution.

Moreover, if it is true that it was the Pléiade who established both the word and the thing "ode" in the French language and literature, it is also true that it was Ronsard who inspired the other members of the Pléiade and was thus, in fact, the "inventor" of the ode. Peletier tells us in his *Art Poètique* how Ronsard, when he was very young, showed him some of his odes at Le Mans and told him that he had decided to write like Horace.[1] Peletier then adopted the idea of writing odes from

[1] Peletier, *L'Art Poètique*, p. 64. Chamard, "Invention Ode," p. 35, thinks that Ronsard and Peletier met when Ronsard, at the age of 19, i.e., in 1543, was getting tonsured and Peletier, aged 26, was secretary to the bishop.

In Laum., *Ed. Crit.*, II, 192–8 and I, 3–8, there are two odes which Ronsard says he wrote in 1540, the latter being a version of the poem that Ronsard published in Peletier's 1547 volume under the title of "Des beautez qu'il voudroit en s'Amie." This ode mentions Peletier. However, this cannot be taken as evidence that Ronsard knew Peletier as early as 1540, even if we accept Ronsard's date as being strictly accurate, since this ode was revised for publication in 1547 when Peletier's name doubtless was added.

The popularity of Horace in the Renaissance was very impressive. There were 100 different editions of his works before 1600, 16 of which were published before 1500. The texts were excellent, painstakingly established by the best humanist scholars, and the editions were elaborately annoted and explicated. Along with the *scholia* there were notes by Cristoforo Landino, who wrote the commentary for the first Florentine edition of 1482, Angelo Poliziano, Desiderius Erasmus, Aldus Manutius, Pietro Crinito, Jason de Nores, Marc Antoine Muret, and Denys Lambin, to mention only the most famous. Moreover the odes were almost invariably accompanied by metrical analyses. Thus Horace was easily accessible.

The Renaissance editions of Pindar have already been described, supra pp. 11–13. They were, in brief, the Aldine (Venice, 1513), which contained only the text chopped up into lines of widely varying lengths and arranged in long, thin strophes, both line and strophe often ending in the middle of a word; the Callierges (Rome, 1515), the first edition to publish the *scholia* and metrical analyses supporting the same interpretation of the versification as the Aldine; and the Cratander (Basel, 1526, reprinted 1528 and 1535), and the Brubacchius (Frankfurt, 1542), both of which were derived from the Callierges.

The third ancient ode writer whom Ronsard decided to imitate, Anacreon, had to wait until 1554 to receive his *editio princeps* from Henry Stephanus the younger.

Ronsard.[1] He later passed on the new enthusiasm to du Bellay.[2] Thus, although Peletier published odes in 1547 and du Bellay in 1549, Ronsard was the first to write them, but shyness, sensitivity, and the influence of Horace kept him from going first into print.[3]

Ronsard's first odes were written in Latin around 1541 under the inspiration of Horace, whom he continued to admire and imitate until the end of his life.[4] Soon, however, Ronsard realized that it was better to be first in France than last in Rome,[5] and he found his true calling writing classically inspired poetry in French. The influence of Horace was followed by that of the neolatin and Italin poets; then, under the tuition of Dorat, by that of Pindar; and finally, after the publication of Stephanus' edition of 1554, by that of Anacreon.

Ronsard was attracted to ancient lyric poetry for its bright, pagan mythology, its glorification of life, and its philosophical reflectiveness. He was tired of the Virgin Mary and allegorical abstractions. He was excited by the brief lyric strophes of Horace, and, later, of Anacreon, with their apparently effortless grace and ease. How clumsy and awkward they made the long French stanzas with their complex, rigid, rime schemes appear, or how contrived the short-lined strophes that all rimed on a single syllable or two! And what a wonder of artistic freedom was revealed in the independently created strophes of Pindar and in their rapturous, rhapsodic style!

[1] Chamard, "Invention Ode," p. 35.

[2] *Ibid.*, p. 42. See du Bellay, *Recueils Lyriques*, ed. Chamard, IV, 43–54.

[3] Ronsard, "Preface Au Lecteur, 1550," Laum., *Ed. Crit.*, I, 45–6, "Ie fu maintesfois auecques prieres admonesté de mes amis faire imprimer ce mien petit labeur, et maintesfois j'ai refusé apreuuant la sentence de mon sententieus Auteur,

Nonumque prematur in annum."

[4] Pierre de Nolhac, *Ronsard et l'Humanisme* (Paris, 1921), pp. 249–56; Chamard, "Invention Ode," p. 34; and Laumonier, *Rons. Poète*, pp. 5, 16.

[5] Nolhac, *Rons et l'Humanisme*, p. 22, quotes Ronsard:

Je fu premierement curieux du Latin:
Mais cognoissant, helas! que *mon cruel destin*
Ne m'avoit dextrement pour le Latin fait naistre,
Je me fey tout François, aimant certe mieux estre
En ma langue ou second, ou le tiers, ou premier
Que d'estre sans honneur à Rome le dernier.

Ronsard, then, chose to imitate the ancient lyric poets to free French poetry from its medieval enslavement to rule and to win the poet's liberty! And it was through his imitation of the ancients that Ronsard was able to enrich French literature with a new genre and a whole new world of subject matter that brought with it a new atmosphere, a new tone, and new methods of expression, particularly images more picturesque and plastic that made a greater appeal both to the imagination and to the senses.[1]

The first published volume to illustrate these new ideas was the *Oeuvres Poètiques* of Jacques Peletier du Mans which appeared in 1547. Besides containing translations of Homer and Vergil and fifteen Petrarchan sonnets, this volume contains eighteen more or less Horatian odes, three of which are "versions," of "Otium divos rogat in patenti" (II, 16), "Quid dedicatum poscit Apollinem" (I, 31), and "Beatus ille qui procul negotiis" (Epode 2). It also contains the first published works of Ronsard and du Bellay, an "ode" by the former and a wholly conventional *dizain* by the latter.

The first of Peletier's ode translations is an attempt to find a French equivalent of the sapphic stanza. Its formal pattern is $AAA_{12}B_6$. The Latin stanza, it will be remembered, has three eleven syllable lines followed by a five syllable line. Peletier's lines with one syllable more, exclusive of feminine endings, seem considerably heavier than the Horatian ones. Yet the compact, closely knit stanza is something new in French literature and not entirely unsuccessful. Moreover the exigencies of its brief form force Peletier to clear, exact expression and a close following of the original, a good discipline for someone who wants to break away from medieval diffuseness. Peletier's other two translations are in less rigorous stanzas and hence are embroidered and diffuse.

Among Peletier's original odes are a long poem on the four seasons that suggests Vergil and Thomson rather than Horace; a long-strophied invitation to Ronsard to come to the country which, in its conversational tone and leisurely, straightforward catalogue of the inevitably Vergilian joys of country life in the spring, suggests the epistle rather than the ode; a proclamation

1 Laumonier, *Rons. Poète*, pp. xxxv–vi.

of the Pléiade programme and point of view addressed to a Latin poet:

> J'escri en langue maternelle,
> Et tasche a la mettre en valeur. . . .
> Mieux vault estre icy des meilleurs,
> Que des mediocres ailleurs,[1]

and a poetical exchange with Ronsard. Typical of the best of the odes is "Des Grans Chaleurs de l'Année 1547." Here, in a long, double stanza ($ABAB_8CDCD_6$) in which French poetry is well at ease, the Horatian formula, its vivid, specific illustrations and its mythological form of expression are made to serve, with lightness and grace, Peletier's witty complaint about the heat and drought:

> L'Humeur de terre est consumée,
> Les champs sont fendus et ouvers,
> Et la liqueur du chaud humée
> Laisse les poissons découvers:
> Les Naiades craintives
> À Phebus se marissent
> Que des fontaines vives
> Les sources se tarissent.
>
> Phébus auteur de medicine,
> Qui toutes choses doiz nourir,
> Tu grilles jusqu' a la racine
> Les plantes prestes a mourir:
> Or maintenant croit on
> Qu'as mis ton char es mains
> D'un autre Phaeton,
> Pour bruller les humains. . . .
>
> Si nous te sommes odieux,
> Et contre nous veux conspirer,
> Pourquoy veux tu aussi les Dieux
> Et les Deesses martirer?
> Maint fleuve en va plaignant,
> Bacchus encore pir,
> Des seps la mort craignant,
> Et Ceres des espiz.

[1] Jacques Peletier du Mans, *Oeuvres Poètiques*, ed. Leon Séché (Paris, 1904), pp. 110–11.

Junon de l'Air haulte princesse,
Envoye nous ta messagere,
Qui a ces ardeurs donne cesse
En attirant pluye legere. . . .[1]

Here Peletier is creating something new for French literature, poetry that takes on a whole additional dimension by absorbing the world of classical mythology, poetry that thus seems more august, more universal. But it is also poetry that lives and breathes, vivified by the realization of new poetic potentialities. Moreover, with the liberation of the spirit has come a new freedom of form, a greater lightness and grace, variety and invention. Yet Peletier is only at the beginning. His book is no revolutionary masterpiece, but merely a tentative, scholarly experiment. The great work is all to come.

Ronsard's "ode" in the same volume, "Des beautez qu'il voudroit en s'Amie,"[2] is written in a newly flexible stanza, $A_{10}ABB_8A_{10}$, but otherwise it is only its tone, the richness and sensuousness of the catalogue-description of the ideal mistress's charms, which reminds us that this poem is written in the pagan Ovidian Renaissance.[3] Apart from its general liberating influence the only trace of classicism here is the specific, picture conclusion which is very much reminiscent of the end of one of Horace's odes, I, 9, "Vides ut alta stet nive candidum." After describing his mistress physically in the medieval tradition from tip to toe, Ronsard describes her manner; it is to be kittenish, teasing, and seductive; and then, in typical Renaissance fashion, her accomplishments; she must know both Petrarch and the *Romance of the Rose* and be able to play the lute. Then he goes on to say,

Quand est de moy, je ne voudroy' changer
Femme telle a l'or estranger,

when she offers her mouth to be kissed or refuses, pretending anger, or when she hides in some corner and surprises me with her embrace[4]:

1 Peletier, *ibid.*, pp. 105–6. 2 *Ibid.*, pp. 107–8.

3 Laumonier, *Rons. Poète*, p. 28, likens this ode to works of Jean Lemaire des Belges, Clement Marot, and Mellin de Sainct-Gelays.

4 The idea of the teasing mistress may have been adapted from one of Secundus' *basia*.

Ou quand en quelque coing cachee,
A l'impourvu accoler me viendroit.

Peletier's reply to this ode,[1] on the beauties and accomplishments of the lover, creates a poetic diptych that reminds us of Marlowe and Raleigh's companion pieces, "The Passionate Shepherd to his Love" and her reply.

These two poems barely hint at the new direction that French literature is about to take. They mark no great departure from Marot or Sainct-Gelays. In fact this whole volume is more conservative than Bernardo Tasso's of 1531, although it stands at the threshold of much more important changes. Thus none of the poems in this volume are "measured to the lyre." Yet *mésurer les vers à la lyre*, i.e., maintain the order of masculine and feminine rimes established in the first stanza throughout the poem so that each strophe is perfectly adapted to the same succession of musical notes, was one of the most characteristic features of the mature poetry of the Pléiade. However, it should be observed that the Pléiade in its early days, in its fight for liberty, specifically rejected such slavery[2] which, by the time of Marot's psalms (*c.* 1540), had become customary for poetry that was written to be sung.[3] Even as late as 1549 du Bellay could write in the *Deffence*,

> Il y en a qui fort supersticieusement entremeslent les vers masculins avecques les feminins, comme on peut voir aux *Psalmes* traduitz par Marot. Ce qu'il a observé . . . afin que plus facilement on les peust chanter sans varier la musique, pour la diversité des mesures qui se trouverroint à la fin des vers. Je trouve cete diligence fort bonne, pourveu que tu n'en faces point de religion jusques a contreindre ta diction pour observer telles choses.[4]

Also in the "Au Lecteur" prefaced to the *Vers Lyriques*[5] of the same year du Bellay tells us that he has not crippled his poetry in order to pamper the performers. (The Pléiade still wrote lyric poetry to be sung.) Thus the odes in Peletier's 1547

1 Peletier, *op. cit.*, pp. 108–9.

2 Laumonier, *Rons. Poète*, pp. 663, 674–5; Chamard, ed. *Deffence*, pp. 291–2, fn. 2, and p. 293, fn. 2.

3 Laumonier, *Rons. Poète*, pp. 652, 654.

4 du Bellay, *Deffence*, ed. Chamard, pp. 290–3.

5 du Bellay, *Oeuvres Poètiques*, ed. Chamard, III, 3.

volume, nine of the thirteen odes in du Bellay's 1549 *Vers Lyriques*, and Ronsard's own early lyrics were not "measured to the lyre."

However, by 1549 Ronsard had changed his mind and come to believe that poetry that was not fit to be sung, in the most exacting sense of that phrase, could not be dignified with the name "ode." Thus in 1550 Ronsard published ninety-four odes all of which were "measured" and he banished the early "odes" to a miscellaneous section of his works:

> Il est certain que telle Ode ["Des beautez qu'il voudroit en s'Amie"] est imparfaite, pour n'estre mesurée, ne propre a la lire, ainsi que l'Ode la requiert, comme sont encores douze, ou treze, que j'ai mises en mon Bocage, sous autre nom que d'Odes, pour cette méme raison, servans de temoignage par ce vice, à leur antiquite.[1]

Similarly du Bellay measured all his later odes. Thus the rigorous observation of an established pattern of masculine and feminine endings became a requirement of French lyric poetry until the time of Victor Hugo and the romantics. However, we must not get ahead of our chronology.

Peletier's *Oeuvres Poètiques*, then, was the pioneer publication of the Pléiade. It was followed in 1549 by du Bellay's *Deffence* which advocated the illustration of the French language by new lyric forms, especially the sonnet and the ode:

> Chante moy ces odes, incognues encor' de la Muse francoyse, d'un luc bien accordé au son de la lyre greque et romaine et qu'il n'y ait vers, ou n'aparoisse quelque vestige de rare et antique erudition.[2]

—and by three volumes in which du Bellay sought to exemplify the new kind of poetry that he was advocating, the first book of *Olive*, a collection of sonnets, the *Vers Lyriques* which contained thirteen odes, and a *Recueil de Poesie* dedicated to his new found protectress, Marguerite de Valois, the king's sister. These three volumes appeared at short intervals in the course of 1549.

The thirteen odes in the *Vers Lyriques* are, broadly speaking, written in the Renaissance ode tradition with which we are

1 Ronsard, "Preface Au Lecteur, 1550," Laum., *Ed. Crit.*, I, 44.

2 du Bellay, *Deffence*, ed. Chamard, pp. 208–9.

already familiar. They also live up to du Bellay's own prescriptions for the ode both as to subject matter,

> Et quand à ce, te fourniront de matiere des louanges des dieux et des hommes virtueux, le discours fatal des choses mondaines, la solicitude des jeunes hommes, comme l'amour, les vins libres, et toute bonne chere,

and style,

> Sur toutes choses, prens garde que ce genre de poeme soit eloigné du vulgaire, enrichy et illustré de mots propres et epithetes non oysifz, orné de graves sentences, et variés de toutes manieres de couleurs et ornamentz poetiques.[1]

Four only of the odes are "measured to the lyre."

The first ode of the volume, "Les Louanges d'Aniou, Au Fleuve de Loyre,"[2] is a type of poem with which we are already familiar from Italo- and Franco-Latin poetry and which was destined to become popular with the Pléiade—in 1550 Ronsard published four similar odes, "Les Louanges de Vandomois," "Au pais de Vandomois," "Au fleuve du Loir," and "A la source du Loir."[3] Du Bellay's praise of Anjou is written in short, seven syllable lines, couplet riming. The ode opens, "O de qui la vive course," with an exhortation of the Loire that implies a river god, to look, as other gods, Ceres and Bacchus, have done, on fertile and happy Anjou. True to his principles, and also to the ancient technique, du Bellay defines Bacchus allusively, "illustrating" his poetry with his "rare et antique erudition," in the manner of Alamanni and of Bernardo Tasso:

> Et cetuy la, qui pour mere
> Eut la cuysse de son pere,
> Le Dieu des Indes vainqueur
> Arrousa de sa liqueur
> Les montz, les vaulx et campaignes
> De ce terroir que tu [la Loire] baignes.[4]

Thus classicizing the French countryside in Macrin's earlier and better manner, du Bellay calls on the Loire to look at the

[1] *Ibid.*, pp. 209–10 and 210–11.

[2] du Bellay, *Oeuvres Poèt.*, ed. Chamard, III, 4–8.

[3] Laum., *Ed. Crit.*, I, 221–5; II, 91–6; II, 104–7; II, 129–32.

[4] *Ibid.*, III, 5.

fauns stag-hunting in the woods, at the beautiful nymphs, and at the demigods pursuing them. This last scene is described with all the detail of an ancient epic simile. We hear the catching breath and see the heaving bosom. Now all the rural tutelary deities are invoked, the nymphs, hamadryads, Priapus, Pales, Flora, and Apollo (the "pasteur Amphrisien") to protect the land from the harshness of drought or frost. Who wants to sing of India or Araby? I will sing of Anjou. When I die may I be buried by a fresh fountain near the Loire; and you, river Loire, shed some tears for me and

> . . . sonne mon bruyt fameux
> A ton rivage ecumeux.[1]

There is more than a hint of one of Macrin's first and most likeable odes, "Ad Petrum Borsalum,"[2] in this conclusion.

The application of classical mythology to a subject of this sort is successful because it is intrinsically appropriate. The pagan gods who had in the Renaissance become a part of every educated man's experience were easily felt to be present on the vine-laden banks of the Loire. Thus the addition of a classical dimension could only enrich one's apprehension of the French countryside. And in an age already eager for *gloire* the prayer to the river to sing the poet's praises did not appear too strained. Du Bellay's first ode, then, is a successful adaptation of the ancient lyric because he has chosen a subject which admits of classical treatment and has only borrowed that which could be assimilated.

In contrast with this ode, du Bellay's second ode illustrates the continuation of medievalism in the poetry of the Pléiade. In picture stanza after picture stanza, rigidly separated, static, and complete, like a series of didactic sculptures or painted allegories, du Bellay develops his sermon theme, "Des Miseres et Fortunes Humains"[3]:

> Bellone seme sang et raige
> Parmy les peuples ça et la,
> Et chasse à la mort maint couraige
> De ce fouet tortu qu'elle a.

[1] *Ibid.*, III, 7. Cf. du Bellay, *ibid.*, V, 264–77; Macrin, *Carm.* (1528), sig. a viii v–b ii r; and Ronsard, Laum., *Ed. Crit.*, V, 233–42, and I, 214–16.

[2] Macrin, *Carm.* (1528), sig. a ii r–v.

[3] du Bellay, *Oeuvres Poètiques*, ed. Chamard, III, 8–11.

Quelques autres venans de naitre,
Avant qu'ilz aillent recontrant
Ce qui malheureux nous fait estre,
Sortent du monde en y entrant.

The poem is superficially classical with Mercury, the conductor of shades, Minos, the judge, Hercules' choice, and Pandora's box. But this sort of classicism, these stock characters, were also found in medieval poetry. Thus, when they are brought in in conjunction with a medieval theme, the wretched lot of mankind, they do not represent anything new. It is the subject and du Bellay's emotional attitude towards it, the feeling of despair, of comfortless in this world, that gives the poem a medieval caste, despite the modern technique, the concise, vivid images, and the new short strophes.

However, du Bellay could treat this sort of theme equally well in the classical manner. When the poet remembers the stoic doctrine that virtue is superior to fortune and the rational, worldly consolation that it is better to be hoping for better fortune than at the height of prosperity fearing its end,[1] Marullus' staff of support in exile, an ode on the imperfection of worldly happiness[2] quite changes its tone. Du Bellay's series of illustrations of the famous Horatian aphorism, "Nihil est ab omni parte beatum,"[3] "Rien n'est heureux de tous poinctz en ce monde," inevitably largely derivative—for there are so many handy texts[4]—is thus completely in the humanist tradition. Du Bellay is not slavish, however, and there are some nice flashes of an almost grotesque wit,

Ne voy-tu pas que les signes des cieux
Sont mutilez de piez, de bras ou d'yeux?

that remind one of France's vigorous medieval sculpture.

Again du Bellay mingles medieval and classical elements in another related ode, "De L'Inconstance des Choses, Au Seigneur Pierre de Ronsard."[5] From medieval iconography he borrows Fortune's ferris-wheel,

[1] Cf. Horace, II, 10.
[2] du Bellay, *Oeuvres Poètiques*, ed. Chamard, III, 46–50.
[3] Horace, II, 16, lines 27–8.
[4] du Bellay borrows from Horace I, 4, and III, 29.
[5] du Bellay, *Oeuvres Poèt.*, ed. Chamard, III, 15–21.

Nul, tant qu'il ne meure,
Heureux ne demeure:
Le sort inconstant
Or' se hausse, et ores
S'abaisse, et encores
Au ciel va montant.[1]

In a later stanza, the "Colosses / En ruines grosses" derive from the long medieval lament, lasting from Alcuin to Petrarch, over the destruction of Rome, "Her very ruins show how great Rome was." But du Bellay incorporates these elements harmoniously in a poem that is basically classical. There are echoes of Vergil[2]

La nuyt froyde et sombre
Couvrant d'obscure umbre
La terre et les cieux,
Aussi doulx que miel
Fait couler du ciel
Le sommeil aux yeux,

and of Flaminio,[3]

Puis le jour luysant
Au labeur duysant
Sa lueur expose,
Et d'un teint divers
Ce grand univers
Tapisse et compose.

1 Despite Horace's

Valet ima summis
Mutare et insignem attenuat deus,
Obscura promens; hinc apicem rapax
Fortuna cum stridore acuto
Sustulit, hic posuisse gaudet.
(I, 34, lines 12–16)

The god has the power to change
The lowest for the highest and to abase the mighty,
Bringing forward the obscure; from one man rapacious
Fortune, with a shrill swoop, sweeps away
The crown, on another she is pleased to place it.

du Bellay's passage about Fortune seems rather to have been inspired by the late medieval and Renaissance iconography of Fortune, in this case, by the wheel symbol. See H. R. Patch's books on the goddess Fortuna.

2 See Vergil, *Aeneid* II, lines 250–1.

3 See Flaminio, *Carm.* (1743), pp. 11–12.

There is a description of the seasons suggested by Horace (IV, 7), but sensitive and independent; a completely original stanza on the impermanence of even the earth's physical features; and a concluding switch from mutability to Horatian *mediocritas*,[1] "Be a bush not an oak, a valley not a mountain . . . ," which is characteristic of du Bellay's frequent careless construction when he makes an uncritical use of classical sources.[2]

Other Horatian odes are "Du Premier Iour de L'An,"[3] a gloomy poem that reflects on man's mortality but finds little real cheer in the traditional fleshly pleasures,

> Les vins, l'amour consolent
> Le triste coeur de l'homme:
> Les ans legiers s'en volent,
> Et la mort nous assome,

and "Du Retour du Printens. A Ian D'Orat,"[4] a description of spring in images of great beauty, with reminiscences of Horace.[5] This ode concludes in typical humanist fashion with the reflection that the year takes our days and months but not our writings. These poems are all written in new short lines and stanzas and are ornamented with classical dignity and sententiousness. There is often, however, an intense feeling of medieval gloom.

The third ode in *Vers Lyriques*, "Les Louanges d'Amour,"[6] is particularly interesting in that it shows, like Bernardo Tasso's "Aurora," how the vernacular poet learned how to write odes from the humanists. Like Tasso's "Aurora" du Bellay's "Louanges d'Amour" is a translation of a humanist ode, Pontano's "De amoris Dominatu."[7] And, like Tasso's poem, du Bellay's ode contains Petrarchan elements which adapt it to

[1] Cf. Horace II, 10, and III, 1.
[2] Cf. du Bellay, "Du Iour des Bacchanales," *Oeuvres Poèt.*, ed. Chamard, III, 29–32.
[3] du Bellay, III, 26–9.
[4] *Ibid.*, III, 33–6. Cf. Laum., *Ed. Crit.*, II, 40–3.
[5] Horace I, 4, and IV, 7 and 12.
[6] du Bellay, *Oeuvres Poèt.*, III, 11–15.
[7] Pontano, *Carm.* IV (Basileae, 1556), pp. 3527–8. For an outline of "De Amoris Dominatu" see supra, pp. 65–6. For a detailed comparison of the two poems see my article in *MLN*, LXXIII (1958), 594–7.

the modern taste. So the introduction, growing out of Pontano's first stanza, develops a familiar medieval setting, the cooling fountain, the friendly shade, and the green fields, and a neo-Petrarchan state, the poet panting in the heat of the fires of love. Those in love get pleasure from speaking of it. Therefore —and here du Bellay picks up Pontano with a prayer to Erato for inspiration—du Bellay begins the praise of love. Most of the rest of the poem is a translation, free in the Renaissance manner, of Pontano. The conclusion, however, like Tasso's conclusion of "Aurora," makes further concessions to contemporary taste. When Pontano, in the course of his description of the powers of love, had reached the point where love led the maid to the marriage couch, he closed his ode with a prayer to love to be kind. It is typical of classical love poetry that it should conclude on a carnal note. That would not do, however, for du Bellay's circle. Therefore, in his third last strophe, du Bellay borrows from *trecento* idealism,[1]

> Amour est tout bon et beau,
>   Son flambeau
> N'enflamme les vicieux:
> Juste est et de simple foy,
>   C'est pourquoy
> Il est tout nu et sans yeux.

There follows a summary praise of love:

> Leurs victorieux charroys
>   Ducz et Roys
> Doyvent a ses sainctz autelz,
> Le poetique ouvrier
>   Son laurier,
> Et les Dames leurs beautez.

Therefore, since we all owe our existence to love, let us adore him. Soon we will be old and the sparks of love will perish. The conclusion is, finally, a bit more than Petrarchan. The modern gallant *can* think of enjoyment.

This ode, along with Ronsard's early "Hinne a la Nuit" published in the third book of odes of 1550, reveals the importance of the neolatins to the Pléiade. Translating Pontano was

[1] See, e.g., Guido Guinizelli's "Al cor gentil ripara sempre amore" and Dante's "Amore e cor gentil sono una cosa" (*Vita Nuova,* xx, 3).

part of their poetic apprenticeship, from him they learnt how to write a new kind of poetry in French, and the fact that this poem was not recognized by some of the most distinguished French scholars as being a translation shows that the absorption of humanism by the Pléiade was complete. Their classicism was no learned veneer, but a part of themselves. It is a tribute to du Bellay's greatness—for so to be able to translate as to create a good poem in one's native language is a mark of greatness—that Chamard could write about du Bellay's "happy inspiration" in his "Louanges d'Amour."[1]

Another of du Bellay's odes on a typical humanist theme is "Du Iour des Bacchanales,"[2] a pastiche of various ancient Dionysiac passages.[3] It does not rise to the level of original creation because du Bellay seems to have been unable to bridge the cultural gap, unable to believe, and thus make us believe, even momentarily, in the ancient god, as Crinito succeeded in doing in his hymn to Bacchus or Flaminio in his to Pan. Thus the ode, though competent, is artificial. It seeks to compensate for its imaginative deficiencies by rhetorical straining:

> Quel bruyt inusité
> A mes oreilles tonne?
> Je suy' tout excité
> De l'horreur qui m'étonne:
> Mon coeur fremist et tremble,
> Evoé, Evoé,
> J'oy la voix (ce me semble)
> D'un cornet enroué.[4]

"Du Iour des Bacchanales" like "De L'Inconstance des Choses," is brought to an end by a sudden shift to an ill-matched source. Adapting the ancient device of breaking the narrative with an exclamation,[5] du Bellay leaves Bacchus

[1] Chamard, *du Bellay*, p. 207.

[2] du Bellay, *Oeuvres Poèt.*, ed. Chamard, III, 29–32.

[3] Chamard, *du Bellay, Oeuvres Poèt.*, III, 29, note, lists the following ancient sources: Horace II, 19; Propertius, III, 17; Ovid, *Ars Amoris*, I, 525–64; *Meta.*, IV, 1–35; *Fasti*, III, 713–90; Seneca, *Oedipus*, 403–508.

[4] Cf. *supra*, p. 83.

[5] See Horace III, 3, which du Bellay translates elsewhere, *Oeuvres Poèt.*, ed. Chamard, III, 43–6, as

> Où vas-tu, Muse? si grand'ire
> Ne convient à la douce Lyre.

fighting against the Titans and echoes Horace's familiar "recepto / dulce mihi furere est amico."[1] Admittedly the connection between the two parts of the poem is obvious, but the poet has not bothered to make it explicit.

The remaining odes of du Bellay's first volume are conventional medieval pieces, like the "Chant du Desesperé,"[2] full of courtly love laments; or conventional classical pieces like "A Une Dame Cruelle et Inexorable,"[3] with its rational attack on the lady's obdurate chastity. The last ode,[4] in true Renaissance fashion, proclaims the inevitable Horatian immortality of poets.

The *Recueil de Poesie* of later in the same year, sent to Madame Marguerite and published by her command, contains some miscellaneous poems, two of which are akin to odes,[5] and sixteen *Vers Lyriques* which are odes. The *Vers Lyriques* begin diplomatically with a tribute, "A La Royne," to Catherine de Medici, and then with a eulogistic dedication to Madame Marguerite.[6] There follows a conventional, Horatian-inspired expression of the poet's aims addressed, also diplomatically, to Mellin de Sainct-Gelays, the reigning court poet.[7] Then "A Madame D'Escrire en Sa Langue"[8] gives poetic expression to the ideas of the *Deffence*:

> Princesse, je ne veulx point suyvre
> D'une telle mer les dangers,
> Aymant mieulx entre les miens vivre
> Que mourir chez les estrangers.

He would follow the examples of Boccaccio, Petrarch, Dante, Bembo, and Sannazaro, all of whom are immortal for their vernacular works.

The fifth ode is addressed "A Tresillustre Prince . . . Cardinal de Guyse" and the sixth "A Monseigneur Reverendiss. Cardinal

1 Horace, II, 7, lines 27–8.

2 du Bellay, *Oeuvres Poèt.*, ed. Chamard, III, 37–9.

3 *Ibid.*, III, 43–6.

4 *Ibid.*, III, 51–4.

5 "Prosphonematique au Roy Treschrestien Henry II," *Oeuvres Poèt.*, ed. Chamard, III, 61–74, and "Chant Triumphal sur Le Voyage de Boulongne," *ibid.*, III, 75–86.

6 du Bellay, *Oeuvres Poèt.*, ed. Chamard, III, 86–91 and 91–3.

7 *Ibid.*, III, 93–7.

8 *Ibid.*, III, 97–100.

de Chastillon," while the seventh celebrates "L'Avantretour en France de Mons. Rev. Card. du Bellay,"[1] the poet's distinguished cousin and later half-hearted patron. Four other bread-and-butter odes promise immortality to the master of the king's household, bid a poet abandon the translation of Homer to celebrate the living exploits of Henry against the English (du Bellay disclaiming the while, in conventional Anacreontic-Horatian fashion, such high abilities himself,

> Mais affin! Luc trop courageux,
> Que tu ne delaisses tes jeux),[2]

celebrate the Valois period as a new Augustan age ("La Louange du Feu Roy Francoys et du Treschrestien Roy Henry"), and address "Madame La Contesse de Tonnere."[3]

The remaining four odes are on familiar classical themes and owe a heavy debt to Horace. "Contre Les Avaritieux"[4] begins like Horace III, 24, with the statement that not all the wealth in the world will save you from death and continues, following its original, to praise the simple life of the nomad Scythians and the Getae. The virtues that he praises, however, are rather more aristocratic and romantic than those of the moral Horace; while the closeness to nature that is characteristic of the Pléiade poets appears in du Bellay's reminder of the soul-corroding effects of cupidity: neither love, wine, good food, the lute, nor birds on a lake can take the hunger for gold from the hearts of the avaricious. Now, still in the same ode, du Bellay switches to another Horatian model, III, 1: Sleep visits the hovels of the poor rather than the palaces of the rich. He who is content with little is not troubled by the rough sea nor the wild winds. Du Bellay pictures the pursuit of wealth with its attendant cares and ends in the odic style with himself, the beloved of the muses, "may the wind blow his troubles to England!"[5]

[1] *Ibid.*, III, 101–4, 104–8, 108–14.

[2] Cf. Horace IV, 8, and Anacreon, "Ἀνὰ βάρβιτον δονήσω," ed. Preisendanz, pp. 50–2. Cf. also Ronsard, Laum., *Ed. Crit.*, VI, 161–2.

[3] du Bellay, III, 128–30, 130–4, 142–4, 145–8.

[4] *Ibid.*, III, 108–19.

[5] Cf. Horace I, 21, and many passages in the humanists.

"A Bouju. Les Conditions du Vray Poete"[1] likewise based on a Horatian original, this time IV, 3, "Quem tu Melpomene," again reveals the Pléiade feeling for nature. Here the poet describes, with sensitive realism, the life that he loves by fountains, streams, and thickets. In typical Horatian fashion du Bellay concludes the ode with a compliment to Madame Marguerite, with whose name he would make the woods echo.

"A Mercure et à Sa Lyre. Pour Adoucir La Cruauté de Sa Dame"[2] is the freshest and most powerful of these Horatian odes. It is a shock to realize that it gains this effect by being a translation of one of Horace's less commonly quoted odes![3] Yet it follows its original faithfully, invoking Mercury to give the poet the power to soften his lady with a song and comparing her to a young mare whose frisking excites all the horses in the country. How homely and non-derivative this image sounds until we look at Horace:

> Quae velut latis equa trima campis
> Ludit exsultim metuitque tangi.

Then du Bellay goes on to tell of the power of poetry which can soften fierce beasts and even joy the hearts of sufferers in hell. By a stroke of genius he moves hence into the admonitory myth of the forty-nine murderous Danaids and of love's martyr, Hypermnestra, a myth whose noble witness to love, powerfully told, could be hoped to produce another example of the power of poetry, the lady's softened heart. How superior this seems to du Bellay's other hackneyed Horatian odes patched together out of the familiar old phrases! And yet the credit for everything but the excellent translation must go to Horace!

Despite some fine passages this second volume of du Bellay's seems to have been a work of opportunism rather than of true inspiration. Written quickly to capitalize on the fame brought by the *Deffence*, it tried to praise the proper people at court and to exemplify further the Pléiade theory of "illustrating" the French language by the adaptation of the classics.

The years of hard study to make up for his neglected youth and the great creative outburst of 1548–9 were too much for du Bellay's health and in 1549 he became seriously ill. His friends

[1] du Bellay III, 120–4. [2] *Ibid.*, III, 138–41. [3] Horace III, 11.

despaired for his life but by June 1550 Ronsard could write joyfully:

> Mortes sont les fièvres cruelles
> Qui rongeoient ses cheres mouelles:
> Son oeil est maintenant pareil
> Aux fleurs que trop les pluyes baignent
> Envieuses de leur vermeil,
> Qui plus gailardes se repeignent
> Aux rayons du nouveau Soleil.

However, this was only a reprieve. In 1551 du Bellay was very ill again and his disease left him deaf like Ronsard and delicate in health for the rest of his brief life.

In 1553 du Bellay accompanied his cousin, the Cardinal du Bellay, to Rome. At first filled with enthusiasm for the eternal city he soon became disgusted with the corruption and intrigue of the successive courts of Julius III, Marcellus II, and Paul IV, and, by 1557, he was glad to return to Paris, although he knew that the hostility of family foes promised continual frustration there. On his return to France he published the poetry that he had written in Rome, *Poemata libri iv*, *Les Antiquitez de Rome*, *Regrets*, and *Divers Jeux Rustiques*. Neither the Latin *Poemata* which contains few odes, nor the *Antiquitez de Rome*, an example of the cult of the Roman ruins that goes back through Rucellai,[1] Poggio,[2] and Petrarch to the early middle ages, nor the *Regrets*, a sonnet sequence of great sensitivity, concern us here. The *Jeux Rustiques*, however, though largely composed of poems in the manner of the neolatin *lusus pastoralis*—indeed the first fourteen of the *Jeux Rustiques* are adaptations of Navagero's *Lusus* of 1530[3]—do contain some odes which we will examine briefly.

The "Hymne de Santé,"[4] dedicated to Robert de La Haye

[1] Bernardo Rucellai, *De Urbe Roma*, written at the end of the fifteenth century but not published until the eighteenth century by J. M. Tartinius in *Rerum Italicarum Scriptores*, II (Florentiae, 1748).

[2] Poggio Bracciolini, *Ruinarum urbis Romae Descriptio* (1430).

[3] Chamard, *Oeuvres Poèt. du Bellay*, V, v.

[4] du Bellay, *Oeuvres Poèt.*, ed. Chamard, V, 264–77. Chamard, *ibid.*, V, 264, note, says that this poem is related to Marot's "Cantique à la Déese Santé." See also Flaminio's "Hymnus in Bonam Valetudinem," supra and *Carm.* (1743), pp. 9–10; Ronsard's "A Phoebus, pour guarir le Roy Charles IX," Laumonier, *Les Oeuvres Complètes de Pierre de Ronsard* (Paris, 1914–19), II, 408–12; and Jean Antoine de Baïf's "Pean Dithyrambique A La Santé," *Euvres en Rime*, ed. Marty-Laveaux (Paris, 1881–90), IV, 294–5.

whose recovery from illness the poet celebrates, possesses the familiar ode characteristics, but it lacks the usual lyric intensity and concentration. Despite some good stanzas the ode lumbers on for fourteen pages at a pedestrian, narrative pace. Du Bellay describes La Haye's illness, how, when he was near death, the laurel withered and Hippocrene dried up. But Apollo saved him. Therefore, praise the poet. Let the Dryads, Naiads, etc., rejoice and sing the praises of Santé, the animating force of Nature, the soul of the universe. Nothing pleases without her. Prometheus stole fire from heaven and disease came to the earth and death quickened her pace. Then Santé came to repair the loss. Therefore let us raise her an altar. Let the nymphs (each of whom is summoned allusively) assemble to sing her praises. Let the poets come too. Now du Bellay asks La Haye to tell him of the banks of the Styx to help him in his translation of the sixth book of the *Aeneid* and also to tell him of the Elysian fields where the great poets are. But, before death comes, let us create poetry that will make us immortal[1]:

Mais si l'homme peult revivre
   Par le livre,
Ton image n'ira pas
Au rang de ces pauvres nues
   Incongnues,
Qui se lamentent là bas.

Length rather than inspiration is the characteristic of the other odes of this volume whose debts to the classics or the Italians is not compensated for by bright flashes of originality. Thus there are tedious odes on the birth of the Duke of Beaumont; on Henry II, the latter adapted from Annibal Caro's "Venite all'ombra de' gran gigle d'oro"; on Paul IV; to the Prince de Melphe, an uninspired pseudo-Pindaric in thirteen "pauses" each of one long and one short stanza[2]; and to Diane de Poitiers, these last, poems that do not live up to the liveliness of the lady.

In 1559 du Bellay wrote an epithalamium for the marriage

1 For the sentiments cf. du Bellay, *Oeuvres Poèt.*, III, 4–8, and Ronsard, Laum., *Ed. Crit.*, II, 40–3, and I, 214–16.

2 For a discussion of du Bellay's indebtedness to Pindar in his ode to the Prince de Melphe see Isidore Silver, "Did Du Bellay know Pindar," *PMLA* 56 (1941), 1007–19.

of his old friend and protectress, Madame Marguerite, to Filiberto Emmanuele, Duke of Savoy. At the same time he wrote a *tombeau* for her brother, Henry II. These were his last works. On January 1st 1560 Joachim du Bellay died of apoplexy in his thirty-fifth year. Ronsard wrote,

> Je pleurais du Bellay qui estoit de mon âge,
> De mon art, de mes moeurs et de mon parentage,
> Lequel apres avoir d'une si docte voix
> Tant de fois rechanté les princes et les rois,
> Est mort pauvre, chétif, sans nulle recompense,
> Sinon un peu d'honneur que luy garde la France.[1]

A generation later Edmund Spenser, in his *envoy* to his translation of du Bellay's *Ruines of Rome*, paid a tribute to

> Bellay, first garland of free Poësie
> That France brought forth, though fruitfull of brave wits,
> Well worthie thou of immortalitie.

However, du Bellay was falling out of print even by the end of the sixteenth century and in the seventeenth century he suffered an eclipse that lasted until Sainte-Beuve began his rehabilitation of the Pléiade in 1828.[2]

What du Bellay had done, however, did not die. The French language never again needed defence against Latin. By du Bellay alone it had been sufficiently "illustrated." Its poetry had been brought up to date, linguistically, prosodically, and stylistically. It had been made superior, even, to what the Italians were doing at the time, so that it was from the Pléiade that the Italians learnt how to write odes. Du Bellay had enriched French poetry with new lyric forms, especially the sonnet and the ode, and with a new kind of prosody characterized by variety and independence in contrast to medieval fixed form. Horace and the Horatian outlook on life had become its familiar, classical realism and classical philosophy, the precise pictorial image, and pagan mythology, its accepted characteristics. And, with the new inspiration had come a new kind of verse freely invented to suit the subject, light, graceful, and song-like. These things du Bellay had been the first to introduce

[1] Quoted by E. Courbet, "notice" on du Bellay in *Poésies Françaises et Latines de Joachim du Bellay*, I (Paris, 1918), xlvii.

[2] In his *Tableau historique et critique de la poésie française et du théatre français au xvie siècle*.

into French poetry with sufficient genius to be influential. Unfortunately his contribution has always been overshadowed by that of his greater contemporary, Ronsard.

The story of Ronsard's exciting youth, of his promising diplomatic career, then of the illness that left him deaf with blighted prospects and only scholarship to turn to,[1] is too well known to be repeated here. Suffice it to recollect that after he was tonsured, Ronsard was invited by Lazare de Baïf to attend the lectures of the celebrated humanist, Jean Dorat, whom Baïf had engaged as tutor for his son, Jean Antoine, and that, when the elder Baïf died in 1547 and Dorat went to be principal of the Collège de Coqueret, Ronsard and Baïf followed him there and later brought du Bellay to join the group.[2]

Under the expert but pedantic tuition of Dorat Ronsard learned rather too much erudite mythology and an admiration for Greek authors that seemed to vary in direct proportion with their difficulty.[3] But from Dorat he also acquired a

[1] Nolhac, *Rons. et l'Human.*, pp. 145, 147, 152, 154, 157, 163, 168, 178, 202, discusses the various learned friendships that Ronsard had throughout his life. Ronsard was always a scholar and a philologian of some pretensions, Nolhac, pp. 133, 141–2. He visited many learned libraries, Nolhac, pp. 75, 135 ff.

[2] These biographical statements are based on Laumonier, *Rons. Poète*, pp. 1–26.

[3] Dorat not only made his students labour through Aeschylus and Pindar, but also, with no discrimination, through Callimachus and Lycophron, see Laumonier, *Rons. Poète*, passim. Ronsard's own remarks about Dorat as a teacher and scholar are illuminating:

> . . . tu brises l'Ignorance,
> Renommé parmy la France
> Comme un oracle des Dieux,
> Pour desnouer aux plus sages
> Les plus ennouez passages
> Des livres laborieux.

A later reference of Ronsard to his studies reflects his schooling with Dorat:

> J'ay l'esprit tout ennuyé
> D'avoir trop estudié
> Les Phaenomenes d'Arate:
> Il est temps que je m'esbate,
> Et que j'aille aux champs jouër.

Admittedly the Renaissance, with its interest in astrology, made Aratus one of its most popular authors. However, the courtiers did not read him in the original as poor Ronsard did. The popularity of Aratus does not alter the fact that Ronsard's classical studies were often unnecessarily tedious.

breadth of view, a loftiness and nobility of style, and a new outlook on life that brought with it a new range of subject matter and a new kind of imagery. That is, from Dorat Ronsard received the education and the inspiration that enabled him to revivify French poetry so that, with the publication of his odes in 1550, a new era for French literature begins.

We now consider that imitation is either a regrettable, if not reprehensible enslavement of one's genius, or mediocrity's substitute for originality. It takes an effort to put oneself in the mind of Ronsard who saw only two courses open to him as a poet, either to continue writing in the French lyric tradition, which would mean imitating his immediate predecessors, or to follow the example of the illustrious Italians who asserted their independence by spurning their recent precursors only to imitate their more remote ancestors. In either case it was a question of imitation—people were not so jealous of the title "original" then as now. The choice lay between the more or less daring forms of it, between a break with the past or a continuation in the old tradition. Thus, when Ronsard chose to imitate the ancients, he was evincing as courageous an originality as any in the sixteenth century.[1] That his hardihood jeopardized his career is illustrated by the well known story of Mellin de Sainct-Gelays' malicious reading of the 1550 volume of odes before the assembled court and of Ronsard's defence by Madame Marguerite and her chancellor, Michel de L'Hospital.[2]

Horace was Ronsard's first and lasting love.[3] He, in his lighter pieces, in his regrets for the ephemerality of youth and

[1] See Ronsard's own statements on the subject, "combien . . . doit on vanter le courreur, qui galopant librement par les campaignes Attiques, et Romaines osa tracer un sentier inconnu pour aller a l'immortalité," and "Donques m'acheminant par un sentier inconnu, et monstrant le moien de suivre Pindare, et Horace . . . ," "Preface Au Lecteur," *Odes* 1550, Laum., *Ed. Crit.*, I, 43 and 45.

[2] Henri Chamard, *Histoire de la Pléiade*, I (Paris, 1939), 362–3 and Laumonier, *Rons. Poète*, pp. 72–3. The story is told by Scevole de Saint-Marthe in his *Elogia*, Nolhac, *Rons. et l'Human.*, pp. 180–2. Nolhac says that the chancellor, Michel de L'Hospital, also defended Ronsard at court.

[3] Laumonier, *Rons. Poète*, p. 47.

beauty and love, where the burden of his song is "and present pleasures chuse," Horace, in his Epicurean praise of the simple life, of nature, of friendship, of conviviality, and of the universal human joys, was closest in spirit to Ronsard. Anacreon, too, was close, and it was for that reason that Ronsard hailed Stephanus' edition with such joy[1] and immediately began writing Anacreontics. But Anacreon could be only a phase; for, after 1500 years of Christianity, the moral undertones of Horace were more lastingly congenial, even to the most pagan of Renaissance poets than the insouciant hedonism of Anacreon. Despite Ronsard's five year enthusiam[2] for Pindar that bore fruit in fifteen triadic odes and left a lasting mark on his more noble lyrics, despite the later desire to imitate Vergil that gave birth to the not regrettably incomplete *Franciade*, neither the genius of Ronsard nor the ethos of the age was in consonance with the heroic. Thus Pindar, and Vergil, too, were only passing phases. Of the other ancient writers, Catullus exerted the most important influence on Ronsard, in occasional poems addressed to friends and in brief love lyrics, and of course Ovid was Ronsard's, as everyman's, master of mythology. The ancient elegists and epigrammatists had their influence, too.

Ronsard's classics, however, were not just the ancients. Apart from Petrarch, whose influence was chiefly exerted in the sonnets, which are not under consideration here, Ronsard's other classics included the neolatin writers Pontano, Marullo, Sannazaro, Bembo, Navagero, Flaminio, Secundus, and Macrin,[3] and, in the particular sphere of the Pindaric, the Italian Alamanni, or the neolatin, Lampridio, depending

[1] In "Nous ne tenons en nostre main," Laum., *Ed. Crit.*, VI, 174–6. See also Ronsard's elegy "A Chrestophe de Choiseul" prefaced to Belleau's 1556 translation of Anacreon and published later in that year in Ronsard's second book of *Hymnes*. Here Ronsard praises Anacreon's gentle sweetness and condemns the arrogance, obscurity, and noisy pretentiousness of Pindar whom no one understands and whose verse is only good for frightening simple school-boys, Laumonier, *Rons. Poète*, pp. 170–1.

[2] Laumonier, *Rons. Poète*, pp. 47 and 58, says that Ronsard's period of Pindaric discipleship was from 1545–6 to 1550–1.

[3] Cuccoli, *Flaminio*, p. 260; Nolhac, *Rons. et l'Human.*, pp. 14–15; Chamard, *Origines de la Poésie Française de la Renaissance*, pp. 299–302.

upon which French scholars you choose to put your faith in.[1]

All of this is not to deny that Ronsard was, despite anything he might say,[2] indebted to many of his French predecessors,[3] especially Marot.

One of the reasons that Ronsard imitated the ancients was so that he could have greater prosodic freedom. Yet, once he had gained this freedom he found that he must limit it by imposing certain rules. Thus his strophes, while freely invented, usually did not exceed twelve lines in length and were, in fact, very often no more than composites of familiar shorter units.[4] Then the length of the individual verse was never less than three or more than twelve syllables, with the short verses, i.e.,

[1] For the possible influence of Alamanni on Ronsard see Nolhac, *Rons. et l'Human.*, p. 47; Carducci, "Ode," p. 275; Vianey and Hauvette quoted in Laumonier, *Rons. Poète*, p. 704; for the possible influence of Lampridio, see Nolhac, pp. 15, 45–8; Laumonier, p. 344, fn. 2. For a refutation of the view that Ronsard was indebted to Alamanni, see Laumonier, p. 704. Nolhac, pp. 45–8, suggests that Ronsard may have been influenced by Lampridio through Dorat who probably knew Lampridio's works in manuscript (we must remember that Lampridio's odes, though written long before, were not published until 1550). Laumonier, *Rons. Poète*, p. 344, fn. 2, agrees with this.

Nolhac's other theory, p. 15 and p. 48, fn. 2, that Ronsard may have been influenced by Lampridio through the volume published by the Chancellor of the University of Paris in 1548, *Doctissimorum nostra aetate Italorum epigrammata*, which contained a few poems by Lampridio is untenable because the selection made of Lampridio there does not include any of the Pindaric odes. Nolhac also, p. 342, suggests that Dorat and his pupils may have got to know the works of Lampridio through Michel de L'Hospital who was a student of Lampridio's at Padua between 1526–32, who writes of Lampridio as a poet, and who says that he studied Pindar.

[2] Ronsard, "Preface Au Lecteur," *Odes*, 1550, Laum., *Ed. Crit.*, I, 44, says "et ne voiant en nos Poëtes François, chose qui fust suffisante d'imiter; j'allai voir les étrangers" and *Ibid.*, I, 45, "l'imitation des nostres m'est tant odieuse (d'autant que la langue est encores en son enfance) que pour cette raison je me suis eloingné d'eus, prenant stile apart, sens apart, euvre apart, ne desirant avoir rien de commun avecq' une si monstreuse erreur."

[3] Chamard, *du Bellay*, p. 76, lists as predecessors of the Pléiade Maurice Scève, Hugues Salel, Antoine Heroet, Mellin de Sainct-Gelays, Jacques Peletier, Guillaume des Autelz.

[4] Laumonier, *Rons. Poète*, p. 673, says that Ronsard only exceeded the twelve verse maximum eleven times. Peletier believed that the strophe should not exceed ten verses and preferred less than ten.

those of three, four, or five syllables, always mixed with longer verses, although the longer verses might be used by themselves to form isometric strophes.[1] In the specific case of the Pindarics Ronsard imitated not only the triadic structure of Pindar but also, to some extent, the physiognomy of the Pindaric ode as it appeared in sixteenth-century editions. To get the visual effect of the Pindaric Ronsard made his stanzas long and his verses short, of six, seven, or eight syllables. However, he did not vary the length of verse within the strophe[2] nor did he go so far as to break words at the ends of lines as some of the English Pindarizers did later. The use of short lines was characteristic of all the early imitators of Pindar and tended to produce monotony and an effect of triviality which was inconsistent with the dignity of the subjects and sentiments of the usual Pindaric.

The fifteen Pindarics were not the only odes that Ronsard composed of double strophic systems. Another dozen odes followed one strophic pattern for the odd numbered stanzas and another for the even. This was in the tradition of some fifteenth-century songs and of some of the psalms of Marot. Such odes were sung to two different melodies.[3]

We have already discussed Ronsard's earliest published ode, "Des beautez qu'il voudroit en s'Amie," which appeared in Peletier's *Oeuvres Poètiques* of 1547. Most of Ronsard's other early odes were published in the *Bocage* of the 1550 edition of the *Odes*, being relegated to that position because they were unmeasured. All but one of these poems is in every real sense an ode. The one exception, "D'un Rossignol abusé"[4] in couplet riming heptasyllables, with its lengthy account of the deceived bird and the somewhat lame analogy with the poet, seems a rather feeble attempt at a fable in the manner of La Fontaine —Horatian influence reveals itself only in the conclusion of the

[1] Laumonier, *Rons. Poète*, pp. 673–4.

[2] Sébilet in his translation of Euripides' *Iphigenia* (1549) was more daring. He used verses that varied in length from two to thirteen syllables, Laum., *Rons. Poète*, p. xxii.

[3] Charles Comte and Paul Laumonier, "Ronsard et Les Musiciens du xvie Siècle, Contribution à l'histoire de la Pléiade," *RHLF*, VII (Paris, 1900), 369, and Laumonier, *Rons. Poète*, pp. 642, 655–7.

[4] Paul Laumonier, *Pierre de Ronsard, Oeuvres Complètes*, Edition Critique, II (Paris, 1924), 165–9.

poem where the poet imagines his prayer answered and pictures himself in the arms of his lady. The other poems of the 1550 *Bocage* exemplify various species of the genre "ode," political, moral, religious, amorous, bacchic, and personal, and are interesting chiefly for the early date of their composition. "Avantentrée du Roi Trescrestien a Paris, L'an 1549"[1] describes the poet's emotions as he awaits the king's triumphal entry into his capital; "Contre la Jeunesse Françoise corrumpue"[2] laments, as Horace did after the disgrace of Carrhae, the inability of the French to win back their trophies from the Spanish because of the moral degeneracy of their youth; "A Dieu Pour La Famine"[3] prays the Lord of Hosts who preserved the Israelites from the Egyptians and rained manna in the desert to feed his people, the French, and afflict only the heathen[4]; one "A Cassandre," "Si cet enfant qui erre / Vagabond par la terre,"[5] written in the Anacreontic, Ovidian, Petrarchan tradition, describes the heat of passion with which Cassandra's beauty inspires the poet; another "A Cassandre," "Le printens vient, naissez fleurettes,"[6] elaborates on that beauty; "Chant de Folie à Bacchus"[7] invokes the god and describes his cult in the language of Horace[8]; "A lui mesme"[9] reproaches himself for his slothful neglect of poetry; and "A son retour de Gascongne, voiant de loin Paris,"[10] tells of the

[1] Laum., *Edition Critique*, I (Paris, 1924), 17–23. Laumonier, *Rons. Poète*, p. 29, says that this ode was published a few days before the king's entry into Paris in June 1549. Nolhac, *Rons. et l'Human.*, p. 107, finds that this ode echoes Callimachus' hymns to Phoebus and Zeus.

[2] Laum., *Ed. Crit.*, II, 189–91.

[3] *Ibid.*, II, 184–6.

[4] Cf. Horace I, 21:

> Hic bellum lacrimosum, hic miseram famem
> Pestemque a populo et principe Caesare in
> Persas atque Britannos
> Vestra motus aget prece.

[5] Laum., *Ed. Crit.*, II, 163–4.

[6] *Ibid.*, II, 187–8.

[7] *Ibid.*, II, 177–80.

[8] Ronsard is particularly indebted to Horace III, 25.

[9] Laum., *Ed. Crit.*, II, 175–7.

[10] *Ibid.*, II, 199–202. Laumonier, *Rons. Poète*, p. 37, and Chamard, *du Bellay*, p. 37, fns. 1 and 5, think that this ode was written towards the end of 1547 or the beginning of 1548 and tells of Ronsard's return from the trip on which he accidentally met du Bellay. This adds extra meaning to his hopes for the future.

poet's mixed emotions on his return to the city, his anticipated joy at the re-encounter of friends and his conviction that he will do great things. Three other poems that appeared in the *Bocage* of 1550 were rehabilitated as odes in later editions,[1] although they retained their basic flaw of not being measured to the lyre. They were "A son Lut,"[2] constructed of two different strophic patterns, which discusses the poet's "election" and his high function as the gods' interpreter; "A Gaspard d'Auvergne,"[3] in triads, which teaches the Horatian lessons, often in Horatian phraseology, of profiting by today, of avoiding the heights, of governing one's will, of being courageous in adversity, and prudent in prosperity; and a second "A Gaspard d'Auvergne,"[4] in unmeasured stanzas, which maintains, again largely in Horatian idiom, the inevitability of fate and the brevity and misery of human life.

Now, with his earliest odes dismissed to the *Bocage* and his life-long enthusiasm for Horace temporarily in abeyance, in the flush of Pindaric pride inspired by Dorat, Ronsard opened his first volume of poetry with thirteen[5] pretentious triadic odes. Because of the poetic genius of Ronsard these were the most important Pindarics published in any language thus far.

Ronsard's Pindarics fall into three roughly equal groups, poems in praise of the royal family, poems in praise of important members of the nobility, and poems in praise of Ronsard's fellow poets. One third of them celebrate what could be considered to be victories, the peace with England, Cerizoles, the *coup de Jarnac*, Madame Marguerite's triumph over Sainct-Gelays and the court poets, and Dorat's over ignorance. The technique of the odes is always the same, mechanically adopted from Pindar. There is the brilliant opening, the myth, the *sententiae*, the comments on the poet's art, his intentions, his inspiration, and his rivals, and the encomium, tempered with counsel, of the chosen hero. The form is triadic and more successful than any of the other modern attempts at the triadic

1 Eg., in that of 1572.

2 Laum., *Ed. Crit.*, II, 155–62.

3 *Ibid.*, II, 169–74.

4 *Ibid.*, II, 180–3.

5 Chamard, *Histoire Pléiade*, I, 340, notes that the "usure" to Carnavalet (I, ode 8) was not yet in triadic form.

in the languages we are discussing here; for Ronsard was able to create and harmoniously couple two different stanzas whose movement was easily caught and readily retained. Thus, despite the complicated structure, we are able to recognize what amounts to a repeated melody and following refrain. The ode, then, has some rhythmic shape, and its sound forms part of the communication and enjoyment of the poem. Unfortunately this enjoyment is limited by the monotony of the prevailingly heptasyllabic or octosyllabic verse which was perhaps partly inspired by the example of Alamanni.

However, it is the content rather than the sound of the odes to which most readers take exception. Ronsard's Pindarics are flatly pedantic. The stanzas, much to the annoyance of his contemporaries, were labelled "strophe," "antistrophe," and "epode," and the *sententiae*, often borrowings from the classics, were indicated by quotation marks. Then, Ronsard tried to recapture Pindar's tone, although the society in which he wrote and Ronsard's position in it, were in no way comparable to Pindar's. Thus when he strives for the heroic he merely sounds strained, when he seeks to be prophetic he becomes heavily didactic, and when he reminds his prince of his debt to poetry he is both sycophantic and vulgar—a poet who writes encomia on commission can maintain his dignity easier than one who writes for patronage. However, in his recreation of some of the myths and in many of the descriptive and reflective passages Ronsard shows his true greatness as a poet. His translations, too, are often incomparable renderings. It is the whole that fails rather than its individual components. Of course there is also much more coherence and connection in Ronsard than there is in Pindar, by no means a fault. With these general introductory remarks let us look at the individual Pindarics.[1]

[1] For a thorough study of very many aspects of Ronsard's imitation of Pindar, see Isidore Silver, *The Pindaric Odes of Ronsard* (Paris, 1937). Silver's study is a sober antidote to impressionistic criticism. Yet *μήδεν ἄγαν*. Silver gives the impression that Ronsard too had a card catalogue of Pindaric phrases with some 12,000 entries. To take an unfair example, Silver, pp. 36–7, says that in the ode to du Bellay, *Odes* I, 11, antistrophe 6, Ronsard's image of rowing his boat over the sea of virtues that covers du Bellay comes from two passages in Pindar, *Pythia*, IV, 202 and *Nemea* IV, 36 ff. That the impartial reader may reach his own conclusion, I shall quote the passage from Ronsard and the two from Pindar, both in Lattimore's

The ode that Ronsard chose in 1560 to put at the head of his works, "Au Roy Henri II de ce nom Sur la Paix faicte entre luy et le Roy d'Angleterre, l'an 1550,"[1] was one of his latest written Pindarics. It was published separately in 1550 after the four books of odes.[2] As the title suggests, peace is the theme of this ode, and the king's peace governs the introductory moralizing and leads into the philosophical digression, itself virtually a myth, on the organization of chaos into creation and the function of peace in the maintenance of the cosmos, a digression which embodies the myth of the Trojan war and the story of the French eponymous hero, Francus.[3] Then the benefits of the

English translation and in the original Greek, so that there can be no questioning of the translation:

Mes doigts ne pourroient se lasser
De faire mon bateau passer
Par les vagues de ton renom
Et ramerois encor, sin-on . . .

and slakeless the oars went dipping from the speed in their hands

ἐιρεσία δ' ὑπεχώρησεν ταχειᾶν ἐκ παλαμᾶν ἄκορος.

(*Pythia* IV, 202)

Still, though the deep sea's water lie
between, resist conspiracy. . . .
ἔμπα, καΐπερ ἔχει βαθεία ποντιὰς ἅλμα
μέσσον, ἀντίτειν' ἐπιβουλίᾳ.

(*Nemea* IV, 36–7)

The card catalogue method with entries made under rowing and sea can produce such absurdities. Surely the "sources" of this imagery lie in the two conceits, that of the poet as boatsman found commonly enough in Pindar and elsewhere in the classical tradition, and that of the sea of virtues, an allegorical figure of the sort found frequently in medieval poetry. We find this sort of imagery in Spenser or in the Capilupi.

For an excellent analysis of the nature of Ronsard's imagery see Chamard, *Histoire de la Pléiade*, I, 351 ff.

[1] Laum., *Ed. Crit.*, III (Paris, 1921), 3–35.

[2] The earliest of Ronsard's Pindaric odes is generally agreed to be the ode on Cerizoles (Laum., *Ed. Crit.*, I, 82–98), which was written about 1546—for a discussion of the date see Chamard, *Hist. Pléiade*, I, 340. The latest was the ode to Michel de L'Hospital (Laum., *Ed. Crit.*, III, 118–63), which was written late in 1550 but not published until 1552. The ode to Henry II, written in 1550 and published independently after the four books of odes, thus comes at almost the end of Ronsard's Pindaric period (Chamard, *Hist. Pléiade*, I, 340).

[3] Laumonier, *Rons. Poète*, p. 302, finds that the prophecy of Cassandra comes from Pindar's fourth *Pythian* and Lycophron's *Alexandra*.

present peace are gratefully recounted, its chief architect, Anne de Montmorency, Constable of France, is praised, and the king's return is celebrated with great joy, but with the *memento mori* that only the poet confers immortality. The penultimate triad lauds the attainments of the youthful monarch and "educates the prince" in practical statecraft. The conclusion combines a prayer for the king with an unabashed request for money.

The ode has "a beginning that shines from afar," a sententious, epigrammatic statement of the theme, inspired by Pindar and Clement Marot,[1]

> Toute royauté qui dedaigne
> L'humble vertu pour sa compaigne,
> Souvent dresse le front trop haut:
> Et de son heur outrecuidée
> Court vague, sans estre guidée
> De la clarté qui lui defaut.

Aphorisms are liberally scattered throughout. The eighth antistrophe opens with a debt to Pindar,

> Nul n'est exent de la fortune,
> Car sans egard elle importune
> Et peuples, et rois et seigneurs.[2]

The eighth epode voices the wisdom both of Homer and of the Psalmist,[3]

> Et qu'esse que des mortels?
> Si au matin ils fleurissent,
> Le soir ils ne sont plus tels,
> Pareils aux champs qui fenissent.

While the ninth antistrophe has its proverbs about princes and

[1] Laumonier, *Oeuvres Complètes de Pierre de Ronsard* (Paris, 1914–19), VII, 223, finds Ronsard here indebted to the 5th *Pythian*, strophe 1, and to the beginning of Marot's Epistle to the Duke d'Enghien on his victory at Cerizoles, the poem that Ronsard dismisses so patronizingly in his ode on Cerizoles. Henceforth this edition of Ronsard will be referred to as Laum., *Oeuvres Rons.* to distinguish it from the *Edition Critique*. Cf. p. 204, fn. 3, supra.

[2] From *Pythia* 3, ep. 4 and *Olympia* 2, ant. and ep. 2, Laum., *Oeuvres Rons.*, VII, 227. The reference is to Montgomery's disgrace from 1540–7.

[3] See psalm 90, verses 5 and 6, and psalm 102, verse 11, and the *Iliad*, VI, 146 ff.

governors,[1] and the tenth strophe about calumniators.[2] Other general truths, about the poet's craft, are taken right out of Pindar and put, as Pindar would have them, in the middle of the poem. In the sixth epode we read,

> Tousjours un propos desplait
> Aus oreilles attendantes,
> Si plein outre reigle il est
> De paroles abondantes.
> Celui qui en peu de vers
> Estraint un sujet divers,
> Se mét au chef la couronne:
> " De ceste fleur que voici,
> " Et de celle, et celle aussi,
> " La mouche son miel façonne.[3]

Then the Pindaric device of interrupting oneself to invoke the Muse to set one straight is called upon to rescue the poet from the Francus myth,

> Muse, repren l'aviron,
> Et racle la prochaine onde
> Qui nous baigne à l'environ
> Sans estre ainsi vagabonde.[4]

The poet's self, again in Pindaric manner intrudes here and there throughout the poem, e.g., in epode eight Ronsard says,

> Pousse ma nef, je serai
> Des premiers qui passerai
> Mes compagnons de vitesse.

The final triad is almost entirely about the poet. All the characteristics of the Pindaric are here, then, except the vitality of Pindar!

Despite all his learning and all his care, indeed, because of them, Ronsard has not created a living poem. We could accept the peculiarity of the triadic form, despite the fact that it appears at its most contrived in this ode,[5] as not being, perhaps, inevitable, but as embodying a convention not unakin to that

[1] *Pythia* I, ant. 5, Laum., *Oeuvres Rons.*, VII, 227.

[2] From Pindar, *Pyth.* 2, str. 3, Laum., *Rons. Poète*, p. 3.

[3] Cf. Pindar, *Pyth.* 9, str. 4 and *Pyth.* 10, ep. 3.

[4] The beginning of epode 6 in Ronsard. Cf. Pindar, *Pyth.* 10, ep. 3.

[5] For a detailed analysis of the metrical structure of the strophes of the "Ode . . . sur la Paix" see Chamard, *Hist. Pl.* I, 346.

of the native French lyric tradition of the middle ages. But the myth within a myth within a myth, recounted at Vergilian rather than Pindaric length and for no very compelling reason, could only be made acceptable by a brilliant treatment of the three threadbare themes, by an evocative image to stimulate the imagination jaded by too many accounts of the Trojan Wars or by the suggestiveness of a slightly new conception. But Ronsard works his way through his myths in a pedestrian fashion and, when he expressly tells us at the beginning of Cassandra's prophecy that Francus did not hear it, we cannot help feeling that, if he was not listening, why should we. This impression of laborious and uninspired pedantry is further enhanced by the clearly marked quotations from ancient authors and by such ink-horn terms as "naufs" (epode 2, line 1) and "dextre" (strophe 7, line 4). On top of this Ronsard's crude demand for a present after 32 verses about himself appears as a sorry vulgarization of Pindar. Thus the poem does not come off. It is not natural nor inspired, but all too mechanically Pindaric.

The second Pindaric ode—I am here following the order in which Ronsard arranged his odes in his latest collected edition—very much briefer, is again addressed to Henry II, the third is appropriately devoted to the praise of the queen, Catherine de Medici, the fourth, scrupulously observing precedence, exalts Mme Marguerite, the new champion of learning, while the fifth, which exercises a certain fascination because of its almost prophetic insight, is a warning to the most powerful prelate in France, Ronsard's schoolmate, Charles de Guise, Cardinal of Lorraine. The fate of his two nephews comes into our minds when we read this short ode admonishing Guise against over-weening ambition, against ὕβρις. Let us quote the closing lines:

Donques, Prelat de bon heur,
Qui tiens le sommet d'honneur,
Et en qui le Roi contemple
Des vertus le vrai exemple,
Sois content d'un si grand bien,
Et ne souhette plus rien. . . .
Cesse de plus rien attendre
Et ne veilles point apprendre
A te faire un nouveau dieu.

History has given force to what was probably no more than another imitation of Pindar.[1]

The first five Pindarics were dedicated to the highest temporal and spiritual powers. The next five Pindarics honour various members of the aristocracy. The first of these, heavily indebted to Pindar, celebrates the victory of François de Bourbon, Comte d'Enghien, over the Spanish and Imperial forces at Cerizoles in the Piedmont in 1544. It was probably written about 1546 and is generally regarded as Ronsard's earliest Pindaric.[2] "Le Victoire de François de Bourbon" opens with a condescending dismissal of Marot's "simple" poem written immediately after the victory and the announcement of Ronsard's intention of writing something truly worthy of the event; for he is more learned and more laborious in his art. Again there is the Pindaric bow with its shafts that will hit the mark and the "well-combed" Muses. Bourbon's earlier martial exploits are alluded to and his feats in the present battle are vividly described in brilliant imagery. Then Ronsard adopts Pindar's conceit[3] of sending a messenger to the underworld to announce to the dead Bourbons the glory of the living representative of their race. The recollection of the noble dead causes Ronsard to end his ode, as Pindar often did, with a reminder that Fortune often fails, that all that is human is mortal, and that only the gods remain impassible. The last epode reads like the concluding lines of a Greek tragedy. There is no easy Christian consolation here:

Autour de la vie humaine
Maint orage va volant,
Qui ores le bien ameine,
Ores le mal violant:

[1] From Pindar, *Ol.* 5, concl., Laum., *Oeuvres Rons.* VII, 230. Silver, *Pindaric Odes Rons.*, pp. 80–1, maintains that this is a shockingly inappropriate and uncritical borrowing from Pindar. I feel, however, that the term "nouveau dieu," while admittedly shocking when applied to a priest, is appropriate in warning a wordly prelate against political ambition, especially one who went, in the intimate circle of the Louvre, by the name of "Mercure" (see Chamard, *Hist. Pléiade* II, 278–9). I do not suppose for one moment that Ronsard is accusing Guise of Messianic aspirations. It will be noted that "dieu" is a term that Ronsard uses of kings (for which, see Silver, p. 79).

[2] Chamard, *Hist. Pléiade* I, 340.

[3] See Pindar, *Ol.* 14, where the conventional Echo is sent and *Ol.* 8, where we have the messenger referred to here, "Ἀγγελία," "the daughter of Mercury who is the nephew of Atlas." Cf. *Pyth.* 5, strophe 4.

La face de la Fortune
Ne se monstre aus Rois toute une,
Et jamais nul ne se treuve
Qui jusqu'à la fin espreuve
L'entiere felicité.
Les hommes journaliers meurent,
Les dieus seulement demeurent
Exentés d'aversité.[1]

The sobriety of the verse, the austerity of the imagery, and the stoicism of the sentiments makes this Ronsard's finest bit of writing in the Pindaric vein. Here Ronsard rises to the level of the great tragedians. He has recaptured the essential spirit of the ancient outlook on life and succeeded in communicating what is universally valid in it in imagery and rhythms as memorable as anything in Greek literature.

The seventh ode, to the Seigneur de Carnavalet, is a *contaminatio* of two odes of Pindar, the tenth and thirteenth *Olympians*, and, like the tenth *Olympian*, it is followed by a "usure," the eighth ode. The ninth ode celebrates the freak duelling victory which has given the French language the proverbial expression "un coup de Jarnac." The tenth ode, "A Michel De L'Hospital, Chancelier de France," is by far the longest and the most important of the Pindaric odes and was considered by his contemporaries to be Ronsard's greatest work.[2] Though it was probably written in 1550 after the ode to Henry II on the peace made with England, it was not published until 1552, in the fifth book of odes.

When Ronsard decided to express in an ode his gratitude to his protector Michel de L'Hospital, what were the considerations that guided his invention? From a close examination of the poem it appears that Ronsard felt that the most appropriate way of praising the chancellor was to reveal, in their greatest beauty, the nobility of the ideals which L'Hospital was defending. Therefore the central passage of the ode must express the

[1] Silver, *Pind. Odes Rons.*, p. 115, finds that lines 1 and 2 echo *Ol.* 7, 24ff.; that line 2 echoes in addition *Pyth.* 3, 104 ff.; that lines 3, 4, and 9 echo *Ol.* 12, 5 ff., with lines 3 and 4 echoing in addition *Ol.* 2, 30 ff. and *Pyth.* 8, 92 ff., and line 9 echoing *Pyth.* 3, 104 ff. and *Ol.* 2, 30 ff.; that line 10 echoes *Pyth.* 8, 92 ff.; and that line 12 echoes frag. 143 (600) in Fennell.

[2] E. Gandar, *Ronsard Considéré comme Imitateur d'Homère et de Pindare* (Metz, 1854), p. 93.

highest humanist concept of the nature of poetry, the Platonic rather than the medieval or Aristotelian. Then, L'Hospital must be praised and Mme Marguerite, the princess whom he served, Ronsard's other defender. She must have the place of honour. Thus the general outline of the middle and end of the ode was determined.

But Ronsard felt himself, and L'Hospital, as his protector, to be the restorers of genuine poetry in France.[1] That is, L'Hospital brought back the Muses at the god-appointed time. This implies destiny and a moment when L'Hospital's soul was created and offers Ronsard an opportunity of praising the chancellor through the vivid imagery of the tenth book of the *Republic*, the account of the Parcae. Then the restoration of true poetry calls for an account of what true poetry was like, i.e., a description of the golden age of antiquity. So the central part of the ode takes its form.

Now, in the first part of the ode there must be a myth, that is a requisite of the genre. And what better subject for the myth than the Muses? There is material about them to draw on in Hesoid and in Pindar's first *Pythian* (where they appear in association with the fallen giants as they do in this ode of Ronsard's), and they would supply an overall unity to the poem, both satisfying the requirements of the genre and supplying a convenient introduction to the real subject of the ode, the nature of true poetry. Furthermore, Hesiod had said "From the Heliconian Muses let us begin to sing" (*Theogony*, line 1), and, later, after their apparition to him,

> and they plucked and gave me a rod, a shoot of sturdy laurel, a marvellous thing, and breathed into me a divine voice to celebrate things that shall be and things that were aforetime; and they bade me sing of the race of the blessed gods that are eternally, but ever to sing of themselves both first and last.[2]
>
> (lines 30–34)

In the *Theogony* Hesoid not only recounted the birth of the

[1] That the middle ages were barren and that the Muses were hidden away somewhere for one thousand years is a humanist commonplace. To take a French example, see Guillaume Budé's *De Studio Litterarum Recte et Commode Institutendo* (Basileae, 1533), dedicated to Francis I, pp. 8–9.

[2] Translation by Hugh G. Evelyn-White in the Loeb library, *Hesiod. The Homeric Hymns* (London and Cambridge, Mass., 1954).

Muses from Memory and Jupiter, he also told how the nine maidens, soon after their birth, went to visit their father in heaven, singing songs. The outline of Ronsard's myth in the popular sense is now fixed. His Muses too will go to visit their father. And where could they better sing their songs, songs that will serve as showpieces of the new art, than at their appearance in court, a tradition of the epic easily adapted to the greater ode which is like it in ethos. Thus the Hesiod-derived visit of the Muses to their father offers Ronsard an opportunity for a virtuoso passage, for a demonstration of what the new poetry can do in the highest vein, for the promise of an epic, in fine, for the gigantomachy borrowed from Hesiod. But a visit to Jupiter on Olympus is a stale theme. Perhaps remembering a few lines from Homer and Aristaeus' underwater visit with his mother, the nymph Cyrene, in Vergil[1] Ronsard decided to send the Muses on their visit to their father when he was a guest of Ocean.

The plan of the ode now unfolds itself: the birth of the Muses, their visit to their father feasting in the palace of Ocean, the songs that they sang, Jupiter's reward, the Muses' gift, the progress of poetry, the Muses' flight to heaven during the dark ages, their restoration to earth by Michel de L'Hospital, Ronsard's attack on his critics, his praise of L'Hospital, and his promise of a *Franciade* to Mme Marguerite.

[1] Laum., *Rons. Poète*, p. 302, says that the description of the banquet of the gods in the palace of Ocean comes from the *Iliad* I (Jupiter among the Ethiopians), XIII (the palace of Neptune), and XXI (Ocean, father of rivers). But the borrowing was not of the order of that from Hesiod. Ronsard found in Homer only a few suggestions on which his imagination worked. To illustrate, the passages concerned are:

> for Zeus went yesterday to Okeanos, unto the noble
> Ethiopians for a feast, and all the gods followed with him.
>
> *Iliad* I, lines 423–4

> and there was his [Poseidon's] famous palace in the
> deeps of the mere, his glistening golden mansions builded,
> imperishable for ever.
>
> *Iliad* XIII, lines 21–2

> the great strength of deep-flowing Ocean, from whom all
> rivers flow and every sea, and all springs and deep wells. . . .
>
> *Iliad* XXI, lines 195–7

I quote from the Lang, Leaf, and Myers translation. For Aristaeus' visit with Cyrene see Vergil, *Fourth Georgic*, lines. 317 ff.

It remained only to find an opening stanza. This must state the occasion and the poet's intention. It must also, to borrow Pindar's image, catch the eye: "The forehead of every work begun must shine from afar" (*Olympia* 6, strophe 1). A common ancient conceit, the poet as gardener of the Muses,[1] gave Ronsard his material. And so a richly textured first stophe opens with the poet wandering through the fields of his Grace beside the Theban spring[2] collecting the fairest blossoms of poetry. Like Pindar and Horace, Ronsard will crown his hero who has brought back a prize, namely the Muses, from Olympus. He will crown him with a triple crown,[3] i.e., with a poem written in triadic verse—the triple crown perhaps also refers to the threefold division of the poem into the myth, the philosophy of poetry, and the praise of his patron.

The dominant idea of the first stanza, then, is the weaving of a poetic crown, and Ronsard conveys this idea not only through words and images, but also through the structure of his verse. Contrary to the main tradition of French prosody, enjambement here interweaves the lines as the poet twines his floral wreath. A trick of Pindar's,[4] too, is used to bind the strophe to the antistrophe; Ronsard ends the one stanza and begins the next with the same word, "Memoire." However, Ronsard unlike Pindar has the device of rime as well as that of position to use in securing his effects. Thus the suspended rime of the third quatrain of the strophe, the switch from the "rimes croisées" of the first two quatrains to the "rimes embrassées" of the third, also throws stress on "Memoire," and helps to effect the link between the two strophes. Similarly, the epode is closely bound to the antistrophe by the relative "En qui." This makes the triad an organic whole and thus fulfils the weaving image of the introductory stanza.

1 See Plato, *Ion.* 534 (where it is the gardens and dells of the Muses); Pindar, *Ol.* 9, lines 27 and 52, *Pyth.* 6, line 2, *Nem.* 6, lines 39–40. Cf. Pindar's image of the poet as a bee skimming from flower to flower, *Pyth.* 10, lines 53–4, an image also found in Horace, *Carm.* IV, 2, lines 27–32 and in Plato.

2 In Pindar, Dirce, near Thebes, is Memory's well and the Muses draw water from it, *Isthmia* 6, lines 77–8.

3 The image of the triple crown, though it is not used in the same sense, is also found in Pindar, *Nem.* 7, lines 77–9.

4 Gilbert Norwood, *Pindar*, p. 2, cites Bury's essay on *Nem.* 9, lines 16 and 17.

The accounts of the birth of the Muses in the first antistrophe and of their sweet song in the first epode are borrowed from Hesiod (*Theog.*, 53–62), as is the *idea* of their visit to their father (see *Theog.*, 68–74) which occupies the following four triads, while the placing of this visit under water may have been suggested by Vergil's *Fourth Georgic*. The details of their trip, however, and the description of the palace of Ocean are Ronsard's own. It was a brilliant idea of Ronsard's to send the Muses first under the sea. Not only did this avoid any monotony, since on Ronsard's thesis of an age of barbarism stretching from the fall of the Roman Empire until 1550, the Muses must later in the poem spend a millennium on Olympus; it also gave Ronsard an opportunity of portraying another realm (we have them all here, heaven and hell, earth and ocean) and of exercising his gift for the description of water. Moreover the Muses then come to the earth from the sea like all other living things.

In this, the most original part of his ode, Ronsard makes us participate in underwater existence through a choice of words that is sensitively exact. Thus, like the Muses we watch the mother's plunge from the outside, but with the Muses we dive into the sea and, as one of them we see the others in their descent, the outlines of their arms confused with the motion in the shifting refractions of the water. A simile borrowed from Homer (*Iliad* xxiv, 80) via Plato's *Ion* (538), gives the Muses time to reach their destination. Now we are on the sea floor. We see Ocean's green enamelled chariot *hanging* beneath the gateway of the pillared palace. With ringing anaphora ("Là pendoit sous le portail . . . ," "Là sont divinement encloses . . . ," "Là les Tritons chassant les fleuves . . . ," "Là ceste troupe est arrivée") Ronsard fixes the scene and emphasizes our presence there in the twilit silence of the ocean depths.

But the poet is not diffuse. As soon as he has created his impression of the ocean he leaves it. We enter the palace to a bustling scene economically described: the first course is being removed, Phoebus sings, Jupiter's eye surveys the assembly, and lights on the new arrivals. The recognition is immediate. The god embraces his daughters and asks them to sing. In a few verses we are in the myths within the myth.

The songs that the Muses sing are of increasing length and

gravity. The first contains the well known myth about the competition of Minerva and Neptune for the possession of Athens; the second, a cosmogony borrowed, selectively, from Hesiod's *Theogony*, lines 722–868; the third, the account of the war of the gods and giants borrowed from the *Theogony*, lines 629–712 with contamination from Horace III, 4, lines 42–64, and Callimachus, *Hymn to Artemis*, lines 57 ff.[1]

The first myth is handled with admirable conciseness. In six lines Ronsard recalls the whole story of the quarrel of Minerva and Neptune. And his account is the more effective for its brevity. Ronsard has made his allusions singularly evocative through the use of the two present participles, "pallissant" and "hanissant," which bring whole scenes of action before our eyes. We see the olive tree paling in the breeze, the spirited horse restive for action. A quarrel in which Neptune was worsted, despite the fact that the outcome is delicately passed over, was somewhat inappropriate to the immediate circumstances of the song; yet it harmonizes with the other two myths to produce a unity with a rising crescendo. Even on the lightest string of the lyre the themes of contention and war are already being sounded.

The second myth approaches the main myth obliquely with a cosmogony which is largely a description of hell with its howling giants and the arsenal of the gods. We are closer now to the theme of quarrel and war, we have been introduced to the chief protagonists, and they have been characterized as monsters and knights. However, a quiet passage intervenes before the gigantomachy. The pageant of night and day in the seventh strophe forms a transition between the descriptions of blackest hell in the sixth epode and of the mountain tops where the war between giants and gods is waged in the seventh antistrophe.

Again, as in the case of the quarrel of Minerva and Neptune, the war between the gods and giants is portrayed with admirable brevity. Where before the two contestants were defined by their gifts, here the two combatants are characterized by their weapons, broken rocks against pointed shafts, the primeval monsters of the earth against the sky gods.

Fortune hovers. The seventh epode skilfully draws out the

[1] Laum., *Oeuvres Rons.* VII, 235 ff.

war, accounts for the passage of time, and prepares us, by its tranquillity, for the clash of conflict in the eighth and ninth triads. Ronsard realizes that psychology and aesthetics demand a rest between the shocks if a work of art is to be effective.

The eighth triad lines up the combatants with their arms. In the ninth triad they meet as armies and in single combat. Here Ronsard draws on Horace and Callimachus to add details to Hesiod's account. The triad ends with the thunderbolt whirling about the heads of the giants.

The tenth strophe begins with the universe on fire. Remnants of that conflagration may be seen today in the Phlegrean Fields. The reference to today, the documentation of the gigantomachy, brings the Muses' song to a strong conclusion, while the description of the smoking, blackened fields leads us back to the quarrel between Minerva and Neptune, to the peaceful olive and the "Futur augure de la guerre," thus unifying and rounding off the series of three myths.

The first part of the ode ends here. Now Ronsard abandons popular Greek mythology—though we are still in the myth in the technical Pindaric sense—for the philosophical consideration of the nature of poetry which occupies the central position in the ode.

Here the choice of Calliope as spokesman was undoubtedly inspired by Hesiod (*Theogony*, line 79). But perhaps Ronsard was also thinking of Ficino's commentary on the *Ion*, that the nine Muses produce the music of the spheres, eight producing eight tones, i.e., the octave, and the ninth a sound that is a sum of the eight, and that Calliope is the ninth Muse whose song is a result of all the songs of the spheres: "octo scilicet sphaerarum tonos, et unum omnium concentum. . . . Calliope Musa vox est ex omnibus resultans sphaerarum vocibus."[1]

Calliope's last request is also based on Hesiod (*Theog.*, lines 79–93) but the emphasis of both position and length placed on the Muse-inspired king probably owes something to Plato's concept of the philosopher king. It is noteworthy that the Maecenas occupies only the penultimate position. Here Ronsard is placing his serious belief before his search for patronage. The other eight requests of the Muses, for Ronsard has found

[1] Marsilio Ficino, *Τοῦ Θείου Πλάτωνος Ἅπαντα τὰ σωζόμενα* . . . (Genevae, 1590), p. 762 F–G.

one each, are based on tradition, but represent Ronsard's concept of the scope of poetry.

Jupiter's reply to the Muses with its unPléiade-like scorn of art in favour of inspiration, its chain of inspiration with the magnet simile, its discussion of the four manias and of the purity of the poet, is all based on Plato[1]; though Pindar also stresses inspiration.

In this central part of the ode, triads eleven to fifteen, Ronsard is somewhat repetitious and verbose. But this is both understandable and pardonable; for here he is setting forth a theory of poetry that is novel in France.[2] He is also giving voice to a new and noble concept of the poet that is not Aristotelian and Horatian but Platonic. Poetry is no longer the art of imitation in words, but a kind of prophecy. The poet is no longer the laborious artist of the *Ars Poetica*, the *Deffence*, and Ronsard's own preface, but a pure soul, divinely possessed. The *μανία ποιητική* is closely related to the *μυστική* and owes something to medieval mysticism. Ronsard's ideal for the poet is impossibly high but it does serve to lift poetry up on to a more exalted plane than heretofore. Now poetry has its justification in France, as it has already had in Italy, as a vocation of the

[1] Chiefly *Phaedrus*, pp. 244–5 and *Ion*, pp. 533 and 535–6. The inspiration of the poet appears passim in Plato, even in hostile passages; see, e.g., *Apol.*, 22 B, *Laws* III, 682 A and IV, 719 B.

[2] The concept of poetry expressed in this ode is a favourite one with the earlier humanists. Its source lies in Ficino's exposition of Plato, particularly in his commentary on the *Ion*. Here we find not only a discussion of divine inspiration and its manner of descent to man but also a clear statement of an idea implicit in Plato, that he who seeks to write poetry without inspiration will produce an empty work: "eum qui sine furore musarum poeticas ad fores accedit, inanem esse ipsum atque eius poesim" (Ficino, *op. cit.*, p. 762 B). Ficino's ideas were elaborated by his followers, especially by those who wrote about poetic theory, e.g., by Bartolomeo Fonzio in his *Orationes . . . In Poeticen* dedicated to Lorenzo de Medici (fols c 5v–c 6r) and by Giampaolo Parisio (Aulus Ianus Parrhasius) in his commentary on Horace's *Ars Poetica* published in Paris in 1533. Here, p. 6, as we might expect where Platonism is wedded with Horatian criticism, the idea of poetry as the source of civilization is stressed and the contributions of the various poets are listed. Parisio also stresses the Platonic idea that the poet must be a good man (p. 8). Sébilet, too, though his ideas are much more old-fashioned than Ronsard's, opened his *Art Poetique Françoys* (Paris, 1549) with a passage on inspiration and the divinity of the poet (p. 3v in the 1555 ed.).

most serious importance. And this affirmation of the divine nature of the poet is reinforced by the prayer for inspiration with which Ronsard ends this passage.

Now the Muses return to earth and Ronsard's progress of poesy begins. The embryo of the progress idea is found in Horace's *Ars Poetica*, lines 391–407, but Ronsard develops it more methodically into the first important example of the progress poem, a genre to become very popular in the eighteenth century.[1]

The Dark Ages, the Muses' flight to heaven, and the long years on Olympus are passed over briefly. The time comes for the fulfilment of Jupiter's prophecy (antistrophe fifteen), for the return of the Muses to earth with their protector. And so Ronsard turns to Plato's *Republic* (X, 621), for his picture of the Parcae spinning L'Hospital's fate. Then Jupiter forms L'Hospital, as Prometheus formed man, from a mass of clay, and he and the Muses fly down to earth. A propitious fire marks their arrival, a contrast with the fire of destruction in the first half of the myth.

Ronsard wisely abandons L'Hospital and the Muses at this stage by seizing on the Pindaric commonplace of the ship off course.[2] A Pindaric discussion of his technique and an attack on his critics follow,[3] then praise of L'Hospital, and finally, skilfully worked in the emphatic position, of Mme Marguerite. Another Pindaric device, with a break in rhythm to correspond with the break in sense, brings the ode to an abrupt conclusion.

When we come to consider the structure of the ode we find that Ronsard like Pindar has no fixed relationship between triad and thought division. Subjects end and new ones begin in the middle of triads. Similarly sentences run on beyond the end of strophes, although only very occasionally in Ronsard. However, new subjects do not begin in the middle of strophes in Ronsard as they do in Pindar. Moreover, Ronsard's strophes themselves regularly break down into a series of metrical units which correspond with the unfolding of the idea. That is, the

[1] Ronsard returns to Hesiod, *Theog.* lines 9–25, for his picture in antistrophe 17 of the shepherd-poets communing with the Muses in solitary places by night.

[2] Cf. Pindar, *Pyth.* 11, ant. 3.

[3] Cf. Pindar, *Nem.* 4, ant. 2.

strophe and antistrophe, whose rime scheme is ABABCDCD-EFFE$_8$ almost invariably divide into three quatrains. The few exceptions occur in catalogue passages as that of the gods (antistrophe 8). Similarly, the epode whose rime scheme is ABBACCDEED$_7$, a quatrain of the octave and the sestet of the normal sonnet, divides in thought into a quatrain and two units of three lines in both of which the D rimes bring to a conclusion the ideas expressed in the preceding couplets (i.e., CC or EE).[1]

To say that Ronsard was here indebted to Hesiod and there to Plato, Pindar, Horace, Callimachus, the Ficinian tradition, etc., is not to say that the ode to Michel de L'Hospital is a pastiche. Horace said that it was better to treat familiar subjects than to attempt novelties and that originality consisted in one's handling of well known material:

> Publica materies privati iuris erit, si
> Non circa vilem patulumque moraberis orbem. . . .
>
> (*Ars Poetica*, 131–2)

Ronsard has followed his advice and has fused his borrowings from the classics into a work that is his own. The synthesis is what is important here, not the source of the various parts.

However, Ronsard's adaptation of ancient material is not always perfect. There are two, possibly three, passages in this ode where an unassimilated borrowing sticks out. Mars "ronflant" (antistrophe 10) seems less offensive to the more robust English taste than to the French, but the particular context in which this borrowing from Pindar appears makes it singularly inappropriate. In the first *Pythian*, both Zeus' eagle and Ares were lulled to sleep by a song that was clearly of the kind that "soothes the savage breast." But here the song, the account of the battle of the gods and giants, is just the sort that should put Mars upon his mettle. If any song is martial this one is. Thus Mars' snoring over his spear—despite the fact that Jupiter *later* describes him as of "mauvais courage" (strophe 12) —is a piece of frigid imitation of Pindar which immediately jars the reader into the realization of the artificiality of the modern Pindaric. Similarly, Ronsard's

[1] There are only two exceptions to this, in epodes 6 and 10. In epode 12 the 4, 3, and 3 order is reversed; i.e., the epode divides ABB/ ACC/ DEED.

Hà, chere Muse, quel Zephire
Souflant trop violentement,
A fait escarter mon nauire
Qui fendoit l'eau si droitement?
(antistrophe 21)

despite the fact that it is sanctioned by an equally digressive Pindar (*Pyth.* 11, antistrophe 3), appears ridiculous. The ship image, in the first place, is already hackneyed. But how can Ronsard refer to his ship cutting straight through the water when he has obviously been tacking for 61 stanzas? Furthermore, as Laumonier has pointed out,[1] Jupiter's leering reference to his seductions is out of keeping with the spirit of the ode. It was an unfortunate borrowing from Callimachus (*Hymn to Artemis*, lines 26–31), and brings out the light and libertine nature of Alexandrian art. There seems to be some confusion, too, in the gigantomachy. Ronsard does not appear to know that Cottus, Briareus, and Gyes, the hundred-handed giants, were on the side of the gods.

These are, however, but four small blemishes in a poem of 816 lines where, for the most part, the poet's inspiration has attained the nobility that the genre he has chosen demands. Certainly for imaginative control and polished finish this is the finest of Ronsard's Pindarics.

The last group of Pindaric odes is addressed to Ronsard's fellow writers. The first, longest, and most ambitious of these is appropriately dedicated to Joachim du Bellay. It is not, however, one of the more appealing poems that Ronsard wrote to his friend and fellow poet. Here, in a not particularly happy imitation of Pindar, Ronsard praises du Bellay through his distinguished but neglectful relatives, the general, Guillaume du Bellay, and the cardinal, Jean. The two opening triads and the single closing one, adorned with reminiscences of Pindar and Horace, praise the two new poets, Ronsard especially:

Par une cheute subite
Encor je n'ai fait nommer
Du nom de Ronsard la mer,
Bien que Pindare j'imite.

[1] Laum., *Oeuvres Rons.* VII, 235.

Horace harpeur Latin,
Etant fils d'un libertin,
Basse et lente avoit audace,
Non pas moi de franche race,
Dont la Grace enfle les sons,
Avec plus horrible aleine,
Affin que Phebus rameine
Par moi ses vieilles chansons,

and criticize their rivals who caw like crows against the royal eagles. The classical ship image, a favourite with Ronsard as with so many other Renaissance humanists, occupies the last two stanzas. There are many allusions and images to ennoble the style and a Pindaric sprinkling of aphorisms, e.g.,

L'homme est fol qui se travaille
Porter en la Mer des eaus,
A Corinthe des vesseaus,[1]

which are well turned in French. However, Ronsard's exaggerated self-praise and his argument of birth against Horace, along with the unnaturalness of the family praise of his close friend du Bellay, make this ode one of his least sympathetic.

"A Bouju, Angevin" thanks a fellow poet for commending him without rancour to Mme Marguerite and, between self-justification and self-praise, lauds his colleague's verses. Though lacking a myth, the ode opens with a proverb, "Le Potier hait le Potier" from Hesiod and Erasmus.[2] It also contains analogous illustrations, and some mythological decoration. The monotriadic "A Jean D'Aurat, Lecteur du Roy" too opens with a proverb,

" Le medecin de la peine
" Est le plaisir qui ameine
" Le repos avecque luy,

and this proverb leads to a series of Pindaric comparisons of poetry to various forms of therapy, to a relaxing bath or a healing ointment![3] But poetry is superior to either of these, and Ronsard's poetry, which soothes kings, was schooled by Dorat who is

1 This is a common Greek and Latin proverb.

2 *Work and Days*, line 25 and Erasmus, *Adagia* (Basileae, 1541), pp. 70–1, Laum., *Rons. Poète*, pp. 306–7.

3 From Pindar, *Nem.* 4, beginning, Silver, *Pind. Odes Rons.*, pp. 40–1.

Renommé parmy la France
Comme un oracle des Dieux,
Pour desnouër aux plus sages
Les plus ennoüez passages
Des liures laborieux.

The ode ends with a comparison of Dorat to Alcaeus. In Ronsard's ode to the other distinguished member of the Coqueret group, Jean Antoine de Baïf, it again seems that the poet's Pindaric self-praise bulks disproportionately large. In this respect Ronsard quite out-Pindars Pindar and we like him distinctly the less for it. The last of the Pindarics, again brief, praises the adaptations from the classics, Greek, Latin, and Italian, made by the architect, Jean Martin, and assures him of his immortality. Like the other Pindarics this ode is starred with *sententiae*, e.g., "L'epreuve est de l'inventeur," a translation of Pindar's "Ἅπαν δ' εὑρόντος ἔργον," *Olympian* 13, epode 1.[1]

Such, then, are Ronsard's Pindaric odes. However great the excitement that they aroused when they were first published in 1550, they have never been popular. Even when Ronsard enjoyed the royal favour, courtiers mocked at his obscure, mythological Pindarics and Ronsard himself soon turned against them. Nevertheless, however over-scholarly and over-ornate, pretentious, pompous, bombastic, and rhetorical Ronsard's Pindarics may have been, and however unpopular, their influence was still very great. Through the stimulus that they gave to François de Malherbe they established classicism firmly and irrevocably in French poetry for almost three centuries. They fixed a tradition of large, formal odes on public affairs, they inculcated the Pindaric prose of the poet-prophet, and they taught the lyric nobility and breadth. Moreover they are not themselves completely without merit. There are many good passages and they have at times a chill beauty. Their chief fault is an over-carefulness of imitation in a kind of poem for which the poet's genius was unsuited. It is unfortunate that these works of his learned and enthusiastic twenties were to cost Ronsard his reputation some fifty years later and blot out, with their shadow, so much that was truly inspired.

[1] Laum., *Rons. Poète*, p. 313.

Now let us consider the other odes of the definitive 1584 edition. Henceforth the odes referred to, unless it is otherwise stated, can be taken to be written in identical stanzas measured to the lyre.

The sixteenth ode of the first book[1] is a good illustration of Ronsard's method of imitation by contamination of various passages of the author who inspires him.[2] This ode, addressed to one "Bertran," opens with an allegorical development of the familiar ship image. The poet is the trafficker of the Muses. His merchandise is not for sale, but he bestows it where he will,[3] and it is a gift which will never perish.

Ronsard illustrates his last statement from Horace (IV, 9) by citing the works of Alcaeus, Pindar, Simonides, Stesichorus, and Anacreon. Most of the rest of the ode, lines 37–68, is a translation of Horace IV, 9, lines 12–44. The conclusion, however, is a composite of Horatian ideas from various sources. Ronsard finds specific examples of Horace's statement in the model ode, "Non possidentem multa vocaveris / Recte beatum" (Horace IV, 9, lines 45–6), in Horace III, 1, lines 17–21, which he adapts as "Damocles with the sword above his head is not hungry, the song of the nightingale brings him no rest"; and in lines 25–32 which become "He who is content does not put to sea, nor does he fear in the summer that his wheat may fail or that his grapes may be burnt by the sun"; in Horace III, 3, lines 1–8, which become "Such a man's strength is not shaken by thunder nor the news of war, by the king's scowling mien nor the threat of pirates"; and in lines 69–72, translated as

> Taisez vous ma Lire mignarde,
> Taisez vous ma Lire jazarde,
> Un si haut chant n'est pas pour vous.

The concluding half stanza, however, "Retournez louer ma Cassandre," although conventional, links this ode with the following one in the collected works in a way unusual in a volume of odes.

Was Ronsard only unwittingly right in maintaining that the

[1] Laum., *Ed. Crit.* I, 138–44.

[2] For a discussion of this technique with a great weight of evidence see Silver, *Pind. Odes Rons.* and "Did Du Bellay know Pindar?"

[3] Inspired by Pindar, *Pyth.* 2, 67–8, and *Isth.* 2, 6–8, Laum., *Oeuvres Rons.* VII, 241.

following ode was the type of poem for which his genius was best fitted? Was he merely repeating a Horatian commonplace without thinking, or was he glad, after all those Pindarics and the dull Horatian pastiche, to take off his singing robes and relax?[1] At any rate the next poem, "A Cassandre,"[2] is the famous "Mignonne, allons voir si la rose," which survived for centuries in the songbooks when Ronsard's name was nothing more than a by-word for bombast.

"Mignonne, allons voir si la rose" is no more original in its conception than the preceding ode. It goes back, through a hundred Renaissance variations on the theme, to Ausonius' famous "De rosis nascentibus."[3] Yet it is not, like the ode to Bertran, a slavish copy of the master. Ronsard's version of the rose-maiden theme has three panels. In the first the poet asks his love to come with him to see the morning's rose whose colour is like hers, in the second they find the rose's petals strewn on the ground, in the third he begs her to enjoy the brief flowering of her beauty before it too falls. The dramatization of the description, comparison, and morality, with the spectator who in the last stanza becomes herself the fast-fading rose, was the master stroke which made Ronsard's poem more touching and immediate than any of the preceding versions.

Mignonne, allon voir si la rose
Qui ce matin avoit declose
Sa robe de pourpre au soleil,
A point perdu, cette vesprée,
Les plis de sa robe pourprée,
Et son teint au vostre pareil.

[1] This statement has a poetic if not literal truth. In fact some three years elapsed between the publication of fourteen of these Pindarics and this ode which first appeared, along with various other odes, in the appendix to the second edition of the *Amours* in 1553.

[2] Laum., *Ed. Crit.* V (Paris, 1928), 196–7.

[3] Laum., *Rons. Poète*, pp. 583–9, has collected Renaissance versions of this theme by Baïf, Desperiers, Sainct-Gelays, Marot, Lemaire, Bernardo Tasso, Muret, Bembo, Secundus, Macrin, Angeriano, Serafino, Pontano, Lorenzo, Marullus, Poliziano. He has also found a similar passage in the *Romance de la Rose*, ed. Lacour, I, lines 68–72, "Cueillez bientost les roses vermeillettes." Before Ausonius the theme was treated by the writers of the *Greek Anthology*, by Ovid (*Ars Amatoria*, III, 59–80), Propertius (*Eleg.* II, 15, lines 23–4 and the conclusion, and IV, 5, lines 57–60), Tibullus (*Eleg.* I, 1, lines 69 ff., and I, 8, 41 ff.), Theocritus (*Idylls* 23), and Mimnermus, frag., quoted by Croiset in *Litterature Grècque* II, 116.

Las, voiés comme en peu d'espace,
Mignonne, elle a dessus la place
Las, las, ses beautés laissé cheoir!
O vraiment maratre Nature,
Puis qu'une telle fleur ne dure
Que du matin jusques au soir!

Donc, si vous me croiés, mignonne:
Tandis que vôtre âge fleuronne
En sa plus verte nouveauté,
Cueillés, cueillés vôtre jeunesse
Comme à cette fleur, la vieillesse
Fera ternir vôtre beauté.

"Mignonne allons voir si la rose" seems very simple and song-like, yet it is ordered by the strictest logic, and it is completely formal and impersonal, as well as being learned, in its treatment of its theme. It is an example of the classical ode technique subtlely adapted to the vernacular song. The theme, classical in origin, but so familiar as to seem popular after all its Renaissance treatments, produced yet another little masterpiece in Herrick's "Gather ye rosebuds while ye may."

All the other poems in the first book are odes which generally lean heavily on classical sources. The most attractive of these, and a considerable artistic achievement, is the "Avant-Venue du Printemps,"[1] an ode which is Horatian in structure and invention, but which contains a generous contamination of Lucretius, Vergil, and Ovid.[2] Yet it is, despite its derivativeness, vividly imagined and lively and vigorous in its description. The coming of spring makes Ronsard think of the spring of the earth and the golden age, then of the jealousy of the gods and the age of bronze,

Lors le printens donna place
Au chaut, au vent, à la glace,
Qui renaissent à leur tour.
Et le sapin des montaignes
Galopa par les campaignes
Qui nous baignent alentour,

[1] Laum., *Ed. Crit.* I, 147–54.

[2] Laum., *Rons. Poète,* p. 440, gives a list of Ronsard's very considerable debts in this poem to Vergil, *Georg.* I, 217; Hor. I, 4; Verg., *Georg.* I, 43, II, 323–35; Lucr. I, 10–20, V, 735; Verg. *Georg.* III, 242 ff., II, 336–40, I, 125 ff.; Ovid, *Metam.* I (the four ages), in this order.

then of the iron age,

> On ouit sonner les armes,
> On ouit par les alarmes
> L'acier tinter durement,
> Et les lames assérées
> Sur les enclumes férrées
> Craqueter horriblement.

Here some of the details, the association of ships with the bronze age and the final thunderbolt, make us think that Ronsard may have had the last stanzas of Horace I, 3, in the back of his mind. The first part of the ode, however, with its lusty vitality, its rich mythology, its poetic diction,[1] and its real observation of nature reminds one of the Elizabethans' particularly happy combination of Ovid and their native lyric tradition, e.g.,

> Toreau,[2] qui desus ta crope
> Enlevas la belle Europe
> Parmi les voies de l'eau,
> Hurte du grand ciel la borne,
> Poussant du bout de ta corne
> Les portes de l'an nouveau.

In the third stanza, when Ronsard bids the ice melt, we notice for the first time what Keats would call Ronsard's gift of negative capability where rivers are concerned. Ronsard is unsurpassed in the description of the sounds, moods, and motions of water:

> Vous nimphes des eaus, qui estes
> Ores prises et subjétes,
> Levez un beau chef dehors:
> Et debridant vostre course
> Bien loin depuis vostre source
> Frapez librement vos bords.

[1] E.g., Laum., *Ed. Crit.* I, 151,

> Adonc la gent enplumée,
> Et la vagabonde armée,

and I, 152, . . . les pleines humides.

[2] Conventionally the sun is in Taurus from April 21st to May 20th.

Now the spring, green, flowery, and gay, overcomes winter with its rain, hail, and wind. The days lengthen, Jupiter fertilizes his bride, Nature wakens love among the creatures, ships bound on the back of the waves, and soldiers pitch their camps—it is the thought of the ships and the soldiers that leads Ronsard into his account of the deterioration of the world, of the opening of Pandora's box, and of the crash of the thunderbolt.

Another ode, to Apollo,[1] opens like the classical and humanist prayer with an invocation of the god by his various titles, a technique that allows much scope for the evocative use of proper names. Like Marullus and Pontano, Crinito and Flaminio, Ronsard is able to bring the gods richly to life in all their pagan, physical beauty:

O Pere, ô Phebus Cynthien,
O saint Apollon Pythien,
Seigneur de Déle, isle divine,
Cyrénean, Patarean,
Par qui le Trepié Thymbrean
Dessous la Custode devine.

Ou soit que Clare, ou que tes seurs
Te detiennent de leurs douceurs,
Ou soit que tu laves en l'onde
D'Eurote clairement roulant
Le crespe honneur du poil coulant
Par flocons de ta teste blonde.[2]

Now the poet prays the god to cure his mistress of a fever[3] and, in doing so, celebrates his powers, alluding to various myths. He asks for medicines famous in mythology, and that

[1] Laum., *Ed. Crit.*, I, 154–9. Laum., *Oeuvres Rons.* VII, 243–4, notes that Apollo's epithets are borrowed from the Homeric *Hymn to Apollo* and from Macrobius I, 17.

[2] For the last two verses cf. Hor. III, 4, lines 61 ff. and IV, 6, 26, Laum., *Oeuvres Rons.* VII, 244.

[3] The lady for whom the poem was originally written was the wife of Nicholas Denisot, Laum., *Oeuvres Rons.* VII, 243. See the notes there for a list of the sources of this ode. Compare this ode with Tibullus' fourth elegy in his fourth book where the poet prays Apollo to come and heal the sick Sulpicia, the mistress of his friend, Cherinthus.

Apollo prepare and apply them. In return he makes a *voeu*.[1] He will build the god a temple. The ode ends in Horatian style with a specific picture of the temple's image. It is an interesting version of the popular, humanist hymn-ode which has been crossed with an occasional poem and a *voeu*, so that the conventional prayer of the hymn has reality and specific content, while the invocation of the gods is made that much more convincing.

Despite Ronsard's two protestations at the beginning of his second book that now he is preparing to celebrate Henry II in the epic strain,[2] there is remarkably little of the high style in this book as compared with the first one. There is practically nothing of the heroic and very little of the more serious Horatian. An unoriginal ode based on Horace I, 24 (on the death of Quintilius Varus) consoles the Queen of Navarre on the death of her nephew, Charles de Valois, Duke of Orleans,[3] the man whom Ronsard served as a page. The duke's youthfulness is mentioned in the beginning—his promise was great—and in the ending—"quem di diligunt adolescens moritur." The centre of the poem, recalling Vergil's apotheoses of Daphnis and Octavian (*Ecl.* 5 and *Georg.* I), pictures the duke in heaven acting as his people's intercessor. "Prophetie du Dieu de la Charente,"[4] again following Horace and Vergil, uses the device of the prophecy of a river god[5] to threaten the

[1] The ode expressing a vow was a favourite with Ronsard. He published four of them in the 1550 ed. of the odes, this present "Veu à Phoebus"; "Veu à Lucine," Laum., *Ed. Crit.* II, 114–17; "Veu au Somme," *ibid.* II, 122–4; and "Ode a Phebus lui vouant ses cheveus," *ibid.* II, 7–9; and six of them in his 1554 *Bocage*: "D'Un Vigneron À Bacus," "D'Un Pecheur Aus Naiades," "D'Une Courtizanne A Venus," "Voeu D'Un Chemineur A Une Fontaine," "D'Un Vaneur De Blé Au Vent Zefire," "D'Un Pasteur Au Dieu Pan." For the texts see Laum., *Ed. Crit.* VI, 16–17; 17–18; 18; 14; 15; 16. Laum., *Rons. Poète*, p. 128, traces the ancestry of the *voeu* back through Navagero's *Lusus pastorales* (ed. princeps, 1530), and Horace's *vota* (III, 18, 22) to the ἀναθήματα of the *Greek Anthology*.

[2] Laum., *Ed. Crit.* I, 167–73 and 174–9.

[3] *Ibid.*, I, 179–83. See Laum.'s note, *Oeuvres Rons.* VII, 247–8.

[4] Laum., *Ed. Crit.* I, 192–6.

[5] See, e.g., Vergil, *Aen.* VIII, lines 31 ff. The ode as a whole is an imitation of Hor. I, 15 where the sea god Nereus predicts to Paris the ruin of Troy, Laum., *Oeuvres Rons.*, VII, 248–9. Laumonier also gives the historical background to the ode.

mutineers of Guyenne with royal punishment. "Contre Les Avaricieus, et ceus qui prochains de la mort batissent"[1] is, as its title suggests, variations on themes from Horace. It is a *contaminatio* of Horace II, 18, III, 16, 24, and 1, in this order. It is written in a double strophic system. Other reflective odes of a somewhat similar sort, assiduously adapting the ancients, denounce the fools who risk their lives at sea to bring home a rich cargo or in the army to win a cold château or who beg worldly wealth from kings and princes when life is ordained short and full of woe and death dogs our footsteps[2]; inveigh against envy and man's unnatural war against his own kind[3]; and complain about the misery of man's lot,[4] often in Horatian idiom but with a cry of pain, with an intensity and despair, that springs from the Biblical and Christian denunciations of this life divorced from their complementary belief in heaven:

> Mon Dieu, que malheureus nous sommes,
> Mon Dieu, que de maus en un tans
> Offencent la race des hommes,
> Semblable aux fueilles du printans,
> Qui, vertes, dedans l'arbre croissent,
> Puis dessous l'Autonne suivant,
> Seiches, sous l'arbre n'apparoissent
> Qu'un jouët remoqué du vent.[5]

Hope is evil. All is vanity. Misery hangs over the young child's head. Death comes to high and low alike in various guises. The serpent has gained eternal youth and sheds his skin each

[1] Laum., *Ed. Crit.* I, 183–8.

[2] *Ibid.*, VI (Paris, 1930), 113–14. Laum. notes, *Oeuvres Rons.* VII, 257, that this is a paraphrase of Bion 5.

[3] Laum., *Ed. Crit.* VI, 116–18. Laum. notes, *Oeuvres Rons.* VII, 258, that this is based on a frag. of Philemon, "Ὦ τρισμακάρια . . ." and a frag. of Menander, "Ἅπαντα τὰ ζῶα . . ."

[4] Laum., *Ed. Crit.* V, 192–6.

[5] Laum., *Rons. Poète*, pp. 108, 112 fn. 2, and 348–9, and *Oeuvres Rons.* VII, 251, notes that the comparison of man's life to leaves comes from the *Iliad*, VI, 146 ff. and from XXI, 464 ff. In the rest of the ode there are debts to Simonides of Ceos, Mimnermus, and Simonides of Amorgos ("Vrayment l'esperance . . . throne de Minos." For the sources see *Lyriques grecs*, Bergk III, 1146, II, 327 and 736), to Hesiod, and to Horace ("Dés ce iour . . . tonneau" from *Works and Days* and Hor. I, 3, 25 ff.).

year,[1] but since the theft of fire, age, disease, and death have been the lot of man.

A few lighter odes have the melancholy Horatian undertone of mortality; indeed melancholy is intrinsic to humanism because all that it loves and studies, all that is human is owing to death, and the humanist's own frail being does not allow him to forget this for long. Thus Ronsard borrows from Horace III, 17, the opening verses of an ode that is more moral and melancholy than its original:

> Si l'oiseau qu'on voit amener
> En fuyant le temps qui ennuye,
> Peut de ces cris acertener
> Du prognostique de la pluye. . . .[2]

Then Ronsard continues in the Horatian vein, "Take advantage of the bad weather to write something that will make you immortal.[3] Then you can drink a fine old wine. You must think of keeping yourself alive now, when you are in good health,"

> Pauure abusé, ne sçais-tu pas
> Qu'il ne faut qu'une maladie
> Pour te mener bien tost là-bas
> D'où iamais ne reuient le pas?[4]

[1] Cf. Ovid, *Ars Amatoria* III, 77, "Anguibus exuitur tenui cum pelle vetustas." Laum., *Oeuvres Rons.* VII, 251, finds that the whole of the strophe, "Ah! que maudite soit l'asnesse," is based on Nicander, *Theriaca*, 343–59.

[2] Laum., *Ed. Crit.* I, 214–16. Cf. du Bellay, *Oeuvres Poèt.*, ed. Chamard, III, 4–8 and V, 264–77 and Laum., *Oeuvres Rons.* II, 424–30.

[3] Ronsard's advice on how to write immortal works,

> Pelle melle dessus la table
> Les livres aussi soient ouvers
> Avecques le luc delectable,
> Fidele compaignon des vers,

reminds one of Horace's advice to the two Pisones in his *Ars Poetica*, lines 268–9,

> Vos exemplaria Graeca
> Nocturna versate manu, versate diurna.

> Turn the pages of your
> Greek Models by night, turn them by day.

[4] Laum., *Ed. Crit.* VI, 103–4. See Laum.'s notes, *Oeuvres Rons.* VII, 254–5 and in *Rons. Poète*, pp. 570 ff.

Again, in a rather grim Anacreontic, Ronsard bids Corydon fill his glass. He would drink to forget his cares. Since he must die some day he wants his life to be short. When youth is gone may death come suddenly.

Of the remaining odes the largest number treat of love. "A Cassandre,"[1]

> La lune est coutumiere
> De naistre tous les mois,

begins with a translation from Catullus, "Vivamus, mea Lesbia, atque amemus," vows the poet's dedication to Cassandra's praises, and proceeds to praise her, borrowing from Secundus, *Basiarum* 6 (lines 4 and 15–16) and 8.[2] The poem ends with an Ovidian-Petrarchan conceit about the archery of her eyes. "Ma petite nimphe Maçée"[3] adapts "Ad Lydiam" of the pseudo-Gallus[4] to describe the beauty of his cruel mistress. A lively, lusty ode with a surprise conclusion[5] tells us

> Si j'ayme depuis n'aguere
> Une belle chamberiere,
> Je ne suis pas à blasmer
> De si bassement aymer.

The poet defends his lowly love with a series of mythological examples and wishes, as the greatest punishment of those who condemn him, that they may never love in low estate! The first six stanzas, fresh and original sounding though they are, and thoroughly in keeping with Ronsard's character, come from Horace II, 4, "Ne sit ancillae." A brief ode addressed to du Bellay,[6] a paraphrase of Bion 4, maintains the close association of the lyre with love—and incidentally explains why Ronsard's

1 Laum., *Ed. Crit.* I, 189–91.

2 Laum., *Rons. Poète*, p. 520 ff. and *Oeuvres Rons.* VII, 248.

3 Laum., *Ed. Crit.* I, 200–3.

4 Laum., *Rons. Poète*, p. 526. See also "pieces justificatives" at the end of Laumonier's book. Also cf. Macrin's "Ad Gelonidem," *Carm.* (1530), II, 28–9.

5 Laum., *Ed. Crit.* X, 133–5. See Laum.'s notes, *Oeuvres Rons.* VII, 256.

6 Laum., *Ed. Crit.* VI, 112–13. See Laum.'s notes, *Oeuvres Rons.* VII, 257.

love poetry remains alive while his heroic odes seem never to have known life:

> quand je veus louër
> Quelque homme ou quelque Dieu, soudain je sens nouër
> Ma langue à mon palais, et ma gorge se bouche:
> Mais quand je veus d'amour ou écrire, ou parler,
> Ma langue se desnouë, et lors je sens couler
> Ma chanson d'elle mesme aisément en la bouche.

Two other poems about love, both addressed to Cassandra, were inspired by the *basia* of Joannes Secundus.[1] Secundus' *basia* are short lyric poems almost entirely devoted to the description of kisses and the largely physical pleasures of love. Although they may often appear to be wholly personal lyrics, strictly occasional, and they usually are conversational in tone, they in fact exploit in succession all the varying aspects of their subject with the cunning and graceful art of the Alexandrians. They are passionate, sensuous, and rich in imagery. They enjoyed a tremendous vogue during the sixteenth century. Ronsard wrote of Secundus:

> Jan Second, de qui la gloire
> N'ira jamais defaillant. . . .
> Et duquel les baizers, ores,
> Pour estre venuz du Ciel,
> En ses vers coulent encores
> Plus doulx que l'Attique miel.[2]

The first of these *baisers* of Ronsard[3] is written in a double strophic system and asks his mistress,

[1] Secundus wrote elegies, funeral pieces, epigrams, epistles, odes, and *sylvae*, as well as *basia*. His odes had nothing to offer to the tradition and therefore were not mentioned above. The new sub-genre of erotic poetry that he created, "the kiss," was inspired by the *Greek Anthology*, Catullus, Tibullus, Ovid, the pseudo-Gallus, Pontano, Marullus, and Sannazaro. See *Joannis Secundi Hagiensis Poetae Elegantissimi opera. nunc secundum in lucem edita* . . . (Parisiis, 1561).

[2] Laum., *Ed. Crit.* III, 181.

[3] *Ibid.*, I, 246–8. From Secundus, *Bas.* 3, 8, 7, 18, 9; Laum., *Rons. Poète*, p. 524. Laum., *Oeuvres Rons.* VII, 254 adds as sources Secundus, *Bas.*, 10; Catullus 7 and 61; and Sannazaro, *Epigr.* 1.

Ma petite colombelle,
Ma petite toute belle,
Mon petit oeil baisez moy:
D'un baiser qui lon tens dure
Poussez hors la peine dure
De mon amoureus esmoi.

Then, with mythological and animal similes, it describes the teasing love-play that excites him in imagination. The other,[1]

Cassandre ne donne pas
Des baisers, mais des appas
Qui vont nourrissant mon ame,

describes the ecstasies of his mistress's kisses. Neither of these poems has the formality and objectivity of the ode, but they are both written in the Renaissance humanist tradition and were too seductive to pass by.

Four odes of the second book are descriptive of nature, of the country around Vendôme, of its forest of Gastine, of the vine flower, the latter ornate with a compact series of flower myths, and of the fountain, Bellerie.[2] "A La Fontaine Bellerie," the first of his odes on this subject, opens with a picture of the fountain, where the nymphs hide and the satyrs pursue, which recalls similar odes of Macrin and du Bellay. However, this is but the façade of Horace's thinly disguised "O Fons Bandusiae"[3] of which the rest of the ode is a translation.

Three different types of poems about drink all have their counterparts in Horace. "Du retour de Maclou de la Haie. A son page," "Fai refreschir le vin, de sorte,"[4] bids his page chill the wine, summon Janne with her lute, and Barbe with her hair twisted like a gay Italian's. They will all sing, dance, and drink; for the day passes and tomorrow is unsure. "A Remy Belleau,"[5]

[1] Laum., *Ed. Crit.* I, 197–9. Laum., *Rons. Poète*, p. 522, finds the source of this lyric in Secundus, *Bas.*, 4, 5, 16.

[2] Laum., *Ed. Crit.* I, 221–5; 243–5; X, 129–32; I, 203–5.

[3] Horace III, 13.

[4] Laum., *Ed. Crit.* I, 207–8. Sources, Horace I, 36, lines 11–16; II, 7, 19 ff.; II, 11, 18 ff.; II, 17; and III, 14, 17 ff.; Laum. VII, 250

[5] Laum., *Ed. Crit.* VII (Paris, 1934), 311–13. See Laum.'s notes, *Oeuvres Rons.* VII, 257.

Tu es un trop sec biberon
Pour un tourneur d'Anacreon,

advises Belleau to drink, but to drink in moderation if he would be a poet; for Bacchus unadulterated spoils the brain. Ronsard tells the illustrative myth about the infant Bacchus who was nursed by the water nymphs. The last of these odes[1] seems to reflect the over-pedantic schooling of Dorat:

J'ay l'esprit tout ennuié
D'avoir trop estudié
Les Phenomenes d'Arate.

Here Ronsard finds study boredom and death ever-threatening. So we must enjoy life. Let Corydon buy wine, and fruits, and vegetables. He will picnic by a murmuring stream!

Most of the remaining odes are translations of Horace or Anacreon.[2]

Ronsard's third book, with a kind of return to the first, and perhaps a reminiscence of Horace's third book with its "Roman" odes, opens with eight odes dedicated to the royal family, all but two of which contain long elaborate myths. These odes were considerably influenced by Pindar, but they strain for their lofty tone and are generally much too long. The only one which is enjoyable to read is "A Monseigneur le Duc d'Orleans."[3] Here a song-like stanza and an occasional pretty image save the ode from tedium:

Comme on void au point du jour
    Tout autour
Rougir la roze espanie,
Et puis on la void au soir
    Se décheoir
A terre toute fanie:

[1] Laum., *Ed. Crit.* VI, 105–7. Laum., *Oeuvres Rons.* VII, 254, notes that this ode is imitated from Stephanus' Anacreon 31 and 15 and echoes Hor. II, 3, lines 9–16, and III, 14, line 17. See also Hor. III, 19, and II, 11.

[2] "Contre Denise Sorciere," Laum., *Ed. Crit.* I, 238–43, and "Palinodie A Denise," *ibid.*, I, 252–7, are derived from Horace's fifth and seventeenth epodes respectively with an admixture of the sixteenth ode of the first book in the latter. Three odes are translated from Anacreon, "Pour boire dessus l'herbe tendre" (*ibid.*, VI, 103–4, from "Ἐπὶ μυρσίναις τερείναις,"), "Du malheur de receuoir" (*ibid.*, VI, 122–4 from "Μεσονυκτίοις ποθ' ὥραις,"), and "La Nature a donné des cornes aus toreaus" (*ibid.*, VI, 115 from "Φύσις κέρατα ταύροις").

[3] Laum., *Ed. Crit.* VII, 55–65.

Ou comme un lis trop lavé,
Agravé
D'une pluyeuse tempeste,
Ou, trop fort du chaut ataint
Perdre teint,
Et languir à basse teste.

These similes have their charm despite their triteness, even though we remember that Ronsard had already used the first in "Mignonne allons voir si la rose" and the second in his poem on du Bellay's convalescence, "Mon ame, il est temps que tu rendes."[1]

In the third book there are the usual types of love poems. One of these[2] warns the young beauty of approaching age and advises her to enjoy herself while she can; another,[3] after two Horatian strophes on the mutability of nature,[4]

Le jour pousse la nuit,
Et la nuit sombre
Pousse le jour qui luit
D'une obscure ombre.

L'autumne suit l'esté,
Et l'âpre rage
Des vens, n'a point été
Apres l'orage,

complains that his love does not change and begs Cupid either to free him of his tormenting passion or show his power by conquering his cruel mistress too. "A Madeleine,"[5] an ode, uses elaborate mythological apparatus borrowed from Ovid to express strong sympathy with and it seems some bitterness at the young woman's marriage with an old man. It is in the medieval tradition of the *chanson de la mal mariée*. "La Deflora-

1 The rose image goes back to Ausonius, the lily to Ovid, *Metam.* X, 190–195; Verg., *Aen.* IX, 435 and XI, 68; Laum., *Oeuvres Rons.* VII, 262.

2 Laum., *Ed. Crit.* II, 33–5. Cf. Hor. IV, 10; Laum. VII, 268.

3 Laum., *Ed. Crit.* II, 51–4.

4 Cf. Hor. *Epod.*, 17, lines 25–6, and *Carm.* II, 9, 18, and IV, 7.

5 Laum., *Ed. Crit.* II, 12–13.

tion De Lede"[1] uses the poet's profession of a Jupiteresque passion as an excuse to tell the myth of Leda at great length. It is an epyllion rather than an ode. The "Complainte de Glaucque a Scylle Nymphe"[2] is not an ode but a piscatory eclogue.

The poems about poetry or the poet are also familiar. So are the philosophical, reflective, and occasional odes. One of Ronsard's most famous nature poems prays to the fountain Bellerie[3] that it may always be an object of rural devotion if he may be freed of his longing to drink there on hot summer days when he burns with fever,

Argentine fonteine vive
De qui le beau crystal courant,
D'une fuite lente, et tardive
Ressuscite le pré mourant.

Quand l'esté ménager moissonne
Le sein de Ceres dévetu,
Et l'aire par compas resonne
Dessous l'épi de blé batu:

A tout jamais puisses-tu estre
En honneur, et religion
Au beuf, et au bouuier champestre
De ta voisine region.

Et la lune d'un oeil prospere
Voie les bouquins amenans
La Nimphe aupres de ton repere
Un bal sur l'herbe demenans,

Comme je desire fonteine
De plus ne songer boire en toi
L'esté, lors que la fièvre ameine
La mort dépite contre moi.

[1] *Ibid.*, II, 67–79. Laum., *Rons. Poète,* pp. 388–9, and Nolhac, *Rons. et l'Human.*, p. 105, find that Ronsard is here indebted to the accounts of the carrying off of Europa by Moschus, Ovid, and Claudian and of the rape of Proserpine by Ovid and Claudian. See also Laum.'s notes, *Oeuvres Rons.* VII, 271.

[2] Laum., *Ed. Crit.* II, 57–60.

[3] *Ibid.*, II, 14–15.

Here we find the Horatian influence and Ronsard's genius at their happiest conjunction. Ronsard's affectionate picture of the vivifying fountain, and his following description of a harvest scene that we all recognize, make the situation so real and familiar that, after a transitional stanza about the worship of fountains, we can easily accept the Horatian nymphs dancing in the moonlight as poetic truth, not mythological ornamentation. Modern life and classical tradition have been perfectly amalgamated here and this adds special poignancy to Ronsard's final prayer, the surprising Horatian concluding turn, that he may no longer yearn to drink from the fountain Bellerie in the summertime when fever brings death near. Classical mythology and conciseness, clear, pictorial imagery, and strongly marked logical development are here all completely subservient to Ronsard's inspiration. In contrast with another successful ode, "Avant-Venue du Printemps,"[1] where Ronsard marshalled his classicism with Ovidian magnificence, for its own sake, in this poem the learned allusions have been managed with a Horatian lightness of touch and have been used solely to communicate, with something of a humorous irony, the poet's own personal feelings. Although this ode is in many ways like Horace's famous Bandusia ode, and although the basic idea, the fevered poet's longing for a cool country fountain, is borrowed from Pontano,[2] "A La Fontaine Bellerie" is by no means an imitation. The classicism here is Ronsard's own, completely mastered and absorbed. It is with "Mignonne allons voir si la rose" one of Ronsard's most successful poems.

Another of Ronsard's loveliest odes, "De La Venue de L'Esté,"[3] describes summer like a Brueghel painting with the same lusty vividness that we found in "Avant-Venue du Printemps":

> Ja-ja les grans chaleurs s'émeuvent,
> Et presque les fleuves ne peuvent
> Leurs peuples escaillés couvrir,
> Ja voit on la plaine alterée
> Par la grande torche aithérée
> De soif se lâcher, et s'ouurir.

[1] *Ibid.*, I, 147–54.

[2] From "Cassim fontem aegrotus alloquitur," G. G. Pontano, *Carm.* (Basileae, 1556), pp. 3293–5. See also "Laudes Casis fontis," *ibid.*, pp. 3295–6. Notes from Laum., *Oeuvres Rons.* VII, 266.

[3] Laum., *Ed. Crit.* II, 23–8.

L'estincelante Canicule,
Qui ard, qui cuist, qui boust, qui brule,
L'esté nous darde de là haut,
Et le souleil qui se promeine
Par les braz du Cancre,[1] rameine
Ces mois tant pourboullis du chaut.

Ici, la diligente troupe
Des ménagers renverse, et coupe
Le poil de Cerés jaunissant, . .

Ce pendant leurs femmes sont prestes
D'assurer au haut de leurs testes
Des plats de bois, ou des baris,
Et fillant, marchent par la plaine
Pour aller apâter la peine
De leurs laborieus maris.

The herdsman rises before dawn and leads his flocks through the plains and woods and along the banks of streams, where the young goats play, crashing their horns together. Then at noon —and the signs of the zodiac change now so that the noon is mid-August[2]—while the cattle rest, their noses pressed to the ground, the herdsman weaves baskets or limes birds or swims, naked like a fish, a homely, yet vivid image, that makes the ode with its grandiose scenic effects and traditional richness, nevertheless close and immediate.

The day lengthens. Under the oaks the cattle chew their cud and the heifers bellow for love, while the herdsman's boy plays his pipe and the sun sinks towards the west. Then the herd is assembled and watered and the flat-nosed band march slowly homeward to the bagpipe's sound.

The poem is pastoral in the broadest sense and owes something to the literary pastoral in its last part. However, the magnificent panorama of the season with its labours and zodiac signs as we find it in medieval sculpture or manuscript illumination has the vastness, grandeur, and elaboration combined

[1] The sun conventionally enters Cancer on June 21st and remains in that constellation through July 20th.

[2] Si l'antique fable est croyable,
Erigone la pitoyable
En telle mois alla luire aux cieux
En forme de vierge.

with the lyricism that only the ode knows, the ode as developed by Pontano and Marullus.

Ronsard's fourth book of odes, most of which was written after his Pindaric enthusiasm had begun to wane, is notable for having only two poems that occupy themselves with the aristocracy.[1] Otherwise the subjects are love, poetry, mutability, and nature. "Le Ravissement de Cephale,"[2] the companion piece to "La Defloration de Lede" of the previous book and like it written in three "poses," is an epyllion with a frame story, the wedding of Peleus and Thetis and the prophecy of the greatness of Achilles, enclosing the myth of Aurora and Cephalus, told as a *chanson de toile* by the nymph Nais during the weaving of Neptune's wedding robes by the Nereids. This is Ronsard's finest feat in mythological writing and in the description of an art object in the "odes." However, as an epyllion it must be passed over.

Two other poems[3] are *voeux*, prayers to deities with promises to be fulfilled if the prayers are answered. A third prayer,[4] to sleep, to bring repose to his sick lady, accompanies its analysis of sleep by compulsory magic rites. It resembles the ancient eclogues about witchraft or some of the incantatory neolatin odes. Then there is an occasional ode which, moralizing about the evils of anger, with illustrative examples, makes peace with Mellin de Sainct-Gelays[5]; a debate between the heart and eyes[6] with the old conceits about love; and an ode, "Au

[1] The two poems are a brief "Au Roy Henry II," Laum., *Ed. Crit.* VII, 90–1, which praises the pillars of the throne, the two soldiers, Montmorency and Guise, and the new Maecenas, the Cardinal of Lorraine, and "Epithalame d'Anthoine de Bourbon, et de Jeanne Royne de Navarre," *ibid.*, I, 9–16, an occasional poem, first published in 1549, based on Theocritus' epithalamium of Helen and Catullus' epithalamium for Julia and Manlius (*Carm.* 62) whence it has borrowed its refrain "O Hymen, Hymenée / Hymen, ô Hymenée," Nolhac, *Rons. et l'Human.*, p. 105.

[2] Laum., *Ed. Crit.* II, 133–47.

[3] "Veu à Lucine," *ibid.*, II, 114–17 and "Veu au Somme," *ibid.*, II, 122–4. As has been noted earlier the *voeu* traces its ancestry back through Navagero's *Lusus pastorales* (1530) and Horace's *vota* (*Carm.* III, 18, 22) to the ἀναθήματα of the *Greek Anthology*.

[4] Laum., *Ed. Crit.*, VII, 198–200.

[5] *Ibid.*, V, 165–74. For sources see Laum.'s notes, *Oeuvres Rons.* VII, 284–5.

[6] Laum., *Ed. Crit.* VI, 250–3. See Laum.'s notes, *Oeuvres Rons.* VII, 285–6, and *Rons. Poète*, pp. 485–7.

Pais de Vandomois (voulant aller en Italie),"[1] expresses joy at the thought of seeing Italy and comments on the educational value of travel.

Of the four main groups of odes in the fourth book, the poems about the poet and poetry are again familiar types. Three of them proclaim the immortality of poetry.[2] A fourth is a kind of pastoral elegy that the poet has written for himself before his death. In "De L'Election De Son Sepulchre"[3] a poet writes of the death of a poet, shepherds speak his eulogy, the dead poet becomes a tutelary deity, in this case a kind of *genius loci*, to whom the shepherds offer yearly sacrifices, and there is a final reconciliation to the fact of death in the classical description of Elysium and in the celebration of the power of poetry. Of course the poem is not a pastoral elegy, and it lacks one of the most important elements of the elegy, namely grief, because Ronsard is not dead. Propertius also wrote a poem (*Elegiarum* II, 13) describing the sort of funeral that he would have, but there is little resemblance between that poem and this.

The mutability odes are also familiar types, frequently borrowing from Horace, and need not be discussed in detail. The theme of one of them,[4]

> Pourquoy, chetif laboureur,
> Trembles tu d'un Empereur . . .
> "Ne scais-tu qu'à tout chaqu'un
> "Le port d'enfer est commun,

calls to mind Shirley's famous lines from *The Contention of Ajax and Ulysses*,

> The glories of our blood and state
> Are shadows, not substantial things;
> There is no armour against fate;

[1] Laum., *Ed. Crit.* II, 91–6. See Laum.'s notes, *Oeuvres Rons.* VII, 275–6.

[2] Laum., *Ed. Crit.* II, 120–2 (see Laum.'s notes, *Oeuvres Rons.* VII, 279–280); VII, 108–10 (Laum. notes, *Oeuvres Rons.* VII, 282, that this ode is based on an epigram of Marullus, *Epigr.* II, "Ad Musas,"); and VI, 161–2.

[3] Laum., *Ed. Crit.* II, 97–103. For a study of the sources see Laum., *Rons. Poète*, p. 369.

[4] Laum., *Ed. Crit.* VII, 103–4. Sources, Pindar, *Isthm.* VI, 42; *Nem.* VII, 19–20 and 30–1; Hor. II, 14, lines 9–12 and III, 1, 9–16, Laum. *Oeuvres Rons.* VII, 281.

Death lays his icy hand on kings:
Sceptre and crown
Must tumble down,
And in the dust be equal made
With the poor crooked scythe and spade.

Another[1] contrasts mortal man with nature and compares his days to the waves of a river,

Ondes, sans fin vous promenés
Et vous menés et ramenés
Vos flots d'un cours qui ne sejourne,
Et moi, sans faire long sejour,
Je m'en vais de nuit et de jour,
Mais comme vous je ne retourne.

But Ronsard manages to lighten the gloom, in the conclusion, by a pretty, if unoriginal compliment to his mistress, mortality's compensation.[2]

The love poems in this book are all Anacreontics, most of them incomparable versions of Anacreon himself,[3] some few,

[1] Laum., *Ed. Crit.* VII, 98–9.

[2] Cf. Ronsard, "Cassandre ne donne pas / Des baisers, mais des apas," *ibid.*, I, 197–9 and Secundus, *Bas.* 4, "Non dat basia, dat Neaera nectar." Both these poems end with a similar conceit.

[3] All but one of the Anacreontics were not added to this book until 1555. The earlier Anacreontic is "Du grand Turc je n'ai souci" (Laum., *Ed. Crit.* V, 79–80), a translation of "*"Ου μοι μέλει τὰ Γυγέω*" and "*Τὸν ἄργυρον τορεύων*" which were printed together as one piece in the *Planudean Anthology* (reprinted four times since the first edition by John Lascaris, Florence, 1494), the source of Ronsard's knowledge of Anacreon before the Stephanus edition of 1554. The other translations from Anacreon are: "Naguiere chanter je voulois" (Laum., *Ed. Crit.* VI, 133–4) from "*Θέλω λέγειν 'Ατρείδας*"; "Le petit enfant Amour" (*ibid.*, VII, 106–7) from "*"Ερως ποτ' ἐν ῥόδοισι*"; "Lors que Bacus entre chés moy" (VI, 243–4) from "*"Οταν βάκχος ἐσέλθῃ*"; "Les Muses lieront un jour" (VI, 253–5) from "*"Αι Μοῦσαι τον "Ερωτα*"; "Pourtant si j'ay le chef plus blanc" (VI, 255–6) from "*Μή με Φύγῃς ὁρῶσα*"; "La terre les eaux va boivant" (VI, 256) from "*'Η γῆ μέλαινα πίνει*"; "Plusiers de leurs cors desnués" (VI, 258–9) from "*"Η Ταντάλου ποτ' ἔστη*"; "Pourquoy comme une ieune poutre" (VI, 259–60) from "*Πῶλε Θρῃκίη, τί δή με*" (Stephanus 1554, not in the Teubner Anacreon); "Ha, si l'or pouvoit alonger" (VI, 260–1) from "*"Ο πλοῦτος εἰ γε Χρυσοῦ*"; "Celuy qui n'ayme est malheureux" (VI, 162–4) from "*Χαλεπὸν τὸ μὴ φιλῆσαι*"; "Verson ces Roses prés ce vin" (VII, 189–92), a *contaminatio* of "*Τὸ ῥόδον τὸ τῶν 'Ερώτων*" and "*Στεφανηφόρου μετ' ἦρος*"; and "Je suis homme né pour mourir" (VII, 195–6) from "*'Επειδὴ βροτὸς ἐτύχθην.*"

versions of other ancient poets,[1] and one of them an original poem based on a Latin distich by the French humanist, Marc Antoine Muret.[2] These are some of Ronsard's most charming works, for Ronsard's genius was thoroughly Alexandrian, and, along with Herrick's, they are the best translations of Anacreon that we have.

The last group of poems are about nature. The only one of these that is really an ode is the "Ode à l'Alouette," which Sells believes is the first skylark poem in the European tradition and which was apparently inspired by the recently published Anacreontic to the cicada.[3] Ronsard's "Ode à l'Alouette" has something in common with Shelley's "To a Skylark." Both poets describe the bird's flight, although Ronsard, like Shakespeare after him,[4] describes it at dawn, while the romantic poet chooses twilight. Then Ronsard, being a nature poet and so interested in the bird itself, also describes its plunge to earth, its nesting, and feeding its young, whereas Shelley, the poet of ideas, allows the physical bird to vanish into the purple sky, leaving only the song. Ronsard also sees the rural occupations of springtime and hears a shepherdess sing as well as the lark, but the bird's song and Shelley's thoughts are alone in the dusk. Both poets share the primitivist outlook and contrast the lark's innocence and joy with man's knowledge and sorrow, but Ronsard, to complain of the misery his mistress causes him, Shelley to desire to know the lark's ecstasy so that he may compel the world to listen to his poetry. Between these two interpretations of the lark lie two hundred and seventy years of human history.

Another of the nature poems and one of Ronsard's greatest

[1] "Venus est par cent mille noms" (VI, 245) is based on a frag. of Sophocles, "Ὦ παῖδες, ἥ τοι," published in the Renaissance in the *Florilegium* of Stobaeus, LXIII, 6, Laum., *Rons. Poète*, p. 124, fn. 3. Another ode (VII, 196–7) takes beginning from Propertius, *Eleg.* II, 12.

[2] Laum., *Ed. Crit.* VII, 105. See note, Laum., *Oeuvres Rons.* VII, 281–2.

[3] For the poem see *Ed. Crit.* VI, 245–7. For Sells' theory of the Anacreontic source of this poem see A. Lytton Sells, *Animal Poetry in French and English Literature and the Greek Tradition* (Bloomington, Ind., 1955), pp. 63–5.

[4] Cf. Hark, hark! the lark at heaven's gate sings
And Phoebus gins arise. *Cymbeline*, II, 3.

lyrics is "Bel aubepin verdissant."[1] Here, in a kind of prayer-ode, Ronsard describes a familiar tree with loving exactitude, a tree that is manifestly mortal like all living things, yet all the more dear because of that. The hawthorne is covered to the end of its branches with a parasitic vine, its foot is half-eaten away by two camps of red ants, and its hollow stump has already found a new tenant, a swarm of wild bees. The nightingale comes there yearly to build his nest, but Ronsard, as pitiless as nature, steals its young. The scene is one of luxuriant life on the bank of a stream, of constant growth and constant decay, of the replacement of the old by the new, and of carelessness about the individual. Then Ronsard, the poet, the giver of eternal life, commands his "Bel Aubepin" to be immortal and so it endures, fixed and unchanged.

The last stanza recalls Horace's *envoi* to his first three books of odes. There the poet's monument, here the hawthorne tree, survives, through the immortal power of poetry, unharmed by storm or wind or the flight of time. But there is a closer parallel to the conclusion of this ode in Horace III, 13, the Bandusia ode, where the poet is explicit about his immortalizing function, "Fies nobilium tu quoque fontium / Me dicente," and in Ronsard's imitation of Horace in "A La Fontaine Bellerie," "Que tu vives par mes vers." Laumonier thinks that the particular source of inspiration for these lines was Flaminio's

> Irrigui fontes, et fontibus addita vallis,
> Cinctaque piniferis silva cacuminibus . . .
> Vivite felices, nec vobis aut gravis aestas,
> Aut nocent saevo frigore tristis hiems,
> Nec lympham quadrupes, nec silvam dura bipennis,
> Nec violet teneras hic lupus acer oves.[2]

> Flowing fountains, and vale of the fountains,
> And forest girt with pine-bearing peaks, . . .
> Live happily, and may the heavy heat of summer do you
> No harm, nor gloomy winter with its cruel frost,
> May the four-footed beast not violate the clear water, nor the hard axe
> The forest, nor the sharp-toothed wolf the tender sheep.

[1] Laum., *Ed. Crit.* VII, 242–4.

[2] M. A. Flaminio, *Carmina* (Florentiae, 1552), p. 267, cited by Laum., *Rons. Poète*, pp. 446–7.

The last of the nature poems in the fourth book of odes, "Dieu vous garde messagers fidelles / Du Printemps vistes arondelles"[1] is a benediction of the living things of spring and a song of joy at the return of the sweet season.

Ronsard's fifth book of odes published in 1552 was little different from the other four. The only unusual poem was "Les Etoiles," a statement of Renaissance astrological belief with illustrations of the various fates of man and a concluding prayer to the stars to favour the French in Poland, which was largely derived from Marullus' "Stellis."[2] Otherwise there were odes to the royal circle, moral odes, bacchics, love poems, and later, several Anacreontics.

Ronsard also wrote hymns, a type of poem that may or may not be lyric[3] and, if lyric, may or may not be composed in the manner of the ode. Here it has been our practice to discuss only the hymns which were written as odes. Thus Ronsard's hymns (1555–6), some to men, but most to God, the saints, the elements, and the virtues, since they were not written in the tradition of the ode, will not be discussed. Ronsard's two books of *Amours* (1552 and 1553) with a few Anacreontic exceptions also contain no odes.

Ronsard as a lyric poet was fundamentally Horatian and *marotique*, if one can use the last adjective to designate the best of the graceful, yet vigorous, French court lyrics inherited from the middle ages and embellished and sophisticated by contact with the Italian Renaissance. However, under the influence of the learned professor, Dorat, he went through a period (approxi-

[1] Laum., *Ed. Crit.* VII, 294–5.

[2] Marullus, *Hymnorum Naturalium* (Parisiis, 1561), pp. 65r–66r.

[3] E.g., the so-called Homeric hymns to Apollo, Hermes, Aphrodite, Dionysus, and Ares are virtually epic fragments; they are long accounts in the epic idiom of some episode in the life of the god. The shorter Homeric hymns to the gods are lyric, and tend to be odic. Like Horace's hymn to Mercury they praise the god by summarizing briefly his powers and functions, and by recounting some incident in his life. They may or may not pray to him to be propitious. The hymns ascribed to Orpheus are brief and odic. The hymns of Callimachus are to the "Orphic" hymns as the Pindaric ode is to the Horatian. They are very big and elaborate, with lengthy myths and a large number of obscure allusions, and yet they still are odes.

mately 1545–51)[1] of devoted imitation of Pindar that brought him jeers during his lifetime,[2] cost him his reputation half a century after his death, and kept him in obscurity for some two centuries. Even today, on hundred and thirty years after Ronsard was restored to the the French literary pantheon through the efforts of Sainte-Beuve, in an age when obscurely allusive, learned, Alexandrian poetry is again in vogue, Ronsard's Pindarics remain in disfavour because of their essential falsity. There is no real reason for their triadic form; there is no real justification for introducing the myths, and the myths themselves are manifestly insincere and lack the power inherent in something that has at least once compelled belief; the poet's priest-prophet posturing seems ridiculous; and some of the allusions are so obscure as to puzzle and frustrate even the classical scholar read in Renaissance literature.[3] Today we feel that Ronsard's first loves, Horace and Marot, along with Pontano and Marullus, Anacreon, the poets of the *Greek Anthology*, and their neolatin imitators, were his truest and most faithful. We prize above all his verses of gay hedonism, his affectionate, sensuous, seductive love lyrics, his keenly observant

[1] Laum., *Rons. Poète*, pp. 171–2, says that Ronsard's enthusiasm for Pindar began to diminish in 1551. First he dropped the triads for long equal strophes, then the vagabond digressions; then he began to prefer the odelette and the *folastrie* to the *ode grave*. His last Pindaric effort was a non-triadic ode to celebrate the royal family in 1554. Laum., *ibid.*, pp. 93–7, maintains that Ronsard travestied Pindar in the anonymous *Livret de Folastries* of 1553. In 1556 Ronsard wrote an elegy to be prefaced to Belleau's translation of Anacreon in which he condemned Pindar's noisy pretentiousness, his arrogance, and obscurity which is only good for frightening simple schoolboys, and announced his preference for the gentle sweetness of Anacreon.

[2] Laum., *Rons. Poète*, p. 117, says that even after Ronsard became reconciled with Sainct-Gelays and became royal favourite, he was still laughed at by many of the courtiers because even his love poems needed a scholarly commentary—the second edition of his *Amours* was published in 1553 with notes by Muret.

[3] E.g., how many readers recognize the allusion in "Fille du neveu d'Atlas," Laum., *Ed. Crit.* I, 88? Even the reader of Pindar would pass over the personnified abstraction, *Αγγελία*, one of the powers or functions of Hermes made into his daughter (at the beginning of the fourth epode of the eighth *Nemean*).

poems about nature, and his classical odes on the ephemerality of youth, beauty, and love, on the uncertainty of tomorrow, and the necessity of profiting by today. Here his own temperament, his personal experiences in the bright, beautiful, but tragic courts of the young Valois and Stuart princes, the native French lyric tradition, and his classical education all conspired most happily to produce real masterpieces. Ronsard's nature poetry, particularly, profited from the realism of the ancients, especially Vergil, which served as a liberating influence from the too-frequent banality of medieval nature descriptions.[1] In this respect he might be compared with the very much slighter English poet, Surry.

Like Pindar, Horace, too, could sometimes do Ronsard harm. Too many odes read like vernacular versions of exercises in Latin verse. The pastiche is dull. Horace has been subjected to the cut and paste too many times before. However, when he turned to straight translation, Ronsard was first rate. His Anacreontics, despite their infidelity, are the best versions that we have of that poet in French.

Although Ronsard was one of the great prosodists of French literature, his metrical innovations were not really new. Everything that he achieved had already been blocked out by his predecessors.[2] The difference between Ronsard and the preceding court poets,[3] Sainct-Gelays and Marot, was one of degree, not of intrinsic nature. Men of the Renaissance that they were, they had already turned to the ancients to "illustrate" French poetry and they wrote classical *chansons* like the

[1] Laum., *Rons. Poète*, p. 454. Laum. points out that Ronsard still associates nature with love as did the medieval lyric poets. However, one should not forget that the ancient poets also associated spring with love, so that this should not be taken as a limitation on his natural realism, but only as a reflection of universal human experience.

Note.—The dismissal of medieval nature descriptions as being conventional is one of those generalizations that are half-true. It applies only to nature in lyric poetry, to the everlasting *reverdie*.

[2] Laum., *Rons. Poète*, pp. 638 ff., "Rhythmique Des Odes Et Chansons De Ronsard," this being the third part of the book.

[3] Laum., *Rons. Poète*, pp. 183 and 203–4, says that Ronsard became court poet on the death of Sainct-Gelays in 1558. Henceforth he wrote quatrains for the comedy-ballet, masquerades, pastorals for royal marriages, and *défis* for tourneys.

classical *canzoni* of their Italian contemporaries.[1] They too reacted against the rigidity of medieval prosody and tried to make French metrics simpler and more flexible. Where Ronsard differed from them was solely in genius. There is one respect, however, in which Ronsard was quite distinct from his predecessors, and that is in the use of words. I am not now thinking of the few inkhorn terms and dialect words for which Ronsard was severely abused for so long by the academicians, but of Ronsard's careful choice of words, of his abhorrence of the cliché and the obvious adjective, and of his tireless search for the meaningful word.[2]

Few poets have known such idolatry as Ronsard did during his lifetime. He was praised not only by the kings and princes whose favour he enjoyed but also by the great critics of the day, the Italians, Castelvetro,[3] Sperone Speroni,[4] and Julius Caesar Scaliger,[5] and the Frenchman, Marc Antoine Muret. In the decade after his first volume was published Mary Stuart spread his influence to Scotland, Muret to Italy, and Marguerite de Valois to the Savoy. In 1565 Ronsard dedicated a book of court entertainments to Queen Elizabeth and perhaps started the vogue for the masque in England. In the 1570's the French

[1] Laum., *Rons. Poète*, pp. xlii–xliii, points out that they used mythological references, learned vocabulary, moral sentences, and all kinds of figures. On p. 293 Laum. lists Ronsard's predecessors who tried to enrich French poetry with the spoils of the ancients: Lemaire des Belges, Marot, Hugues Salel, Sainct-Gelays, Lazare de Baïf, Charles Fontaine, Despériers, and Peletier.

[2] See Ronsard, *Abbrégé* (1565), p. 7v, where he warns the Abbé Del Bene against using such expressions as "la rivière coulante" and "la verde ramée" where the epithet is one that would be normally understood and suggests instead expressions such as "le ciel vouté."

[3] Nolhac, *Ronsard et ses Contemporains Italiens*, pp. 3–4, and *Ronsard et l'Humanisme*, p. 226, and F. Neri, *Il Chiabrera e la Pléiade Francese* (Torino, 1920), pp. 5 ff., state that Castelvetro was the first Italian to mention Ronsard whom he lavishly praised in 1559 at the expense of Annibal Caro.

[4] See Nolhac, *Rons. et l'Human.*, p. 228.

[5] J. C. Scaliger dedicated his *Anacreontica* to Ronsard, addressing him as

> Son of the measureless Ether,
> You who are prodigal of wit and govern the Muses,
> O glory of golden song,

Poemata (n.p., 1574), p. 472.

court carried his works with them into Poland. Even during his lifetime Ronsard became a classic to be studied in the schools and universities in Germany, the Low Countries, Poland, England, and Scotland where his glory continually grew as he fell in favour at home.[1] Soon he had imitators abroad, Chiabrera in Italy, Weckherlin and Opitz in Germany, Van Hout in Holland, Kochanowski in Poland, and Rosenhane in Sweden.[1] Ronsard's glory was great, but short lived. With Malherbe he fell out of favour. Early in the seventeenth century he ceased to be reprinted and, apart from a few lyrics that lived in the popular song-books, his name survived only as a by-word for bombast, obscurity, and bad taste.[2] A quatrain that appeared at the head of Ronsard's 1578 edition turned out to be strangely prophetic:

> Les François qui mes vers liront,
> S'ils ne sont et Grecs et Romains,
> Au lieu de ce livre ils n'auront
> Qu'un pesant faix entre les mains.[3]

With the decline of broad humanist learning and the knowledge of Greek in the seventeenth century, Ronsard's poems in fact became "un pesant faix entre les mains." Ronsard, following Pindar and Horace, had compared himself to a bee:

> Mon Passerat, je resemble à l'abeille
> Qui va cueillant tantost la fleur vermeille,
> Tantost la jaune, errant de pré en pré
> Où plus les fleurs fleurissent à son gré,
> Contre l'Hyver amassant force vivres.
> Ainsi lisant et *fueilletant mes livres*,
> J'amasse, trie et choisis le plus beau,
> Qu'en cent couleurs je peints en un tableau.
> Tantost en l'autre, et prompt en ma peinture
> Sans me forcer j'imite la nature.[4]

In the seventeenth century in France palates were no longer educated to appreciate the honey.

[1] See Laum., *Rons Poète*, p. 729 and Laum., ed., *La Vie de Pierre de Ronsard de Claude Binet* [first edition 1586] (Paris, 1910), pp. 43, 208–10; Nolhac, *Rons. et l'Human.*, pp. 205 ff., and *Rons. et ses Contemporains Italiens*, pp. 4–5; Toffanin, *Cinquecento*, pp. 626 ff. For Ronsard's French followers see M. Raymond, *L'Influence de Ronsard*, 2 vols. (Paris, 1927).

[2] See Laum., *Rons. Poète*, p. 722.

[3] Quoted in Nolhac, *Rons. et l'Human.*, p. 129.

[4] *Ibid.*, pp. 129–30.

There was no baroque period in French literature.[1] The Renaissance led straight to neoclassicism. Despite the lionization of Marino by the French Court, there was no school in France to correspond with that of the English metaphysicals. *Preciosité* was a lesser and different thing. The seventeenth century was heralded in France by the appearance of a "correct" poet, François de Malherbe (*c.* 1558–1628).

Malherbe was neither fertile of imagination nor warm of temperament.[2] He was a late-developing, crotchety character with a circle of admiring young poets to whom he set himself up as the arbiter, not of elegance, but of correctness. In some respects, he recalls Dr. Johnson, without the latter's warmth, humanity, and generosity. Indeed, while some of the anecdotes about him reveal a laconic wit not unlike the doctor's, most of the stories about Malherbe suggest a singularly unpleasant personality.

Malherbe's chief preoccupations were with purity of language and clarity of diction. He wrote little, wrote slowly, and with great difficulty. Poetry was always imposed upon him by external obligation. It did not come from internal compulsion. Even counting the pieces that he did not acknowledge and the poems that he left incomplete, Malherbe left only thirteen odes, some verses for court entertainments, a few sonnets, epigrams, songs, consolations, three paraphrases of the Psalms, and an early translation from Tansillo. It is chiefly on the odes that his reputation rests.

In writing the odes, Malherbe looked back fifty years to the young Ronsard, and in many respects he was, in his odes, a follower of Ronsard, particularly of Ronsard as he revised himself for the 1584 edition.[3] Already by 1584 the principles

[1] See M. Raymond, *Baroque et Renaissance Poétique* (Paris, 1955); Raymond Lebègue, *La Poésie Française de 1560 à 1630, II, Malherbe et Son Temps* (Paris, 1951), pp. 15–19, 84.

[2] See Racan's *Mémoires Pour La Vie de M. de Malherbe.*

[3] Note some of Ronsard's revisions of "Avant-Venue du Printemps" (Laum., *Ed. Crit.* I, 147–54):

> Et le sapin des montaignes
> Galopa par les campaignes
> Qui nous baignent alentour,
>
> (lls. 94–6)

was revised to read

that are associated with the name of Malherbe were pretty well established.[1] The popularity of stoicism and of Lipsian rhetoric made clarity and reasonableness the great virtues of a literary work. The appeal to the imagination and the senses was abandoned in favour of an address to the intellect.

During the second half of the sixteenth century poetry had also become serious. From 1555–6 onwards, after Ronsard's hymns were published, and under Italian influence, religious poetry came into vogue. During the same period, heroic poetry was coming to the fore and amorous poetry and the personal lyric were falling out of favour. There were almost no odes written during this half century. Ronsard's abandonment of the ode finished it. Ronsard himself had mocked the Pindaric and soon no-one else attempted it. With the Pindaric went the serious ode. The lighter ode, along with all other forms of poetry whose sole aim was to delight, was not much practised.[2]

Enfin Malherbe vint. He saw that the ode, as adapted by Ronsard, but purged of his extravagances, and submitted to the modern rational discipline, was the ideal vehicle for the official poetry that he felt called upon to write. Thus, he

Et le sapin des valées
Sauta sur les eaux salées
Qui nous baignent à l'entour.

"L'acier tinter durement" (l. 99) was changed to "Rompre harnois et couteaux" and

Et les lames assérées
Sur les enclumes férrées
Craqueter horriblement

was changed to

Et les lames acerées
Sur les enclumes férrées
S'amollir souz les marteaux,

a factually correct but how much less vivid expression!

Again in "De La Venue de L'Esté" in the early version the Dog Star "L'esté nous darde de là haut" and it brings back "Ces mois tant pourbouillis du chaut." For the 1584 edition these two lines were changed to read "L'ardeur nous lance de là haut" and "Tels iours recuits d'extreme chaud."

[1] Lebègue, p. 83; René Fromilhague, *Malherbe Technique et Creation Poétique* (Paris, 1954), pp. 13 ff., 70–80.

[2] Lebègue, pp. 30–1; Fromilhague, pp. 63–7.

borrowed his strophes from Ronsard, but shunned the triadic structure. He chose the same sort of official themes as Ronsard in his Pindaric odes, but never allowed mythology to triumph over the matter at hand. And he was careful to use only those myths that a courtier might recognize. He, too, larded his odes with *sententiae*, but much more sparingly. And he adopted Ronsard's trick, copied from Horace, of plunging *in medias res*. He even echoed Ronsard occasionally, both his moralities and his myths,[1] perhaps because they were well known, perhaps because they saved Malherbe the trouble of finding ideas of his own—Malherbe's imagination was so infertile that he even used some of his occasional poems, including one on the death of a friend's daughter, several times over![2] In his first important ode, on the coming of Marie de Medici, he went so far as to use a mythological conceit as Ronsard might have done.

In general, however, Malherbe banished all fiction and all fanciful forms of expression from his poetry as being contrary to reason and manifest fact. Mythology, however, was occasionally useful to supply well-known examples of the stock virtues and vices. Achilles was the great warrior, Hercules the strong man, and the Titans the impious rebels, i.e., the Protestants. These were the myths that Malherbe used most commonly. Malherbe never enlarged upon his myths through a love of their intrinsic beauty as did Ronsard; they never formed the subject or core of a poem. Rather the names of mythological personages were used by Malherbe in almost the same spirit as personified abstractions.

While Malherbe was never learned or pedantic like Ronsard, he also never sought to affect our sensibilities. He chose his words for their intellectual content, not for their emotional aura. He never described nature—indeed he deplored detailed descriptions[3]—and he used very little visual imagery. His

[1] Compare "A La Reine," lls. 38–40 with Ronsard, "Le Ravissement de Cephale"; "A Monseigneur Le Duc de Bellegarde," lls. 41–4 with Ronsard, "A Michel de L'Hospital," strophe 1; "Ode Pour Le Roy Allant Chastier La Rebellion Des Rochelois," lls. 73–88 with Ronsard, "A Michel de l'Hospital," antistrophe 8–strophe 10; "Au Roy Henry Le Grand sur La Prise de Marseille," lls. 31–4 with Ronsard, Laum., *Ed. Crit.* VII, 98–9, lls. 25–8.

[2] Fromilhague, pp. 130–3; Lebègue, p. 22.

[3] Lebègue, p. 10.

imagery, rather, tended to be of the abstract, allegorical sort. Like Bernardo Tasso he was very fond of the ship image, the storm and the harbour or calm.[1] He often used personifications to convey ideas.

Malherbe's poetry was the poetry of statement, not the poetry of evocation. And his poetry was very like prose both in its vocabulary, which reflected, as far as possible, normal usage, and in its syntax, which did not violate the natural forms of the language. Herein lies Malherbe's chief claim to greatness as a poet. Despite an occasional flat line which reads like prose,[2] Malherbe has succeeded, for the most part, in giving ordinary words and ordinary constructions the elevation peculiar to poetry. He had done this through an economy of expression and through an exquisite choice of words which has permitted him to maintain regular patterns of syllables and rimes without taking liberties with the syntax of the language. Malherbe's is, in one sense, the most natural of poetry. It is not very exciting, but it has a quiet strength.

The one subject about which Malherbe really cared, apart from correct language, was the welfare of France, the end of civil war and of religious dissension, the establishment of a strong monarchy with an assured succession, and the triumph of French arms over her neighbours'. These were the themes, oft repeated, of his best poetry, and they inspired him with a grave and serious tone which still earns him the admiration of critics, even though his reputation as a poet has been in eclipse since the early nineteenth century.[3]

Malherbe's earliest and latest odes were his finest. He was over forty when he wrote his first complete ode and his second original poem. The coming of a queen who promised the

[1] Fromilhague, p. 52.

[2] E.g.,

> L'espine suit la rose, et ceux qui sont contens
> Ne le sont pas long-temps,
>
> "Victoire de la Constance," lls. 15–16
>
> Mais quoy que vous ayez, vous n'avez point Caliste,
> Et moy je ne voy rien, quand je ne la voy pas,
>
> "Sonnet V," lls. 13–14

It is interesting to note that this kind of prosaic poetry was written in Latin as early as the middle of the sixteenth century. See Fabricius, supra, pp. 136–7.

[3] Raymond, pp. 154–5; Lebègue, p. 5.

kingdom an heir and stable government was the theme that inspired him to his first published work. In his favourite *dizain* of octosyllables borrowed from Ronsard (ABABCCDEED), a flexible stanza that lent itself to various effects, Malherbe saluted Mary of Medici on her passage through Aix in the year 1600.

The people's joy and the troubles that have harassed them in the past are bound up together, as they inevitably would be psychologically, in the first two stanzas. Then the poet praises the queen in his characteristic impersonal hyperbole. The sincerity of his feelings towards the queen are evident, but his expressions are all conventional: the sun has never seen her like, she surpasses Venus, Diana, and Aurora. He touches on her ancestry and her moral character. Her family does not make her proud, the Graces speak through her lips, her brow confesses her innocence.

To bolster up a theme rather thin, Malherbe, like Rubens later when he was treating Mary of Medici, resorts to mythology. The queen had been delayed by storms on her passage to France. Neptune, enamoured of her beauty, was reluctant to let her go. The conceit is elaborated as it might have been by Ronsard or the Petrarchans and it occupies two stanzas, a lot of space for Malherbe to spend on mythological fictions. Now the queen has arrived. Poetic licence is tempered by reason. "Les fleurs naissent à sa rencontre"—"Dans les coeurs et dans les esprits."

Malherbe addresses the princess in two stanzas harking back to the first two stanzas, rejoicing over the promise of an end to France's troubles. The prospect of an heir who will bring glory to French arms and conquer the Turks occupies another two stanzas. Now at last Malherbe is free to treat the subject which is at the moment of prime importance to a man of sober thought, the safety of the king's person. This theme occupies the whole last half of the ode, lines 120–230.

The prospect of an end to civil dissension, real hope at last, puts added stress on the terrible peril in which the kingdom still stands. The coming of the princess means the ultimate security of the monarchy. But the king must live a while or the kingdom may be reduced to anarchy again. Henry, upon whom all happiness depends, must be persuaded to trust to the new bastion of his marriage and to risk his life no more in military campaigns. As is often the case with ode writers, Malherbe becomes strangely prophetic when he warns Henry to be careful on all sides. Achilles was killed by his least redoubtable enemy. Even with the most brilliant captain there is always the possibility of a Paris, or a Ravaillac! So strongly does Malherbe feel that the fate of France depends upon the life of a single man that he virtually accuses Henry of impious ambition (lls. 205–10). The king must now retire to a happy private life and leave conquest to his successful generals. The conclusion is strong and specific, all the more powerful for its restrained expression,

> Et Soissons, fatal aux superbes,
> Fera chercher parmi les herbes
> En quelle place fut Turin.

This is a successful official ode. It celebrates a particular occasion and it interprets its wider meaning. It has lessons for the young queen, the king, and the people of France. It remains of interest today because it successfully recreates the anxieties, tensions, and uncertainties of a crucial period in French history. It is not an ode full of showy set pieces like Ronsard's famous ode to Michel de l'Hospital—we do not remember lovely images nor epigrammatic turns of phrase—but it is a more serious work. It gains its effect through the poet's conviction of the importance of what he has to say and his restrained earnestness in saying it.

A greater ode, without the frivolity of conventional compliment and mythological conceit, is Malherbe's last work, his "Ode Pour Le Roy Allant Chastier La Rebellion Des Rochelois Et Chasser Les Anglois Qui En Leur Faveur Estoient Descendus En L'Isle De Ré." In a stanza reminiscent of the Latin sapphic, one of Horace's favourites, Malherbe calls on the king to crush the last rebel outpost in France. The theme as well as the stanza is Horatian.

In many ways this ode is a departure from Malherbe's mature work. Here he does not shun sensuous and emotional appeal. In the opening stanza Louis is called upon to strike with his thunder and, in the heavy strokes of the "d" alliteration, we feel that the king beats down the rebellion and stills the discord in his kingdom. We would not have expected that Malherbe could make such an effective use of this figure of sound:

> Donq un nouveau labeur à tes armes s'appreste;
> Pren ta foudre, Louys, et va comm' un lion
> Donner le dernier coup à la derniere teste
> De la rebellion.

The discreet allusion to the rebellion as a hydra, something monstrous, in keeping with his later references to the Protestants as giants, is also unusually effective.

Two stanzas later the duration of the rebellion is expressed in concrete visual imagery, conventional to be sure, but still more vivid than is typical of Malherbe:

> Le centiesme decembre a les plaines ternies
> Et le centiesme avril les a peintes de fleurs.

This has the ring of Herrick. The fortifications of La Rochelle, too, are described in pictorial imagery. Here a grotesque baroque conceit following the prosaic reality of the second verse heightens the effect of the two-fold allusion to the Giants and the Babylonians in the first line of the stanza:

> Ils ont beau vers le ciel leurs murailles accroistre,
> Beau d'un soin assidu travailler à leurs forts,
> Et creuser leurs fossez jusqu' à faire paroistre
> Le jour entre les morts.

The passing references to the Protestants as Giants in the first part of the poem controls the imagery of the extended simile in the middle of the ode where Malherbe, taking inspiration from Ronsard's ode to Michel de l'Hospital, describes the Gigantomachy to urge Louis to realize the same sort of victory over his enemies. The last quarter of the ode, in Ronsard's Pindaric manner is devoted to the poet. Malherbe, now seventy, reflects on a glorious death and regrets that he cannot serve as a soldier, but

> Mars est comme l'Amour: ses travaux et ses peines
> Veulent de jeunes gens.

In two magnificent stanzas with well-founded pride he boasts that his intellectual powers have not failed:

> Je suis vaincu du temps, je cede à ses outrages;
> Mon esprit seulement, exempt de sa rigueur,
> A de quoy tesmoigner en ses derniers ouvrages
> Sa premiere vigueur.
>
> Les puissantes faveurs dont Parnasse m'honore
> Non loin de mon berceau commencerent leur cours;
> Je les posseday jeune, et les possede encore
> A la fin de mes jours.

With these gifts he will glorify Louis, as no poet can do, so that his renown will reach the farthest corners of the earth:

> Par eux [mes vers] de tes beaux faicts la terre sera pleine,
> Et les peuples du Nil qui les auront ouys,
> Donneront de l'encens, comme ceux de la Seine,
> Aux autels de Louys.

Was the extraordinarily emphatic position of the king's name suggested to Malherbe by Horace's tremendous conclusion to the second ode of his first book, "Te duce Caesar"? Everywhere in this ode Malherbe is specific and pictorial like Horace.

The "Ode for the King" with its sober dignity, its nobility of tone, its restrained severity against the Protestants, so much more effective than hysterical ranting, its single-minded attachment to the tranquillity of the kingdom, its pictorial technique, and its occasional epigrammatic turn of phrase is Malherbe's most Horatian, indeed the only one of his odes which, for economy and sustained intensity, could be compared with Horace's patriotic odes.

Malherbe's other odes are "Prière Pour Le Roy Allant en Limozin" (pp. 13–18), "Ode Sur L'Attentat Commis En La Personne De Sa Majesté Le 19 De Décembre 1605" (pp. 18–26), "Ode Au Feu Roy Sur L'Heureux Succez Du Voyage De Sedan" (pp. 28–36), "A Monseigneur Le Duc De Bellegarde Grand Escuyer De France" (pp. 37–48), "A La Reine Sur Les Heureux Succez De Sa Regence" (pp. 56–62), "A La Reine Mere Du Roy Pendant Sa Regence" (pp. 62–4), "Sur Le Marriage Du Roy Et De La Reine" (pp. 75–7), "Fragment d'Ode" (against the mignons of Henry III) (pp. 155–6), "Au

Roy Henry Le Grand Sur La Prise de Marseille" (frag.) (pp. 156–8), "Sur le Même Sujet" (frag.) (pp. 158–9), and "Pour La Reine Mere Du Roy Pendant Sa Regence" (frag.) (pp. 167–174). The subjects are not of great interest today and there is little variety of treatment. The odes to Henry IV are highly repetitious. Mary of Medici seems to have offered a happier inspiration than Malherbe's other subjects.

Malherbe, along with his pupils Maynard and Racan, gave the French ode its definitive form until the romantic movement. It was a soberer form than Ronsard's, less fanciful, more serious, a cold address to the intellect rather than an appeal to the imagination, a form of "lyric" poetry which virtually banished personal emotion, which shunned particular imagery, which became in fact a kind of eloquence characterized by discipline, vigour, exactness of expression, and logical clarity. Inspiration yielded to impeccable purity of form.[1]

[1] Lebègue, pp. 41–2.

Chapter 6

THE ENGLISH ODE

IT is a familiar fact of English literary history that the period from the death of Chaucer in 1400 until the publication of the *Shepheards Calendar* in 1579 is one of literary barrenness, whose vast Sahara is relieved by few green oases—and these offer salvation to the soul but no comfort to the body. Chaucer's merry caravan of pilgrims has disappeared into eternity and we are left for nearly two hundred years with the empty winds and the drought stricken sands; for, after the deposition and murder of her anointed king in 1399, England was desolated at home by a century of civil war and, despite Henry V's brilliant victory at Agincourt, disgraced and defeated abroad. Thus, in the course of the fifteenth century, England lost not only France but also what we now feel to be more important, her fourteenth-century promise of an early Renaissance. There was little to foster the arts and civilization in the rude and savage age of Warwick the Kingmaker (1428–71). And so, despite "good" Duke Humphrey's efforts to introduce the new learning into England and despite the brief flowering of humanism under Grocyn, Linacre, Colet, More, and Erasmus at the turn of the sixteenth century, a period when Cornish's music, King's College and Henry VII's chapels, and Wiat and Surry's lyrics held golden promise, culture in England was blasted by political, and then religious, conflict from the reign of King Richard II until the middle years of Elizabeth. It was only after the great queen had been twenty years on the throne that poetry began to flourish in England, and it was then that

Spenser looked back to Chaucer to find the continuity of the tradition. The poetry of Chaucer's successor, John Lydgate (1370?–1451?), had, with the *Falls of Princes*, dominated the whole of the English barren period and culminated in the early Elizabethan *Mirror for Magistrates*. Now that a new poetic impulse had come, the English poets turned away from him to the more cheerful Chaucer and, like Chaucer, to the French and the Italians, for their inspiration.

There have been many studies of the influence of the French and the Italians, and of the Italians through the French, upon the English during the Renaissance.[1] These show the specifically Italian influence to be greater in the early period, with the French influence steadily growing to reach its acme in the reigns of the two Charleses. The state of affairs can best be illustrated from two well known literary sources, Roger Ascham's attack, in *The Scholemaster* (1565), on the fashionable young man of his day, "l'inglese italianato è un diabolo incarnato," and Ben Jonson's epigram on the "English Mounsieur" (1616):

> Would you beleeve, when you this Mounsieur see,
> That his whole body should speake french, not he?
> That so much scarfe of France, and hat, and fether,
> And shooe, and tye, and garter should come hether,
> And land on one, whose face durst never bee
> Toward the sea, farther than halfe-way tree?
> That he, untravell'd, should be french so much
> As french-men in his companie, should seeme dutch?
> Or had his father, when he did him get,
> The french disease, with which he labours yet?
> Or hung some Mounsieur's picture on the wall,
> By which his damme conceiv'd him clothes and all?

[1] See, e.g., A. Lytton Sells, *The Italian Influence in English Poetry* (Bloomington, Ind., 1955); Antero Meozzi, *Azione e diffusione della letteratura italiana in Europa* (Pisa, 1932), p. 48; Mary Augusta Scott, *Elizabethan Translations from the Italian* (Boston, 1916); Alfred Horatio Upham, *The French Influence In English Literature From The Accession of Elizabeth to the Restoration* (New York, 1908); Sidney Lee, *Elizabethan Sonnets*, 2 vols. (Westminster, 1900); and *The French Renaissance in England* (Oxford, 1910); Charles Edward Mallet, *A History of the University of Oxford* I (London, 1924); and James Bass Mullinger, *The University of Cambridge From the Earliest Times to the Royal Injunctions of 1535* I (Cambridge, 1873).

Or is it some french statue? No: 'T doth move,
And stoupe, and cringe. O then, it needs must prove
The new french-taylors motion, monthly made,
Daily to turne in Paule, and help the trade.[1]

Since the ode enters English literary history in this later period it comes under the auspices of the French. However, once the English began emulating the Pléiade and writing odes, their classical education founded by the great humanists of the beginning of the sixteenth century soon caused them to go from the French to the ancient and neolatin poets for their models. Thus the characteristic English ode derives its irregular form from the school experimentation in Latin verse, its elevation, dignity, and high seriousness from Pindar, and its knowledge of how to universalize a contemporary theme from the humanists. There is a minor tradition deriving from Horace, of moral odes composed in restrained classical taste and written in neat, brief stanzas. There is a more minor stream yet, tumbling down in silvery laughter from the far-off spring of Anacreon. But the main tradition of the English ode is Pindaric, and unmistakably seventeenth century in origin. The typical English ode is marked by the broken line, the fervid emotionalism, the pompousness, and the lavish decoration of the baroque period and the developed classical tradition which gave it birth.

John Sootherne is usually given the credit for having introduced the ode into English literature by virtue of his clumsy, and unacknowledged, versions of Ronsard in *Pandora: The Musique of the Beautie of His Mistress Diana* (1584). He rightly says "that never man before, / Now in England, knewe Pindars string."[2] But we may legitimately wonder if they were much the wiser after Sootherne's volume appeared. The obvious external characteristic of the Pindaric was there, the triadic structure, imitated from Ronsard, although not exactly imitated, with the result that the odes were slightly irregular, the strophes and antistrophes not being exactly alike throughout the poems. But there was nothing of the spirit of Pindar and there was no inspiration or poetry in these versions to

[1] *Poems of Ben Jonson*, ed. George Burke Johnston (London, 1954).

[2] Sootherne, Ode 1, epode 3, quoted by Robert Shafer, *The English Ode to 1660* (Princeton, 1918), p. 46.

popularize the new way of writing. It is not surprising that Sootherne's volume had little, if any, influence.

The other author who is commonly given credit for having introduced the ode into England is Edmund Spenser, with his *Epithalamium* of 1594. The *Epithalamium*'s claim to being an ode is that it is an occasional lyric poem, written in an elevated style, celebrating an event generalized to appear of vast importance. Thus it resembles an ode. But the epithalamium like the sonnet, the usual elegy, whether amorous or funeral, and the ancient type of epigram, has so long been discriminated from the large lyric genre that there seems little point in removing it from its historical sub-genre and throwing it back into the less differentiated mass, especially when this reclassification will offer no new key to the interpretation of the poem, nor will the *Epithalamium*'s inclusion among English odes contribute to the clarification of that already confused genre. Therefore it is our opinion that the *Epithalamium* should continue to be an epithalamium and not be forced to be an ode.

A third man whom nobody seems to notice in this connection is Barnabe Barnes (1569?–1609). In *Parthenophil and Parthenophe* (1593), along with madrigals, elegies, sonnets, sestinas, and *canzoni*, Barnes published a series of poems called *Odes Pastoral* which tend to resemble the neolatin *lusus pastoralis* or the Italian pastoral sonnet or *canzone*. Most of Barnes' poems, however, are lower in style than their Italian counterparts—usually the country bumpkins are described with the crude and lusty vigour of a Flemish painting, e.g.,

> The Shepherds poopen in their pipe,
> One leads his wench a Country Round;
> Another sits upon the ground,
> And doth his beard from drivel wipe,
> Because he would be handsome found.[1]

Some of these pastoral "odes" are *canzoni* in form, i.e., poems composed of a series of long like stanzas completed by a brief *envoy*. Others are sestinas. Some are in the Petrarchan tradition with a weeping lover, sighing nature, and an oh so cruel mistress. Others belong to the echo type favoured by the troubadours. There is a vow to Bacchus of a sort familiar from

[1] Lee, *Elizabethan Sonnets* I, 287.

Horace, the neolatins, and Ronsard[1]; a rimeless poem with a Petrarchan lover which is written in a stanza which suggests the sapphic, ABC_4D_2[2]; another called "Asclepiad" that does *not* recall the ancient metre[3]; and a group of poems inspired by or translated from Anacreon.[4] Barnes' odes, although they are infinitely more attractive to read and more pleasing to the ear than Sootherne's, introduce little that is new into the English lyric tradition but a label.

Another figure which stands at the threshold of the English ode is Thomas Campion (1567–1620). His songs, epigrams set to airs, are almost odes—indeed there is a hymn in a successful English sapphic stanza among them,

> Come, let us sound with melody, the praises
> Of the King's King, th'omnipotent Creator,
> Author of number, that hath all the world in
> Harmony framed.[5]

However, Campion, although he could write in the manner of Anacreon and Secundus and even of Ronsard, and although he sometimes echoed Horace and Catullus, always preferred the slighter form of the epigram to the more elaborate form of the ode.

With Michael Drayton (1563–1631), however, we come to a man who wrote some genuine odes, although we would not allow him that title for all of the poems for which he claims it in the 1606 and 1619 editions of *Poems Lyrick and Pastorall*. We cannot accept Drayton's typical sixteenth-century equation of ode with song.[6] In an address "To the Reader" Drayton says:

> Odes I have called these my few Poems; which how happie soever they prove, yet Criticisme it selfe cannot say, that the Name is wrongfully usurped: For . . . an Ode is known to have been properly a Song, moduled to the ancient Harpe, and neither too short-breathed, as hasting to the end, nor composed of the longest

[1] *Ibid.*, I, 277.

[2] *Ibid.*, I, 306–7.

[3] *Ibid.*, I, 308.

[4] *Ibid.*, I, 282, 289–91, 293, 304–6.

[5] Thomas Campion, *Songs and Masques* . . . , ed. A. H. Bullen (London, 1903), pp. 22–3.

[6] Cf., e.g., Shakespeare, *Love's Labour Lost* IV, iii, 99 and *As You Like It* III, ii, 384.

Verses, as unfit for the sudden Turnes and loftie Tricks with which Apollo used to manage it. They are (as the Learned say) divers: Some transcendently loftie, and farre more high than the Epick (commonly called the Heroique Poeme) witnesse those of the inimitable Pindarus, consecrated to the glorie and renowne of such as returned in triumph from Olympus, Elis, Isthmus, or the like: Others, among the Greekes are amorous, soft, and made for Chambers, as other for Theaters; as were Anacreon's, the very Delicacies of the Grecian Erato, which Muse seemed to have beene the Minion of that Teian old Man, which composed them: Of a mixed kinde were Horaces, and [these] may truely therefore be called his mixed; whatsoever else are mine, little partaking of the high Dialect of the first:

> Though we be all to seeke
> Of *Pindar*, that great Greeke.

Nor altogether of Anacreon, the Arguments being Amorous, Morall, or what else the Muse pleaseth,

and later,

> . . . the last Ode of this Number, or if thou wilt, Ballad . . . for both the great Master of Italian Rymes, Petrarch, and our Chaucer, and other of the upper House of the Muses, have thought their Canzons honoured in the Title of a Ballad. . . .[1]

The first of the *Poems Lyrick and Pastorall*, however, "To Himselfe, and the Harpe,"[2] is a genuine ode written in a short stanza ($AABAB_3$) which recalls the Horatian. Its subject is the poet's intention of reviving ancient lyric poetry. In the Renaissance manner Drayton stresses the importance of divine inspiration, driving his point home with an illustrative myth briefly told. Then he illustrates the power of poetry by allusions to David and Orpheus, tells of the invention of the lyre by Mercury and the miracles it has performed, and alludes to the long history of poetry among the British, Greeks, Romans, Irish, and English. We have met many times before in the Renaissance the association of David with the ode. The inclusion of the ancient British and Old English poets here is quite new and points forward to the mid-eighteenth century

[1] *The Works of Michael Drayton*, edited by J. William Hebel, II (Oxford, 1932), 345–6.

[2] *Ibid.*, II, 347–9.

Norse odes of Thomas Warton, Sr., and to Gray's "The Bard." This ode, like so much of Drayton's work, is unfortunately marred by a careless use of language, contorted syntax, and consequent obscurity.

Drayton's second ode, "To the New Yeere,"[1] in the romance six ($AABCCB_3$) with a profusion of feminine endings, prays the New Year, represented by the image of Janus, to give of his store to the poet's mistress, "Idea,"

> Give her th'Eoan brightnesse,
> Wing'd with that subtill lightnesse,
> That doth trans-pierce the Ayre;
> The Roses of the Morning
> The rising Heav'n adorning
> To mesh with flames of Hayre.

"Give her the music of the spheres and the spheres themselves for earrings, and give me the power to describe her beauty,"

> Her Bosome full of Blisses,
> By nature made for Kisses,
> So pure and wond'rous cleere,
> Whereas a thousand Graces
> Behold their lovely Faces,
> As they are bathing there.

The ode ends with the poet's complaint about his bleeding heart, his mistress's coldness, and his fire, and proclaims his determination to make his lady's name immortal, more lasting than one carved in adamant—a fate often denied kings. Here the Petrarchan idealization of woman with its accompanying heats and frosts and its sweet prettiness has been transformed by Elizabethan vigour and extravagance and under the ennobling influence of the greater ode. Roses of the garden are not good enough for the poet's mistress, he will give her the roses of the morning; he will rob the whole cosmos to deck his love; the ringing spheres shall make her pendants! The deities of the pagans shall serve the English beauty! Not three but one thousand Graces shall bathe in her bosom and there find the reflection of their beauty! Here we have Drayton at his virile best.

[1] *Ibid.*, II, 350–2.

The third ode,[1] "To His Valentine," has the same golden Elizabethan richness. In a stanza that tends to divide like that of the *canzone* ($ABABACCB_3$) Drayton invokes the Muse to wake the morn; for today is St. Valentine's day. He pictures his mistress in her tower. If he could enter in a shower of rain as Jove did! Using a vivid form of the verb like Navagero he imagines what he *will* do:

Her Canopie Ile draw,
With spangled Plumes bedight,
No Mortall ever saw
So ravishing a sight;
That it the Gods might awe,
And pow'rfully trans-pierce
The Globie Universe,
Out-shooting ev'ry Light.

My Lips Ile softly lay
Upon her heav'nly Cheeke,
Dy'd like the dawning Day,
As polish'd Ivorie sleeke:
And in her Eare Ile say;
O' thou bright Morning-Starre,
'Tis I that come so farre,
My Valentine to seeke.

There seems to be a suggestion of Apuleius' Cupid and Psyche here and perhaps a reminiscence of Wiat's lyric "They flee from me that sometime did me seek."

Now the lover tells his lady that this is the day when the birds choose their mates. "Let us follow suit. We can teach them about love; we have more senses than they and reason too. We will kiss until we swoon and laugh at those who choose their Valentines by lot." The poet prays St. Valentine that he may spend the morning thus. Otherwise he tells the Muse not to waken the day.

The obvious affinities of this poem are with medieval poetry. We think of Chaucer's *Parlement of Fowles* and of the *aubade*. Yet this poem is more than medieval. It marks the beginning in English literature of the adaptation of medieval tradition and the fashionable new classical style to one another. It

[1] *Ibid.*, II, 352–4.

resembles both the humanist ode describing a love dream and that describing a popular festival. Although it is much more personal than Marullus' May Day ode and even more personal than Herrick's "Corinna's going a-maying," yet it possesses enough ode characteristics to keep its place with these two poems. Despite the intimacy that it pleads for it is, in its invention and in its organization of its material, a formal address to his mistress celebrating a particular occasion, it generalizes its emotion by myth, parallel and contrary example, as did the ancient ode, and it classicizes itself by opening and closing addresses to the Muse.

Many of the other poems in Drayton's *Poems Lyrick and Pastorall* are not odes, although they seek to introduce other august traditions, Petrarchan and Anacreontic, into English literature. They may best be described by Lewis's adjective, "drab."[1] Also dull is the faithfully odic "The Sacrifice to Apollo,"[2] an undistinguished exercise on a common ancient and humanist theme. Better are the odes written more particularly in imitation of Horace: "An Ode Written in the Peake"[3] which describes the wet and stormy autumn in Derbyshire, pictures the sunny south near the Thames or Cam, and yet finds consolation in the north's beautiful scenery, Buxton's delicious baths, the strong ale, noble cheer, and the ubiquitous Muse; "To His Rival"[4] which recalls Horace's "Quis multa gracilis te puer in rosa"; and "A Hymne to His Ladies Birthplace" which celebrates Coventry once famous for Godiva, now famous for Idea.[5]

Last of these Horatian odes is the well-known "To the Virginian Voyage."[6] This ode, inspired by Hakluyt's description of the Virginian expedition, opens with a rousing exhortation to the settlers:

> You brave Heroique Minds,
> Worthy your Countries Name,
> That Honour still pursue,
> Goe, and subdue,
> Whilst loyt'ring Hinds
> Lurke here at home, with shame.

[1] I am borrowing the term from C. S. Lewis, *English Literature in the Sixteenth Century* (Oxford, 1954).
[2] *Works Drayton* II, 357–8.
[3] *Ibid.*, II, 365–6.
[4] *Ibid.*, II, 368–9.
[5] *Ibid.*, II, 373–4.
[6] *Ibid.*, II, 363–4.

There follows a lively account of the voyage, interrupted by a description of Virginia based on classical pictures of the golden age which stands as a myth in relation to the whole. Then comes advice to the settlers, and praise of Hakluyt, who inspires in men's minds the noble desire for fame.

Here we have a thoroughly modern and original ode, a formal lyric celebration of a public event written in the spirit of Horace's Roman odes but based on a modern source and adapted to the modern taste. The firmness of outline and the clarity and economy of expression were learnt from Horace. But Drayton's debt does not go beyond that. Here there is none of the imitation of irrelevant superficialities that we have found so often in the Renaissance ode.

The last of these poems of Drayton, "To the Cambro-Britans, and their HARPE, his Ballad of AGINCOURT,"[1] is, as its title suggests, intended to be written in the traditional, i.e., medieval, English style of celebrating an outstanding event. It is meant to illustrate Drayton's statement made in the preface and in the first ode that the British and English wrote odes as well as the Latins and Greeks. Thus this "ode" is dedicated to those who still practise the indigenous art, the Welsh harpers. The poem professes to be a ballad and it has many ballad characteristics: the relatively brief description of heroic action, the abrupt beginning, the use of aorist past and vivid present tenses, dialogue, exclamation, liveliness, vigour, and an exalted heroic tone. On the other hand it is longer, has more detailed and scientific descriptions of the movements of the British troops, of the various commands, and of the battle strategy, and it is written in a more lengthy stanza than is usual with the ballad. The stanza, $AAA_3B_2CCC_3B_2$, rather suggests a romance, or medieval epic, and the fulness of treatment, a lay. There is nothing at all classical about the poem. Therefore, since the poet maintains that it was written in the ballad tradition, and since it is solely a description of heroic action, it cannot be called an ode.

Drayton, then, is the first proper ode writer in English. Yet, although his definition of the ode is in many ways perceptive, his all-inclusive use of the term does much to destroy its value. His practice of the ode, which makes no distinction between

[1] *Ibid.*, II, 375–8.

the new classically inspired and the old familiar lyric poetry; between typical songs and love poems flaunting only Petrarchan conceits, and formal poems on public events; and, in the case of the public poems, between those written in the new style and those in the old; between a "Virginian Voyage" and a "Ballad of Agincourt," Drayton's illustrations of the "ode," do little to establish it as a new genre in English poetry. Drayton represents the first stage of the introduction of the ode into English literature, when the fashionable new term is used for almost everything that is in any sense lyric. However, Drayton did write some genuine odes, and these mark the beginning of a new tradition in English literature. Henceforth the progress of assimilation was destined to be very rapid. Half a century after Drayton had published his odes the ode became the most popular lyric form in English.

Although Ben Jonson (1572/3–1637) as a poet was not primarily an ode writer, there are a few more odes scattered through this work than through Drayton's, and these are much more classical. Among Jonson's epigrams, sometimes addressed to real people but more frequently to such "humorous" types as Doctor Empirick, Brayne-Hardie, Don Surly, Banck the Usurer, Captaine Hazard the Cheater, Groyne, Gut, etc.—epigrams that unfortunately do not live up to their colourful titles, for Jonson seems to lack the quickness and sparkle of the wit—is a thoroughly Horatian ode, thoroughly englished. "Inviting a friend to supper"[1] is written on a Horatian theme and expresses the Horatian ideal of simple social pleasures, a good companion, good food and drink, literature, and honest conversation—there will be no character assassination here! However, the ode is much more independent of any Horatian original and much more closely adapted to Jonson's native culture than similar poems by Ronsard, for example. Although token respect is paid to Horace's ideal meal—there will be olives, capers, and salad—Jonson does not disappoint his English friend by suggesting that that will be all. In addition there will be mutton, hen, rabbits, larks, and perhaps also partridge, pheasant, woodcock, goodwit, knat, raile, and ruffe, followed by cheese and fruit, and washed down with

[1] *Poems of Ben Jonson*, ed. George Burke Johnston (London, 1954), pp. 50–1.

canary. This ode is written in decasyllabic couplets, as are most of the epigrams, a fact which underlines the kinship between Jonson's epigrams and his odes—yet Ronsard, too, wrote odes in heroic couplets.

Another poem that may be considered to be an ode, this time in the collection called *The Forrest*, "To Penshurst,"[1] is likewise written in heroic couplets. This ode, largely descriptive of the manor, of its woods and waters, of the game birds bright and brittle as in a still life, of the fish, and fruits, the happy tenants, and the generous lord, recounts one particular event, Penshurst's reception of King James on a hunting trip, and finds in the Sidneys' way of life the pattern of excellence for the aristocracy.

This same collection, *The Forrest*, ends with the first poem that Jonson clearly labels ode, "Ode. To Sir William Sydney, on his Birth-day."[2] This ode, Pindaric in its stanza form, $A_5B_4CC_1B_3ADDE_2E_5$, which looks much more revolutionary on the printed page than its metrical analysis would suggest, skilfully adapts the ancient ode to modern exigencies. It opens conversationally in the midst of action, vividly but casually described. It is Sidney's birthday celebration. The poet asks for a cup from the Thespian well that he may tell Sidney the meaning of the day and say something for him to reflect on later. He has come of age. Now he must *will* great achievement; he cannot rest on his ancestors' laurels,

> For they, that swell
> With dust of ancestors, in graves but dwell.

He must learn how to be great, from his forebears, *now*,

> And he that stayes
> To live untill to morrow' hath lost two dayes.

In honour alone man lives,

> . . . Then
> The Birth-day shines, when logs not burne, but men

The ode as a whole, perhaps because of its limber structure and its concern with aristocratic ideals, suggests Pindar rather than Horace as a source of inspiration. Certainly the abundant

[1] *Ibid.*, pp. 76–9.
[2] *Ibid.*, pp. 100–1.

pictorial imagery and the scattering of aphorisms is common to both ancient poets.

Jonson's *Under-Wood* is a miscellaneous collection, mostly of lyric poetry of various sorts. It begins with a few hymns, which are followed by *amores*, idylls of the *Anthology* type, *basia*, pastorals, songs, epistles, epitaphs, elegies, sonnets, epigrams, a dedication, an epithalamium, various short occasional poems, some odes, and a few versions of Horace. "An Ode. To himselfe,"[1] discusses his poetic inactivity, ascribed to an unappreciative age, in an irregular-looking stanza, $ABBAAB_3B_6$, inspired by Pindar. The ode, however, is written in the Horatian moral tradition; from Horace Jonson has learnt the brief, undeveloped allusions and economical images, the compressions, the mythology, and the moralizing. Typical of both the ancient ode tradition and contemporary metaphysical poetry is the attention-catching, opening rhetorical question which is followed by aphorisms,

Where do'st thou carelesse lie
Buried in ease and sloth?
Knowledge, that sleepes, doth die, ...

The reference at the end of stanza two to "chattring Pies" is an allusion to Pindar,[2] but Jonson is much the crueller to his rivals, who are not only cacaphonous but dirty birds. Jonson's concluding self-exhortation to

sing high and aloofe,
Safe from the wolves black jaw, and the dull Asses Hoofe,

suggests many of Crinito's poems about himself as a poet in an uncongenial age. However, Jonson's imagery is vivid and personal rather than derivative and Horatian, as Crinito's invariably is in such passages.

"An Ode to James Earl of Desmond Writ in Queene Elizabeth's Time, since Lost, And Recovered"[3] is written in a long, *canzone*-like stanza, $A_4BA_5BCC_4DD_2E_5E_2F_5E_2F_6$. It has the strained rhetorical beginning that Pindar unfortunately too

[1] *Ibid.*, pp. 150–1.

[2] Pindar, *Olympia* 2, strophe 5.

[3] *Poems Jonson*, pp. 152–4.

often inspired in his imitators. We recognize, too, an echo of Horace's ever popular "Exegi monumentum."

Where art thou, Genius? I should use
Thy present Aide: Arise invention,
Wake, and put on the wings of Pindars Muse,
  To towre with my intention
High, as his mind, that doth advance
Her upright head, above the reach of Chance,
  Or the times envie:
  Cynthius, I applie
My bolder numbers to thy golden Lyre:
  O, then inspire
Thy Priest in this strange rapture; heat my braine
  With Delphick fire:
That I may sing my thoughts, in some unvulgar straine.

The Pindaric influence persists, leading to further bombastic invocations, sudden aphorisms, e.g., "Palme growes straight though handled ne'er so rude,"[1] strange mythological references, slightly obscure allusions to Desmond's political career, and final advice. The imagery is at times metaphysical.[2]

"An Ode,"[3] a brief conversational address to a convalescing friend, gives Horatian advice on restraining ambition and stewarding what has been gained. It suggests Ronsard's ode to the Cardinal de Guise, but it is quite independent. A second "An Ode"[4] is written in the style of Ronsard's *Amours*. Here Jonson lists the mistresses of great poets, whom they have made famous. To this list he will add Celia; for, although he is much inferior to these others as a poet, yet Celia's superior beauty will make his poem the best. This is a favourite humanist sort of conceit, one that we have already met in Bernardo Tasso, for example, in "per la navigazione del Card. di Tournon."[5]

"An Ode, or Song, by all the Muses IN CELEBRATION OF HER MAJESTIES BIRTHDAY. 1630"[6] is written in the popular romance six (AABCCB3) that Drayton had already

1 *Ibid.*, p. 153, line 26.
2 See, e.g., stanza 3.
3 *Poems Jonson*, pp. 154–5.
4 *Ibid.*, pp. 155–6.
5 Bernardo Tasso, *Rime* II (Bergamo, 1749), 328–9.
6 *Poems Jonson*, pp. 207–8.

used for the ode. Here we have a lively, spirited celebration of Queen Henrietta Maria's twenty-second birthday written in nine stanzas apportioned to the nine Muses. Each stanza carefully maintains the proper decorum. Thus Clio, the Muse of history, opens with

> Up publicke Joy, remember
> This sixteenth of November,
> Some brave un-common way:
> And though the Parish-steeple
> Be silent, to the people
> Ring thou it Holy-day.

She is followed by Melpomene, the Muse of tragedy who speaks of the thunder of a royal salute; Thalia, the Muse of comedy, who describes the popular celebration, the merry music and dancing; Euterpe, the Muse of lyric poetry, who tells how the singing of the people enchants the angels from their spheres; Terpsichore, the Muse of dancing, who describes the pomp of Mary,

> The Daughter of great Harry!
> And Sister to just Lewis!

Erato, the Muse of erotic poetry, who finds the Mary of this sea island fairer than the Cyprian Queen of Love; Calliope, the Muse of epic poetry, who sees the noble king, her husband, triumphant in the tournament; Urania, the Muse of astronomy, who announces that time has now measured the queen's twenty-second year; and Polyhymnia, the Muse of the hymn, who sings a song of thanksgiving because the queen has borne England an heir. The technique, the relation of the particular event celebrated both to the people as a whole, to national history, to the divine government of the world, and to scientific cosmology, the portrayal of the event in each of its aspects, the succession of vivid pictures, the brief images and frequent allusions, the praise of Mary through her father, her brother, her husband, and her son, the opening and closing of the ode on the theme of public joy for the particular occurrence, all these characteristics are Pindaric in inspiration, although Pindar here is completely mastered and made to serve Jonson's purpose. This is a highly successful birthday ode. It suggests comparison with Dryden's "Alexander's Feast."

Pindaric both in form and invention is Jonson's well-known ode "To the Immortall Memorie, and Friendship of that Noble Paire, Sir Lucius Cary, and Sir H. Morison."[1] The terms that Jonson uses to denote the different parts of his triads "Turne," "Counter-turn," and "Stand" immediately recall Minturno's "volta," "rivolta," and "stanza," and suggest that Jonson may have borrowed his terms from the Italian whose Aristotelian criticism undoubtedly attracted him. Otherwise, however, this poem reveals no specific debts to any particular part of the Pindaric tradition. It is written in riming couplets arranged in stanzas which are made to look Pindaric by varying lengths of line, $AA_4BB_5CC_3DD_4EE_5$. The ode opens Pindarically with a symbol, an account of a prodigy recorded in Livy, of a child who, born at the very moment of Hannibal's destruction of Saguntum, took one look about him and returned to his mother's womb to die. The first "turne" concludes,

> How summ'd a circle didst thou leave man-kind
> Of deepest lore, could we the center find!

In the first "counter-turne" Jonson tries to find the "centre" and in the first "stand" he concludes that it is this: that it is its quality not its length that stamps life with its value. He illustrates this point by a counter-myth of a man who lived sixty years too long. The second "turne" develops, in accents of almost Wordsworthian righteousness—or, should we say here, Browningesque?—the story of this man, showing how his early promise succumbed to worldly corruption. The second "counter-turne" now contrasts Morison:

> Alas, but Morison fell young:
> Hee never fell, thou fall'st, my tongue.
> Hee stood, a Souldier to the last right end,
> A perfect Patriot, and a noble friend,
> But most a vertuous Sonne.
> All Offices were done
> By him, so ample, full, and round,
> In weight, in measure, number, sound,
> As though his age imperfect might appeare,
> His life was of Humanitie the Spheare.

Now we have returned to the introductory symbol; Morison's

[1] *Ibid.*, pp. 210–14.

life like that of the infant was complete and perfect. The second "stand" mocks the idea that a long tale of miseries is a long life and, like the first "stand," insists that life is measured by its quality, not by its quantity.

The third "turne," closely linked to the second "stand" as the second "turne" was linked to the first "stand"—for Jonson follows Pindar's organic method of development—now gives full development to this theme that has hitherto sounded in the background. In the exact centre of the poem come the famous words:

It is not growing like a tree
In bulke, doth make man better bee:
Or standing long an Oake, three hundred yeare,
To fall a logge, at last, dry, bald, and seare:
A Lillie of a Day,
Is fairer farre, in May,
Although it fall, and die that night;
It was the Plant, and flowre of light.
In small proportions, we just beauties see:
And in short measures, life may perfect bee.

Now, with his point firmly established, Jonson can dismiss the idea of mourning over Morison's death. He bids the surviving friend, Cary, be glad, call for wine, and garland his head; for Morison is not dead, but gone to eternal life.

As the first half of the poem was concerned with life, so the second half is concerned with friendship. Thus the third "stand" likens the Morison-Cary friendship to that of the Dioscuri. The fourth "turne" and "counter-turne" describe the noble friendship more fully, explain its origin philosophically, and proclaim it as a pattern of excellence. The final "stand," linking the two themes of life and friendship, and returning to the beginning symbol of completeness in little, states that the friendship was perfect and so ended ere manhood began.

This ode, although it has many of the Pindaric fundamentals and even such superficialities as run-on lines and stanzas, with words broken in the middle,[1] is, in its perfect balance and

[1] Cf. Jonson, *Poems*, p. 213, lines 84–5. Here the name Ben Jonson is broken up between the end of the third "counter-turne" and the beginning of the third "stand."

symmetry neither Pindaric nor Horatian but a superb example of Jonson's Palladian neoclassicism.

"To the Right Honourable Hierome, L. Weston. An Ode Gratulatorie. For his returne from his Embassie. 1632,"[1] written in tail-rimed stanzas, consists of an "epic" simile and its application: as the earth joys in spring so his friends joy in Weston's return. Four others of Jonson's odes are versions of Horace.[2] The last of these takes us from *The Under-Wood* into the *Miscellany*.

The *Miscellany* contains a brief incantatory "Hymn to Diana,"[3] "Queene, and Huntresse, chaste, and faire," which is taken from *Cynthias Revells*. It is written in the ode tradition. Also in the *Miscellany* are "Ode. Enthousiastike,"[4] which seems to be neither an ode nor enthusiastic, at least not in the etymological sense of divinely inspired; an "Ode. Allegorike"[5] which contains a long and laboured account of a metamorphosis and a not too clear allegory; and the famous preface to the 1623 folio, "To the Memory of my Beloved, the Author, Mr. William Shakespeare: and what he hath left us."[6] This ode is perhaps the greatest tribute made by one poet to another and one of the ablest pieces of criticism of a great man by a contemporary that exists. However, our job here is not to evaluate Jonson as a critic but to analyse this poem as an ode. The ode, then, opens with a direct address to Shakespeare, whom Jonson says no man nor Muse can praise too much. Then, in Pindaric fashion, Jonson interrupts himself. This is what any man might say, the ignorant, the fondly blind, even the malicious. Like Pindar he discusses his technique. He will begin anew. With exclamations he bids Shakespeare rise. His place is not among the dead, not even by the side of England's greatest poets. He is alive as long as his book lives. Now Jonson compares Shakespeare with the other great dramatists, both in Tragedy and in Comedy, and he bids Britain triumph in the greatest of them all. He praises Shakespeare's writing, both for its "nature" and its art, and he discusses poetic composition, out of Horace. Finally, in the peroration, Jonson hails Shakespeare as the Swan of Avon; he

[1] Jonson, *Poems*, pp. 217–18.
[2] *Ibid.*, pp. 251–3, 254–5, 255–6, 283.
[3] *Ibid.*, pp. 261–2.
[4] *Ibid.*, pp. 263–4.
[5] *Ibid.*, pp. 265–9.
[6] *Ibid.*, pp. 285–7.

sees him as a constellation in the sky; and he bids him shed his influence upon the British stage. Again this ode, while remaining a distinctly original poem, has all the characteristics of the ancient and humanist ode.

Jonson's last two odes, "Ode to Himselfe,"[1] and "Ode,"[2] are both complaints about the degenerate taste of the age reminiscent of the earlier ode on the same theme. They are in no way extraordinary.

A classical weight and dignity, then, and a rational, restrained style were Jonson's chief contributions to the English ode tradition. If he introduced Pindar, it was really Horace whom he propagated. Many of the more sober odes of the seventeenth and eighteenth centuries were thus indebted to him, including Marvell's magnificent "Horatian Ode upon Cromwell's Return from Ireland."

The ode was not intimate or informal enough for the cavalier poets. None of them favoured it and few of them essayed it. Lord Herbert of Cherbury (1583–1648) wrote two poems that he called odes. "An Ode Upon A Question Moved, Whether Love Should Continue For Ever,"[3] after a classically inspired, mythological statement that it is spring, begins as though it were going to be a sentimental eighteenth-century "ballad,"

When with a love none can express,
That mutually happy pair,
Melander and Celinda fair,
The season with their loves did bless,

but quickly turns into a long, dry, dull discussion of love which suggests most disadvantageous comparisons with Donne's "The Ecstacie." This poem is by no means an ode in the classical sense. Neither is it an ode in the Elizabethan sense. There is nothing song-like about it. Indeed there seems to have been no music whatsoever in the soul of the inventor of deism, as a glance at his other "ode," "Of Our Sense Of Sin,"[4] will corroborate. This "poem" is an illustration of Lord Herbert's

[1] *Ibid.*, pp. 298–300.

[2] *Ibid.*, pp. 316–17.

[3] Lord Herbert, *Minor Poets of the Seventeenth Century*, Everyman Library (London and New York, 1953), pp. 43–7.

[4] Lord Herbert, *ibid.*, p. 60.

criticism of himself, that he "Add[s] feet unto round prose."[1] It is a bit of commonplace and prosaic philosophizing made palatable neither by imagery nor by variety of thought. The editor says that it was once ascribed to Donne. Such an ascription seems incredible; for there is nothing of Donne's poetry, of his imagination, music, intensity, or compression in this dreary little piece.

Thomas Carew (1595?–1639) was a travelled man, he knew neolatin and Italian literature and criticism,[2] and he was aware of the contemporary vogue of the ode,[3] yet, although he uses classical literature to enrich his poetry with allusions, he never imitates the characteristic classical lyric form, the ode. Neither does John Suckling (1609–42). Richard Lovelace (1618–57), although he knew neolatin, Italian,[4] and French literature and even wrote a few poems that he called odes or epodes, did not contribute to the ode tradition either. His odes are merely songs[5] or Petrarchan occasional poems,[6] while his epodes can only maintain their claim to that title by ingenious argumentation.[7]

Robert Herrick (1591–1674), however, is England's first and only Anacreontic poet.[8] Although he was very much influenced by Horace and was occasionally indebted to Catullus or Ovid, although he could once be metaphysical[9] and was another time shockingly baroque,[10] in his slight and graceful lyrics, Herrick is fundamentally Anacreontic—indeed Herrick must be unique in being able to write on the same theme as Anacreon with an even greater brevity.

One of the most treasured parts of Herrick's works, however, derives neither from Anacreon nor Horace but from the

[1] *Ibid.*, p. 30.

[2] Thomas Carew, *Minor Poets of the Seventeenth Century*, p. 142.

[3] Carew, *Ibid.*, p. 123.

[4] See Richard Lovelace, *Minor Poets*, p. 360 ff.

[5] See, e.g., Lovelace, *ibid.*, pp. 249–50 and 268–9.

[6] See, e.g., Lovelace, *ibid.*, pp. 267–8.

[7] See, e.g., Lovelace, *ibid.*, p. 292. Is this poem called an epode because her "cruelty" is attacked?

[8] For Herrick's life and a discussion of him as a poet see Flores Delattre, *Robert Herrick* (Paris, 1911).

[9] See *The Poetical Works of Robert Herrick*, ed. F. W. Moorman (London, New York, Toronto, 1947), p. 104, "Primroses."

[10] *Ibid.*, p. 366, on Jesus' foreskin.

pastoral tradition as exemplified by Drayton. Herrick is the great recorder of the country life of Merry England, of the folk festivals and the round of seasonal activities,

> I sing of *Brooks*, of *Blossomes*, *Birds*, and *Bowers*:
> Of *April*, *May*, of *June*, and *July*-Flowers.
> I sing of *May-Poles*, *Hock-carts*, *Wassails*, *Wakes*,
> Of *Bride-grooms*, *Brides*, and of their *Bridall-cakes*.
> I write of *Youth*, of *Love*, and have Accesse
> By these, to sing of cleanly-*Wantonnesse*.
> I sing of *Dewes*, of *Raines*, and piece by piece
> Of *Balme*, of *Oyle*, of *Spice*, and *Amber-Greece*.
> I sing of *Times trans-shifting*; and I write
> How *Roses* first came *Red*, and *Lillies White*.
> I write of *Groves*, of *Twilights*, and I sing
> The Court of *Mab*, and of the *Fairie-King*.
> I write of *Hell*; I sing (and ever shall)
> Of *Heaven*, and hope to have it after all.[1]

Herrick's most famous poem and the most famous Anacreontic in the English language is "To the Virgins to make much of Time,"[2]

> Gather ye Rose-buds while ye may,
> Old Time is still a flying:
> And this same flower that smiles to day,
> To morrow will be dying.
>
> The glorious Lamp of Heaven, the Sun,
> The higher he's a getting;
> The sooner will his Race be run,
> And neerer he's to Setting.
>
> That Age is best, which is the first,
> When Youth and Blood are warmer;
> But being spent, the worse, and worst
> Times still succeed the former.
>
> Then be not coy, but use your time;
> And while ye may, goe marry:
> For having lost but once your prime,
> You may for ever tarry.

[1] *Ibid.*, p. 5.
[2] *Ibid.*, p. 84.

This poem, as song-like as Ronsard's "Mignonne, allons voir si la rose" or Waller's "Go, lovely Rose!" is, in its invention and disposition, in its two analogous illustrations of its theme, Ausonius' comparison of life to a flower and Catullus' to the course of the sun, in its clear expression of the application of the illustrations to human life, here with perhaps an echo of Horace II, 11, and in its final pointing up of the moral in a concluding stanza giving practical, mundane advice, much more classical an ode than the other two.

A very similar ode is "To a Bed of Tulips."[1] Slightly different is "To Daffadills,"[2]

Faire Daffadills, we weep to see
  You haste away so soone:
As yet the early-rising Sun
  Has not attain'd his Noone.
    Stay, stay,
  Untill the hasting day
    Has run
  But to the Even-song;
And, having pray'd together, we
  Will goe with you along.

We have short time to stay, as you,
  We have as short a Spring;
As quick a growth to meet Decay,
  As you, or any thing.
    We die,
  As your hours doe, and drie
    Away,
  Like to the Summers raine;
Or as the pearles of Morning dew
  Ne'r to be found againe.

This ode is obviously indebted to Ausonius' "De rosis nascentibus" with its flowers in the morning, but it applies the lesson of the flowers, reinforced by Scriptural sounding comparisons of human life to summer rain and the dew of the morning, to all of mankind. However, despite the sacerdotal reference to Even-song, the spirit of this poem is as pagan as that of the

[1] *Ibid.*, p. 183.
[2] *Ibid.*, p. 125.

other two, as a glance at the same conceit in the Prayer Book will immediately illustrate:

> Man that is born of woman hath but a short time to live, and is full of misery. He cometh up, and is cut down, like a flower; he fleeth as it were a shadow, and never continueth in one stay.

"To Blossoms,"[1]

> Faire pledges of a fruitfull Tree,
> Why do yee fall so fast?

is a similar ode with a similar lesson to that of "To Daffadills". Here there is perhaps a touch of indebtedness to Ronsard's "Mignonne, allons voir si la rose"—compare Herrick's

> What, were yee borne to be
> An houre or half's delight;
> And so to bid goodnight?
> 'Twas pitie Nature brought yee forth
> Merely to shew your worth,
> And lose you quite,

with Ronsard's

> O vrayment marastre Nature,
> Puis qu'une telle fleur ne dure
> Que du matin jusques au soir!

The last of these flower pieces, except for the Ovidian "Metamorphoses,"[2] which are epigrams, and the aesthetic poem, "The Lilly in a Christal," is "To Primroses fill'd with morning-dew,"[3] a typical seventeenth-century sermon illustration of the text, "In sorrow shalt thou bring forth." However, Herrick's discussion of the meaning of the dew on the new-born primroses, although rather witty in the metaphysical manner, is too tender and emotional and not sufficiently piercing or passionate to be typically metaphysical.

Herrick wrote many Anacreontics directly inspired either by Anacreon himself or by the *Anthology*, Secundus, or Ronsard,[4] e.g.,

[1] *Ibid.*, p. 175. [2] See, e.g., *ibid.*, pp. 74, 105. [3] *Ibid.*, p. 104.

[4] *Ibid.*, pp. 16, "Me thought (last night) love in an anger came"; 18, "Old wives have often told, how they"; 20, "I dream'd we both were in a bed"; 26–7, "One silent night of late"; 31–2, "About the sweet bag of a

Born I was to be old,
And for to die here.
After that, in the mould
Long for to lye here.

But before that day comes,
Still I be Bousing;
For I know, in the Tombs,
There's no Carousing.

---

1 I held Love's head while it did ake;
But so it chanc't to be;
The cruell paine did his for sake,
And forthwith came to me.

2 Ai me! How shal my griefe be stil'd?
Or where else shall we find
One like to me, who must be kill'd
For being too-too-kind?

---

1 I plaid with Love, as with the fire
The wanton Satyre did;
Nor did I know, or co'd descry
What under there was hid.

2 That Satyre he but burnt his lips;
(But min's the greater smart)
For kissing Loves dissembling chips,
The fire scortcht my heart.

In the *Hesperides* there are also many poems that seem to echo Horace or owe some debt to him,[1] including the epistle, "A

Bee"; 39, "Come, skilfull *Lupo*, now, and take"; 50, "Cupid as he lay among"; 65, "I feare no Earthly Powers"; 71, "As Julia once a-slumb'ring lay"; 96, "As lately I a Garland bound"; 100, "Fly to my Mistresse, pretty pilfring Bee"; 186, "Born I was to be old"; 189, "Borne I was to meet with Age"; 192, "Fly me not, though I be gray"; 195, "I held Love's head while it did ake"; 200, "I plaid with Love, as with the fire"; 219, "1. A Christal Viol *Cupid* brought"; 234, "Let us now take time, and play"; 270, "Maidens tell me I am old"; 276, "Love in a showre of Blossomes came"; 288–9, "Love, like a Beggar, came to me." The quotations are from pages 195, 186, and 200, respectively.

[1] *Ibid.*, pp. 21, 22, 32, 143, 212, 242–3.

Country life: To his Brother, M. Tho: Herrick,"[1] which is written in the English equivalent of the elegiac couplet, A_5A_4, and utters the conventional Horatian moralities about the superiority of rural innocence and contentment over the unhappy pursuit of fortune in the world. Horatian, too, is "To live merrily, and to trust to Good Verses,"[2] an ode which also owes a suggestion to Ronsard. It is the spring:

Now is the time for mirth,
Nor cheek, or tongue be dumbe:
For with the flowrie earth,
The golden pomp is come.[3]

The golden pomp is come;
For now each tree do's weare
(Made of her pap and Gum)
Rich beads of *Amber* here.

Now raignes the *Rose*, and now
Th' Arabian Dew besmears
My uncontrolled brow,
And my retorted haires.[4]

"I will drink to Homer," says Herrick merrily, and his verses reflect his good humour and high spirits:

Homer, this Health to thee,
In *Sack* of such a kind,
That it wo'd make thee see,
Though thou wert ne'r so blind.

Next, to Vergil, Ovid, and Catullus. And now the roof is reeling and the poet in a bacchanalian ecstasy drinks to Propertius and then to Tibullus. Then comes the reflection,

Behold *Tibullus* lies,
Here burnt, whose smal return
Of ashes, scarce suffice
To fill a little Urne.

[1] *Ibid.*, pp. 35–8. One of his earliest poems, Delattre, p. 282.

[2] *Ibid.*, pp. 80–1.

[3] A translation of Ovid's "aurea pompa venit," *Amores* III, 2, 44, noted by Delattre, p. 412.

[4] This latinism, a literal transl. from Martial VI, 39, 6 (Delattre's note, p. 66, fn. 1), mars an otherwise extremely attractive poem.

Trust to good Verses then[1];
They onely will aspire,
When Pyamids, as men,
Are lost, i' th' funeral fire.

And when all Bodies meet
In Lethe to be drown'd;
Then onely Numbers sweet,
With endless life are crown'd.

The ode recalls Ronsard's "Nous ne tenons en nostre main"[2] and "Mon ame, il est temps que tu rendes,"[3] but Herrick's ode is more luxuriously poetic, has the appearance of greater spontaneity, seems closer to life, smells less of the lamp, and sounds the moral note more lightly and more delicately than Ronsard is ever capable of doing. Here we recognize not only the familiar Horatian ideas and the Horatian linear pattern of development through image to philosophical reflection, but also, in the second last stanza, the reference to Horace's famous prediction of his own immortality (III, 30).

A similar ode in thought, though not in development, is "His Poetrie his Pillar,"[4] the only example in Herrick of the popular baroque *tour de force* of poems shaped so as to represent their subjects physically. Here each stanza and the poem as a whole is shaped like a pillar. The theme is a familiar Horatian one and echoes III, 30. "An Ode to Sir Clipsebie Crew"[5] returns to the "live merrily" theme. This ode, an invitation to a friend to come to dinner, a favourite theme of Horace's, in the Horatian manner describes the treatment that he may expect, the good cheer, the best meat, an ever-blazing fire, lots of wine, and rollicking toasts to the ancient poets, Anacreon and Horace. In his typical light and graceful manner Herrick, in the conclusion of the ode, makes it possible for his friend to decline the invitation:

Take Horse, and come; or be so kind,
To send your mind

1 From Ovid, *Am.* III, 9, 39, Delattre, p. 412.
2 Laum., *Ed. Crit.* VI, 174–6.
3 *Ibid.*, II, 40–3.
4 *Poems Herrick*, Moorman, p. 85.
5 *Ibid.*, pp. 195–6.

(Though but in Numbers few)
And I shall think I have the heart,
Or part
Of *Clipseby Crew*.

Jonson had already written a similar Horatian invitation in English, but without Herrick's delicacy and ease.

"Comfort to a Lady upon the Death of her Husband,"[1] like Bernardo Tasso's similar ode to Vittoria Colonna,[2] is reminiscent of Horace II, 9, "Non semper imbres nubibus hispidos," but it has Herrick's characteristic brevity and his golden Elizabethan richness of description. Another ode, Horatian in sentiment, is "The Country Life, to the honoured M. End. Porter, Groome of the Bed-Chamber to His Maj."[3] Here, after an introduction inspired by Horace I, 1,

Sweet Country life, to such unknown,
Whose lives are others, not their own! . . .
Thou never plow'st the Oceans foame
To seek, and bring rough Pepper home.

and the voicing of the Horatian ideal of contentment, we have a Vergilian description of the joys and duties of country life:

When now the Cock (the Plow-mans Horne)
Calls forth the lilly-wristed Morne;
Then to the corn-fields thou dost goe,
Which though well soyl'd, yet thou dost know,
That the best compost for the Lands
Is the wise Masters Feet, and Hands,

and Herrick's own individual idealization of the popular English festivals:

For Sports, for Pagentrie, and Playes,
Thou hast thy Eves, and Holydayes:
On which the young men and maids meet
To exercise their dancing feet:
Tripping the comely country round,
With Daffadills and Daisies crown'd.
Thy Wakes, thy Quintels, here thou hast,
Thy May-poles too with Garlands grac't:

[1] *Ibid.*, p. 105.
[2] B. Tasso, *Hinni et ode* (1534), p. 79v.
[3] *Poetical Works Herrick*, Moorman, pp. 225–7.

Thy Morris-dance; thy Whitsun-ale;
Thy Sheering-feast, which never faile.
Thy Harvest home; thy Wassaile bowle,
That's tost up after Fox i' th' Hole.
Thy Mummeries; thy Twelfe-tide Kings
And Queenes; thy Christmas revellings:
Thy Nut-browne mirth; thy Russet wit;
And no man payes too deare for it;
To these, thou hast thy times to goe
And trace the Hare i' th' trecherous Snow. . . .

This ode, written in riming couplets, though octosyllabic, not decasyllabic, with its catalogue-like, yet unreal description of country life and bucolic contentment in some idyllic Arcadia where crops never fail and there is no blight or drought is Herrick's most neoclassical poem. It is interesting to compare this "Country Life" dedicated to Endimion Porter with the previously mentioned one to Herrick's brother, Thomas. Both of these poems are concerned with the description of rural life and its moral values, and both echo Horace, but the present ode, after the introductory, exclamatory quatrain stating its subject, is almost entirely pictorial, whereas the earlier epistle is almost wholly sententious. It is a moral lecture with illustrations. It uses the didactic technique of exposition and exhortation rather than the more subtle method of moral persuasion through attractive portrayal. It is because the one is mainly overt and the other mainly implied argumentation that the one is an epistle and the other an ode. It is significant that the epistle is double the length of the ode and is written in a metre that resembles the elegiac couplet.

"An Ode to Master Endymion Porter, upon his Brothers death"[1] is an unusual sort of ode. Like the funeral elegy it is divided between lamentation over the loss occasioned by death, and reconciliation to it, but here the reconciliation is accomplished by the dead brother's place in Herrick's life being filled by Herrick's friend, Porter. And this substitution is not effected with sufficient delicacy. The unfortunate phrase, "The debt is paid," although it probably refers only to Herrick's debt of gratitude to Porter for giving him his sympathy and understanding at a time when he needed them—as other

[1] *Ibid.*, p. 72.

passages where the same conceit is used would suggest[1]—introduces a distateful commercial element into the poem. We feel that Herrick is too willing either to accept one life in return for another or to indulge in fulsome flattery of his friend. However, perhaps this is to misread the poem slightly; for the emphasis throughout is on Herrick's own emotions and not on the events which elicit them. Thus the ode opens, calling to mind both Horace II, 9 and Catullus 5, line 4, "Soles occidere, et redire possunt," with the familiar contrast between man's life and the sun. In the second, well-known stanza Herrick affirms that *he* is dead—or virtually so:

> Alas for me! that I have lost
> E'en all almost:
> Sunk is my sight; set is my Sun;
> And all the loome of life undone:
> The staffe, the Elme, the prop, the shelt'ring wall
> Whereon my Vine did crawle,
> Now, now, blowne downe; needs must the old stock fall.

In the third stanza he springs like a phoenix from his ashes because Porter the Preserver stands by. In the fourth stanza he gives thanks to his friend, thus repaying *his* debt. The technique is that of the ode; the formal treatment of the theme, its objectification by analogy and metaphor, by literary, cosmological, and mythical relations, its concentration, brevity, pictorial sequence, and its opening and closing commonplaces are all typical.

Other odes of a familiar type are "Farewell Frost, or welcome the Spring,"[2] in which the coming of spring after winter gives hope of peace after war; "The bad season makes the Poet sad,"[3] in which the poet says that he can no longer sing because the times are out of tune, but that if harmony returned to the kingdom he could still "Knock at a Starre with my exalted Head";

[1] Cf. *ibid.*, p. 94, line 10, "He payes the halfe, who do's confesse the Debt," and p. 338, "Thanksgiving for the former, doth invite / God to bestow a second benefit."

[2] *Ibid.*, p. 221.

[3] *Ibid.*, p. 211. Cf. "To his Friend, on the untuneable Times," pp. 84–5 and "On himselfe," p. 131. See also Ben Jonson, *Poems* (1954), pp. 298–300 and 316–17, and Abraham Cowley, "Preface," *Poems*, ed. A. R. Waller (Cambridge, 1905), pp. 7–8.

and "To Musique, to becalme his Fever,"[1] an ode on the healing power of music. An unusual poem suggested by Martial[2] is "The Lilly in a Christal,"[3] a series of pictorial illustrations of the aesthetic proposition that beauty half-seen and half-suggested is the most potent. With this ode may be compared the briefer epigrams, "Art above Nature, to Julia,"[4]

> I must confesse, mine eye and heart
> Dotes less on Nature, then on Art,

and the contrasting "Clothes do but cheat and cousen us,"[5]

> For as my Heart, ene so mine Eye
> Is wone with flesh, not *Drapery*.

Disappointing is "An Ode of the Birth of our Saviour,"[6] in which Herrick contrasts Jesus' actual birthplace with the rich one people would make him nowadays. It is a bit too saccharine and pretty. Herrick lacks the strength for such a theme.

"Corinna's going a Maying"[7] is written on the same theme as "To the Virgins, to make much of Time" and is, with it, Herrick's most famous poem. The treatment of the *carpe diem* theme in "Corinna," however, is very different from the treatment of it in "Gather ye Rosebuds." Here Herrick adapts the *aubade* to describe, with some metaphysical wit, the maying and the mating that goes with it. Then he bids his mistress *carpe florem*. The conversational opening, with its learning and affectionate raillery, is typically metaphysical,

> Get up, get up for shame, the Blooming Morne
> Upon her wings presents the god unshorne,
> See how *Aurora* throwes her faire
> Fresh-quilted colours through the aire:
> Get up, sweet Slug-a-bed, and see
> The Dew-bespangling Herbe and Tree.
> Each Flower has wept, and bow'd toward the East,
> Above an houre since; yet you not drest
> Nay! not so much as out of bed?

[1] *Poetical Works Herrick*, Moorman, p. 95. Cf. "To Musick," p. 67, "To Musick, to becalme a sweet-sick-youth," p. 99, and "To Musick, A Song," p. 103.

[2] See Martial VIII, 68, 5–8, Delattre, p. 415.

[3] *Ibid.*, pp. 75–6.

[4] *Ibid.*, p. 200.

[5] *Ibid.*, p. 154.

[6] *Ibid.*, p. 335.

[7] *Ibid.*, pp. 68–9.

Metaphysical, too, is the final, Horatian-Ausonian stanza with its shocking participle "decaying,"

> Then while time serves, and we are but decaying;
> Come, my *Corinna*, come, let's goe a Maying.

Otherwise the poem, with its realistic and objective account of village festivities, with its warmth and gaiety and music, illustrates the particularly happy results that may be obtained by adaptation rather than imitation of the ancients. Herrick has achieved the same kind of success here as Drayton did in his odes to the New Year and on St. Valentine's day.

Another ode, "The Hock-Cart, or Harvest Home: To the Right Honourable, Mildmay, Earle of Westmorland,"[1] though more straightforward in structure, resembles "Corinna" in being a description of a folk festival, the harvest home. Written in octosyllabic couplets with some poetic diction, e.g., the farmers are called "Sons of Summer," and vivid personification, e.g., "Smirking Wine," this ode reminds us at times of Milton in *L'Allegro*. The ode opens with an invocation of the farmers,

> Crown'd with the eares of corne, now come,
> And, to the Pipe, sing Harvest home.

and of the earl,

> Come forth, my Lord, and see the Cart
> Drest up with all the Country Art.

This leads into a description of the harvest procession, the peasants' clowning, the manor hall feast, and the rounds of drinking. The speech-making naturally offers occasion for the moral conclusion.

The last of these odes which describe popular festivals is "A New-yeares gift sent to Sir Simeon Steward."[2] It is like the preceding ode in being a description of festivities (this time of the Christmas–New Year's celebrations), written in octosyllabic couplets, and garnished with Miltonic personifications, e.g., "Bucksome meat and capring Wine." However, both in invention and structure it is more Horatian. The ode opens

[1] *Ibid.*, pp. 100–2.
[2] *Ibid.*, pp. 126–7.

its advocacy of the whole-hearted enjoyment of present pleasures with a passage that recalls Horace.[1]

No newes of Navies burnt at Seas;
No noise of late spawn'd *Tittyries*:
No closset plot, or open vent,
That frights men with a Parliament:
No new devise, or late found trick,
To read by th' Starres, the Kingdoms sick:
No ginne to catch the State, or wring
The free-born Nosthrills of the King,
We send to you; but here a jolly
Verse crown'd with Yvie, and with Holly.

Then, in Herrick's typical manner, it describes the traditional festivities of the twelve days of Christmas,

Of Christmas sports, the *Wassell-boule*.
That tost up, after *Fox-i' th' hole* :
Of *Blind-man-buffe*, and of the care
That young men have to shoot the *Mare*:
Of Twelf-Tide Cakes, of Pease, and Beanes
Wherewith ye make those merry Sceanes,
When as ye chuse your King and Queen,
And cry out, *Hey, for our town green.*
Of Ash-heapes, in the which ye use
Husbands and Wives by streakes to chuse:
Of crackling Laurell, which fore-sounds,
A Plentious harvest to your grounds. . . .

As the ode requires there are timely admonitions, to forget the troubles of the past and look to the New Year,

Then as ye sit about your embers,
Call not to mind those fled Decembers;
But think on these, that are t'appeare,
As Daughters to the instant yeare:
Sit crown'd with Rose-buds, and carouse,
Till *Liber Pater* twirles the house
About your eares; and lay upon
The yeare (your cares) that's fled and gon.

The poem ends with the poet's request to be remembered in their toasts,

[1] Cf. the opening of Horace II, 11. See also I, 26 and III, 29.

Read then, and when your faces shine
With bucksome meat and capring Wine:
Remember us in Cups full crown'd,
And let our Citie-health go round.

Of Herrick's remaining poems, almost all are epigrams in the ancient sense.

Herrick, although he invented one type of ode in English, was destined, partly because of the time he was born, partly because of his unusual qualities as a poet, to have no followers; he was a unique phenomenon in English literature. Never again was there an English poet born who was so consummate a classicist, so perfect an artist, and such a forthright lover of the good, physical things of life: food, drink, women, and the age-old round of country labours and festivities.

Milton's early (1631) companion pieces, *L'Allegro* and *Il Penseroso*, on the characters of mirth and melancholy, link him with Herrick as the delineator of Merry and Anglican England. In *L'Allegro* as in "The Hock-Cart," "A New-yeares gift," and "The Country Life to Endimion Porter" we have a description of the beauties and joys, pleasures and entertainments, of early seventeenth-century England. Like Herrick's poems, too, *L'Allegro* is written in the spirit of the ancient ode but in a style that foreshadows the later classicism, in octosyllabic couplets with emblematic personifications. However, Milton is, as we would expect, more classical than Herrick both as to those things that we associate with English neo-classicism and as regards that which is characteristically ancient and humanistic. Already in this early work we observe Milton's oft-noted generality, his characteristic painting of abstract, idealized scenes: the hunter's horn rings

From the side of *some* hoar hill . . .

line 55

And *every* shepherd tells his tale
Under *the hawthorn in the dale*.[1]

lines 67–8

The poet's eye moves over an imagined, abstract, and inclusive list of topographical features, significantly referred to in the plural and organized into a "landskip,"

[1] The italics are mine.

Russet lawns, and fallows gray,
Where the nibbling flocks do stray;
Mountains, on whose barren breast
The labouring clouds do often rest:
Meadows trim with Daisies pide,
Shallow Brooks, and Rivers wide,
Towers, and Battlements it sees
Boosom'd high in tufted Trees.

lines 71–9

Herrick's pictures, though they too foreshadow Augustan abstraction, seem always to spring from a series of particular scenes vividly remembered and never pushed too far into the background by the generalizing habit of mind. Thus recollections of particular experiences and actual beasts seem to come to Herrick's mind when he writes in a similar passage,

. . . then to th'enameld Meads
Thou go'st. . . .
And smell'st the breath of great-ey'd Kine,
Sweet as the blossomes of the Vine.
Here thou behold'st thy large sleek Neat
Unto the Dew-laps up in meat:
And, as thou look'st, the wanton Steere,
The Heifer, Cow, and Oxe draw neere
To make a pleasing pastime there.
These seen, thou go'st to view thy flocks
Of sheep, (safe from the Wolfe and Fox)
And find'st their bellies there as full
Of short sweet grasse, as backs with wool.
And leav'st them (as they feed and fill)
A Shepherd piping on a hill.[1]

It is surprising, however, to find that Herrick is, in these poems, more didactic than Milton. On the other hand Milton's structure is formally closer to that of the ancients. In *L'Allegro* we notice the conventions of the ancient hymn-ode conscientiously observed as they are nowhere in Herrick. Here we find the exorcism of Mirth's opponent, Melancholy, who is identified by her parentage, birth-place, and those things associated with her (lines 1–10). Then there is the invocation of the deity hymned, Mirth, who is identified and whose nature is defined

[1] *Poetical Works Herrick*, p. 226.

by two alternative birth-myths (lines 11–34). This is followed by a further defining description, of Mirth's *comitatus* or pomp (lines 25–36). Finally comes the poet's prayer to be admitted to the goddess's company and enjoy the benefits that she bestows, the conventional classical proviso or talisman against ὕβρις (lines (37–40). These are all elements that we have noted often before in both ancient and humanist hymns. In the last two lines of this introduction we find an echo of Marlowe's "Passionate Shepherd to his Love,"

> To live with her, and live with thee,
> In unreproved pleasures free,

a reference that is picked up again in the concluding couplet,

> These delights if thou canst give,
> Mirth, with thee I mean to live.

The body of the poem thus framed is a description of that which Mirth leads us to perceive and enjoy; for Milton has chosen to portray Mirth, philosophically considered as an attitude of mind, through the actions of one who possesses it, much as Dürer portrayed Melancholia. That is Milton describes Mirth in typical ode fashion through a series of pictures.

L'Allegro's companion piece, *Il Penseroso*, replying as it does in every way to its predecessor, refuting the claims of Mirth, invoking Melancholy, and viewing life under the pale caste of thought, expressing the outlook of the introvert, not the extravert, of one who has been betrayed to a lingering book and wrapt up in a gown, is also an ode. This is not to say, however, that Milton thought of either *L'Allegro* or *Il Penseroso* as odes. For him they were poetic refurbishments, made with some help from the popular modern "character," of old school exercises of a very ancient type inherited from sophistic Greece and Imperial Rome and represented by his first prolusion. Milton did not foresee that *L'Allegro* and *Il Penseroso* would be among the progenitors of the favourite eighteenth-century odes on "moral" abstractions or that *Il Penseroso* would one day help to form a graveyard school and father much melancholy poetry.

Now let us return to Milton's first work (1629), his ode, "On The Morning Of Christ's Nativity." In this first, fervent expression of youthful genius, in the enthusiastic young poet's celebration of the infant Jesus, we have the greatest ode in the English language, an ode in which the most beautiful of all themes is given worthy expression. The poet's ability to treat a subject on a universal scale and express the meaning of an event in cosmological and political, in theological and human terms, the completeness of the vision in which scenes of nature, works of art, medieval philosophy, classical literature, and the study of ancient religions all make their contributions, with harmony and ease, to the telling of the simple, familiar Bible story, already reveal the potentiality of *Paradise Lost*. But this is a youthful work and lyrical, and so we still have the short lines and oft-repeated music of the song and the sweet enchantment of rime—the stanza is made up of a romance six with a concluding couplet of a short, four-foot line followed by a round Alexandrine ($AA_3B_5CC_3B_5D_4D_6$). There is also much of the traditional English poetry-making alliteration and assonance. We do not yet hear the mighty-mouthed organ voice of England, but still the almost Elizabethan singer. And this Elizabethan music is exquisitely appropriate to the Christmas theme. The poetry, too, has the golden Elizabethan quality, the pictorial vividness and the evocative images.

The hymn or Christmas carol, two hundred and sixteen lines in length, has a formal introduction of four heavier stanzas in rime royal ($ABABBC_5C_6$) stating the occasion with the usual Christian paradoxes, invoking the Heavenly Muse, asking for a present to lay at the feet of the Infant God,

> Now while the Heav'n by the Suns team untrod,
> Hath took no print of the approaching light,
> And all the spangled host keep watch in squadrons bright,

and begging that he may anticipate the wise men with his work of divine inspiration. This proemium announces the contrast that is to be basic to the hymn, the brightness associated with Jesus and the darkness associated with man and this world:

> He . . .
> Forsook the Courts of everlasting Day,
> And chose with us a darksom House of mortal Clay.

The hymn itself opens in true ode fashion with a real picture of this world at the time that Jesus was born, the cold, darkness, and disharmony ("It was the Winter wilde"), and of the lowly scene of his birth ("All meanly wrapt in the rude manger lies"). Then Nature appears, *natura naturata, this world*, which partakes of man's imperfection and sin, but which also can be restored —as she is symbolically in stanza two, with the white snow which vests her with purity and hides her irregularities, her physical deformities—and so is pictured as a Magdalene:

> Nature in aw to him,
> Had doff't her gawdy trim,
> With her great Master so to sympathize.
> It was no season then for her
> To wanton with the Sun her lusty Paramour.

With these words we have already left the particular scene and begun its interpretation.

In the second stanza Nature "woos the gentle air / To hide her guilty front with innocent snow" and already we note the miracle of the birth making itself felt on the rudeness of the elements; the air has become gentle, soothed by love, and snow will soon abate the harshness of the cold. Then, in the third stanza, the divine power is exercised overtly. Universal peace is struck throughout the lands:

> But he her fears to cease,
> Sent down the meek-eyd Peace:
> She crown'd with Olive green, came softly sliding
> Down through the turning sphear,
> His ready Harbinger,
> With Turtle wing the amorous clouds dividing;
> And waving wide her mirtle wand,
> She strikes a universal Peace through Sea and Land.

The ethereal picture of the descent of Peace is followed by another picture, of iron-age peace on earth:

> No War, or Battails sound,
> Was heard the World around:
> The idle spear and shield were high up hung;
> The hooked Chariot stood
> Unstain'd with hostile blood;
> The Trumpet spake not to the armed throng;
> And Kings sate still with awfull eye,
> As if they surely knew their sovran Lord was by.

This last line takes us back to the Christ child. Now Milton emphasizes the deep peace that his birth brought to earth:

The windes with wonder whist,
Smoothly the waters kist,
  Whispering new joyes to the milde Ocean,
Who now hath quite forgot to rave,
While Birds of Calm sit brooding on the charmed wave.

The Stars with deep amaze
Stand fixt in stedfast gaze,
  Bending one way their pretious influence
And will not take their flight,
For all the morning light,
  Or *Lucifer* that often warn'd them thence;
But in their glimmering Orbs did glow,
Untill their Lord himself bespake, and bid them go.

During this first section of the hymn there have been no colours but white and green and the pale gold of stars in darkness, there has been no sound but the soft voice of Nature and the whisper of the winds, and no motion but the sliding of Peace down through the turning spheres. All has been fixed with the permanence of a series of painted panels which move with our imaginations, and yet are for ever still. And this painted quality persists throughout the ode, with a thinness and a flatness which gives the scenes a timeless quality and an ethereal beauty removed from earthly three-dimensionalism. But now, for a moment, there is light, people, conversation, music, and the radiant vision of the shepherds. The second part of the hymn is taken up with the first proclamation of the birth of Christ. The darkness lightens.

The Shepherds on the Lawn,
Or eer the point of dawn,
  Sate simply chatting in a rustick row;
Full little thought they than,
That the mighty *Pan*[1]
  Was kindly com to live with them below:
Perhaps their loves, or else their sheep,
Was all that did their silly thoughts so busie keep.

[1] For Pan as Christ see Albert S. Cook, "Notes on Milton's Nativity Ode" *Transactions of the Connecticut Academy of Arts and Sciences* XV (1909), 335–8.

Then the divine music is heard. Nature, this time *Natura naturans*, the goddess who governs, with delegated powers, beneath the sphere of the moon, almost thinks that the end of her reign has come, that she is being replaced by a more perfect harmony between earth and heaven. Now the sound grows into sight.

> The helmed Cherubim
> And sworded Seraphim,
> Are seen in glittering ranks with wings displaid,
> Harping in loud and solemn quire,
> With unexpressive notes to Heav'ns new-born Heir.

The geometric austerity of the picture, the only colour that of flashing brightness, and the music that is pure of the taint of human passions,[1] make the portrayal of the angels magnificently convincing. We return to their music never heard before

> But when of old the sons of morning sung,
> While the Creator Great
> His constellations set,
> And the well-balanc't world on hinges hung,
> And cast the dark foundations deep,
> And bid the weltring waves their oozy channel keep.

This is a new creation of the world! And now, in almost the central stanza of the ode, Milton calls for the Christmas bells:

> Ring out ye Crystall sphears,
> Once bless our human ears,
> (If ye have power to touch our senses so)
> And let your silver chime
> Move in melodious time;
> And let the Base of Heav'ns deep Organ blow,
> And with your ninefold harmony
> Make up full consort to th' Angelick symphony.

If men could hear these divine harmonies for long—we refer back to Nature's wondering if she had been superseded—the golden age would return to the earth, vanity and sin would perish, hell would "leave her dolorous mansions to the peering day," Truth, Justice, and Mercy would descend to man, orbed

[1] Cf. Milton's use of "unexpressive" in *Lycidas*,

> And hears the unexpressive nuptial song,
> In the blest kingdoms meek of joy and love.

in the rainbow, fulfilling God's promise to Noah, and Heaven's gates would lean open wide.

But that cannot be. Man first must be redeemed. The smiling Babe must hang upon the bitter cross. This stanza acts as a transition between the second section of the ode with its brilliance and music and the third section with its dissonance and darkness. The Last Judgment must precede the New Jerusalem. The third section opens with the thunder of doomsday, with red fire, smoke, and earthquake, and the throne of Jehovah spread in the middle air. There is only a glimpse of terror, only the sounding of a note; for this is a song and this day marks the beginning of our Redemption. Thus the rest of this section is concerned with the effects of the birth of the Christ child on the powers of evil and the deities of paganism. And yet the third movement of this ode is not too terrible, so as to destroy the earlier moods of peace and joy. There is lusty vigour in the description of the feline frustration of

Th' old Dragon under ground
In straiter limits bound,
Not half so far casts his usurped sway,
And, wrath to see his Kingdom fail,
Swindges the scaly Horrour of his foulded tail,

and a pale, minor key beauty in the confusion of the fair, yet deceitful, young gods of Greece:

The Oracles are dumm,
No voice or hideous humm
Runs through the arched roof in words deceiving.
Apollo from his shrine
Can no more divine,
With hollow shreik the steep of *Delphos* leaving,
No nightly trance, or breathed spell,
Inspire's the pale-ey'd Priest from the prophetic cell.

The lonely mountains o'er
And the resounding shore,
A voice of weeping heard, and loud lament;
From haunted spring, and dale
Edg'd with poplar pale,
The parting Genius is with sighing sent,
With flowre-inwov'n tresses torn
The Nimphs in twilight shade of tangled thickets mourn.

Omens startle the superstitious Romans with their narrower cults and more earthbound religion:

In consecrated Earth,
And on the holy Hearth,
The *Lars*, and *Lemures* moan with midnight plaint,
In Urns, and Altars round,
A drear, and dying sound
Affrights the *Flamins* at their service quaint;
And the chill Marble seems to sweat,
While each peculiar power forgoes his wonted seat.

The scene progressively darkens and the tension mounts. The weird Semitic deities and the animal gods of Egypt forsake their grotesque devotees in the black, flickering shadows, mid the barbaric clash of cymbals:

And sullen *Moloch* fled,
Hath left in shadows dred,
His burning Idol all of blackest hue,
In vain with Cymbals ring,
They call the grisly king,
In dismall dance about the furnace blue;
The brutish gods of *Nile* as fast,
Isis and *Orus*, and the Dog *Anubis* haste.

Nor is *Orisis* seen
In *Memphian* Grove, or Green,
Trampling the unshower'd Grasse with lowings loud:
Nor can he be at rest
Within his sacred chest,
Naught but profoundest Hell can be his shroud,
In vain with Timbrel'd Anthems dark
The sable-stoled Sorcerers bear his worshipt Ark.

He feels from *Juda*'s Land
The dredded Infants hand,
The rayes of *Bethlehem* blind his dusky eyn,
Nor all the gods beside,
Longer dare abide,
Not *Typhon* huge ending in snaky twine;
Our Babe to show his Godhead true,
Can in his swadling bands controul the damned crew.

With the allusion to Hercules in his crib, who is made a kind of prefiguration of Christ, we return to the infant Jesus and to the particular occasion. We have been reminded of what the Redemption must mean, of the necessary conflict of light with darkness. And that is enough.

Now the sun rises red on the first Christian day. This is not the terrible, smoky red of the Last Judgment scene, but the radiant red of hope and good cheer, the red of the joy of high feasts. Now, with the strengthening light the powers of evil are dispersed:

> So when the Sun in bed,
> Curtain'd with cloudy red,
>   Pillows his chin upon an Orient wave.
> The flocking shadows pale,
> Troop to th' infernall jail;
>   Each fetter'd Ghost slips to his severall grave,
> And the yellow-skirted *Fayes*
> Fly after the Night-steeds, leaving their Moon-lov'd maze.

And so the Babe is put to rest and

> Heav'ns youngest teemed Star,
> Hath fixt her polisht Car,
>   Her sleeping Lord with Handmaid Lamp attending
> And all about the Courtly Stable,
> Bright-harnest Angels sit in order serviceable.

The mean, dark stable scene of the first stanza has been transfigured with glory. The red sun glitters on the white snow, the new star sheds its pale rays above, and shining angels flash their diamond brilliance about the stable. In this concluding section we have returned, too, from the metaphysical and supernatural worlds to the human for which, primarily, the birth has taken place. The sun and star are personified and the angels are courtiers waiting on their king.

The "Nativity Ode" is the masterpiece of youth and hope. It is significant that *Paradise Lost* is the work of Milton's old age.

Milton's other odes are far less interesting and much inferior. The attempted but unfinished companion piece to the "Nativity Ode," "The Passion," written in a heavy stanza similar to that of the introduction to the "Nativity Ode" ($ABBAAC_5C_6$), suffers from baroque extravagance and bombast, from too oft-repeated frenzies of grief and too much melodramatic posing. It is interesting to note here, as in *Il Penseroso*, early examples of the conventions of later melancholy poetry:

> Befriend me, Night, best patroness of grief:
> Over the pole thy thickest mantle throw,
> And work my flatter'd fancy to belief,
> That heaven and earth are colour'd with my woe;
> My sorrows are too dark for day to know:
> The leaves should all be black whereon I write:
> And letters, where my tears have wash'd, a wannish white.

This introduction has a Shakespearian ring. Another baroque piece in one long irregular stanza ($ABCBACC_5DD_3CE_5F_3F_2$-$F_3G_5HIHGII_6JJ_3IK_5L_3L_2K_3$) is the ode—we will give it that title rather than epigram because of its formal elaboration of its theme and its conscious pretence—"Upon the Circumcision." Here the Christmas angels are invoked to weep with man at this, the first shedding of Christ's blood for us in his earliest infancy. This takes us to the thin centre bit of the poem. In the last part of the poem the meaning of the circumcision is explained with rhetorical play on the phrase, " O more exceeding love or law more just!" The sentiments expressed are extravagant and the ode is frigid.

A much finer piece of writing is the ode "On The Death Of A Fair Infant, Dying Of A Cough." This ode, written in the stanza of the introduction to the "Nativity Ode" ($ABABBC_5C_6$), creates a myth, which calls to mind Bernardo Tasso's conceit on the drowning of his friend's brother,[1] to explain the death of the summer born baby at winter's kiss, adduces the analogical myth of Apollo and Hyacinth, affirms that the child is not dead, for she never was mortal, speculates on her immortal identity, regrets that she did not stay to reform the world to goodness, and entreats the mother to bear God's will with patience that she may have another child. The characteristics of the funerary ode are evident.

"On Time," like "Upon the Circumcision," is a brief, epigram-like ode in a single, irregular-shaped stanza ($ABABC_5$-$DDC_3EEF_5F_4GG_5H_3H_5I_3IG_5J_4J_5G_6$). However, there is some-

[1] See B. Tasso, *Rime* (Bergamo, 1749), p. 250.

thing of metaphysical wit here that suggests Donne; Milton bids time quicken her pace, gobbling up what is merely mortal, what is time herself; for then there will be eternal bliss,

> Then all this Earthy grosnes quit,
> Attir'd with Stars, we shall for ever sit,
> Triumphing over Death, and Chance, and thee, O Time.

We think of Donne's "Death, be not proud." A similar ode in a similar sort of stanza (ABABCCD$_5$D$_3$EFFGGH$_5$HI$_4$JJKKLM-NNOOP$_5$P$_6$), "At A Solemn Music" reveals, as in the "Nativity Ode," Milton's skill in the description of musical concerts and the characteristic emphasis on design rather than on colour in his pictures. Here Milton bids Verse and Voice unite to represent the song of heaven, that we may again learn the harmony we knew before the fall and so be restored to our God. Finally there is "An Epitaph On The Marchioness of Winchester," a funerary ode in the form of an epitaph,

> This rich marble doth inter
> The honour'd wife of Winchester.

The ode opens with a panegyric of the lady's noble ancestry and of her virtues and charms, describes, in mythological terms, her wedding, the birth of her son, and the second fatal child-bed, compares her life to a carnation's, bids her rest in peace, strews her grave with flowers, and then pictures her in glory in heaven like Rachel, the mother of Joseph, who also died at the birth of her second child.

Milton's odes were few, but he established the great tradition in English. His masterpiece, the "Nativity Ode," revealed how the fusion of traditional English with learned humanist elements could produce a new kind of lyric in English, close and song-like, yet majestic and grandiose. Milton showed how the modern poet could resume the Pindaric role by choosing the most serious and universal of themes and treating them with an all-embracing knowledge.[1] He demonstrated how learning

[1] Gilbert Highet, *The Classical Tradition* (Oxford, 1949), p. 237, quotes D. M. Robinson, *Pindar*, pp. 26 ff., as saying that Milton bought a copy of Pindar shortly before he wrote the "Nativity Ode." Milton's Pindar, now in the Harvard library, is carefully annotated, showing that Milton studied him closely.

could extend the scope of lyric poetry and give it new solidity and breadth. The medieval carol had described the birth of Christ and proclaimed our redemption. Under classical influence Milton went farther than that in his Nativity ode. Over and over again he departed from the actual birth scene to investigate, with specific, pictorial illustrations in the typical ode fashion, another facet of its meaning: of its meaning to the physical cosmos and to the spiritual powers that govern it; of its meaning to the princes of the earth; to the powers of darkness and evil; to the old religions, the old cultures, and the old civilizations of the Mediterranean world; and to all of mankind. With only a few allusions and pictures he made a grand synthesis of the whole of human experience so that it all became part of the one Christian story.

Then, in his descriptions of the two aspects of personality, "l'allegro" and "il penseroso," in his catalogue thoroughness, in his consistent pictorialness that led him to create allegorical figures that give brief, specific, visual, yet not particular expressions of his meaning, and in his use of riming couplets, Milton looks forward to the neoclassical ode, particularly to the ode to an abstraction. He also, both in *Il Penseroso* and "The Passion," lent his tremendous influence to the propagation of the cult of melancholy which was to become so important in English literature during the eighteenth century. Finally, Milton is the first English poet to follow the lead of the neolatins and to write an irregular ode. In this he was soon followed by Crashaw, then by Cowley, and then by the main English lyric tradition.

Anglo-Latin poetry has not been mentioned earlier because England, unlike Italy and France, did not express her first Renaissance creative impulse in Latin.[1] Sixteenth-century English poets never competed for the dubious honour of being last in Rome. Thus the first poetry written in England inspired

[1] Admittedly there was a certain amount of neolatin poetry written in England throughout the sixteenth century from the reign of Henry VIII onwards. But from the beginning the important poets wrote in English and Anglo-Latin verse, never, except in Milton's *Epitaphium Damonis*, attained the high quality of the Italian. For Anglo-Latin verse see Leicester Bradner, *Musae Anglicanae: A History of Anglo-Latin Poetry 1500–1925* (New York, 1940).

by the classics and by humanist imitations of them was written in English. It was only with the greater sophistication and erudition of the seventeenth century that English poets began writing in Latin, and then it was chiefly under university influence, and very few distinguished works were produced. The most pretentious Anglo-Latin work was Cowley's six books of *Plants* (1668), an exercise in the hellenistic didactic poem, a genre never widely popular. The most successful Anglo-Latin poem was Milton's *Epitaphium Damonis* (1639?), a kind of pastoral elegy on the death of his talented young Italian friend, Charles Diodati. Since Anglo-Latin poetry has been comprehensively treated by Leicester Bradner in *Musae Anglicanae* (New York, 1940), only a summary of the facts relevant to this study will be given here.

Perhaps the most important characteristic of the late developing Anglo-Latin lyric is its preoccupation with eccentricities of form. It not only favoured the shaped poems of the Alexandrians and very late Latins; it also created novel strophic forms through original combinations of ancient verses or stanzas. We note the first sign of this in a book written for Winchester School by Richard Willis (*c.* 1545–*c.* 1600), sometime professor of rhetoric at Perugia. Willis's *Poematum Liber* (1573) begins with a series of poems in symbolic shapes, altars, wings, swords, pastoral pipes, etc. Then there are illustrations of the various types of lyric poetry, odes, hymns, dramatic choruses, etc., and of the various appropriate metres, hexameters, sapphics, iambics, hendecasyllabics, glyconics, different kinds of couplets, sapphic and alcaic stanzas, and riming verse. The book concludes with a description of "epimicton" and examples of mixed metres in Greek and in Latin, e.g., a dactylic hexameter coupled with a dactylic pentamenter and an iambic senarius.[1] This book of Willis's is undoubtedly indebted to Julius Caesar Scaliger's *Poetics* (Geneva, 1561), an encyclopedia of ancient metrics which illustrates every metre known, even from fragments, which combines them in verse samplers, and which, in its description of the liberties of the choral ode and dithyramb, suggests novelties which go beyond classical authority.[2] Much of the Latin lyric poetry written in England from the end of the sixteenth century to the middle of the

[1] *Ibid.*, pp. 34–5. [2] Bradner, p. 103.

eighteenth was written in the unorthodox forms practised in the schools. Dr. Johnson blamed Cowley for the horror of the irregular *Latin* ode,[1] but it now seems more probable that the school exercises in Latin verse were responsible for the irregular *English* ode; although undoubtedly the real vogue of the one, with the success of Cowley's Pindarics, influenced the practice of the other.

The chief outlet for Anglo-Latin poetry was the university memorial volume,[2] a fact which, in itself, shows how unpopular and how academic Anglo-Latin verse actually was. The first of these volumes was *Academiae Cantabrigiae lachrymae*, 1587, a memorial volume on the death of Sir Philip Sidney. Although the verse here was poor the idea caught on and soon both the universities were issuing volumes to commemorate important public events, especially the births, deaths, and marriages of princes, victories won, and peace obtained. The poetry in these volumes was written not only in Latin but also in Greek, Hebrew, Celtic, Old English, Arabic, Persian, and Coptic, languages that princes were politely held to comprehend. In the eighteenth century poems in English were admitted, a language only slightly more familiar to the Hanoverians.

In these volumes, and in the independently published Anglo-Latin poetry, Bradner finds four different types of non-classical Latin verse, as well as the conventional sort, of which the pastoral elegy was most popular in the first half of the seventeenth century and the Horatian ode in the second.[3] The four unconventional kinds of Latin poetry are the mixed ode made up of various classical metres, the ode composed of newly invented but symmetrical stanzas, the dithyramb, and free verse.

The mixed ode, which occurs as early as 1603 in the volumes on the death of Queen Elizabeth and is, throughout the whole period, very popular for learned poetry, consists of a mixture of various classical stanzas or of metrical units normally used only by themselves in homogeneous wholes: e.g., the "Carolus redux" (1623) by William Axon of New College contains nine

[1] Samuel Johnson, "Cowley," *Lives of the English Poets*, Everyman ed. (London and New York, 1950), I, 32.

[2] For the various anniversary volumes see Bradner, pp. 36, 60–2, 99–102.

[3] *Ibid.*, p. 101.

different metres in thirty lines, hexameters, sapphic stanzas, hendecasyllabics, iambics, lesser asclepiads, lesser alcaics, lesser sapphics, cretics, and adonics.

The second type of non-classical Latin verse is made up of a series of identical stanzas, the stanzas themselves being composed of novel combinations of correct classical lines. Such verse was used in the Latin translations of Spenser's *Shepheards Calendar*; in Andrew Willett's *Sacrorum emblematum centuria una* (*c.* 1596), a collection of English emblem poems with Latin translations in which the many original stanza forms of the English are imitated in Latin by such couplet combinations as a hendecasyllabic and an adonic or an asclepiad and a dactyllic dimeter; in the incidental verse to John Barclay's Latin novel, *Argenis*, where the songs are composed of stanzas created by various combinations of hendecasyllabics, asclepiads, glyconics, sapphics, and adonics; in the anonymous *Nova Solyma* of 1648 in which original stanzas are composed of hendecasyllabics, asclepiads, glyconics, and pherecratics; and in Milton's Latin ode to John Rouse (1646, but not published until 1673), the librarian of the Bodleian. Milton's ode to Rouse consists of three strophes and antistrophes followed by an epode. The strophes are composed of unfamiliar combinations of Latin verses, perhaps inspired by the Greek. Moreover, the strophes and antistrophes are not exactly alike throughout, but Milton, as he says himself in a note, has divided the verses for the propriety of reading rather than for the observance of ancient rules of versification.

The dithyrambs, hypothetical imitations of the strophic form of the Dionysiac hymns of the Greeks, none of which has survived, are written in a mixture of correct classical lines of varying lengths ungrouped into stanzas. In appearance they resemble the Italian madrigals which they, however, usually exceed in length. Bradner states that the dithyramb came to England through the works of such neolatin poets as Andrea Dazzi and Théodore de Bèze,[1] and on the authority of Scaliger's *Poetics*. For Dazzi and Bèze he cites only one short poem each which is written in a novel form and I have certainly not been able to find any more. It seems more likely, then, that

[1] *Ibid.*, p. 108.

the dithyramb grew out of the various attempts by Benedetto Lampridio to reproduce the Pindaric and by Pietro Crinito to create new Latin strophes,[1] as well as from the encouragement of Scaliger's *Poetics*. Later, in the early seventeenth century, there was also the example of Daniel Heinsius. The Latin dithyramb first appears in England in the anniversary volumes of the 1630's, in the *Flos Britannicus* of 1636, and in the *Musarum Oxoniensium* of 1638.

Free Latin verse differs from these other three licentious varieties by being composed of a mixture of correct and incorrect classical lines. It is only the presence of classically unscannable lines that distinguishes free verse from the dithyramb, which it otherwise resembles. Free verse came late to England. Bradner finds the first example in Robert Waring's elegy, shaped like a tombstone inscription, in *Jonsonus Virbius*, 1638.[2]

We have already, in the neolatin chapter, seen examples both of mixed odes, e.g., in Filelfo, and of odes in which the conventional resources of classical metrics have been used to create wholly unconventional strophes, e.g., in Crinito and Lampridio. Because of its importance in the formal history of the English ode let us now look, for here the appearance is the most important thing, at a typical dithyramb. I quote the shortest one at hand, Heinsius' "Lusus ad apiculas":

Mellificae volucres,
Quae per purpureas rosas,
Violasque amaracumque
Tepidique dona veris,
Legitis suave nectar,
Tenerae cives,
Et seduli coloni,
Et incolae beati
Horrorum redolentium,
Gens divino
Ebria rore;
Agite, o meae volucres, age, gens vaga nemorum.
Agite hinc abite cunctae,
Et tumulum magni cingite Lipsiadae.
Illic domum laresque

[1] See supra, pp. 105–9 and pp. 85–6, 93, 96–7.
[2] *Ibid.*, pp. 103–9. For Milton's ode to Rouse see also p. 116.

Vobis figite, figite:
Illic vestri
Copia mellis,
Haereditasque fertur ad vos denuo
Debita, quam vobis quondam sublegerat ille.
At invidos malosque,
Et quem non Venus aurea,
Quem non amat Cupido,
Quem non amant lepores,
Quem non amat venustas,
Quem non amat Suada,
Illis acutis protinus
Figite cuspidibus.
Ut si quis malus impiusque, tendit
Mel illud roseumque nectar, illas
Coeli delicias cibosque Divum,
Impii male vellicare morsu;
Protinus undique et undique et undique et
 undique punctus,
Calamisque, vocibusque
Et eruditis morsibus,
Concidat extincto victima Lipsiadae.[1]

Heinsius' dithyramb may serve as an example both of the dithyramb and of free verse; for the difference between the two is merely technical and they can be treated as one as far as their influence upon English verse is concerned.

The Anglo-Latin poets were influenced by Vergil, Ovid, and Horace, in that order of importance, and by the writers of the *Greek Anthology*, both as to form and, in the case of elegies, epigrams, and lighter lyrics, also as to manner. The chief neolatin poets, particularly the Italian ones, and the two Dutchmen, Secundus and Heinsius, were known and appreciated in England. There were many editions of their individual works as well as Gruter's tremendous anthologies in which they could be read. The French and German neolatin poets were little known, the latter only by scholars who had studied in Germany.[2] On the whole neolatin writers had little influence on Anglo-Latin. Rather, Anglo-Latin verse tended to resemble contemporary English verse. Thus the first Anglo-Latin mixed

[1] *Danielis Heinsii Poematum editio nova* (Amstelodami, 1649), pp. 68–9.
[2] Bradner, p. 6.

odes appeared in translations from the English, where they imitated English stanza forms, e.g., in John Dove's Latin translation of the *Shepheards Calendar*, *c.* 1584. On the other hand it seems likely that their university exercises in irregular Latin verse suggested to English poets the writing of irregular verse in English. Certainly Milton's "Upon the Circumcision," "On Time," and "At A Solemn Music" suggest, in their form, in their single, long, irregularly shaped strophe, the spurious Latin dithyramb—as well as the madrigal of Marino.

Richard Crashaw (1612–49)[1] first appears as an Anglo-Latin writer, as the author of a collection of Jesuit-inspired *Epigrammata Sacra* (1634), a series of ingenious reflections usually on the physical facts of various New Testament texts.[2] The quatrain on Luke 11, 27, which Crashaw himself translated into English will serve as a convenient example of his epigrammatic style:

Et quid si biberet Jesus vel ab ubere vestro?
  Quid facit ad vestram, quòd bibit ille, sitim?
Ubera mox sua et Hic (ô quàm non lactea!) pandet:
  E nato Mater tum bibet ipsa suo.

Suppose he had been Tabled at thy Teates,
  Thy hunger feeles not what he eates:
Hee'l have his Teat e're long (a bloody one)
  The Mother then must suck the Son.[3]

Although this astounding conceit is no more than a vivid assertion of the familiar doctrines of the Redemption and Transubstantiation, which do not normally shock anyone, yet the very literalness of their expression, the picture of Jesus' spear-opened breast and his blood-sucking mother, is so shocking that the modern mind draws back in repulsion and the

[1] For the facts about Crashaw's life and for a criticism of his poetry see L. C. Martin, *The Poems English, Latin, and Greek of Richard Crashaw* (Oxford, 1927), introduction, pp. xv–xlii; R. C. Wallerstein, *Richard Crashaw, A Study in Style and Poetic Development* (Madison, 1935); and A. Warren, *Richard Crashaw, A Study of Baroque Sensibility* (Louisiana State University, 1939).

[2] For a discussion of the technique of Crashaw's Latin epigrams see Wallerstein, *Crashaw*, pp. 61–3 and 108; Warren, *Crashaw*, pp. 117, 163, 173, 192–3.

[3] Martin, *Poems Crashaw*, pp. 40 and 94.

image fails in its anagogical duty. An epigram on almost the same theme by the Jesuit poet François Remond[1] is much tamer stuff; for here it is the poet who is sustained both by the milk of the mother and the blood of the son. Expressed thus, the theme of the different nourishment offered by the mother and the son makes no more than a clever and somewhat frigid conceit, especially when the theme is developed and varied over an expanse of twelve lines. Crashaw, by making the mother who had cherished his life, drink from the bleeding breast of her dying son, puts the maximum of emphasis on the bitter sacrifice of the Son of God. For ingenuity and daring, for sheer baroqueness, Crashaw puts all rivals in the pale. Crashaw gains immeasurably in power, too, by his brevity. One couplet is enough to mark the bounds of normal human love, another to show the extent of divine love. Crashaw's other epigrams tend to be extravagantly baroque, often in the same way. Some few exchange a fleshly sensationalism for dialectical quibbles. This type of religiosity is so exotic, so foreign to the English mind that Crashaw's Latin epigrams are rarely read with real sympathy.

In addition to epigrams Crashaw's next two volumes, *The Delights of the Muses* of 1646 and 1648 contain the more conventional type of Latin poem, sapphic and alcaic odes, glyconics, hendecasyllabics, hexameters, and elegiac couplets. They also contain examples of the dithyramb and free verse. Since Crashaw's conventional Latin poetry is undistinguished, we will consider only his dithyrambs, which are at least of historical importance, and his free verse. The piece in free verse,[2] like Waring's pioneer example in *Jonsonus Virbius*, is a lengthy epitaph and may owe some of its peculiarities to an effort to approximate the physical appearance of the funerary inscription. Otherwise it looks like a rather odd dithyramb. "Epitaphium in Dominum Herrisium"[3] appeared in *The Delights of the Muses* of 1646. The four dithyrambs which were added to *The Delights of the Muses* in 1648, formally resemble the Heinsius example above, except that they are briefer, each being twenty-two lines in length, and thus even more like the

[1] Franciscus Remondus, S. J., *Carmina* (Viennae, 1617), p. 9.

[2] Bradner, p. 110.

[3] Martin, *Poems Crashaw*, pp. 164–6.

madrigal. To illustrate Crashaw's mixture of metres we will analyse the first of the dithyrambs, "In Apollinem depereuntem Daphnen."[1] This poem is composed, in this order, of an adonic; a dactylic penthemim; a pherecratic; a glyconic; a dactylic tetrameter; a dactylic hexameter; a trochaic dimeter catalectic; an iambic dimeter; an iambic dimeter hypermetric; an iambic trimeter catalectic; an iambic trimeter acatalectic; a first asclepiad; a sapphic; a greater alcaic; a lesser alcaic; a fifth asclepiad; an iambic dimeter catalectic; a greater sapphic; a verse composed of three lesser ionics; a greater archilochian; a verse composed of a dactylic penthemim and an iambic dimeter, the second line of the third archilochian strophe; and a verse composed of an iambic dimeter and a dactylic penthemim, the second line of the second archilochian strophe. In this one poem Crashaw has all but exhausted the metrical resources of Horace, skilfully grouping structurally similar metres into a prosodic sampler. This, with permissible substitutions, is the metrical pattern for the three other dithyrambs, a fact which suggests that Crashaw may have been trying to create a new stanza form for Latin verse.

As to content, the dithyrambs each describe a scene from classical literature and then toy with it and analyse it with baroque wit and an ingenuity that recalls decadent scholastic speculation. These dithyrambs call to mind the popular seventeenth-century emblem book.[2] Indeed we wonder that Crashaw with his talent for "drawing, limming, and graving"[3] did not illustrate them, especially since he had already written:

> I Paint so ill, my peece had need to bee
> Painted againe by some good Poesie.
> I write so ill, my slender Line is scarce
> So much as th' Picture of a well-lim'd verse.[4]

None of these dithyrambs is an ode.

A sixth poem, like the dithyrambs in form, but half the

[1] *Ibid.*, p. 222.

[2] For the emblem book see Wallerstein, *Crashaw*, pp. 114–24, Warren, *Crashaw*, pp. 75–6, and Mario Praz, *Studies in Seventeenth Century Imagery*.

[3] Martin, *Poems Crashaw*, p. 416.

[4] *Ibid.*, p. 156, from *The Delights of the Muses*, 1646.

length, is a conceited epigram on the Phoenix[1] one of Crashaw's favourite themes.

The form of the dithyramb and the technique of the epigram are of first importance to Crashaw's English odes. Some odes are composed of irregular stanzas with constantly changing metres which, as most of these were later printed as one solid piece, may be considered to be super-dithyrambs. Others are composed of a series of stanza length epigrams, of parallel, conceited variations on the single theme which supplies the unity to the whole. We will examine this latter type of ode first of all. Here there is little, if any development or progression of thought throughout the poem and no subordination of ideas. Each stanza stands independently. As in Pindar the style is paratactic, but, unlike Pindar's, most of these odes are static, there is no action or story, only wit and highly refined emotion. Such an ode is "The Weeper,"[2] the first poem in the 1646 *Steps to the Temple.* Here the amount of thought progression is very slight, and, where it exists, consists only in the linking of related groups of conceits. A glance at the poem will illustrate this. The first stanza of "The Weeper," in a series of images, defines the subject of the ode, the weeping eyes of Mary Magdalene. The second stanza, a perfect baroque epigram, declares that the eyes are sowers of stars. The third stanza affirms that these stars, like the stars of heaven, only appear to fall. The fourth stanza makes the startling statement,

> Upwards thou dost weepe,
> Heavens bosome drinks the gentle streame.
> Where th' milky rivers meet,
> Thine Crawles above and is the Creame.
> Heaven, of such fair floods as this,
> Heaven the Christall Ocean is.

Again we have the typical Crashaw epigram, the fantastic conceit loaded with literary and theological allusions and the mouth-sensuous imagery. In other places Crashaw revels in the imagination of blood; here it is cream whose sensuous

[1] *Ibid.*, pp. 224–5.

[2] *Ibid.*, pp. 79–83. See Warren, *Crashaw*, p. 134 ff., for a discussion of previous Magdalene literature. Wallerstein, p. 56, finds various sources in Marino and in some of the Jesuit epigrammatists for parts of this poem.

quality is admirably suggested by the verb "crawls." The allusion to the Milky Way recalls the ancient myth of Hercules and Juno known in the Renaissance, as Ronsard, Rubens, and Herrick testify.[1] According to this myth the infant Hercules, Jupiter's illegitimate son by the mortal Alcmena, was placed at the sleeping Juno's breast that he might suck her milk and gain immortality. Juno, sensing the strange baby, pulled her breast away and the spilt drops of milk, flying across the sky, formed the Milky Way.[2] The Milky Way then became the highway of gods and heroes to the palace of Jupiter.[3] As the Milky Way was the pathway to heaven for the pagan hero, so the tears of the repentant have always been regarded as the Christian way to God.[4] The efficacy of tears was particularly emphasized in the late middle ages[5] and in Crashaw's baroque period which in many ways referred back to it.[6] We find a

[1] See Laumonier, *Oeuvres Ronsard* II, 223–4; Herrick, Moorman, pp. 74 and 96; and Rubens' "Juno allaitant Hercule," Musées Royaux des Beaux Arts, Brussels, painting number 814.

[2] See Robert Graves, *The Greek Myths*, Penguin Book II (1955), 90, 93, 94. See also Migne, *Patrologia Latina*, XC, *Bedae Ven. Operum Pars I . . . De Natura Rerum*, gloss of Bridefertus on Chapt. 18: "When Hercules was placed by the sleeping Juno to suck the divine milk, she was aroused and realized that it was not her own son and drew away. Then drops of milk were scattered through the heavens and created the Milky Way."

[3] See, e.g., Ovid, *Meta.* I, lines 168–71: "This is the gods' way to the royal palace, the dwelling place of the mighty Thunderer." Note that in the seventh book of *Paradise Lost*, at the end of the sixth day, Creation finished, the son and angels return to heaven by the Milky Way. Note too that Marvell uses the Milky Way figuratively for the Christian's pathway to heaven:

There the milky way doth lye;
'Tis a sure but rugged way,
That leads to Everlasting day,

"A *Dialogue between* Thyrsis *and* Dorinda"

[4] Cf., e.g., Goffridus Abbas Vindocinensis (eleventh century) in Migne, *Patrologia Latina* CLVII, 271:

> We do not read there that she spoke, but wept; and nevertheless we believe that she spoke exceedingly well, but with tears rather than with words. For with the good Lord the speech of tears is wonderfully fruitful. . . . To be sure, the prayers of tears are considerably better than those of words. For he who prays with words sometimes offends; but the tear knows not how to offend.

[5] J. Huizinga, *The Waning of the Middle Ages*, a Doubleday Anchor Book (Garden City, New York, 1954), pp. 191–2.

[6] See, e.g., Donne's "A Valediction: Of Weeping" and *passim* in his poetry.

weakened form of this doctrine in eighteenth-century sentimentalism. So, then, Magdalene's tears may be compared with the Milky Way, they flow up to God and they are the sinner's road to heaven.[1] But they are superior to the Milky Way as the new dispensation is to the old. Therefore they crawl above and are the cream. Perhaps Marlowe's lines in *Hero and Leander*:

> Forth from these two translucent cisterns brake
> A stream of liquid pearl, which down her face
> Made milk-white paths, whereon the gods might trace
> To Jove's high court,[2]

mark the transition stage between the Hercules myth and Magdalene's tears.

The first four stanzas, then, form a related series of conceits. The next two stanzas are again related to each other and are linked to the preceding four stanzas by the last two lines of the fourth stanza quoted above: "Magdalene's tears are the waters of Heaven." This conceit is developed in the next two epigrammatic stanzas which picture the drawers of this heavenly water. Here we are reminded of Herrick's epigram:

> Teares, though th'are here below the sinners brine,
> Above they are the Angels spiced wine.[3]

The rest of the ode consists of a series of ingenious and widely varied conceits about Magdalene's tears, some of them forming

[1] See Honorius Agustodunensis (twelfth century), Migne, *Patrologia Latina* CLXXII, 981, where Magdalen is spoken of as Jesus' apostle to the apostles, since it was she who announced his resurrection to the apostles: as death was brought into the world by woman, so eternal life was announced by woman. See also Goffridus Abbas Vindocinensis, Migne, CLVII, 273:

> Let us invoke her especially [after Jesus and the Virgin] . . . that, through her holy intercession she should make her intercessor intercede for us sinners, that he should grant the remission of our sins, and that he should receive us within the gates of paradise.

and 274:

> Her prayer is the medicine for sin, her tongue has become the dutiful doorkeeper of heaven. She opens the gate to everyone who is perfectly repentent, no sinner is excluded by her.

[2] *The Works of Christopher Marlowe*, ed. F. Cunningham (London, 1874), p. 200a.

[3] Moorman, *Herrick's Poems*, p. 223.

stanzas quite unrelated to anything before or after in the poem, others clustering together in groups. Anything that has any element of likeness in it may be compared with the weeping Magdalene's tears; for the universe is still God's greatest parable and thus any one part of it may contribute to the explanation of any other part. The images are usually drawn from literature or intellectual experience rather than from life, there is little visualization, and the colours are limited to gold, red, and pale. However, Crashaw's visual deficiency is compensated for by his tactile sensuousness and the sweet music of his lines. Thus the pretty but frigid conceit of stanza seven is saved by the warmth and sensuousness of the adjective "nuzzel'd," by the slightly hypnotic effect of the repetition of "The dew no more will," and by the music of long vowels, alliteration, and liquid consonants:

The dew no more will weepe,
The Primroses pale cheeks to decke,
The dew no more will sleepe,
Nuzzel'd in the Lillies necke.
Much rather would it tremble heere,
And leave them both to bee thy Teare.

The ode as a whole is marred by disorganization and repetition. "The Amber-weeping Tree" of stanza eight is little differentiated from "The Balsame-sweating bough" of stanza twelve, a fact that Crashaw recognized when, in the second version of this poem in the *Carmen Deo Nostro* of 1652,[1] he omitted stanza eight. Indeed a comparison of these two versions of "The Weeper" will reveal how anarchistic its structure is. The stanzas can be shuffled about without any apparent disharmony. Thus the first five stanzas of both versions are alike, but after stanza five the second version places stanza ten of the 1646 version, then stanzas nine, seven, twelve, and thirteen, a new stanza which serves as a sort of link with the following stanza six, then stanzas fourteen and fifteen. Of the first part of the original poem stanzas eight and eleven are omitted. After stanza fifteen of the 1646 version (stanza fourteen of the 1652 version) the 1652 version inserts eight new stanzas partly inspired by different neolatin religious epigrams.[2] Then follow

[1] Martin, *Poems Crashaw*, pp. 309–14.
[2] *Ibid.*, pp. 448–9.

the old stanzas nineteen, eighteen, and sixteen revised, stanza twenty, a new stanza, stanzas twenty-one, twenty-two, and twenty-three revised, and a new conclusion. From the second part of the poem stanza seventeen is omitted. Although the new version of "The Weeper" has thus, happily, a better grouping of stanzas, a more logical line of development, and clearer connections, and so is structurally superior, it is also more florid and more ornately baroque than the earlier version and so has an even more unsympathetic suggestion of meretricious art. The stanza form of "The Weeper," $A_3B_4A_3B_4CC_4$, with its concluding couplet, emphasizes the isolation of each of its parts and tends to create epigrammatic units.

Crashaw's next ode, "The Teare,"[1] is written in the same stanza as "The Weeper" and like it is constructed of a series of epigrammatic reflections on Mary's tear. There is, inevitably, the impression of repetitiousness: for Crashaw's material for imagery was rather scanty and the sun, rose, and Aurora appear too soon again. "On the wounds of our crucified Lord,"[2] in an alternately riming quatrain, $ABAB_4$, is an expanded epigram. Again we have blood and tears, roses and pearls, and Mary Magdalene.[3] Another of the epigram-built, emblem book odes, "Easter day,"[4] consists of a series of ingenious meditations, not without true wit, on the miracle of Easter. The longer stanza and the varying length of line, $A_4B_3A_6C_4B_2C_6$, allow each idea a fuller development than was possible in the previous odes, suggest more the rhythm of reflection, and do not break the ode down into a series of highly polished parts, but rather tend to bind it together into an organic whole. The last in this group of epigram odes is "On the bleeding wounds of our crucified Lord,"[5] revised in the *Carmen Deo Nostro* as "Upon The Bleeding Crucifix. A Song."[6] Again there is a succession of witty meditations whose order is changed from one version to the other with ease, and again there is much blood and tears, red and roses:

1 *Ibid.*, pp. 84–5. Wallerstein, p. 56, finds some sources for this ode in Marino and the Jesuit epigrammatists.

2 Martin, *Poems Crawshaw*, p. 99.

3 Wallerstein, p. 97, finds specific indebtedness here to Marino.

4 Martin, *Poems Crashaw*, p. 100.

5 *Ibid.*, pp. 101–2.

6 *Ibid.*, pp. 288–9.

Water'd by the showres they bring,
The Thornes that thy blest browes encloses
(A cruell and a costly spring)
Conceive proud hopes of proving Roses.

The last conceit, like many of Crashaw's extravagances, is firmly based on medieval Catholic tradition. We find roses blooming on the crown of thorns in "De Corona Spinea," a medieval hymn found in the modern breviairies,

Reddening with the blood of Christ
Its spikes are changed to roses,
With branches fairer than the palm,
The thorn is more fit for triumphs,[1]

and in John of Hoveden's famous Latin *Philomena*,

The royal head stiffens beneath the thorn,
The rose groans on the thorn's spear . . .
A dreadful image, the thorn sucks
The golden honies of frankincense;
The king of virtues, all perfumed,
Grows red in his thorny diadem.[2]

An ode somewhat similar to this epigrammatic group which, however, does have stanza sequences, is "An Himne for the Circumcision day of our Lord,"[3] which celebrates a favourite baroque poetic theme. There is again much red, gold, purple, and white, laces, jewels, jewel cabinets, the sun, and the exotic east. There is no natural imagery and little that is clearly visualized, but a rich profusion of artistic treasure and all the suggestiveness that goes with it.[4] This ode was revised slightly for *Carmen Deo Nostro*.

Quite a different sort of ode is "A Hymne of the Nativity, sung by the Shepheards,"[5] a choral ode with two soloists, Tityrus and Thyrsis, drawn from the pastoral tradition which has, as one would expect in the case of a learned poet like Crashaw, moulded the form of the Christmas carol. The chorus

[1] H. A. Daniel, *Thesaurus Hymnologicus* II (Halis, 1841), 360.
[2] Ed. C. Blume (Leipzig, 1930), Stanzas 140–2.
[3] *Ibid.*, pp. 141–2.
[4] *Ibid.*, pp. 251–2.
[5] *Ibid.*, pp. 106–8.

of shepherds sings to wake the sun and bids Tityrus and Thyrsis tell them where they have been and what they have seen, a familiar device in the pastoral. The shepherds then take their turns describing the events at Bethlehem, often with sensuous delight, occasionally with metaphysical wit, e.g.,

> I saw the curl'd drops, soft and slow
> Come hovering o're the places head,
> Offring their whitest sheets of snow,
> To furnish the faire Infants Bed.
> Forbeare (said I) be not too bold,
> Your fleece is white, but 'tis too cold. . . .
>
> The Babe no sooner 'gan to seeke,
> Where to lay his lovely head,
> But streight his eyes advis'd his Cheeke,
> 'Twixt Mothers Brests to goe to bed.
> Sweet choice (said I) no way but so,
> Not to lye cold, yet sleepe in snow.

A final chorus welcomes the child, using Crashaw's typical imagery, gold and silk, milk, tears, rosebuds, diamonds, April showers, May flowers, and silver doves. There is an occasional uncommon but marvellously expressive image:

> Welcome (though not to those gay flyes
> Guilded i' th' Beams of Earthly Kings
> Slippery soules in smiling eyes),

and the sweetly intoxicating music of alliteration, skilfully varied vowel sounds, and smoothly running lines that avoid hiatus, characteristics that become dominant in Crashaw's later poetry.[1] The stanza, after an introductory quatrain, $AABB_4$, is $ABABCC_4$, a form that lends itself to statement and recapitulation or precision, which nicely rounds off each swelling of the music, and which need not break the poem up into isolated epigrams if the author has some plan of development as Crashaw had here. This ode was revised for *Carmen Deo Nostro*,[2] given a couple of extra stanzas and choral repetitions, so that it became a grandiose baroque hymn looking forward to Dryden's *Alexander's Feast*.

1 See Warren, p. 108.
2 Martin, *Poems Crashaw*, pp. 248–51.

Apart from two psalms, one in stanzas, $A_5B_4A_5B_4CC_4$,[1] the other in octosyllabic couplets,[2] an early (1635) neoclassical-type ode in decasyllabic couplets "On a Treatise of Charity,"[3] and the antiphonal "On Hope, By way of Question and Answer, betweene A. Cowley, and R. Crashaw,"[4] an exercise in metaphysical dialectic whose tone and form are set by Cowley, an interesting piece of work since it shows Crashaw much more witty under Cowley's influence than he is on his own and writing in a longer and more elaborate stanza, $A_4ABB_5CC_4D_5D_2EE_5$, than he ever invents for himself, the remaining odes of *Steps to the Temple* are written in irregular verse apparently inspired by the neolatin mixed odes and dithyrambs, by the vernacular mixed odes[5] whether medieval or humanist inspired, and perhaps something indebted to the form of the Italian madrigal and even to the neolatin triadic Pindaric.

The first of these irregular odes is "On a prayer booke sent to Mrs. M. R."[6] Let us look at the metre. After an epigrammatic, emblem book quatrain on the prayer book, $A_5B_2B_3A_5$, there follows:

stanza 2	$A_5AB_4B_5C_4CDDEE_5$
stanza 3	$AA_4B_2C_4B_2C_4$
stanza 4	$AA_2BC_4B_2CDD_4$
stanza 5	$A_2AB_3B_2$
stanza 6	$A_2A_3B_4C_4B_3C_4DD_5E_5F_4G_3G_2$
stanza 7	$A_5BB_4C_4C_2A_4D_2D_3A_4$
stanza 8	$A_3A_2B_3B_5CDCCD_4$
stanza 9	$ABAB_4C_5C_4D_2D_5$
stanza 10	$A_4A_5B_3B_4$
stanza 11	$A_4BA_3B_5C_3C_5$
stanza 12	$A_3A_4B_2B_3C_3D_3C_2E_2E_4$
stanza 13	$A_5B_4C_3BCD_2DEEF_4GG_2HFH_4$
stanza 14	$AAB_4C_2C_3DD_5EEF_4G_2GF_4$

[1] *Ibid.*, pp. 104–5. [2] *Ibid.*, pp. 103–4.
[3] *Ibid.*, pp. 137–9. [4] *Ibid.*, pp. 143–5.
[5] Several lyrics of Herbert's used two different stanza patterns, e.g.,"The Church-Floor," "An Offering," "Vanitie," Bradner, p. 110. Herbert also wrote one Latin mixed ode, "Ad Joannem Donne."
[6] Martin, *Poems Crashaw*, pp. 126–30.

Although, because of the particular placing of the verses on the printed page, it is hard to be positive exactly where every stanza begins, and there might be one stanza more or less, yet this outline gives a fair impression of the irregular form of the ode. It is significant that in the revised version of this poem in *Carmen Deo Nostro*[1] the verses are printed in a continuous piece which does look like the neolatin mixed ode, a very long dithyramb, or even a Pindaric. As to content, after a series of varied epigrammatic definitions of the prayer book, all of them military conceits presumably originally inspired by St. Paul's description of the armour of the Christian, there follows spiritual advice, illustrated by the parable of the wise and foolish virgins interpreted in the spirit of medieval Latin and baroque mysticism.[2] Christ is the lover of the soul and she who is prepared to receive him enjoys soft, St. Theresa-like ecstasies:

> . . . the sacred store
> Of hidden sweets, and holy joyes,
> Words which are not heard with eares,
> (These tumultuous shops of noise)
> Effectuall whispers whose still voyce,
> The soule it selfe more feeles then heares.
>
> Amorous Languishments, Luminous trances,
> Sights which are not seen with eyes,
> Spirituall and soule peircing glances.
> Whose pure and subtle lightning, flies
> Home to the heart, and setts the house on fire;
> And melts it downe in sweet desire:
> Yet doth not stay
> To aske the windowes leave, to passe that way.
> Delicious deaths, soft exhalations
> Of soule; deare, and divine annihilations.
> A thousand unknowne rites
> Of joyes, and rarifyed delights.
>
> An hundred thousand loves and graces,
> And many a misticke thing,
> Which the divine embraces
> Of the deare spowse of spirits with them will bring.

[1] *Ibid.*, pp. 328–31.
[2] For amorous religious poetry of the middle ages see Remy de Gourmont, *Le Latin Mystique* (Paris, 1892).

There is less visual imagery than usual, but no change in Crashaw's characteristic vague but emotive collection of sweets whose richness is reinforced by the music of alliteration.

Another of the irregular odes, "In memory of the Vertuous and Learned Lady Madre de Teresa that sought an early Martyrdome,"[1] again printed in stanzas of very varying lengths in 1646 and as a continuous piece in 1652,[2] has more development than any other of Crashaw's odes because it is based on the *Vida* of St. Theresa and tells a story with comment. The central incident of this ode on the life and works of St. Theresa is her childhood determination to become a martyr among the Moors. Her would-be martyrdom at the Moorish knife is contrasted with the ecstatic deaths reserved for her at the hands of divine Love who turns his seraphim into Ovidian-Petrarchan archers, a happier St. Sebastian firing squad.[3] Then, at last, St. Theresa joins the virgins in heaven where she is honoured with the fruits of her works. There are the usual images of sound, particularly alliteration, and there is considerable anaphora.

[1] Martin, *Poems Crashaw*, pp. 131–6.

[2] *Ibid.*, pp. 316–21.

[3] For the nature of the conceit cf. Marino's madrigal about Mary Magdalene, "Lachrymis cepit rigare Pedes eius," *Rime* (Venetia, 1608), p. 182:

> You have already struck me
> Heavenly Archer, to give me life:
> I feel the shaft of your
> Divine love in my heart,

and Crashaw's "St. Theresa," *Steps to the Temple* (1646), Martin, *Poems Crashaw*, pp. 133–4:

> Thou are Loves victim, and must dye
> A death more misticall and high.
> Into Loves hand thou shalt let fall,
> A still surviving funerall.
>
> His is the dart must make the death
> Whose stroake shall taste thy hallowed breath.

Note the greater richness and sensuouness of Crawshaw's style and the much intenser feeling. For a contrast of Marino's and Crashaw's styles see Wallerstein, pp. 74–81, and M. Praz, *Secentismo e Marinismo in Inghilterra* (Firenze, 1925). Cf. also the whole ode "The Flaming Heart," *Carmen Deo Nostro* (1652), Martin, *Poems Crashaw*, pp. 324–7, which is based upon this same Ovidian conceit, as is Bernini's statue of St. Theresa and the Cupid-seraph.

There is also the usual rich but limited, glamorous but unreal imagery, the imagery of baroque art, blood and diadems, knives, darts, and flames, incense, angels, moons, and stars, crowns, tears, gems, virgins, roses, light, and the Lamb. There are some unforgettable figures, e.g.,

> We'll see him take a private seat,
> And make his mansion in the milde
> And milky soule of a soft childe,

the occasional aphorism, e.g.,

> Tis love, not yeares, or Limbes, that can
> Make the martyr or the man,

and some examples of real wit, e.g.,

> All thy sorrows here shall shine,
> And thy sufferings bee divine;
> Teares shall take comfort, and turne Gems.
> And wrongs repent to diadems.

The last of these irregular odes, "On the Assumption," was, like the other two, stanzaic in 1646 and monostrophic in 1652.[1] This ode, the sweetest and most song-like of all, was written on a theme for which Crashaw's emotion-laden, imprecise poetic vocabulary that rouses a thousand beautiful and reverent emotions and never fixes the imagination earth-bound on any clearly defined object or scene, was exquisitely fitted. Here, following an old medieval tradition,[2] Crashaw lyrically dramatizes the Assumption as the wooing of the Virgin by the sighing dove:

> . . . rise up my Love,
> Rise up my faire, my spotlesse one,
> The Winter's past, the raine is gone:
> The Spring is come, the Flowers appeare,
> No sweets since thou art wanting here.

[1] See, respectively, Martin, *Poems Crashaw*, pp. 139–41, and pp. 304–6.

[2] See "Veni, Coronaberis" (A Song of Great Sweetness from Christ and His Daintest Dam),

> Surge mea sponsa, swete in sizt, . . .
> Come, clenner þan cristal, to my cage;
> Columba mea, y þee calle.

Hymns to the Virgin and Christ, F. J. Furnivall, EETS 24 (London, 1867), pp. 1–3.

Come away my Love,
Come away my Dove
cast off delay:
The Court of Heav'n is come,
To wait upon thee home:
Come away, come away.

The Dove calls again. Mary is carried up to heaven and the ode ends in a crescendo of her praise:

Mary, men and Angels sing,
Maria Mother of our King.

The reminiscences of the *Song of Songs* add to the emotional aura of Crashaw's own favourite words, light, stars, crystal, Milky Way, silver dove, spring, flowers, fair, golden, wings, bright, hearts, eyes, lips, song, sweetness, crown, radiant, white, breast, and angels. Alliteration and anaphora enrich the music of metre and rime. Although the opening is witty,

Harke shee is called, the parting houre is come,
Take thy farewel poore world, heaven must go home,

there is little cleverness here to interrupt the lyricism of the ode.

The companion piece to *Steps to the Temple*, *The Delights of the Muses* of 1646, contains a number of secular odes none of which attains the stature of the best religious pieces. One of the most pleasant of these odes is "In the praise of the Spring"[1] based on Vergil, *Georgics* II, 323–45. There is nothing out of the way here but some singularly felicitous phrasing, e.g.,

No loane shade, but rings
With chatting Birds delicious murmurings.

This ode, as is frequently the case in adaptations of Vergil, is written in heroic couplets. Three other odes, the first two in decasyllabic couplets and the last in octosyllabic, bear the mark of Donne. "On a foule Morning, being then to take a journey"[2] has the abrupt, Donnian conversational opening, the question and raillery. However, Crashaw does not dare take the sun to task as Donne would have done and the rest of the poem with its poetic diction and its generalized vocabulary

[1] *Ibid.*, pp. 155–6.
[2] *Ibid.*, pp. 181–2.

is rather neoclassical. The couplets are not yet Augustan and the language is too lush, but this ode reminds us that the future is always forming in the present. Another ode, "To the Morning. Satisfaction for sleepe,"[1] has the same sort of conversational opening, questions, and exclamations, but none of Donne's vigour. Instead it has some tasteless excesses in classical allusion:

And pointing to dull *Morpheus*, bids me take
My owne *Apollo*, try if I can make
His *Lethe* be my *Helicon*,

too heavily ornamented lines in which every noun must have its adjective, and Crashaw's familiar, pretty, but, without the strength of the religious theme and emotion, somewhat ineffectual vocabulary. "In praise of Lessius his rule of health,"[2] in octosyllabic couplets, not only uses the Donnian conversational method, here questions throughout, but also, largely because of the subject, has a rougher, more masculine, less poetic vocabulary than is usual with Crashaw. The most conventional ode of the volume, "Upon the Duke of Yorke his Birth. A Panegyricke,"[3] written in heroic couplets, is the type of pompous laureate ode that we have met before and will meet often again. The remaining poems that may be considered to be odic are all funerary pieces and seem inappropriate to a collection entitled *The Delights of the Muses*. Written in couplets, four of them in octosyllabic, two in decasyllabic, these six odes on the deaths of three Cambridge fellows[4] express the universal sense of tragedy with echoes of Horace, mythological allusions and occasional conversational familiarity that recalls Donne. The first and best of these, "Upon the Death of a Gentleman," is metaphysical. The others are inclined to be over-lush, Crashaw's fatal fault.

The 1648 edition of *The Delights of the Muses* added the five Latin dithyrambs already mentioned, an alcaic ode addressed to the queen,[5] various other Latin verses, and an English ode "Upon two greene Apricockes sent to Cowley by Sir Crashaw."[6] Written in decasyllabic couplets this ode tends, like the previous exchange with Cowley, to be more densely meta-

[1] *Ibid.*, pp. 183–5. [2] *Ibid.*, pp. 156–8. [3] *Ibid.*, pp. 176–81.
[4] *Ibid.*, pp. 166–74 and 175–6. [5] *Ibid.*, pp. 214–15. [6] *Ibid.*, pp. 220–1.

physical than Crashaw's other poetry. Martin's suggestion[1] that the "apricockes" are poems seems a very good one, and would put this ode in a familiar sub-genre.

With the *Carmen Deo Nostro* (1652) we return to Crashaw's religious poetry and his important odes. While some of these are revised versions of the odes of the 1646 *Steps to the Temple* and as such have been mentioned earlier, there are some half a dozen new odes here. All but one of them is irregular. The rimes in these, as in the earlier irregular odes, tend to be in couplets, although there are occasional crossed rimes, while some verses are left entirely without rime. The lines vary in length from seven feet to one, the majority being two, three, four, or five feet in length. The long lines are mingled with the short and both parts of a riming couplet are not necessarily of the same length.

The first of these odes, "To The Name Above Every Name, The Name of Iesus A Hymn"[2] is a grandiose baroque work of art, an overpowering chorale in which every musical voice of the universe is summoned to join. Here, with all the august formalities of Pindar and the exalting ecstasies of the mystic,[3] Crashaw hymns the name of God in an intoxicating outpouring of vague, non-visual, evocative words, in a never pausing flood of mellifluous song that overpowers thought.[4] This is auditory *colorismo*: as in Rubens' paintings form is lost in the mad motion of colour, so in Crashaw's later poetry meaning is swept away by the freshet of sound. The ode to "The Name of Iesus" opens with a Pindaric statement of subject,

> I sing the NAME which None can say
> But touch't by An interiour RAY:
> The Name of our New PEACE: our Good:
> Our Blisse: and Supernaturall Blood:
> The Name of ALL our Liues and Loues.

This is followed by a series of invocations, not of Muses but of the dove souls of the elect. Again we have the appositional

[1] *Ibid.*, p. xxxiv. [2] *Ibid.*, pp. 239–45.

[3] For the excitement aroused by the sight of the name of Jesus see Huizinga, *The Waning of the Middle Ages*, p. 200.

[4] For a discussion of the music of Crashaw's verse see Warren, pp. 108, 168, 173. As Warren has pointed out, p. 168, the effect of a never pausing flow of words is partly achieved by alliterative ligatures between verses.

style which does much to rush one on past the meaning while the sound intoxication builds up. Then Crashaw invokes his own Platonic-winged soul,

> Awake, My glory. SOVL . . .
> Awake and sing
> And be All WING.

Continuing the Platonic train of thought he asks his soul what it recollects of its parent heaven. Now he finds himself insufficient for his theme. And so, still borrowing from Plato, he sends his soul to request

> Great NATVRE for the KEY of her huge Chest
> Of Heauns, the self-inuoluing Sett of Sphears . . .
> Then rouse the nest
> Of nimble ART, and trauerse round
> The Aiery Shop of soul-appeasing Sound:
> And . . .
> . . . warn each seuerall kind
> And shape of sweetness, Be they such
> As sigh with supple wind
> Or answer Artfull Touch,
> That they conuene and come away
> To wait at the loue-crowned Doores of
> This Illustrious DAY. . . .
> Wake LVTE and HARP
> And euery sweet-lipp't Thing
> That talkes with tunefull string;
> Start into life, And leap with me
> Into a hasty Fitt-tun'd Harmony . . .
> Wake . . .
> . . . All Things that Are,
> Or, what's the same,
> Are Musicall; . . .
> Come, ye soft ministers of sweet sad mirth,
> Bring All your household stuffe of Heaun on earth;
> O you, my Soul's most certain Wings,
> Complaining Pipes, and prattling Strings,
> Bring All the store
> Of SWEETS you haue; And murmur that you haue
> no more.
> Come, nere to part,
> NATVRE and ART! . . .

Bring All the powres of Praise
Your Prouinces of well-vouted WORLDS can raise;
Bring all your LVTES and HARPS of HEAVN and
EARTH;
What e're cooperates to The common mirthe
Vessells of vocall Ioyes,
Or you, more noble Architects of Intellectual Noise,
Cymballs of Heau'n, or Humane sphears,
Solliciters of SOVLES or EARES; . . .
Cheer thee my HEART!
For Thou too hast thy Part
And Place in the Great Throng
Of This vnbounded All-imbracing SONG.[1]

Having summoned his musicians in this long, melodious passage, Crashaw now, still observing classical conventions, makes the proviso, "si fas est," "May it be no wrong," and apologizes, in the fullest sense of the word, for the less than celestial music. Now the pagan as well as Christian ritual formulas dispensed with, the poet summons the deity, the Name of Jesus, with the dove-like wooing of "The Assumption," "Dearest Sweet, and come away." He pictures the world's *desiderium* for the Name of Jesus in the natural imagery of the sky-god worshipper, reminiscent of Tasso's "Ad Nubes," simultaneously glancing at the Greek myth that symbolizes the relationship of earth and sky, the myth of Zeus and Danae:

Lo how the thirsty Lands
Gasp for thy Golden Showres! with long streatch't Hands
Lo how the laboring EARTH
That hopes to be
All Heauen by THEE,
Leapes at thy Birth.

The golden shower also suggests the common representation of the Name of Jesus surrounded by gold, and then the favourite baroque sun image as a symbol of the deity. Thus the golden shower controls the next two lines with their rising sun:

The' attending WORLD, to wait they Rise,
First turn'd to eyes.

[1] I have here made excerpts from some sixty lines.

Now the Name of Jesus comes and, like an Ovidian god, it has its *comitatus* and its pomp.

The excitement rises as Crashaw prays the god to fill our whole beings sensuously. He longs for the days of martyrdoms and the weapons that open bleeding breasts. Here he returns to his earlier conceited manner and his favourite imagery, the ruby east, blood, and roses, with a reminiscence, perhaps, of Marino's relatively sober and emotionless madrigal "Alla lancia di Longino":

Lance, sweet lance,
  Lance no more, but key,
  Yours is not to pierce,
  But sweetly to open,
  See, you open, and what treasure,
  Treasure, which has waters of silver, and blood of gold.[1]

The ode ends in a wonderful picture of the Last Judgment when

They that by Love's mild Dictate now
  Will not adore thee,
Shall Then with Iust Confusion, bow
  And break before thee.

The ode moves through many moods from pompous formality, through self-abandon to sound, drunken joy, dark strife, and glorious bloodshed, to awful but tranquil reverence in the vision of the apocalypse, and everywhere the metres and the vowel sounds co-operate with the words to express the changing emotions. Although for the most part of this ode we are in the world of sound—then of smell—in a world without colour, the conclusion of the ode is composed of three contrasting panels coloured with appropriate emotions, dark with fortitude, red with joy, and bright with faith.

The second of these irregular odes, "In The Glorious EPIPHANIE Of Our Lord God, A Hymn. Sung As By The Three Kings"[2] is a cantata, a typical baroque musical form. Here the verses, sweetly and tumultuously intoxicating as in the ode to "The Name of Jesus," are distributed between the three kings and a chorus. Much of the poem (lines 1–83, 112–29, 230–54, and *passim* elsewhere) is taken up with the

[1] Gian Battista Marino, *Rime* (Venetia, 1608), p. 162.

[2] Martin, *Poems Crashaw*, pp. 254–61.

favourite baroque sun symbolism which we also noticed both in Crashaw's and in Milton's "Nativity" odes. Here, too, as in Milton's "Nativity" ode, the pagan animal gods are overcome by the fair, new manifestation of the true divinity, and the meaning of the birth, the Redemption, the crucifixion, is told. But, whereas in Milton there was only a reminder of the pain and suffering, and then back to the joy of Christmas, Crashaw develops the theme at length. He seizes on the Good Friday eclipse as an opportunity for wit, which his well established sun image easily makes possible:

The shutting of his eye shall open Theirs.
As by a fair-ey'd fallacy of day
Miss-ledde before they lost their way,
So shall they, by the seasonable fright,
Of an unseasonable night,
Loosing it once again, stumble' on true Light
And as before his too-bright eye
Was Their more blind idolatry,
So his officious blindness now shall be
Their black, but faithfull perspectiue of thee
His new prodigious night,
Their new and admirable light;
The supernaturall DAWN of Thy pure day.

The rest of the ode before the final chorus in which God is hailed as Hyperion is taken up with elaborations of these conceits.

Another of the irregular odes, "Charitas Nimia. Or The Dear Bargain"[1] is a long series of variations on the Scriptural text, "What is man that thou art mindful of him":

Lord, what is man? why should he coste thee
So dear? what had his ruin lost thee?
Lord what is man? that thou hast ouerbought
So much a thing of nought?

Occasionally the variations tend to be pretty Alexandrian or Ovidian conceits:

Loue is too kind, I see; and can
Make but a simple merchant man.
'Twas for such sorry merchandise
Bold Painters haue putt out his Eyes.

[1] *Ibid.*, pp. 280–2.

There are seraphims and the swinging spheres, the conventional Renaissance correspondences, the king and the sun, and the Christian wolf and the white, blood-stained Lamb.

"Sancta Maria Dolorum Or The Mother Of Sorrows," another of the irregular odes, is "A Patheticall descant vpon the deuout Plainsong of Stabat Mater Dolorosa."[1] The words "patheticall descant" are the key to this ode; for the old hymn has been given all the popular seventeenth-century pathos; it has been modernized by the Jesuit-advocated exercise of sympathetic imagination that is typical of Crashaw.[2] We may feel that it is not improved by its ornate, baroque emotionalism nor by its elaboration with such Ovidian or Marinistic clevernesses as,

> His Nailes write swords in her, which soon her heart
> Payes back, with more than their own smart
> Her SWORDS, still growing with his pain,
> Turn SPEARES, and straight come home again,

nor by its intensification with Crashaw's favourite, vampirish assertion of the doctrine of Transubstantiation:

> O let me suck the wine
> So long of this chast vine
> Till drunk of the dear wounds, I be
> A lost Thing to the world, as it to me.[3]

The last of the irregular odes is "To The Same Party [i.e., to the young woman to whom he gave the prayer book] Councel Concerning Her Choice."[4] This poem continues with the imagery of the "Prayer-book Ode," to which it is here a companion piece. Jesus the bridegroom, the lover of the soul, of the first poem, suggests to Crashaw his own John Alden role as the spokesman of his lord in the second. Again the young lady is called away from

[1] *Ibid.*, pp. 284–7.

[2] Wallerstein, p. 104, finds that Crashaw is here indebted to Marino's version of "Stabat Mater." For a description of St. Ignatius Loyola's *Spiritual Exercises* see Warren, pp. 65–9.

[3] Cf. Martin, *Poems Crashaw*, p. 293, lines 45 ff., and the epigrams on pp. 94 and 40.

[4] *Ibid.*, pp. 331–3.

. . . painted shapes
Peacocks and Apes,
Illustrious flyes,
Guilded dunghills, glorious LYES,
Goodly surmises
And deep disguises,
Oathes of water, words of wind

to the golden court of the heavenly lover.

We have already seen one adaptation of a medieval hymn in the irregular ode, "Sancta Maria Dolorum." Crashaw wrote several other versions of medieval hymns equally free and in the modern taste. The most interesting of these are the two versions of hymns of St. Thomas which maintain the angelic doctor's doctrinal clarity and even follow his text rather closely while still using the sensational language of the baroque poet. Thus in "The Hymn of Sainte Thomas In Adoration Of The Blessed Sacrament,"[1] there is justification in St. Thomas for the bestiary lore,

O soft self-wounding Pelican!
Whose brest weepes Balm for wounded man,

and even for Crawshaw's ever shocking blood imagery,

Ah this way bend thy benign floud
To' a bleeding Heart that gaspes for blood.

However, Crashaw, without formalizing and elaborating it into an ode and without departing too far from the saint's text, has added an emotional colouring that has made St. Thomas's dry and rational, lawyer-languaged prayer into the devout outpouring of a fervent soul. The other version of a hymn of St. Thomas's, "Laude Sion Salvatorem. The Hymn For the Bl. Sacrament,"[2] in stanzas composed of octosyllabic couplets, is a formal ode with invocation, statement of subject, discussion of technique, and teaching by allusion and analogy. It takes from its original a witty, at times daring, yet exceedingly clear exposition of the doctrine of Transubstantiation:

Lo the new LAW of a new LORD
With a new Lamb blesses the Board.
The aged Pascha pleads not yeares

[1] *Ibid.*, pp. 292–3. [2] *Ibid.*, pp. 294–7.

But spyes loue's dawn, and disappeares.
Types yeild to TRVTHES; shades shrink away;
And their NIGHT dyes into our Day.

But lest THAT dy too, we are bid
Euer to doe what he once did.
And by a mindfull, mystick breath
That we may liue, reuiue his DEATH,
With a well-bles't bread and wine
Transsum'd, and taught to turn divine.

The last of Crashaw's odes, "The Flaming Heart Vpon The Book and Picture of the seraphical saint Teresa, (As She Is Vsually Expressed with a Seraphim biside her.),"[1] in octosyllabic couplets with occasional decasyllabics, is, in its first and earlier part, written in the style of the 1646 odes. Here again is the series of lengthy and ingenious elaborations, variations on the fairly obvious conceit:

That is a SERAPHIM, they say
And this the great TERESIA.
Readers, be rul'd by me; and make
Here a well-plac't and wise mistake
You must transpose the picture quite,
And spell it wrong to read it right,
Read HIM for her, and her for him;
And call the SAINT the SERAPHIM.

The seraph is, as in Bernini's group, a very Ovidian Cupid and there are some supra-Ovidian clevernesses here that cannot fail to arouse admiration though they may not inspire the devotion that Crashaw obviously felt, e.g.,

Painter, what didst thou vnderstand
To put her dart into his hand?
See, euen the yeares and size of him
Showes this the mother SERAPHIM.
This is the mistresse flame; and duteous he
Her happy fire-works, here, comes down to see.

There is Crashaw's usual flaming, bright vision of things divine,

But had thy pale-fac't purple took
Fire from the burning cheeks of that bright Booke

[1] *Ibid.*, pp. 324–7. Cf. Propertius' elegy on a painting of Cupid, II, 12.

Thou wouldst on her haue heap't vp all
That could be found SERAPHICALL;
What e're this youth of fire weares fair,
Rosy fingers, radiant hair,
Glowing cheek, and glistering wings,
All those fair and flagrant things,
But before all, that fiery DART
Had fill'd the Hand of this great HEART.

Again we find the peculiarly baroque cult of wounds and hearts and a great deal of daring wit, e.g.,

Vndresse thy Seraphim into MINE.

In the later part of the poem there is a final litany to St. Theresa which exploits all the power of the liturgical form:

O thou vndaunted daughter of desires!
By all thy dowr of LIGHTS and FIRES;
By all the eagle in thee, all the doue;
By all thy liues and deaths of loue;
By thy larg draughts of intellectual day,
And by thy thirsts of loue more large then they;
By all thy brim-fill'd Bowles of feirce desire
By thy last Morning's draught of liquid fire;
By the full kingdome of that finall kisse
That seiz'd thy parting Soul, and seal'd thee his;
By all the heau'ns thou hast in him
(Fair sister of the SERAPHIM!)
By all of HIM we haue in THEE;
Leaue nothing of my SELF in me.
Let me so read thy life, that I
Vnto all life of mine may dy.

Richard Crashaw is the first English poet whom we honour chiefly as an ode writer. Although his older yet longer lived contemporary, Robert Herrick, also wrote odes, bits of light, bright, Anacreontic song and pastoral pieces about Merry England, these form a relatively small part of his output. Herrick was primarily an epigrammatist rather than an ode writer. Crashaw, on the other hand, while he indulged in the contemporary vogue and wrote Jesuit inspired epigrams in his youth, early abandoned his childish toys to serve his God in great sense symphonies of adoration, to hymn him in gorgeous, baroque odes. Thus the bulk of Crashaw's work, and the most important part poetically, is his odes. Milton also wrote odes, big and serious, as we have seen, but his odes were very few in number and insignificant beside his greatest work, so that he lives in our minds as an epic poet. Thus Crashaw is the first English poet whom we classify as an ode writer.

However, although Crashaw was England's first important ode writer, it is not to him that we are indebted for the tremendous popularity of the ode in England from the second half of the seventeenth century through the middle of the nineteenth. Crashaw was too exotic—and a papist as well!—to command a large following in England. Generally his work was forgotten and neglected except by a fellow Catholic like Pope.[1] Abraham Cowley (1618–67), however, Crashaw's younger contemporary and friend, was the man eminently fitted to introduce a new poetic form and establish it in vogue in mid-seventeenth-century England. Cowley was the man of his age. He was the witty follower of Donne, the Muse's Hannibal,[2] who audaciously blasted his way through the conventional barriers to expression. He was, too, the forerunner of the Augustans, the rational man, the stoic, the friend of scientific speculation. And he was safely Anglican and Royalist (although there were final doubts about his fidelity—how else explain the "Brutus" ode?). Cowley was all that a poet should be to win acceptance in his time. And so it is from Cowley, England's "Anacreon, Horace, and Pindar, as well as Vergil and Ovid,"[3] that the English ode tradition stems.

1 See Pope's criticism of Crashaw in a letter to Henry Cromwell, No. 11, 1710, *The Works of Alexander Pope*, ed. J. W. Croker and Rev. W. Elwin, VI (London, 1871), 109 ff.

2 Borrowed from A. H. Nethercot, the author of the standard critical biography of Cowley by that title, and from Cowley's "The Motto," *Miscellanies, The Poems of Abraham Cowley*, ed. A. R. Waller (Cambridge, 1905), p. 15.

3 See Cowley's epitaph on the monument erected to him in Westminster Abbey by George, Duke of Buckingham, August 3, 1667:

Anglorum Pindarus, Flaccus, Maro
Deliciae, Deus, Desiderium Aevi sui . . .
Aurea dum volitant late tua scripta per orbem
Et Fama aeternum vives Divine Poeta . . . ,

and his biographer, Bishop Thomas Sprat's ode "Upon the Poems of the English Ovid, Anacreon, Pindar, and Virgil, Abraham Cowley, in Imitation of His Own Pindaric Odes."

Cowley went to Westminster School about 1628 when he was ten years of age.[1] Three years later he had produced a sheaf of verses which circulated two years in manuscript before they were published in the first volume of *Poeticall Blossoms* in 1633.[2] These early verses were largely inspired by Spenser. In 1636, however, he celebrated his going up to Trinity College, Cambridge, by publishing a second edition of *Poeticall Blossoms* enlarged by seven Horatian inspired odes.[3] These odes are creditable works for one so young and show a remarkable facility in verse. They are, of course, unoriginal. They ring the familiar changes on the familiar Horatian themes. But they do it well, and that is the best that can be said of many Renaissance Horatians. The book was so successful that a third edition appeared in 1637. It is little wonder, then, that the Latin epigrammatist and aspiring English poet, Richard Crashaw, newly appointed fellow of Peterhouse,[4] should seek out the friendship of the bright young undergraduate, exchange verses with him, with Cowley setting the form, be it noted, and later send him his poems for correction.[5]

While he was at Cambridge Cowley wrote three Latin plays, began his religious epic, *Davideis* (1638),[6] continued with his odes,[7] and delivered a political broadside, *The Puritan and the Papist* (1643). With other Royalists and Anglicans Cowley left Cambridge for Oxford in 1644 and then Oxford for Paris,

[1] A. H. Nethercot, *Abraham Cowley. The Muse's Hannibal* (London, 1931), p. 13.

[2] *Ibid.*, pp. 22–3.

[3] "Ode I. On the praise of Poetry," "That a pleasant Poverty is to be preferred before discontented Riches," "To his Mistris," "On the uncertainty of Fortune," "In commendation of the time we live under the Reign of our gracious K, Charles," "Upon the shortness of Mans life," and "A Vote."

[4] Martin, *Poems Crashaw*, p. 418.

[5] I am accepting Martin's interpretation of the "two greene Apricockes," *Works Crashaw*, p. xxxiv.

[6] Nethercot, *Muse's Hannibal*, pp. 49–52.

[7] Nethercot, pp. 46–8 and 76, says that Cowley wrote occasional poems in Latin and English for the University volumes, Συνωδία, 1637, and *Voces Voticae*, 1640, and various pieces that later appeared in his *Miscellanies*, notably those that concerned his friend, William Hervey, "Of Wit" and "The Motto," *c.* 1637–8, and "On the Death of Mr. William Hervey," 1642.

where he worked as a cipher clerk for the Queen, enjoyed the company of Davenant, Denham, Hobbes, Waller, Evelyn, and Crashaw in the Louvre,[1] and wrote *The Mistress* under the influence of Donne, whose *Poems* had been published in 1633. *The Mistress* is a collection of metaphysical *Amours*. Here long conventional themes, shocking cavalier carelessness, and witty cleverness appear in all their cultivated superficiality. There is no genuine passion. Dr. Johnson, however, was overly harsh with Cowley when he said that *The Mistress* "might have been written for penance by a hermit, or for hire by a philosophical rhymer who had only heard of another sex."[2]

Some of the eighty-two poems of *The Mistress* are written in octosyllabic couplets, others in decasyllabic, but the very large majority are stanzaic and most of the stanza patterns are unique. Here Cowley exhibits a great metrical virtuosity and perfects an apprenticeship which is to serve him in good stead in his attempt to invent a new English poetic form. It is significant of a trend towards the ode, towards a larger and looser poetic form that gives the author unlimited liberty of expression, that Donne's lyrics, the love poems of the cavaliers, and this collection of Cowley's are written in stanzas rather than in the exacting sonnet form.

Most of *The Mistress* does not concern us here. However, there are a couple of odes that deserve passing mention, "Against Hope," Cowley's contribution to the debate with Crashaw published in *Steps to the Temple* in 1646, a contrasting companion piece, "For Hope,"[3] "Beauty,"[4]

> *Beauty*, thou wild fantastick Ape.
> Who dost in ev'ry Country change thy shape,

a metaphysical ode on an abstraction written in Crashaw's appositional, variational style but with much more intellection, and very much less feeling, and "Maidenhead,"[5] a typically shocking, iconoclastic, cavalier ode. All of these odes are in stanzas.

1 Nethercot, *Muse's Hannibal*, pp. 94–6.
2 Samuel Johnson, *The Lives of the English Poets* (Everyman ed.), I, 28.
3 Waller, *Poems Cowley*, pp. 109–10 and 110–11 respectively.
4 *Ibid.*, pp. 116–17.
5 *Ibid.*, pp. 129–30.

The Mistress was followed by the *Anacreontiques*,[1] where Cowley's particular talents appeared to the greatest advantage. Here there was no call for deep personal feeling. Here an ease in verse, shining superficiality, and a dash of modern wit were the ideal qualifications. A convenient example of Cowley's Anacreontic style is "Drinking,"[2] a version of the Anacreontic, "'*Η γῆ μέλαινα πίνει*,"[3] which we have already seen in a version by Ronsard, "La terre les eaux va boyvant"[4]:

The thirsty *Earth* soaks up the *Rain*,
And drinks, and gapes for drink again.
The *Plants* suck in the *Earth*, and are
With constant drinking fresh and fair.
The *Sea* itself, which one would think
Should have but little need of *Drink*,
Drinks ten thousand *Rivers* up,
So fill'd that they or'eflow the *Cup*.
The busie *Sun* (and one would guess
By's drunken fiery face no less)
Drinks up the *Sea*, and when h'as done,
The *Moon* and *Stars* drink up the *Sun*.
They drink and dance by their own light,
They drink and revel all the night.
Nothing in *Nature's Sober* found,

[1] Nethercot, *Muse's Hannibal*, p. 107.

[2] Waller, *Poems Cowley*, p. 51. Cowley's other versions of Anacreon are "Love" (Waller, p. 50), based on "*Θέλω λέγειν Ἀτρείδας*"; "Beauty" (pp. 51–2) inspired by "*Φύσις κέρατα ταύροις*"; "The Duel" (pp. 52–3) from "*Θέλω, Θέλω Φιλῆσαι*"; "Age" (p. 53) from "*Λέγουσιν αἱ γυναῖκες*"; "The Account" (pp. 53–4) from "'*Ει Φύλλα πάντα δένδρων*"; "Gold" (p. 55) from "*Χαλεπὸν τὸ μὴ Φιλῆσαι*"; "The Epicure" (pp. 55–6) from "*Οὔ μοι μέλει τὰ Γύγεω*"; "Another" (pp. 56) from "'*Επὶ μυρσίναις τερείναις*"; "The Grasshopper" (p. 57) from "*Μακαρίζομέν σε τέττιξ*"; and "The Swallow" (p. 58) from "*Τί σοι Θέλεις ποιήσω*." The last of Cowley's Anacreontics is an "Elegie upon Anacreon, Who was choaked by a Grape-Stone" (pp. 59–62), a description of Anacreon's poetry and character spoken by the god of love in octosyllabic couplets.

[3] *Ἡ γῆ μέλαινα πίνει*
πίνει δὲ δένδρε' αὖ γῆν
πίνει Θάλασσ' ἀναύρους,
ὁ δ' ἥλιος Θάλασσαν,
τὸν δ' ἥλιον σελήνη.
τί μοι μάχεσθ', ἑταῖροι,
καὐτῷ Θέλοντι πίνειν;

[4] Laum., *Ed. Crit. de Ronsard*, VI, 256, "La terre les eaux va boyvant."

But an eternal *Health* goes round,
Fill up the Bowl then, fill it high,
Fill all the Glasses there, for why
Should every creature drink but *I*,
Why, *Man of Morals*, tell me why?

Here Cowley has blown out his original emphasizing each of its points in the manner of the baroque artist. Where the Greek says simply, "The black earth drinks," and Ronsard, often diffuse, although with Renaissance largeness and decorativeness rather than with baroque heavy stress, translates this simply as "La terre les eaux va boyvant," Cowley writes,

The thirsty *Earth* soaks up the *Rain*,
And drinks, and gapes for drink again.

And so it goes. The Greek sea drinks the air. The English sea, with different geography, quite rationally swallows up rivers. The sun drinks up the sea. So, says Cowley with typical English wit, that must explain his fiery complexion. Cowley's additions to "Ἡ γῆ μέλαινα πίνει" are all consistent with this being a version, but they have tended to make "Drinking" a poem of a particular age whereas Ronsard's "La terre les eaux va boyvant" can be accepted more or less as a translation today. Cowley's method of translation by adaptation is in accordance with the best theory of the day. We will see more of it later.

The Anacreontics form part of Cowley's *Miscellanies* which were written for the most part between 1642 and 1650.[1] The first of these, the introductory "The Motto,"[2] in the English elegiac couplet, expressing Cowley's craving for fame and his well known determination to essay something extraordinary,

Yet I must on; what sound is't strikes mine ear?
Sure I *Fames Trumpet* hear.
It sounds like the *last Trumpet*; for it can
Raise up the *bur'ied Man*.
Unpast *Alpes* stop me, but I'll cut through all,
And march, the *Muses Hannibal*,

was written as early as 1637–8[3] when Cowley was strongly

1 Nethercot, *Muse's Hannibal*, pp. 108–9.
2 Waller, pp. 15–16.
3 Nethercot, pp. 47–8.

under the influence of Donne. Though not intrinsically different from such a prefatory ode contrasting the poet's aims with those of other men as Horace's "Maecenas atavis edite regibus" (Carm. I, 1) and therefore a strong contender for the title "ode," Cowley undoubtedly thought of this poem as an elegy. Mottoes were usually elegies in Latin and written in couplets, and Cowley has used the same metre in English, a metre which never occurs in his odes, which, except for the Anacreontics, tend to be written in stanzas. Moreover, the metre has determined the style which tends to be more economical than that of the stanza poems, or even of the pieces in symmetrical couplets which can run on and on. The greater terseness, the difference in the amount of elaboration and illustration in the poem, can be shown by comparing "The Motto" with the following, clearly marked "Ode. Of Wit,"[1] written about the same time.[2] Here, in a stanza, $A_5A_4B_5B_4CC_4DD_5$, composed of a double elegiac couplet followed by one octosyllabic and one decasyllabic couplet, a stanza already used in *The Mistress*,[3] Cowley searches out the definition of wit with the subtle logic and strange linking of disparates, the conversational familiarity, the cynicism, and the satire, typical of the metaphysical poets:

Tell me, O tell, what kind of thing is *Wit*,
  Thou who *Master* art of it.
For the *First matter* loves *Variety* less;
Less *Women* love't, either in *Love* or *Dress*.
  A thousand different shapes it bears,
  Comely in thousand shapes appears.
Yonder we saw it plain; and here 'tis now,
Like *Spirits* in a *Place*, we know not *How*.

The organization, however, is that of an *Ars Poetica*, of which this might well be a part:

'Tis not a *Tale*, 'tis not a *Jest*
Admir'd with *Laughter* at a feast,
Nor florid *Talk* which can that *Title* gain;
The *Proofs* of *Wit* for ever must remain.

'Tis not to force some lifeless *Verses* meet
With their five gowty feet.

[1] Waller, *Poems Cowley*, pp. 16–18. [2] Nethercot, pp. 47–8.
[3] *Ibid.*, pp. 142–3, "The Gazers."

All ev'ry where, like *Mans*, must be the *Soul*,
And *Reason* the *Inferior Powers* controul. . . .

Yet 'tis not to adorn, and gild each part;
That shows more *Cost*, then *Art*.
Jewels at *Nose* and *Lips* but ill appear;
Rather then *all things Wit*, let *none* be there.
Several *Lights* will not be seen,
If there be nothing else between.
Men doubt, because they stand so think i' th' skie,
If those be *Stars* which paint the *Galaxie*. . . .

'Tis not when two like words make up one noise;
Jests for *Dutch Men*, and *English Boys*. . . .

'Tis not such *Lines* as almost crack the *Stage*
When *Bajazet* begins to rage.
Nor a tall *Meta'phor* in the *Bombast way*,
Nor the dry chips of short lung'd *Seneca*.

Here we can see the difference of style, the greater fulness of development of each idea, the greater looseness and prolixity, concomitant with the stanza rather than the couplet unit, that distinguishes this ode from the preceding elegy.

Other odes in Cowley's *Miscellanies* are "On his Majesties Return out of Scotland," "Ode," "Friendship in Absence," "To a Lady who made Posies for Rings," "Ode. In imitation of Horaces Ode. Quis multa gracilis te puer in rosa . . . ," "The Tree of Knowledge," and "Reason. The use of it in Divine Matters."[1] All of these poems are written in symmetrical stanzas, six to eight lines in length, usually at least half in couplet rimes, the rest in crossed, in a mixture of four or five foot verses, with occasional sixes or threes and the odd feminine ending. Except for the version of Horace they all, including the convivial "Ode,"

Here's to thee *Dick*; this whining *Love* despise;
Pledge me, my *Friend*, and drink till thou be'st *wise*.

develop their themes in a series of metaphysical conceits, of witty reflections on the subject at hand. Sometimes the influence of Donne is apparent in an abrupt, conversational opening

[1] *Ibid.*, pp. 22–4, 26, 27–8, 30–1, 37–8, 45–6, 46–7.

that, with a question or exclamation, immediately alerts the attention of the reader. Other odes, "To the Lord Falkland, For his safe Return from the Northern Expedition against the Scots," "On the Death of Mr. Jordan," "On the Death of Sir Henry Wootton," "On the Death of Sir Anthony Vandike, The famous Painter," "To the Bishop of Lincoln, Upon his Enlargement out of the Tower," "To Sir William Davenant. Upon his two first Books of Gondibert, finished before his voyage to America," and "On the Death of Mr. Crashaw,"[1] are written in heroic couplets but in the same conceited style and with the same fantastic wit as the stanzaic odes. The subjects, as is apparent from the subtitles, are typically odic; these are the sorts of occasions normally celebrated in formal verse. The ode on the death of Crashaw may be taken as representative. The first strophe, for the couplets here are grouped, sounds all the motifs of the whole:

> *Poet* and *Saint:* to thee alone are given
> The two most sacred *Names* of *Earth* and *Heaven* . . .
> Long did the *Muses* banisht *Slaves* abide,
> And built vain *Pyramids* to mortal pride;
> Like *Moses* Thou (though Spells and Charms withstand)
> Hast brought them nobly home back to their *Holy Land.*

The second strophe varies the first; Crashaw was as angelic alive as dead, although poetry had fallen into bondage to paganism. The third strophe compares Crashaw as a divine poet to the Virgin Mary; for they both contained the godhead. The fourth strophe is perhaps Cowley's most brilliant piece of metaphysical writing. Here the audacious conceits are admirably adapted to their function, to express the nature of Crashaw and to describe his death. Here there is a close and exact parallel between image and event, a choice of concepts consonant with Crashaw's own personality, and a greater sensuousness, again suggestive of Crashaw, than is usual in Cowley:

> How well (blest Swan) did Fate contrive thy death;
> And made thee render up thy tuneful breath
> In thy great *Mistress* Arms? thou most divine
> And richest *Off'ering* of *Loretto's Shrine*!
> Where like some holy *Sacrifice* t'expire,

[1] *Ibid.*, pp. 19–20, 21–2, 20, 24–5, 28–30, 42–3, 48–9.

A *Fever* burns thee, and *Love* lights the *Fire*.
Angels (they say) brought the fam'ed *Chappel* there,
And bore the sacred Load in Triumph through the air.
'Tis surer much they brought thee there, and *They*,
And *Thou*, their charge, went *singing* all the way.

The concluding four lines referring to the Catholic belief that the Virgin's house was miraculously transported to Loreto lead naturally into the discussion of religious belief in the fifth strophe. Here Cowley, the Anglican, apologizes for Crashaw's Catholicism with the deistic tolerance of the coming age:

Pardon, my *Mother Church*, if I consent
That *Angels* led him when from thee he went,
For even in *Error* sure no *Danger* is
When joyn'd with so much *Piety* as *His*. . . .
His *Faith* perhaps in some nice Tenents might
Be wrong; his *Life*, I'm sure, was *in the right*.
And I my self a *Catholic* will be,
So far at least, great *Saint*, to *Pray* to thee.

Thus the sixth and final strophe salutes the poets' saint, prays him to save Cowley from various earthly adversaries, all personified abstractions, describes Crashaw in life as a heaven-ascending Elijah, and begs him now to inspire Cowley with his spiritual exaltation.

And now we come to the epoch-making *Pindarique Odes, Written in Imitation of the Stile and Manner of the Odes of Pindar.* "In a place, where he had no other Books to direct him,"[1] presumably when he was royalist agent in Jersey in 1651,[2] Cowley found Pindar. He was immediately enthralled by his rapturous style of writing, by the broken outpouring of melody like a bird's song, by the force and daring of his teeming imagination, and by his Olympian confidence and apartness. There had never been poet like this! Here was an authority to answer the needs of the aesthetic of the age. Here was a model for liberty, originality, and gorgeous pomp. And so, "Having then considered at leisure the height of his Invention, and the Majesty of his Style, he try'd immediately to imitate it in

1 Bishop Thomas Sprat, "An Account of the Life and Writings of Mr Abraham Cowley," *The Works of Mr Abraham Cowley*, 6th ed. (London, 1680), fol. b 2v.

2 Nethercot, *Muse's Hannibal*, pp. 128 and 135.

English."[1] Up-to-date on the latest theories of translation,[2] Cowley did not attempt any slavish copying of Pindar. The translator's duty was to translate, bodily, the illustrious of one age into the next, in this case, to reincarnate Pindar in the seventeenth century, to show how he would write if he were alive today.[3] Such a theory always has its supporters and has much to be said for it. Its disadvantages are obvious. Certain ages are congenial to certain poets, they form their genius to produce everlasting works. In other ages the same men might not be poets or they might not draw from the world around them the sustenance to make them great. And of course the kind of modern man that they are made depends upon the genius of their adaptor. A commonplace mind will make a commonplace creation. At any rate the individuality, the unique quality of the old master will probably be lost sight of.

So it is with Cowley's Pindarics. Cowley had the talent to express his age, better than even Milton could, in many things that were good, but in nothing that was great. Thus he was immensely popular. Thus he could present Pindar to his countrymen clad with perfect correctness "in an English habit"

[1] Bishop Thomas Sprat, "An Account of the Life and Writings of Mr Abraham Cowley," *The Works of Mr Abraham Cowley*, 6th ed. (London, 1680), fol. b 2v.

[2] J. E. Spingarn, "Jacobean and Caroline Criticism," chapt. 11, *CHEL* VII (Cambridge, 1911), 263–4, says that Perrot d'Ablancourt (1606–64), a prolific French translator, set the vogue for translations that were modern adaptations. It was under his influence that Fanshawe translated Guarini's *Il Pastor Fido* (1647), and that Sir Johns Davies wrote the prefatory verses:

> That servile path thou nobly dost decline
> Of tracing word by word and line by line...
> A new and nobler way thou dost pursue
> To make Translations and Translators too;
> They but preserve the Ashes, Thou the Flame,
> True to his sense but truer to his fame.

It was also under his influence that Denham wrote the prose preface to his *Essay on Translation* (1656) in which he stated that the modern ideal for translation was adaptation. Something of this method of translation had already been seen in Chapman's *Iliad* and *Odyssey* which were adapted to the popular modern stoicism, Douglas Bush, *English Literature in the Earlier Seventeenth Century* (Oxford, 1945), pp. 61–2.

[3] See Cowley's preface to his *Pindarique Odes* (1656), Waller, *Poems Cowley*, pp. 155–6.

and train him to be flawless in English manners. But he also could not make Pindar a greater genius than Cowley was. So Cowley could create a new and popular genre, the English Pindaric, but he could not become another Pindar in seventeenth-century England.

Now let us look at Cowley's Pindarics. They are, as were Ronsard's, fifteen in number, seemingly a coincidence. The first two are translations, in the modern fashion, of two of Pindar's odes, the second *Olympian*, and the first *Nemean*, the third is a version of Horace's praise of Pindar (*Carm.* IV, 2), and the last two, "The 34. Chapter of the Prophet Isaiah" and "The Plagues of Egypt" are based on the Bible. The rest, except for "The Exstacie," which was in part inspired by a neolatin poem by Casimir,[1] are original. Cowley's Pindarics are written, as were Crashaw's odes,[2] in irregular strophes with couplet rimes, thus combining the repetition of terminal sound, homoioteleuton, which marks off the musical phrases and makes this poetry, with the variation in length of phrase and the freedom from any exigent repetitive pattern which is characteristic of natural utterance or, as Sprat put it in his "Life," of prose.[3] Thus the ordering poetic principle is kept, while the poet has still the maximum freedom to express his inspiration. This was the first rule of dress that Cowley decreed for Pindar, wisely rejecting the no longer functional triads and deciding, perhaps influenced by Horace's description of Pindar's style, that symmetrical strophes would be too tame an attire for the passionate poet of almost heroic Greece. This

1 Mathias Casimir Sarbiewski, S.J., "E rebus humanis excessus," *Lyricorum libri IV* (Antverpiae, 1632), pp. 52–4.

2 Other seventeenth-century English poems written in irregular verse apart from Crashaw's odes are:
Michael Drayton's "The Crier," John Donne's "The Dissolution," John Milton's "Upon the Circumcision," "On Time," and "At A Solemn Music," George Herbert's "The Collar," William Cartwright's "Ariadne Deserted by Theseus as She Sits upon a Rock in the Island Naxos, Thus Complains," Robert Herrick's "Connubii Flores," Henry Vaughan's "Resurrection and Immortality," "The Holy Communion," and "Affliction," and Jeremy Taylor's *Festival Hymns*, twenty-three out of twenty-four of which are in non-stanzaic irregular verse.

3 Bishop Thomas Sprat, "An Account of the Life and Writings of Mr Abraham Cowley," *The Works of Mr Abraham Cowley*, 6th ed. (London, 1680), fol. b 2v.

metrical form that Cowley chose has also the advantage of being adapted to all manner of subjects,[1] since its one characteristic is being chameleon. This need not mean, as Dr. Johnson wittily but rather unfairly remarked, "that what is fit for anything can fit nothing well."[2]

Irregular verse, then, was part of Pindar's modern dress. Metaphysical wit was another. Here was the equivalent guise for a darting, coruscating imagination playing in fire over the whole rich tradition of his people. To Cowley, Donne had the modern Pindaric imagination. His sweep over all the subjects of modern knowledge, scholastic speculation and scientific investigation, was the equivalent of Pindar's masterful survey of ancient mythology. And so the seventeenth-century Pindar put on metaphysical wit.

But Cowley had found Pindar almost a raving madman.[3] What could be done about that? Surely he would not be so wild in mid-seventeenth-century England where inspiration was learning to walk hand in hand with sober judgment and sweet reasonableness? The modern Pindar must be civilized and taught to avoid logical lapses. Thus all his Cowleyan utterances, including the translations, are carefully concatenated pieces of argument. Pindar's manner needs a bit of polish too, a few of the Ovidian graces so popular in the Renaissance to take away any harshness and austerity and make it all brilliant and smooth. Thus Pindar "in an *English habit*" quite naturally meant for Cowley all the things most popular in the middle of the seventeenth century, irregular verse that both suggested inspiration and gave inspiration its freest play, metaphysical wit and wide-ranging learning that gave the poet mastery of the universe, orderliness in both rime and thought that showed that the poet, too, was participating in the triumph of reason and knew that irregularity must be kept under control, and an occasional elegance of ornament that befitted the cultivated and refined.

[1] Bishop Thomas Sprat, "An Account of the Life and Writings of Mr Abraham Cowley," *The Works of Mr Abraham Cowley*, 6th ed. (London, 1680), fol. b 2v.

[2] Johnson, "Cowley," *Lives Poets* I, 31.

[3] See Cowley's preface to his *Pindarique Odes* in Waller, *Poems Cowley*, p. 155.

Needless to say Cowley's Pindaric licence was not due to ignorance of the true nature of his poet. In an earlier chapter we have described some of the editions of Pindar that were available to Cowley.[1] There were also the excellent editions of Erasmus Schmidt (1616) and Iohannes Benedictus (1620), both of them copiously annotated from the *scholia*, both containing a life of Pindar, a description of the Greek games, an explanation of the triadic structure of the odes, and a Latin prose metaphrase. In addition, each ode in the Schmidt edition was preceded by an elaborate and highly complex rhetorical analysis, by an argument, and by an illustration of its *regular* metrical pattern. In the Benedictus edition each ode was prefaced by an explanation, and surrounded by its two Latin translations; for Benedictus added a paraphrase to Schmidt's metaphrase. In both editions Pindar's verse was printed in long, thin, irregularly shaped strophes with words sometimes broken at the ends of lines or stanzas. Apart from their different interpretations of the versification, which, however, they always treated as regular, these two editions of Pindar gave as sound and scholarly a picture of the poet as the Christ edition of 1896. Now, as will be seen from a quick glance at the notes, with their quotations of the Greek and Latin texts, that follow Cowley's two translations of Pindar, Cowley used the Benedictus edition for his studies. Thus he knew exactly what he was about when he made his own peculiar translations of Pindar. The seeming vagaries of Cowley, then, were not due to ignorance but to the most careful deliberation, in full knowledge of his subject. Far from being able to be patronizing towards him many a modern critic might well envy Cowley his classical scholarship.

Since Cowley's adaptations of Pindar founded a new style in the English ode they are deserving of close attention. Thus we will examine "The Second Olympique Ode of Pindar."[2] This ode, in the original, five triads or fifteen strophes long, has been rearranged by Cowley into eleven irregular but self-contained unified stanzas through the running together of parts of two or three Pindaric strophes on the same theme. Thus the flow, the organic unity of Pindar has been broken to produce a series of

[1] See p. 205, fn. 1.

[2] Waller, *Poems Cowley*, pp. 157–62.

clearly defined, logical entities. The ode is followed by copious and learned notes that discuss interpretation, justify the translation, etc.

Since Cowley's first stanza follows the first strophe of Pindar, it will be instructive to quote them together:

Queen of all Harmonious things,
Dancing Words, and *Speaking Strings*,
What *God*, what *Hero* wilt thou sing?
What happy *Man* to *equal* glories bring?
  Begin, begin thy noble choice,
And let the Hills around reflect the *Image* of thy *Voice*.
  Pisa does to *Jove* belong,
  Jove and *Pisa* claim thy Song.
The fair *First-fruits* of *War*, th'*Olympique Games*,
  Alcides offered up to *Jove*:
  Alcides too thy strings may move;
But, oh, what *Man* to join with these can worthy prove!
Join *Theron* boldly to their sacred *Names*;
        Theron the next honour claims;
        Theron to no *man* gives place,
Is first in *Pisa*'s, and in *Virtue*'s Race;
        Theron there, and he alone,
Ev'n his own swift *Forefathers* has outgone.

'Αναξιφόρμιγγες ὕμνοι,
τίνα θεόν, τίν' ἥρωα, τίνα δ' ἄνδρα κελαδήσομεν;
ἦτοι Πίσα μὲν Διός· 'Ολυμπιάδα δ' ἔστασεν 'Ηρακλέης
ἀκρόθινα πολέμου·
Θήρωνα δὲ τετραορίας ἕνεκα νικαφόρου
γεγωνητέον, ὄπιν δίκαιον ξένων,
ἔρεισμ' 'Ακράγαντος,
εὐωνύμων τε πατέρων ἄωτον ὀρθόπολιν.

(My songs, lords of the lyre,
Which of the gods, what hero, what mortal shall we
  celebrate?
Zeus has Pisa; but Herakles founded the Olympiad
out of spoils of his warfare:
but Theron, for his victory with chariot-four, is the man
we must sing now, him of the kind regard to strangers,
the tower Akragantine,
choice bud of a high line guarding the city.)[1]

[1] From Richmond Lattimore's translation, as in chapter 2.

Now let us examine the departures in Cowley's translation in detail. Cowley's own note on line one suffices:

> Whereas *Pindar* addresses himself to his *Song*, I change it to his *Muse*; which methinks, is better called 'Αναξιφορμιγξ, ["lord of the lyre"] then the ode which she makes[1]

So the logical Muse has become "lady of the lyre." But what does the simple phrase mean? It means that the Muse is mistress of the spoken poetry and the vibrating strings. Yet the words do not just speak, but, in the exuberance of poetic expression, in the joy of celebrating the victory, they dance; it is the words that dance on the moving fingers and tremulous chords; it is they that dance, up and down, quick and slow, in the changing tones and tempos; it is the words that dance with the nimble notes on the printed page. So the Muse, then, is queen of "dancing words." But what of the strings? Now, in the surrealistic shattering of the images and more expressive reassemblage that Cowley makes here, it is the strings that speak—for the music expresses the meaning—and, bound together by a semi-alliteration, the "speaking strings" couple with the "dancing words" to form a kind of hendiadys.

The next two lines, three and four, give a more typical illustration of Cowley's translation technique, his fondness for padding: "to *equal* glories bring" of line four is only a variation on "wilt thou sing" of line three. The fifth line—and again this is typical of Cowley—is a logical addition emphasizing the connection between the introductory questions and the following divine, heroic, and human trinity, while the sixth line, as Cowley honestly admits, is borrowed from Horace to round off in fulness the introductory part of the stanza. Now the eighth and eleventh lines explain the exact relationship, to the preceding verses, of the ninth and tenth lines, respectively, while the tenth line emphasizes the connection, only implicit in Pindar, between Zeus and Heracles. The last seven lines introduce and praise Theron, substituting for Pindar's specific citation of, "the victor in the four horse chariot race, the hospitable man, the bulwark of Agrigentum, the finest flower of an illustrious line, and the defender of his native city," a series of vague, abstract phrases that could apply to almost any of the

1 Waller, *Poems Cowley*, p. 163.

victors. Such is one aspect of Cowley's translation technique.

Let us now look at the prosodic structure of the stanza to see what it contributes to the interpretation; for since Cowley, in the form that he has adopted, is obliged neither to fill out decasyllabic lines nor to adapt his thought to a prescribed pattern of rime, we may reasonably expect that variations in line length or exceptions to the prevailing couplet rime are determined by the exigencies of expression and are, therefore, part of the meaning. The symbolic representation of the stanza is $AAB_4B_5/C_4C_7/DD_4/E_5FF_4F_6/E_5EG_4G_5H_4H_5$. Vertical lines mark the limits of the sentences. Here we notice that the first period, invoking the Muse in one rime and posing the question of what god, hero, man she would sing in another, is rounded off and concluded by a longer line which brings this second rime to an end. Then the transitional second sentence, which concludes the introductory material of the poem and leads into the second part of the stanza, closes, appropriately, with an even longer line to mark a heavier stop. It is also in rime self-sufficient. Next the first of the trinity of subjects, Jove, is disposed of neatly in two brief statements riming together in a short couplet. The fourth period, which finally introduces the occasion of the ode, the Olympic Games, which treats the second person of the trinity and connects him both with the god and with the man, is appropriately twice as long as the preceding one. It rimes together the two octosyllabic lines dealing with Heracles and Jove and the longer concluding line leading up to the introduction of the man, while leaving the decasyllabic line referring to the Olympic Games standing at the head, and, for the moment, unrimed. The next sentence, however, opens with Theron, the man of the ode, who is linked by rime, in an answering decasyllabic verse, with the Olympic Games, the occasion of the ode, thus completing the introductory summary of the subject matter of the ode and the suspended rime scheme. However, a little more must be said about Theron; therefore, linking the dilation of the subject with the preceding part of the poem, the second unit of this sentence, a mere variation on the first, rimes with it in a shorter line (E_4). A second variation, leading, however, into the explicit relation of Theron to the games, fills an equally short verse (G_4) but rimes with the conclusion of the thought in the following line (G_5). The final couplet links Theron's achievements in the games with those of his ancestors, brings this stanza to a conclusion and leads into the next. It therefore ends with the rounding decasyllabic line but not with the completing and discontinuous Alexandrine or heptameter.

The same general qualities may be seen in Cowley's second stanza, again conveniently based on only one stanza of Pindar:

They through rough ways, o're many stops they past,
    Till on the fatal bank at last
They *Agrigentum* built, the beauteous *Eye*
    Of *fair-fac'ed Sicilie*,
Which does it self i' th' *River* by
    With *Pride and Joy* espy.
Then chearful *Notes* their *Painted Years* did sing,
And *Wealth* was one, and *Honour* th'other *Wing*.
Their genuine *Virtues* did more sweet and clear,
    In *Fortunes* graceful dress appear.
    To which great *Son* of *Rhea*, say
The *Firm Word* which forbids things to *Decay*.
    If in *Olympus Top*, where Thou
    Sit'st to behold thy Sacred *Show*,
    If in *Alpheus* silver flight,
    If in *my Verse* thou dost delight,
    My Verse, O *Rhea's Son*, which is
    Lofty as *that*, and *smooth* as *This*.

καμόντες οἳ πολλὰ θυμῷ
ἱερὸν ἔσχον οἴχημα ποταμοῦ, Σικελίας τ' ἔσαν
ὀφθαλμός, αἰὼν δ' ἔφεπε μόρσιμος, πλοῦτόν τε καὶ χάριν ἄγων
γνησίαις ἐπ' ἀρεταῖς.
ἀλλ' ὦ Κρόνιε παῖ Ῥέας, ἕδος Ὀλύμπου νέμων
ἀέθλων τε κορυφὰν πόρον τ' Ἀλφεοῦ,
ἰανθεὶς ἀοιδαῖς
εὔφρων ἄρουραν ἔτι πατρίαν σφίσιν κόμισον

(In strong toil of spirit
they were the eye of Sicily, they beside the river kept
the sacred house; their doom drew on, bringing wealth and
    delight near by valor in their blood.
But, O Kronios, Rhea's son, guarding Olympos' throne
and the games' glory and the Alpheus crossing,
in mild mood for the song's sake
kind keep for them always the land of their fathers. . . .)

Into the first two lines Cowley incorporates extraneous information further elaborated in the notes. In lines three and four Cowley's logic again triumphs, "I rather chuse to call *Agrigentum*, then *Therons* Ancestors (as Pindar does) the *Eye* of *Sicilie*. The Metaphor in this sense is more natural."[1] We might also add that it is more commonplace, as Cowley's citation of parallel expressions substantiates.[2] In Pindar's simple phraseology we feel the hard work of Theron's ancestors, the deserved triumph, and their shining glory when they were the living, vital, expressive part of Sicily, when they were that towards which everyone looked for the interpretation of the island, its brightest and most precious spot. Cowley's expression is not so strong because it is more conventional and less individual. Still Cowley's development of the germ in "holy river city" is not without its effectiveness and is more pictorial than is usual with him, while the adjective "painted" to describe the years of their prosperity, of wealth and grace, was a stroke of genius. The adjective is wonderfully expressive both of Pindar's text and of an era of wealth and culture, while its static quality suggests duration and causes us to pause over centuries of greatness. Coupled with cheerful notes, singing, and wings of wealth and honour, the painted years not only suggest a grandiose, highly coloured Renaissance painting on a public theme, but also a kind of bird of paradise, a symbolic bird that exists in eternity, untouched by time. For the rest of the stanza we may note the contrast between Pindar's packed and condensed style and Cowley's greater looseness and expansiveness, his plodding logic, and his fondness for adjectival ornamentation, never meaningless but always decorative rather than essential, like the details of baroque art. The last two lines drawing a parallel, not found in Pindar, between the poet's verse and Olympus and the Alpheus, were inevitable in Cowley who, as Dryden said, "cou'd never forgive any conceit which came in his way."[3]

Now if we look at the prosodic pattern we notice the same inter-relation of it with the meaning as we saw in stanza one. The formula for the stanza is $A_5A_4B_5B_3B_4B_3CCD_5DE_4E_5FF$-

[1] *Ibid.*, p. 163. [2] *Ibid.*, p. 164.

[3] Quoted by Bush, *Eng. Lit. 17th Cent.*, p. 157.

$GGHH_4$. The long first line describes the wandering and hardship of the ancestors, the shorter second line the end of their trials—where they stopped short, so does the line. The third line, again long, describes the task of building the city. The alternating shorter and short lines all riming together with line three tell what the built city was like, completing the picture, giving it detail and ornament, quickening it into life. Then the couplet of long lines following on the short lines perfect the picture and give it permanence in long drawn out years of prosperity. An elegiac couplet (D_5D_4), really a variation, brings the first part of the stanza to a conclusion. Then the short eleventh line with its abruptness gives earnestness, urgency, and intensity to the prayer to god, while the following long twelfth line expresses the permanence for which the poet prays. The conventional "ifs" of the prayer are all expressed in symmetrical short lines matching that which introduced the prayer.

And so the ode goes. Everywhere Pindar is adapted to the new taste. He is trimmed, rearranged, interpreted, given explanatory connections, and embellished with "all we can adde to him by our wit or invention (not deserting still his subject)."[1] Thus even the concluding stanza is adorned with a bit of popular satire, the "character" of the debtors:

> But in this thankless *world* the *Givers*
> Are *env'ed* ev'en by the *Receivers*.
> 'Tis now the *cheap* and *frugal* fashion,
> Rather to *Hide* than *Pay* the *Obligation*.
> Nay 'tis much worse than so,
> It now an *Artifice* does grow,
> *Wrongs* and *outrages* to do,
> Lest men should think we *ow*.

The ode as a whole, though often decorated, is deficient in visual imagery and vague and inexact compared with its original. The factual details of Pindar are generally left out and the adjectives that Cowley uses tend to be imprecise. There is much light, implicit or explicit: "eye, fair-fac'ed, river, clear, Olympus top, Alpheus silver flight, illustrious, shine, brightly, chrystal, blew-ey'd, seas, lightnings, bright, sea, sun,

1 Cowley's preface to his *Pindarique Odes*, Waller, *Poems Cowley*, p. 155.

fair, waves, day, glories, air, unexhausted light, the god-like suns unwearied sight, lamp, silver rivers, beauteous, white, Castalian waters"; but there is little colour and when it does occur it is primary and conventional, and thus has a weakened colour content: painted, bleed, golden, furnace, enamell'd, jewels, flames of day. Generally Cowley's images appeal to the intellect, not to the senses, and there is little emotional impact in the non-visual images, vague modifiers, general statements, or abstract words. Cowley, Milton's contemporary, without being blind, is as lacking in visualization, and a very good case could be made for his being the author of T. S. Eliot's "dissociated sensibility."[1] The most notable thing about this

[1] It would seem that the "dissociation of sensibility" was produced by the popular stoicism, by the growing scientific outlook and the distrust of the imagination, by rationalism, deism, and the natural revulsion, in troubled times, from any further emotional excitement, in short, by the whole temper of the age, rather than by anyone's weak eyesight. L. Zanta, *La Renaissance du Stoicisme au xvie Siècle* (Paris, 1914), pp. 336–7, states that neostoic insensibility, impassivity, produced the reasonable lovers of the seventeenth century, Corneille's heroes, the rationalism of Descartes, and the determinism of Spinoza. Joan Bennet, "The Evolution of seventeen century prose," *RES* XVII (1941), 287, says that Hobbes in the *Leviathan* (1651) attacked rhetoric because it affects the emotions not the reason, and figurative language because it affects the passions. For Hobbes the virtues of a word were two—perspicuity and decorum—and these, significantly, are Lipsian, stoic virtues (see Justus Lipsius, *Institutio Oratoria, Opera Omnia* . . . , I (Antverpiae, 1637), 536). See also M. W. Croll, "Juste Lipse et le Mouvement Anticicéronien à la Fin du XVIe et au début du XVIIe Siècle," *Revue du Seizième Siècle* II (1914), "Attic Prose in the Seventeenth Century," *SP* XVIII (1921), 79–128, "Muret and the History of Attic Prose," *PMLA* XXXIX (1924), 254–309, "The Baroque Style in Prose," *A Miscellany in Honor of Frederick Klaeber*, ed. Kemp Malone and Martin B. Ruud (Minneapolis, 1929); D. C. Allen, "Style and Certitude," *ELH* XV (1948), 167–75; G. Williamson, "The Senecan Style in the Seventeenth Century," *PQ* XV (1936); and R. F. Jones, "Science and English Prose Style in the Third Quarter of the Seventeenth Century," *PMLA* XLV (1930). R. F. Jones, *PMLA* XLV, 993–6, gives examples of Glanville's versions of the same passage before and after the establishment of the Royal Society.

Note that Cowley's idea of how one should prepare onself for writing is like the deists' idea of how one should think about religion: "The truth is, for a man to write well, it is necessary to be in good humour," "Preface," 1656 volume, Waller, *Poems Cowley*, p. 8, and

> There is nothing that requires so much serenity and chearfulness of *Spirit*; it must not be either overwhelmed with the cares of *Life*, or overcast with the *Clouds of Melancholy* and *Sorrow*, or shaken and disturbed

Pindaric ode, however, is the intimate connection between metre and meaning, the way one reinforces the other.

The same kind of analysis could be made of Cowley's translation of "The First Nemean Ode of Pindar."[1] When we read Pindar, we have a very clear and exact idea of the Hercules story. The circumstantial details, the names of the people involved, the bareness of ornament, all make the account realistic and convincing—we can well believe that it happened. When we read Cowley's translation we know that we are in the world of mythology. Here is the story abstracted from reality and prettily decorated, a sugar-plum for the children. There are some nice touches, like the description of the serpents from the baby Hercules' point of view,

> . . . the mighty *Infant smil'd.*
> The *mighty Infant* seem'd well pleas'd
> At his gay gilded foes,
> And as their spotted necks up to the *Cradle* rose,
> With his young warlike hands on both he seis'd;
> In vain they rag'd, in vain they hist,
> In vain their armed *Tails* they twist,
> And angry *Circles* cast about,
> Black *Blood*, and fiery *Breath*, and poys'nous *Soul* he
> squeezes out.

Here the last line reminds us that Spenser was Cowley's first love. But the whole lacks the force of the original. Throughout this ode, as in the previous one, Cowley incorporates notes, supplies connections,[2] amplifies and varies his text, gives every noun its adjective, introduces his favourite allegorical figures and witty conceits wherever he can, and enriches Pindar with the spoils of his vast erudition. Thus the mention of Sicily

with the storms of injurious *Fortune*; it must like the *Halcyon*, have *fair weather* to breed in. The *Soul* must be filled with bright and delightful *Idaea's*, when it undertakes to communicate delight to others; which is the main end of Poesie. One may see through the stile of *Ovid de Trist.* the humbled and dejected condition of *Spirit* with which he wrote it; there scarce remains any footsteps of that *Genius*. . . . The *cold* of the Countrey had strucken through all his faculties, and benummed the very *feet* of his *Verses*. *Ibid.*, p. 7.

1 Waller, *Poems Cowley*, pp. 170–4.

2 See Cowley's note, Waller, *Poems Cowley*, p. 177, at top.

naturally suggests the incorporation of a bit from Claudian's *De Raptu Proserpinae*,[1] while the concluding reference to Hercules in heaven, rather restrained in Pindar,

> and, feasting beside Kronian Zeus,
> should praise the high design of the gods,

is smartened up by Cowley, with a witty reference to Hercules' labours and with perhaps a reminiscence of Ronsard,[2]

> Walk with ineffable Delight
> Through the thick *Groves* of never-withering *Light*,
> And as he walks affright
> The *Lyon* and the *Bear*,
> *Bull*, *Centaur*, *Scorpion*, all the *radiant Monsters* there.

Similar to his Pindaric translations is Cowley's version of the Pindaric half of Horace's second ode of the fourth book, "Pindarum quisque studet semulari." Again Cowley selects from his author, makes additions to him from his general knowledge of classical antiquity, and suppresses parts that he thinks make for unnecessary complication, here the reference to the battle of the Lapiths and Centaurs,[3] which he perhaps considers would be burdensome to his reader. Again the raw material is reorganized by Cowley into unified strophes, and again there is an absence of visual imagery, but an abundance of indefinite adjectives with no specific content but a certain intellectual aura. Let us, for example, compare Cowley's version of the well-known flood simile with the original. Horace writes

> Monte decurrens velut amnis, imbres
> Quem super notas aluere ripas,
> Fervet immensusque ruit profundo
> Pindarus ore,
>
> Laurea donandus Apollinari,
> Seu per audacis nova dithyrambos
> Verba devolvit numerisque fertur
> Lege solutis.

[1] See Waller, *Poems Cowley*, p. 171 and the notes on p. 175.

[2] See the conclusion of "A Son Lict," Laum., *Ed. Crit. de Ronsard* I, 257–9.

[3] See Horace, *Carm.*, IV, 2, lines 14–15.

Cowley's version is as follows:

Pindars unnavigable Song
Like a swoln *Flood* from some steep *Mountain* pours along,
The *Ocean* meets with such a *Voice*
From his enlarged *Mouth*, as drowns the *Oceans* noise.

So *Pindar* does new *Words* and *Figures* roul
Down his impetuous *Dithyrambique Tide*,
Which in no *Channel* deigns t'abide,
Which neither *Banks* nor *Dikes* controul.

Here Cowley has added the adjective "unnavigable," not unhappily, as the logical bond between the first and second strophes. He has also added a series of weak, conventional adjectives, "swoln" to "flood" and "steep" to "mountain"; he has introduced an ocean whose sound, in baroque hyperbole, is drowned by the torrent's roar; and he has varied the statement that the river has left its channel, stating that it is beyond the control of both nature ("Banks") and art ("Dikes"). Thus, by diffusing our attention, by preoccupying it with an ocean, a river mouth, banks, and dikes, as well as with the flooding stream, by leading us to its end in the sea and then taking us back over its course, and by interrupting the simile by its careful application, Cowley has lost the realism, the immediacy, and the emotional power of Horace. While Cowley's long, pompous lines are obviously rhetorical and thus sound artificial, Horace's simple stanza, "Monte decurrens . . . ," with remarkable skill, easily contains a seeming closeness to the facts in the figure, an immediate emotional reaction, and a strikingly economical application of the image. Horace describes the river as we would see it, and he does this with consummate skill. The first line gives us the mountain, the river tumbling down, and the rain. The "notas" of the second line suggests a personal observer and an emotional reaction: this is something beyond his ken, "super notas"—as is often with Horace two words that are juxtaposed interfecundate one another—something which he can observe but does not understand. And his introduction of a personal reaction adds meaning to the remaining words describing the river. The personal involvement makes "fervet" more vivid; we see more clearly the boiling, seething mass of water. It also makes it more frightening. And the fear broadens with the adjective "immensus." Here is the wild, uncontrollable unknown, beyond the measurement, and hence understanding, of the mind of man. It rushes by, "ruit," and it is deep, "profundo." Only now with "Pindarus" do we realize that the last two lines of the quatrain, apparently continuing the river image, have, in fact, been its application to Pindar. Thus Horace by his placing of the two words, "Pindarus ore" has succeeded in getting double value out of "Fervet immensusque ruit profundo."

As was the case in the other translations, Cowley uses length of verse and rime relations to co-operate in the expression of the meaning. By breaking the pattern in the baroque manner, Cowley catches our attention and secures emphasis. The brief first line succinctly stating the theme is thrown into relief by the following long line varying it,

> *Pindar* is imitable by none;
> The *Phoenix Pindar* is a vast *Species alone*,

and generally throughout the ode new subjects are introduced by short lines which break the rhythm, while old subjects are disposed of in long lines.

"The Resurrection,"[1] Cowley's first original Pindaric, is written in the usual irregular stanzas decreed by the exigencies of free expression, and with an invention that, in the author's opinion, "is truly *Pindarical*, falling from one thing into another, after his *Enthusiastical manner*."[2] Put more bluntly, the ode is poorly planned out of incompatible material that was allowed to come together because of Cowley's self-surrender to what he felt was Pindar's associational method. This abandonment to Pindar's "usual manner of being transported with any good Hint that meets him in his way"[3] leads Cowley on with a certain *élan* through three stanzas and then brings him to an impasse where he must resort to the transparent subterfuge of being too overwhelmed by inspiration to continue. Thus the fourth stanza begins

> Stop, stop, my *Muse*, allay thy vig'orous heat,
> Kindled at a *Hint* so Great,

1 Waller, pp. 182–3. 2 *Ibid.*, p. 183, note by Cowley.
3 *Ibid.*, p. 170, Cowley's introductory note.

and concludes the poem with a long drawn out analogy in which all possible parallels are worked in, between his Pindaric poetic inspiration and a high-spirited steed.

The poem suffers from lack of unity. Stanza one, the first half of stanza two, and stanza four all discuss poetry, while the second half of stanza two and stanza three describe the resurrection; but the concept of poetry of the first part is quite different from that of the second, and the intervening material in no way makes a transition, but in fact tends to annul the vaunted value of poetry completely. There is an incompatibility between the first stanza's claim for poetry, that it preserves man's memory while time lasts, and thus panders to earthly pride, and the vivid picture in the third stanza of the panic-stricken souls at doomsday who fear punishment for just such things, for worldliness and vanity and pride. There is an equal incompatibility between the first stanza's claim that poetry is the nurse of virtue and the fourth stanza's arrestation of the doomsday description, which might have been thought to have the power to turn some delinquent soul into the paths of righteousness.

The first stanza on the favourite bardic and Renaissance theme that poetry nurtures virtue and confers immortality is, in its beginning, a bit of embroidery on a passage from Pindar, helpfully quoted by Cowley in his notes, and, in its conclusion, a recast of the beginning of Horace's famous *envoi* at the end of the third book of the *Carmina*. "Exegi monumentum aere perennius." The values throughout this classically inspired stanza are, up to the last couplet, pagan and secular. The last couplet, however, introduces the Christian concept of an end to the world.

The second stanza, after a conventional odic beginning, "Begin the *Song*, and strike the *Living Lyre*," develops further the ideas of the last half of the first stanza, the Ovidian dance of the years during which poetry, and in particular his poetry lasts, and the final day on which the world ends, when the music of the spheres shall cease and nature, divinely built like ancient Troy, shall, in a similar fashion, perish in conflagration. Here we notice echoes of the Revelation of St. John the Divine: with "then all the wide extended *Sky*... shall dy," compare "And the heaven departed as a scroll when it is rolled together."[1]

[1] Revelation, 6, verse 14.

The third stanza describing the resurrection of the dead as God might see it combines religious doctrine with modern scientific thought in a way typical of Cowley:

> Then shall the scatter'ed *Atomes* crowding come
> Back to their *Ancient Home*,
> Some from *Birds*, from *Fishes* some,
> Some from *Earth*, and some from *Seas*,
> Some from *Beasts*, and some from *Trees*.
> Some descend from *Clouds* on high,
> Some from *Metals* upwards fly,
> And where th'*attending Soul* naked, and shivering stands,
> Meet, salute, and joyn their hands.
> As disperst *Souldiers* at the *Trumpets* call,
> Hast to their *Colours* all.

The movement is swift, the description vivid, and the comparison of the dispersed atoms flocking to the naked soul, to soldiers crowding to the standard at the call to arms is truly brilliant. The stanza as a whole, however, is marred by a trivial conclusion where Cowley falls into a bathetic—largely because it is inconsonant with the previous scientific description—comparison of the greater with the less, a frequent fault for which Dr. Johnson chastised him.[1] Here it is the mountains which are compared to very mice-like men,

> To *Mountains* they for shelter pray,
> The *Mountains* shake, and run about no less confus'd then *They*.

St. John on Patmos had a nobler vision:

> . . . and every mountain and island were moved out of their places. And the kings of the earth, and the great men, and the rich men, and the chief captains, and the mighty men, and every bondman, and every free man, hid themselves in the dens and in the rocks of the mountains;
> And said to the mountains and rocks, Fall on us, and hide us from the face of him that sitteth on the throne, and from the wrath of the Lamb, . . .[2]

And every island fled away, and the mountains were not found.[3]

[1] Johnson, "Cowley," *Lives Poets* I, 18.
[2] Revelation, 6, verses 14–16.
[3] *Ibid.*, 16, verse 20.

So far Cowley has followed his will-o'-the-wisp Pindaric associationism, perhaps hoping that a surrender to it would lead him to something great. Instead it has only led him to the point where he can go no farther because he has nothing to say. Thus he hides his imaginative barrenness, his lack of inspiration, under the claim of overpowering inspiration,

> Stop, stop, my *Muse* . . .
> Hold thy *Pindarique Pegasus* closely in,
> Which does to rage begin.

Now, as we read through the elaborately worked out and varied conceit of the fourth stanza we feel, behind the meretricious art of the poet, an empty mind. Cowley had nothing very definite to express in this poem and it is for that reason that "The Resurrection," despite a fine third stanza, is, as a whole, a failure. As in the previous odes of Cowley that we have seen, metre and rime here form part of the ideas that they express.

A very much more successful ode is "The Muse."[1] Although the Ovidian pomp of the Muse[2] suggested by a passage from Pindar[3] has little meaning—the Muse drives in a chariot with Nature as her postillion, Art as the coachman, a six-horse team composed of Phansie and Judgment, Wit and Elegance, Memory and Invention to draw her, and "airy Footmen," Figures, Conceits, Raptures, Sentences, Innocent Loves, pleasant Truths, and useful Lies to accompany her—the description of the range of the Muse, through the real world and that of the imagination, through past, future, and present constitutes a clearly thought out and vividly expressed, if not highly original, essay on the power of poetry. It is regrettable that the allegorical "art," the technical introduction, was not more meaningful. This ode is written with Cowley's usual erudition, there is the usual variation, e.g., the idea that poetry stops time and fixes the transient for ever is expressed in six different visual images in the last stanza, and again there is the harmony between meaning and metre.

Cowley's finest Pindaric, in which no part fails, is his ode in praise of the philosopher, Thomas Hobbes.[4] Here there is unity

[1] Waller, *Poems Cowley*, pp. 184–6. [2] Cf. Ovid, *Amores* I, 3.

[3] See Cowley's own note, Waller, pp. 186–7.

[4] Waller, pp. 188–90.

of theme, skilful development, and a completeness that links the concluding sentence with the opening. Here the previous state of philosophy and the achievement of Hobbes are described in a most memorable variety of images that, in this case, are quite appropriately largely intellectual, rather than visual. Hobbes's achievement, like that of the Greek athlete, is fixed in the tradition of his people, who are here all his intellectual forbears, Aristotle, the Greeks, Romans, Arabs, and the Schoolmen. It is given universal significance by being compared both to Columbus's discovery of the new world, one of the greatest modern achievements, and to the shield of Aeneas, one of the greatest ancient creations.[1] Here Cowley's great knowledge, his wide-ranging imagination, and his metaphysical wit conspire together to produce the happiest results. The pun on "body" which relegates all philosophies other than Hobbes's to the charnel house is Cowley's most effective, while his characterization of the current state of philosophy reveals what Johnson would describe as true wit:

We break up *Tombs* with *Sacrilegious hand*;
Old *Rubbish* we remove;
To walk in *Ruines*, like vain *Ghosts*, we love,
And with fond *Divining Wands*
We search among the *Dead*
For Treasures *Buried*,
Whilst still the *Liberal Earth* does hold
So many *Virgin Mines* of *undiscover'ed Gold*.

And, as was remarked earlier, the end of the poem is skilfully turned back towards the beginning by Cowley's conclusion that Hobbes's youthfulness, with his intellectual fire undiminished despite his snowy head—here there is a comparison to Mount Etna which Cowley admits in the notes[2] was inspired by Claudian—is a sign that he will live for ever and that, therefore, his philosophy will never be, like the others, a body dead, but will always possess a living soul.

In this ode, as elsewhere, there is the same closeness between

[1] See Cowley's note, *ibid.*, p. 191, and his evaluation of Vergil in "The Resurrection," p. 182, where his *Aeneid* is taken as the type of the supreme human creation, "And *Virgils* sacred *work* shall dy."

[2] Waller, *Poems Cowley*, p. 191.

matter and metre. In the first stanza, e.g., represented as $A_4BB_3B_4A_5A_3C_3CC_5D_3DAAEEE_5$, A_4 introduces the general subject of the ode, philosophy, the three short B rimes dispose of other philosophies, while the returning A rimes bring us back to the subject, here the more specific subject, of the ode, the philosophy of Hobbes. The short C line, as is Cowley's wont, attracts our attention to a new subject, which is developed in the following two decasyllabic lines riming with it, the poet's incompetence to know the truth. Another short line, D_3, introduces what is, however, the poet's opinion, another new subject that is developed in a series of decasyllabic lines. Similarly, in the second stanza, $AAABB_5C_6CCDD_5EE_4E_6FF_3$-$G_4G_6$, a series of long lines expresses the long supremacy of Aristotelian philosophy. The first group of three tells of Aristotle under the Greeks; the first couplet, of Aristotle and the Roman Empire; the second triplet, introduced by an Alexandrine which shifts us to an entirely different culture, of the spread of Aristotelianism by the Arabs; while the last couplet begins a parallel between decaying political empires and philosophies, a parallel that is completed in the short E couplet. Then Aristotelianism finally perishes in the E Alexandrine. The last quatrain is merely a variation on the theme of the death of Aristotelianism, a summary of what has gone before, characteristic of Cowley.[1] The two short F verses tell how trivial it became in the final stage of degeneracy, the longer G_4 emphasizes its death, and the second Alexandrine tells of its complete dissolution and evaporation. And so one could go on throughout the ode.

The ode "Destinie"[2] is an original exercise on the popular Horatian theme, "Quem tu Melpomene,"[3] so often essayed in the Renaissance. The ode has an arresting beginning, inspired by several learned sources, as Cowley is careful to point out.[4] There is an abrupt, Donnian conversational opening that

[1] See, e.g., "The Praise of Pindar," *ibid.*, p. 178, stanza 1, lines 8–11 (though this is borrowed from Horace, the arrangement is Cowley's), p. 179, stanza 2, lines 9–12, and stanza 3, lines 9–12; "To Dr. Scarborough," p. 198, stanza 1, lines 17–20.

[2] Waller, *Poems Cowley*, pp. 192–4.

[3] Horace, *Carm.* IV, 3.

[4] Waller, p. 194 notes.

catches the attention, especially because of its implication that the poet has surprised something abnormal

> *Strange* and *unnatural*! lets stay and see
> This *Pageant* of a *Prodigie*,

and then the conceit, vividly worked out, with a certain amount of "negative capability" on the part of the poet, of the chess game that plays itself.[1] The second stanza cleverly puts the case for determinism. The third stanza, a mosaic of Horace[2] with a bit of bestiary lore[3] and Christian theology,[4] tells us of Cowley's destiny; while the fourth stanza moans over the misfortunes of those claimed by the Muses and tries to find consolation in the company that he keeps "from *Homer* down to *Ben*."

"Brutus,"[5] a Pindaric ode on a favourite Renaissance theme, since it was written during the period of the Commonwealth and very likely when Cowley was in Cromwell's prison as a Royalist spy or when he was out on probation and a thousand pound bond put up by Dr. Scarborough,[6] was a politically unfortunate work. Whatever services he had previously rendered, the restored Charles could hardly be expected to reward lavishly the man who had written,

> From the strict rule some think that thou didst swerve
> (*Mistaken Honest men*) in *Caesars* blood;
> What *Mercy* could the *Tyrants Life* deserve, . . .
> There's none but *Brutus* could deserve
> That all men else should *wish* to *serve*,
> And *Caesars* usurpt place to him should proffer;
> None can deserve't but he who would *refuse* the *offer*.

[1] Keats said that the poet must be able to become the bird pecking in the gravel. Cowley here becomes the chessman swept into the bag and the spectator of the perfidiousness of the king.

[2] I.e., Horace, *Carm.* IV, 3; I, 1; and II, 16.

[3]

> . . . and my *Head*
> With her own *Hands* she *Fashioned*

seems to be a reference to the popular belief that the mother bear licks her young into shape.

[4] Cowley gives the standard interpretation of the meaning of the Circumcision.

[5] Waller, *Poems Cowley*, pp. 195–7.

[6] See Sprat's life of Cowley prefixed to the sixth edition of *The Works of Mr Abraham Cowley* (London, 1680), fol. a 3r–v.

The ode as a whole is based on Shakespeare's *Julius Caesar*, perhaps Cowley's way of giving himself some protection.

Cowley's other important Pindaric is his ode in honour of Dr. Scarborough.[1] Here the figures, manipulated with the most astonishing ingenuity and virtuosity, are almost all derived from either war or medicine, as being appropriate to the man and his age, to the man whose whole life was devoted to the solution of the health problems of a war-torn nation. As civil war is to the nation so is disease to man, and vice versa. This conceit, based on both traditional political and medical theory and on an analogy that goes back to Plato's *Republic*, controls the imagery of the first part of the ode and exerts some influence throughout. Thus, in the third line of the first stanza we have "*Epidemick War*," in the eighth, "It, like a *Plague*, infected all the *Aire*," in the twelfth and thirteenth, "*Diseases* rage / Their *Civil Wars* in *Man* to wage," and in the sixteenth, "*Medi'cine* and a *Counter-poyson* to the Age," where the state in civil war is regarded as being diseased. Then, in the second stanza, Cowley writes,

> The subtle *Ague*, that for *sureness* sake
> Takes its own times th' assault to make,
> And at each *battery* the whole *Fort* does shake,
> When thy strong *Guards*, and *works* it spies,
> *Trembles* for it *self*, and *flies*,

and a little later,

> The cruel *Stone* . . .
> Thou *break'st* and *meltest* by learn'd *Juyces* force,
> (A greater work, though short the way appear,
> Then *Hannibals* by *Vinegar*),

another military comparison, although in this case not an allusion to a civil war. In the third stanza Cowley speaks of syphilis establishing a "*Tyrannie*" here, of Scarborough's succouring the "besieged Heart," and of disease being called "Leagion," a military metaphor as well as a Biblical echo. In the fifth stanza Scarborough has made a "*Conquest*" of learning, but in the sixth stanza he, like all mortals must die:

[1] Waller, *Poems Cowley*, pp. 197–200.

And all thy noble *Reparations* sink
Into the sure-wrought *Mine* of treacherous *Mortality*.
Like *Archimedes*, hon'orably in vain,
Thou holdst out *Towns* that must at last be *ta'ne*,
And *Thou* thy self their great *Defender* slain.

A relationship that parallels that of civil war to the nation and disease to the body is that of flood to the land and it supplies images that at any time may be used to explain any one of the other relationships. Thus in the first stanza Cowley writes,

When *Slaughter* all the while
Seem'd like its *Sea*, *embracing* round the *Isle*,
With *Tempests*, and *red waves*, *Noise*, and *Affright*?

and in the second,

The *Inundations* of all *Liquid pain*,
And *Deluge Dropsie* thou do'est *drain*.

Comparisons drawn from other sources of course there are; for all that Cowley, with his wit and learning, can bestow upon his Pindaric will not make it a richer work than it would have been in its own country.[1] Where Pindar made mythological allusions Cowley makes allusions to all branches of modern science, in the broadest sense of that term. Thus Scarborough's treatment of the fevered patient is compared to the goldsmith's work (stanza 2, lines 3–8), the persistent "stone" is compared to that of Sisyphus (stanza 2, lines 14–16), and Scarborough's treatment of it to Hannibal's device to break through the Alps (stanza 2, lines 17–19), and to Moses' miracle in producing water from the rock (stanza 2, lines 21–2)—references to art, mythology, "history," and the Bible all in one stanza that is dominated by the war and flood images. Similarly, in the third stanza Syphilis is Columbus, Europe or England his America, and his empire like that of the Spaniard, while Cowley may have had in mind the myth of Aphrodite's virginity-restoring bath[2] when he wrote the daring lines,

[1] See Cowley's "Preface" to his Pindaric Odes in Waller, p. 155.
[2] See Graves, *Greek Myths* I, 51, 52.

The *Indian Son* of *Lust*, . . .
  Is so quite rooted out by Thee,
  That thy *Patients* seem to be
Restor'ed not to *Health* onely, but *Virginitie*.

Moreover, in the second part of the third stanza there are references to Aaron and Phineas; in the fourth stanza there is a reference to Archimedes' glass; in the fifth to Apollo, to the stock comic character of the *medicus*, and to Hippocrates' aphorism, "Ars longa, vita brevis"; and in the sixth to Archimede's death, banking, and commerce, the latter favourite subjects of the metaphysical poets.

The ode as a whole, fortunately, does not, "after Pindar's enthusiastical manner fall from one thing into another"[1] without any organization at all, any more than Pindar's own odes ever did. After an attention-catching beginning with exclamations and rhetorical questions the first stanza introduces the war-torn nation and the healing man, summarizing the doctor's achievement in the typical concluding quatrain,

Scarce could the *Sword* dispatch more to the *Grave*,
  Then *Thou* didst *save*;
By wondrous *Art*, and by successful *care*
The *Ruines* of a *Civil War* thou dost *alone repair*.

Then the second stanza praises his achievements against disorders connected with the four elements, water, fire, air (if the "subtle" ague with its shaking and sibilant alliteration could be ascribed to the air), and earth. The third stanza tells of Dr. Scarborough's success against the two great epidemic diseases, syphilis and the plague. Since the doctor must give medicines the fourth stanza treats of his pharmaceutical knowledge. And now we can turn to the doctor in his private person. Here, in the fifth stanza, we find that Scarborough is a two-fold follower of Apollo; for not only is he a physican, but also a man of civility and learning. It is here that the comic doctor appears,

    Thou'rt by this noble Mixture free
From the *Physitians* frequent *Maladie*,
    Fantastick Incivilitie,
There are who all their *Patients* chagrin have
As if they *took* each morn worse *potions* then they
    gave.

1 See Cowley's first note to "The Resurrection," Waller, p. 183.

The final stanza, midst much imagery about man's mortality, makes the Horatian plea that the doctor will take a little relaxation and spare some of himself for his friends. It ends in a gloomy epigram,

> Let *Nature*, and let *Art* do what they please,
> When all's done, *Life is an Incurable Disease.*

Another metaphysical ode in the spirit of Donne or Rochester and with the same dread of death that the metaphysicals felt is "Life and Fame."[1] This poem is loaded with riches from learned sources and yet it is Cowley's own and at times most effective. In the first line there is a startling conceit drawn from the traditional mythological accounts of creation; in the third and fifth lines there are echoes of Pindar, "τὶ δὲ τὶς, τί δ' οὔτις" and "σκιᾶς ὄναρ ἄνθρωπος"[2]; in the fourth line there is perhaps a reference to Francis Bacon[3]; the seventh, eighth, and ninth lines reveal scientific learning, and the tenth and eleventh philosophic knowledge:

> Oh Life, thou *Nothings younger Brother*!
> So *like*, that one might take *One* for the *other*!
> What's *Some Body*, or *No Body*?
> In all the *Cobwebs* of the *Schoolmens* trade,
> We no such nice *Distinctions* woven see,
> As 'tis *To be*, or *Not to Be*.
> *Dream* of a *Shadow*! a *Reflection* made
> From the false glories of the gay *reflected Bow*,
> Is a more *solid* thing then *Thou*.
> Vain weak-built *Isthmus*, which dost proudly rise
> Up betwixt *two Eternities*.

In the second stanza there is an anti-Renaissance hopelessness about the survival of man's works that presages Shelley. Compare

> Some with vast costly *Tombs* would purchase it,
> And by the *proofs* of *Death* pretend to *Live*.
> *Here lies the Great*—False *Marble*, where?
> Nothing but *small*, and *sordid Dust* lies there. . . .

[1] Waller, *Poems Cowley*, pp. 201–3.
[2] Pindar, *Pyth.*, 8, epode 5.
[3] See Francis Bacon, *The Advancement of Learning*, ed. W. A. Wright (Oxford, 1900), pp. 31–2.

So he who on th'*Egyptian* shore,
Was slain so many hundred years before,
Lives still (Oh Life most *happy* and most *dear*!
Oh *Life* that *Epicures* envy to hear!)
Lives in the *dropping Ruines* of his *Amphitheater*.

with

. . . Two vast and trunkless legs of stone
Stand in the desert. Near them, on the sand,
Half sunk, a shattered visage lies, . . .
And on the pedestal these words appear:
"My name is Ozymandias, king of kings:
Look on my works, ye Mighty, and despair!"
Nothing beside remains. Round the decay
Of that colossal wreck, boundless and bare
The lone and level sands stretch far away.

The third and final stanza makes a vigorous attack, in the correct philosophical manner, on the belief that men live in report and in the memories of men:

But, Oh ye learned men, explain,
What *Essence*, what *Existence* this,
What *Substance*, what *Subsistence*, what *Hypostasis*
In *Six poor Letters* is?
In those alone does the *Great Caesar* live,
'Tis all the *Conquered World* could give.

The end of the stanza

Who his *To-Morrow* would bestow,
For all old *Homer's Life* e're since he *Dy'ed* till *now*,

reminds us of what Homer himself said about death in the person of the dead Achilles in the eleventh book of the *Odyssey*: "Rather would I be a bond-servant in the house of a landless man . . . than lord of all the departed."

"The Extasie"[1] is a strange ode. Though it is Cowley's most Pindaric in structure—the last half is a "myth" from which we do not return—it is written in practically symmetrical stanzas, not in the broken lines that we would expect that this theme above all others would demand. This ode purports to be a

1 Waller, *Poems Cowley*, pp. 204–6.

description of an ecstatic experience which Cowley had, but it is quite devoid of religious feeling. In the opening stanza a rather mannered courtesy jostles a bit uncomfortably with an apparent echo of Crashaw's "Assumption" ode,

> I leave Mortality, and things below;
> I have no time in *Compliments* to wast,
> *Farewel* to 'ye all in hast,
> For I am *call'd* to go.

This is followed by a picture that appears to be borrowed from contemporary paintings of the Assumption,

> A *Whirlwind* bears up my dull Feet,
> Th' officious *Clouds* beneath them meet.

Then there is a rather satirical Brobdingnagian comment on the smallness of Britain,

> Where shal I find the noble *Brittish* Land?
> Lo, I at last a *Northern Spec* espie,
> Which in the *Sea* doth lie,
> And seems a *Grain* o' th' *Sand*!
> For this will any *sin*, or *Bleed*?
> Of *Civil Wars* is this the *Meed*?
> And is it this, alas, which we
> (Oh *Irony* of *Words*!) do call *Great Britanie*?

The following three stanzas contain a lively, vigorous, scientific description of the poet's passage through the various spheres. Here, except for one petty lapse when the sphere of fire is compared with that which burned in his breast as an earthly lover, medieval tradition is adapted to modern astronomical discovery. So far the reader has the impression that this is going to be an imaginary voyage in the manner of Lucian's *Vera Historia*, an early essay at science fiction—yet he has an uncomfortable feeling about the beginning. But suddenly, in the sixth stanza, its meaning becomes shockingly apparent with the reference to St. Paul as Cowley's predecessor there in that vague place that he has reached where "*Angels* and *God* is here." And then we plunge into the analogous myth, the story of Elijah and his chariot. Still there is no religious feeling but a concentration on the artistic beauties of the chariot and the startling spectacle that it created in the sky. Cowley's sudden change of subject in stanza six, as soon as he had reached heaven, and his expressed ignorance about where Elijah actually went in stanza eleven add further to the apparent incompatibility between the religious theme and Cowley's attitude towards it. Cowley's statement that he had an ecstatic experience or even could imagine one and his comparison of himself to both St. Paul and Elijah, when he is so manifestly incapable of any real religious feeling, strikes us as being empty bombast. Here we find the beginning of the rhetorical posturing and the inflated egoism that were such a bane to the later seventeenth-century and eighteenth-century English odes. The incompatibilities make this ode meaningless. The fact that this poem was partly inspired by "E rebus humanis excessus"[1] by the Polish poet, Casimir, does not excuse its faults; for Cowley rushed in where the Jesuit feared to tread and himself added the St. Paul and Elijah comparisons. Indeed only the opening of Cowley's ode was actually based on Casimir's.

"The Extasie" has, however, its fine bits of description and its daring conceits, e.g.,

> Without *affright* or *wonder*
> I meet *Clouds* charg'd with *Thunder*,
> And *Lightnings* in my way
> Like harmless *Lambent Fiers* about my Temples play,

and later, describing Elijah's chariot,

> 'Twas gawdy all, and rich in every part,
> Of *Essences* of *Gems*, and *Spirit* of *Gold*
> Was its *substantial mold*:
> Drawn forth by *Chimique Angels* art.
> Here with *Moon-beams* 'twas *silver'd* bright,
> There double-*gilt* with the *Suns* light
> And mystique Shapes cut round in it,
> *Figures* that did transcend a *Vulgar Angels* wit.

As one might expect, Cowley here exploits to the full all the possible oxymora and paradoxes of a Christian theme, e.g.,

> How small the biggest Parts of *Earths* proud *Tittle* show

[1] Matthias Casimir Sarbiewski, S. J., *Lyricorum libri iv* (Antverpiae, 1632), pp. 52–4.

and

The mighty' *Elijah* mounted so on high,
That second Man, who *leapt* the *Ditch* where all
The rest of Mankind *fall*,
And went not *downwards* to the *skie*.

"To the New Year,"[1] again in irregular stanzas with following notes, consists of a series of commonplace reflections on the uncertainty of man's fate. It becomes memorable only in the last stanza:

In whatsoever *Character*;
The *Book* of *Fate* is writ,
'Tis well we *understand* not it,
We should grow *Mad* with *little learning* there.
Upon the *Brink* of every *Ill* we did *Foresee*,
Undecently and foolishlie
We should stand shivering, and but slowly venter
The *Fatal Flood* to enter,
Since *willing*, or *unwilling* we must do it,
They feel least *cold* and *pain* who *plunge* at once into it.

The last of Cowley's independent Pindarics, a metaphysical ode in the manner of "Life and Fame" and "Destinie," "Life,"[2] again written in irregular stanzas and followed by learned notes, develops the Christian paradox that life is death and death is life, although Cowley attributes his particular source of inspiration to Euripides' reflection,

Τίς οἶδεν εἰ τὸ ζῆν μέν ἐστι κατθανεῖν
τὸ κατθανεῖν δὲ ζῆν;[3]

Cowley's other two Pindarics are both based on the Bible, in accordance with the theory, growing in popularity since the Council of Trent, that religion is the true subject of poetry—note Cowley's praise of Crashaw, in the elegy on his death, for restoring poetry to her true domain,[4] his remarks in his general preface to the 1656 edition of his poems,[5] and his introduction

[1] Waller, pp. 206–8.
[2] *Ibid.*, pp. 209–10.
[3] Cowley's note, *Ibid.*, p. 211.
[4] *Ibid.*, p. 48.
[5] *Ibid.*, pp. 12–13

of the religious epic into English; for his *Davideis* (1656) preceded Milton's *Paradise Lost* (1667). Of the two Biblical Pindarics just mentioned, "The 34. Chapter of the Prophet Isaiah,"[1] might be considered to be an ode of the sort of Gray's "The Bard"; for it uses the ode technique and is written in irregular stanzas. Here is the opening that "shines from afar"[2] and the rich adornment of the theme from a wide range of knowledge. This poem, however, is not "on" anything as odes usually are, but merely contains a prophecy. Here, as in the versions of Pindar, Cowley has added and subtracted what has seemed fit and he has supplied connections and interpretations to make his general message better understood.[3] "The Plagues of Egypt,"[4] however, despite the irregular verse, the embroidery on the theme, the metaphysical wit, and the rhetorical tricks, is not an ode but a straightforward narrative account of historical events.

After his imprisonment and release (1655) and his publication of his 1656 book of poetry containing the fruits of twenty years' work, his *Miscellanies*, his *Anacreontiques*, his *Amores* called *The Mistress*, his revolutionary *Pindariques*, and his abortive religious epic, *Davideis*, Cowley did very little else of importance. Perhaps under the influence of Dr. Scarborough and the necessity of making a living in Commonwealth England, Cowley satisfied a life-long interest in science, took a degree in medicine (Oxford, 1657), and began practising as a doctor. In the 1660's he wrote a long didactic Latin treatise on the properties of plants, on the model of Alexandrine and Renaissance didactic poems like Aratus' *Phaimomena* or Fracastoro's *Syphilis*, and he was one of the founding spirits of the Royal Society in 1662. Disappointed in his hopes at the Restoration, Cowley nevertheless received a small piece of land in payment for his Royalist services. Retiring there to lead the life of a country gentleman he caught a fever and died (1667).

In this last decade of his life Cowley wrote his familiar essays, but little lyric poetry, only a handful of conventional

1 *Ibid.*, pp. 211–14. 2 Pindar, *Ol.* 6.

3 See Cowley's own statements, Waller, p. 214, note 1; p. 215, notes 1, 4; p. 216, general note on stanza 3, notes 2, 3; pp. 216–17, note 4; and p. 217, note 6.

4 Waller, pp. 219–31.

Latin verses and a baker's dozen of English odes, mostly irregular Pindarics. Of these the most interesting is the latest one, "To the Royal Society,"[1] written to be prefaced to Sprat's history of 1667.

With his Pindaric odes Cowley created a new English poetic form, the formal lyric, on a serious subject or a significant occasion, studied, grandiose, and magniloquent, yet brightly decorated, lively, and enthusiastic. He established the etiquette for the rhetorical, public tribute to the moment, and he naturally established it in the baroque taste. First of all there must be enthusiasm, god-given excitement at the noble thought or the important event celebrated. Then there must be irregular verse, the phrasing of unpremeditated inspiration and of heartfelt sincerity, metric expressionism. This had the aesthetic advantage of being able to manipulate the attention of the auditors to secure the desired emotional response and it was, at the same time, through its variety, constantly pleasing to the ear[2]—many of Cowley's odes and those of his followers were sung to music.[3] Then there must be wit. Wit finds out new truth in flashes of insight, fixes the universal meaning of the subject celebrated, constantly titillates the minds of the audience with strange novelties, and honours the occasion with bunting and garlands and a glittering display of intellectual pyrotechnics. But there must be reason and logic, too, behind the apparant fantasy and extravagance; for it is the duty of the public poet to have something serious to say. That the style should be repetitious, full of variations and amplifications, that the ode should be loose, large, and leisurely, was only

[1] *Ibid.*, pp. 448–53.

[2] See Sprat's "Life," *Cowley's Works*, 6th ed. (London, 1680), fol. b 2v:

> Besides this they will find, that the frequent alteration of the Rhythm and Feet, affects the mind with a more various delight, while it is soon apt to be try'd by the settled pace of any one constant measure,

and fol. b 1 v:

> If his Verses in some places seem not as soft and flowing as some would have them, it was his choice not his fault. He knew that in diverting mens minds, there should be the same variety observ'd as in the prospects of their Eyes: where a Rock, a Precipice, or a rising Wave, is often more delightful than a smooth, even ground, or a calm Sea.

[3] J. Loiseau, *Abraham Cowley, Sa Vie, Son Oeuvre* (Paris, 1931), p. 665, lists a number of settings of Cowley's odes.

natural considering the public rather than private nature of the utterance. That the imagery should be intellectual rather than sensuous, that no aspect of experience or its accompanying vocabulary should be debarred, and that there should be a fondness for general adjectives, abstract nouns, and classifying plurals was also to be expected in the modern age of reason and the Royal Society. Thus it was that Cowley fulfilled the needs of his age shaping the materials at hand to form both what the public wanted and what their poets could produce. The spate of Cowleyan Pindarics during the next half century witnesses to this.

CONCLUSION

THE history of the ode is the history of classicism forming a new type of lyric out of modern and ancient materials to express a new outlook on life, the outlook itself one born of humanism and the Renaissance. It was an outlook that was at once more egotistical than the medieval one and that yet saw the self in a larger context. The self became more important in Renaissance poetry because it became bigger. But, because the individual was recognized to be related to a vaster range of human experience than previously, to society and history, to mythology and nature, and to literary tradition, Renaissance poetry became less personal, intimate, and emotional than medieval poetry, more rational and critical. Its aim was to be universal.

However, despite this effort to take a wider, rational view of experience, the Italians did not suddenly become stoics in the middle of the fifteenth century. The revival of stoicism came more than a century later. Thus, in the wider view the experience itself and the emotion aroused by it were not lost. Rather, vernacular poetry taught the revived Latin how to express the greater range of sensibility of modern man. Under the influence of Christianity man was more emotional now than fifteen hundred years ago, and accustomed to value emotion and give it expression. Hence Latin must learn how to express the new Christian idealization of love, the sanctified joys of the family and home, the more personal feeling of the existence of a supernatural behind the shows of nature, and the fervour of religious belief. The neolatin poetry of the humanists achieved all this and, from the synthesis of two cultures and their modes of expression created a new type of poem, the ode. The Pléiade, perhaps learning something from the Italian pioneer, Alamanni, then adapted the ode to vernacular literature, to a more popular idiom and to a potentially wider audience. They were able to show a new way to the Italians, unable to surmount, by themselves, their two great traditions, the humanist, in Latin, and the Petrarchan, in Italian. They also set the English on the way of the ode. The English, however, once given the initial impulse, turned rather to the classics themselves and to the humanists, to the Latin and Greek heavily emphasized in their education, for their inspiration. Thus Drayton, Jonson, Herrick, Milton, Crashaw, and Cowley drew directly on ancient and neolatin sources.

Much of the history of the vernacular ode from the time of Ronsard onwards is a history of the attempt to create a modern Pindaric. Ronsard tried it, Chiabrera tried it, but Cowley was the only one to succeed. He created exactly what his baroque period wanted. He suited the great English neoclassicists, too. He wrote an ode that was formal, grandiose, highly decorated, emotional, and learned. A modern feeling that it was also frigid is completely irrelevant. Cowley sought a complete fusion of meaning and metre. Under the influence of Pindar he went much farther than the Pléiade in an effort to free the poet's inspiration from the fetters of form. With Cowley the inspiration and the form were one. The meaning demanded the metre, the metre expressed the meaning. And, since Cowley was writing in a rhetorical, declamatory age, and in the person of the poet who addresses his nation, there were many exclamations and many arresting gestures. Like the baroque architect, Cowley repeatedly broke his line to emphasize his idea. The Cowleyan Pindaric, then, admirably suited the baroque period in England, and even thrived, transplanted abroad, in Italy. It also suited English neoclassicism; for here was Longinus' sublime classical poet adapted to English. These were the accents of enthusiasm, and in the harmony of life, of home and garden, dress and manners, art, science, and religion that rationalism had created there was an unexpected need for emotional abandon. Beneath the timeless white wig passion was growing and intellectualism was being abandoned for psychology. Cowley with his irregular ode offered a well-sanctioned escape valve to the neoclassicist. The sentimental novel was to offer another.

So, for fifty years after the publication of his *Pindarique Odes* in 1656, the Pindaric ode was wildly popular in England. And its excesses were great. It was inevitable that there should be some reaction. In 1706, in a "Discourse on the Pindaric Ode" prefixed to two new sample Pindarics, William Congreve cried out against this exaggerated libertinism, reminded the English that Pindar was strictly regular in form, and advocated some coherence in the ode through the use of regular stanzas. The stanza would, naturally, be freely invented for the individual poem and could be as original as one wished, but, once invented for the poem, it must be maintained throughout. The ode was still to retain its enthusiasm, given form by a more regular art, and its classical and humanist grandeur.

Cowleyan Pindarics continued to be written in undecreased volume for the first quarter of the eighteenth century and, although they declined in both number and importance as the century wore on, every boy and girl was still writing them in Johnson's day, and they finally emerged again, much modified by their passage through the eighteenth century, in the English romantic movement. Meantime, however, what turned out to be the *avant-garde* poets began following Congreve's example and writing odes in regular stanzas, usually by no means revolutionary in form. A poet like Young still used the ode, in stanzas now, with more than Cowleyan bombast and almost as much wit, to celebrate public themes, and there still were the anniversary volumes, the annuals, and the magazines with their occasional public poems. But now new subjects came to the fore. The influence of Milton's *L'Allegro* and *Il Penseroso* and the new interest in psychology produced a series of odes on allegorical abstractions, which were also psychological realities. There were odes on melancholy, and fear, and the passions. This fresh, new subject matter gave the imagination full play and the best poetry of the middle of the eighteenth century was of this sort, the poetry of the three Wartons and of William Collins. Gray's first odes were more conventional: the odes on spring and on a distant prospect of Eton College, and the charming, mock-heroic, moral, occasional poem on the drowning of Walpole's cat. These odes were all written in the classical and humanist traditions as they had come down through the most cultivated authors. Then Gray, too, like Congreve and Cowley, and Ronsard before them, read Pindar, and the old mania took hold. He would create a new, more noble, and dignified form for English literature! The unfortunate results were *The Bard* and *The Progress of Poesy* of 1757. These odes were immediately attacked as obscure and their adverse reception virtually closed Gray's poetic career. He later wrote a couple of Norse odes following the direction of Thomas Warton, senior, and the suggestion of Michael Drayton, but that was all. Gray's two Pindarics, however, did point the way back to the large, irregular form of the ode; for, although they were written in regular triads themselves, the individual strophes were long and contained much metrical variety.

So the ode went through the eighteenth century associated with what was new and progressive, what was free and inspired. Thus it was one of the forms chosen by the English romantics for some of the greatest lyric poetry in our literature and so it was passed on to the Victorians. This study of the origin and development of the ode may help to illuminate their poetry.

BIBLIOGRAPHY

Aigaliers, Pierre Delaudun d'. L'art poètique françois. Paris, 1598.

Alamanni, Luigi. Opere Toscane. Firenze, 1532. 2 vols.

—— Versi e prose. Firenze, 1859.

Alberti, Leon Battista. Opera inedita. Firenze, 1890.

—— Opere volgari, ed. Anicio Bonucci. Firenze, 1843–9. 5 vols.

Allen, Don Cameron. Style and certitude. ELH, XV (1948), 167–75.

Anacreon. Teubner text, ed. C. Preisendanz. Leipzig, 1912.

—— Ed. H. Stephanus. Lutetiae, 1554.

Aneau, Barthélemy. Attrib. Le Quintil Horatien. Paris, 1550.

Ariosto, Ludovico. Jo. Baptistae Pignae Carminum libri 4 . . . Caelii Calcagnini carm. lib. III. Ludovici Areosti Carm. lib. II. Venetiis, 1554.

Atanagi, Dionigi. Editor. De le rime di diversi nobili poeti toscani. Venetia, 1565.

Ausonius. Opuscula. Teubner text, ed. R. Peiper. Lipsiae, 1886.

Autelz, Guillaume des. Réplique aux furieuses défenses de Louis Meigret. Lyon, 1550.

Bacon, Francis. The advancement of learning, ed. W. A. Wright. Oxford, 1900.

Baïf, Jean Antoine de. Carmina. Lutetiae, 1577.

—— Euvres en rime, ed. Charles Marty-Laveaux. Paris, 1881–1890. 5 vols.

Bandini. Catalogus Codicum Laurentium. Florentiae, 1764, 1770. 3 vols.

Barbato, Petronio. Rime. Foligno, n.d. Imprimatur 1711.

Battista, G. Delle poesie meliche. Venezia, 1653.

Belleau, Remy, tr. Les odes d'Anacréon Téien. Paris, 1556.

Oeuvres poètiques, ed. Charles Marty-Laveaux. Paris, 1878. 2 vols.

Belloni, Antonio. Il seicento. Milano, 1943.

Bembo, Pietro. Carmina 5 illustrium poetarum, Bembi, Naugerii, Castilioni, Cottae, Flamini. Venetiis, 1548.

—— Carmina 5 illustrium poetarum, Bembi, Naugerii, Castilioni, Casae, Politiani, Sadoleti, Lampridii, Flaminii. Bergomi, 1753.

—— Prose . . . della volgar lingua. Vinegia, 1525.

—— Rime. Vinegia, 1540.

Benivieni, G. Opere. Vinegia, 1524.

Bennet, Joan. Evolution of seventeenth century prose. RES, XVII (1941).

Bennett, Charles E. and John Carew Rolfe, edd. Horace. The Complete Works. Boston, New York, and Chicago, 1901.

Bèze, Théodore de. Poemata. Lutetiae, 1548.

Binet, Claude. La vie de Pierre de Ronsard, ed. Paul Laumonier. Paris, 1910 (1st ed. 1586).

Blanchemain, Prosper, ed. Oeuvres complètes de Ronsard. Paris, 1857.

—— ed. Oeuvres complètes de Mellin de Sainct-Gelays. Paris, 1873.

Boeckh, A. Pindari carmina. 2 vols. Gothae et Erefordiae, 1830.

Bonucci, Anicio, ed. Opere volgari di Leon Battista Alberti. Firenze, 1843–9. 5 vols.

Bottari, Giovanni Gaetano, ed. Carmina illustrium poetarum italorum. Florentiae, 1719–26. 11 vols.

Bottiglione, Gino. La lirica latina in Firenze nella seconda metà del secolo XV. Annali della regia scuola normale superiore di Pisa, XXV. Pisa, 1913.

Bourbon, Nicholas, the elder. Nugarum. Paris, 1533.

Braccius, Alexander. Carmina, ed. Alexander Perosa. Firenze, 1944.

Bradner, Leicester, Musae Anglicanae: a history of anglo-latin poetry, 1500–1925. New York, 1940.

Brittain, F. The medieval latin and romance lyric. Cambridge, 1934.

Bullen, A. H., ed. Thomas Campion's Songs and Masques. London, 1903.

Brooks, C. and J. E. Hardy. Poems of Mr. John Milton, the 1645 edition, with Essays in Analysis. New York, 1951.

Budé, G. De studio litterarum. Basileae, 1533.

Bury, J. B. The Nemean odes of Pindar. London, 1890.

Bush, Douglas. English literature in the earlier seventeenth century. 1600–1660. Oxford, 1945.

Campanus, Joannis Antonius. Epistolae et poemata. Lipsiae, 1707.

Campion, Thomas. Songs and masques, ed. A. H. Bullen. London, 1903.

Capello, Bernardo. Rime. Venetia, 1550.
Capilupo, Camillus. Capiluporum carmina. Romae, 1590.
Capilupo, Hippolytus. Capiluporum carmina. Romae, 1590.
Capilupo, Julius. Capiluporum carmina. Romae, 1590.
Capilupo, Lelius. Capiluporum carmina. Romae, 1590.
Carducci, Giosuè, ed. Collezione di opere inedite o rare di scrittori italiani dal XIII al XVI secolo. Bologna, 1895–8. 6 vols.
—— Delle poesie latine d'Ariosto. Bologna, 1875.
—— Dello svolgimento dell' ode in Italia, in Poesia e Storia. Opere, XVI. Bologna, 1905.
—— Discorsi letterari e storici. Opere I. Bologna, 1905.
—— Il Poliziano e l'umanesimo. Bologna, 1905.
—— La gioventù de Ludovico Ariosto e la poesia latina a Ferrara. Opere, XV. Bologna, 1905.
—— Odi barbare. Opere, XVII. Bologna, 1907.
—— La poesia barbara nei secoli XV e XVI. Bologna, 1861.
—— Primavera e fiore della lirica italiana. Bologna, 1905.
Carew, Thomas. Minor poets of the seventeenth century. Everyman library. London and New York, 1953.
Cariteo, Benedetto Gareth, detto il. Opere. Napoli, 1506.
Caro, Annibal. Rime. Venetia, 1572.
Casa, Giovanni della. Carmina 5 illustrium poetarum, Bembi, Naugerii, Castilioni, Casae, Politiani, Sadoleti, Lampridii, Flaminii. Bergomi, 1753.
—— Opere, I. Venezia, 1752.
Casimir, Matthias Casimir Sarbiewski, S. J. Lyricorum libri IV. Antverpiae, 1632.
Casoni, Guido. Ode. Venetia, 1605.
Castiglione, Baldassare. Carmina 5 illustrium poetarum.... Venetiis, 1548, and Bergomi, 1753.
Chamard, Henri, ed. du Bellay's La deffense et illustration de la langue françoise. Paris, 1904.
—— Introduction à l'histoire de la Pléiade. Extrait du bulletin de l'université de Lille, 2e série. Lille, 1899.
—— Joachim du Bellay. Paris, 1900.
—— L'invention de l'ode. *RHLF*, VI (1899).
—— ed. Oeuvres poètiques de Joachim du Bellay. Paris, 1912. 5 vols.
—— Origines de la poésie française de la renaissance. Histoire de la Pléiade. Paris, 1939. 2 vols.
Chiabrera, Gabriello. Rime, I. Milano, 1807.
—— Rime, Roma, 1718. 3 vols.
Christ, W. Pindari Carmina. Lipsiae, 1896.
Ciampoli, G. Rime Scelte. Roma, 1648.

Comte, Charles and Paul Laumonier. Ronsard et les musiciens du XVIe siècle, *RHLF*, VII (1900), 341–81.

Cook, Albert S. "Notes on Milton's Nativity Ode," Transactions of the Connecticut Academy of Arts and Sciences, XV (1909), 307–68.

Cornford, F. M. The origin of Attic comedy. Cambridge, 1934.

Costanzo, Angelo di. Rime. Padova, 1738.

Cotta, Joannis. Actii Synceri Sannazari Odae. Eiusdem elegia de malo Punico. Ioannis Cottae carmina. M. Antonii Flaminii carmina. Venetiis, 1529.

—— Carmina 5 illustrium poetarum . . . Venetiis, 1548.

—— Carmina. Bassani, 1802.

—— Doctissimorum nostra aetate italorum epigrammata. Lutetiae, n.d. [1548].

Couderc, Camille. Les poésies d'un florentin à la cour de France, Bartolomeo Delbene. Extract from GSLI, XVII. Torino, 1891.

Courbet, E. Poésies françaises et latines de Joachim du Bellay. I. Paris, 1918.

Cowley, Abraham. Essays, plays, and sundry verses, ed. A. R. Waller. Cambridge, 1906.

—— Poemata latina. London, 1668.

—— Poems, ed. A. R. Waller. Cambridge, 1906.

—— Works, ed. with "life" by Bishop Thomas Sprat. London, 1680 (1st ed. 1668).

Crashaw, Richard. The poems, English, Latin, and Greek, ed. L. C. Martin. Oxford, 1927.

Crinito, Pietro Del Riccio, detto. Opera Omnia. Lugduni, 1559.

Croce, Benedetto. Poeti e scrittori del pieno e del tardo rinascimento. Bari, 1945. 2 vols.

—— Storia della età barocca in Italia. Pensiero, poesia, e letteratura, vita morale. Bari, 1929.

Croiset, Alfred. La poésie du Pindare et le lyricisme grec. Paris, 1880.

—— Manuel d'histoire de la litterature grecque. Paris, 1901.

Croll, Maurice. Attic prose in the seventeenth century. SP, XVIII (1921), 79–128.

—— Cadence in English oratorical prose. SP, XVI (1919).

—— Juste Lipse et le mouvement anticicéronien à la fin du xvie et au début du xviie siècle. Revue du seizième siècle, II (1914).

—— Muret and the history of Attic prose. PMLA, XXXIX (1924), 254–309.

—— The baroque style in prose. Studies in English philology. A miscellany in honor of Frederick Klaeber, edd. Kemp Malone and Martin B. Ruud. Minneapolis, 1929.

Cuccoli, Ercole. Marc Antonio Flaminio. Bologna, 1897.

Cunningham, F. The Works of Christopher Marlowe. London, 1874.

Daniel, H. A. Thesaurus Hymnologicus. Halis, 1841, 4 vols.

Dazzi, Andrea. Poemata. Florentiae, 1549.

Deboulle, A. Anacréon et les poèmes Anacréontiques. Texte grec avec les traductions et imitations des poètes du xvie siècle. Havre, 1891.

Delattre, Flores. Robert Herrick. Paris, 1911.

Del Bene, Bartolomeo. Rime. Livorno, 1799.

Dissen. Commentarius in Pindari Carmina, in Boeckh's ed., vol. 2.

Dolce, Ludovico. Raccolta di diversi illustri poeti. Vinegia, 1565. 2 vols.

Dolet, Etienne. Carminum libri IV. Lugduni, 1538.

Donadoni, F. Breve storia della letteratura italiana. Milano, 1951.

Dorat, Jean. Poematia . . . Lutetiae Parisior, 1586.

—— Oeuvres poètiques, ed. Charles Marty-Laveaux. Paris, 1875.

Du Bellay, Jean. Poemata, with Salmon Macrin's Odarum libri III. Paris, 1546.

Du Bellay, Joachim. La deffense et illustration de la langue françoise, ed. Henri Chamard. Paris, 1904.

—— Oeuvres Poètiques, ed. Henri Chamard. Paris, 1912, 5 vols.

—— Poèsies françaises et latines, with a life by E. Courbet. Paris, 1918. 2 vols.

Dumaine, R. Ronsard et les musiciens du xvie siècle. Dieppe, 1925.

Ellinger, Georg. Geschichte der Neulateinischen Literatur Deutschlands im Sechzehnten Jahrhundert. Italien und der deutsche umanesimus in der neulateinischen lyrick. Berlin and Leipzig, 1929. 2 vols.

Esdaille, Arundell. The sources of English literature. Cambridge, 1928.

Fabricius Chemnicensis, Georgius. Odarum libri tres ad deum omnipotentem. Basileae, 1552.

Farnell, L. R. The works of Pindar. London, 1930–2. 3 vols.

Fennell, C. A. M. Pindar: Nemean and Isthmian Odes. Cambridge, 1883.

—— Pindar: Olympian and Pythian Odes. Cambridge, 1893.

Fiamma, G. Rime Spirituali. Venice, 1606.

Ficino, M. *Τοῦ Θείου Πλάτωνος Ἅπαντα τὰ σωζόμενα* . . . Genevae, 1590.

Filelfo, Francesco. Conviviorum. Coloniae, 1537.

—— Odae. n.p. [Brixiae], 1497.

Flamini, Francesco. La lirica toscana del rinascimento anteriore ai tempi del Magnifico. Annali della regia schuola normale superiore di Pisa, XVII. Pisa, 1891.

—— Leonardo di Piero Dati . . . GSLI, XVI (Torino, 1890), 1–107.

—— Peregrino Allio, umanista, poeta. Pisa, 1893.

—— Studi di storia letteraria italiana e straniera. Livorno, 1895.

—— Varia. Livorno, 1905.

Flaminio, Gabriel. Flaminiorum Forocorneliensium carmina. Patavii, 1743.

Flaminio, Giovanni. Flaminiorum Forocorneliensium carmina. Patavii, 1743.

Flaminio, Marc Antonio. Actii Synceri Sannazarii odae. eiusdem elegia de malo punico. Ioannis Cottae carmina. M. Antonii Flaminii carmina. Venetiis, 1529.

—— Carmina 5 illustrium poetarum. . . . Venetiis, 1548.

—— Carmina 5 illustrium poetarum. . . . Bergomi, 1753.

—— Carminum liber ultimus eius amicorum cura. Venetiis, 1552.

—— Carmina, with Fracastoro, Cotta, Bonfadio, Fumano, Archi Comite, Bembo, Navagero, Castiglione. Veronae, 1740.

—— De rebus divinis carmina ad Margaritam Henrici Gallorum regis sororem. Parisiis, 1551.

—— Doctissimorum nostra aetate italorum epigrammata. M. Antonii Flaminii libri duo. Marii Molsae liber unus. Andreae Naugerii liber unus. Io. Cottae, Lampridii, Sadoleti et aliorum. Lutetiae, n.d. [1548].

—— Flaminiorum Forocorneliensium carmina. Patavii, 1743.

—— In librum psalmorum brevis explanatio. Parisiis, 1546.

—— Michael Tarchaniotae Marulli neniae. eiusdem epigrammata nunquam alias impressa. M. Antonii Flaminii adulescentis amoenissimi carminum libellus. Fano, 1515.

—— Paraphrasis ad xxx psalmos. Florentiae, 1552.

Flaminio, Marc Antonio and Francesco Spinula, Davidis regis et vatis inclyti psalmi. Basileae, 1558.

Fraccarolli, G. Le odi di Pindaro. Verona, 1894.

Fracastoro, H. Naugerius. Opera. Venetiis, 1555.

—— Poemata omnia. Patavii, 1718.

Frank, T. Catullus and Horace. New York, 1928.

Fresnaye, Vauquelin de la. L'art poètique. Paris, 1885 (1st ed. 1605).

Fromilhague, René. Malherbe. Technique et création poétique. Paris, 1954.

Furnivall, F. J. ed. Hymns to the Virgin and Christ. EETS 24. London, 1867.

Galletti, A. La lirica volgare nel '500. Nuova Antologia (1929), 266–8.

Gandar, E. Ronsard considéré comme imitateur d'Homère et de Pindare. Metz, 1854.
Gareth, Benedetto, detto il Cariteo or Chariteo. Rime. Napoli, 1892.
Gherus, Ranutius (Jan Gruter). Delitiae C poetarum gallorum. n.p. [Frankfurt], 1609, 6 vols.
Gildersleeve, Basil L. The Olympian and Pythian odes. London, 1892.
Gourmont, Remy de. Le latin mystique. Paris, 1892.
Graf, Arturo. Il fenomeno del secentismo. Nuova Antologia, CXIX (1905), 353–82.
Graves, Robert. The Greek Myths. Penguin Book. II (1955).
Greco, L'Orlandino del. Alcune rime. Marsala, 1889.
Gruter, Jan. Delitiae CC italorum poetarum. n.p. [Frankfurt], 1608. 6 vols.
—— Delitiae C poetarum belgicorum. Francofurti, 1614. 7 vols.
—— Delitiae poetarum germanorum. Francofurti, 1612. 16 vols.
Hardy, J. E. and C. Brooks. Poems of Mr. John Milton, the 1645 ed. with essays in criticism. New York, 1951.
Harrison, T. P. The pastoral elegy. Austin, Texas, 1939.
Hauvette, H. Un exilé florentin à la cour de France au XVIe siècle: Luigi Alamanni. Sa vie et son oeuvre. Paris, 1903.
Heinsius, Daniel. Poematum. Amstelodami, 1649.
Herbert, Lord. Minor poets of the seventeenth century. Everyman library. London and New York, 1953.
Herrick, Robert. Poems, ed. F. W. Moorman. Oxford, 1947.
Hesiod. Hesiod. The Homeric Hymns. tr. H. G. Evelyn-White. Loeb Library. London and Cambridge, Mass., 1954.
Highet, G. The Classical Tradition. Oxford, 1949.
Horace. The complete works, edd. Charles E. Bennett and John Carew Rolfe. Boston, New York, Chicago, 1901.
Hoveden, John J. Philomena. ed. C. Blume in Hymnologische Beiträge, IV. Leipzig, 1930.
Huizinga, Jan. The waning of the middle ages. Doubleday Anchor Book. Garden City, N.Y., 1954.
Jebb, R. C. The growth and influence of classical Greek poetry. Boston, 1893.
Johnson, Samuel. The lives of the English poets. Everyman library. 2 vols.
Johnston, George Burke, ed. Poems of Ben Jonson. London, 1954.
Jonson, Ben. Discoveries, ed. Maurice Castelain. Paris, n.d. [1906] (1st ed. 1640–1).
—— Poems, ed. G. B. Johnston. London, 1954.

Jones, R. F. Science and English prose style in the third quarter of the seventeenth century. PMLA, XLV (1930).
—— Science and language. JEGP, XXXI (1932).
—— The attack on pulpit eloquence. JEGP, XXX (1931).
—— The moral sense of simplicity. Studies in honor of Frederick W. Shipley. St. Louis, 1942.
Kane, E. A. Gongorism and the golden age: a study of exuberance and unrestraint in the arts. Chapel Hill, 1928.
Lampridio, Benedetto. Carmina, ed. Ludovico Dolce. Venetia, 1550.
—— Carmina 5 illustrium poetarum. . . . Bergomi, 1753.
—— Doctissimorum nostra aetate italorum epigrammata. Lutetiae, n.d. [1548].
Landino, Cristoforo. Carmina omnia, ed. Alexander Perosa. Florentiae, 1939.
Lattimore, Richmond, tr. The odes of Pindar. Chicago, 1947.
Laumonier, Paul, ed. Claude Binet, La vie de Pierre de Ronsard. Paris, 1910 (1st ed. 1586).
—— ed. Les oeuvres poètiques de Jacques Peletier du Mans. Paris, 1904 (1st ed. 1547).
—— ed. Les oeuvres complètes de Pierre de Ronsard. Paris, 1914–19.
—— ed. Pierre de Ronsard. Oeuvres Complètes, Edition Critique. Paris, 1914–.
—— Ronsard poète lyrique. Paris, 1923.
Laumonier, Paul and Charles Comte. Ronsard et les musiciens du xvie siècle. Contribution à l'histoire de la Pléiade. RHLF, VII (Paris, 1900).
Lebègue, Raymond. La Poésie Française de 1560 à 1630, II, Malherbe et son Temps. (Paris, 1951).
Lee, Sidney. Elizabethan Sonnets. Westminster, 1900. 2 vols.
—— The French Renaissance in England. Oxford, 1910.
Leishmann, J. B. Metaphysical poets. Oxford, 1934.
Lemaire de Belges, Jean. La concorde des deux langages, ed. J. Stécher. Paris, 1885. III.
Lewis, C. S. English literature in the sixteenth century. Oxford, 1954.
Lipsius, Justus. Opera Omnia. Antverpiae, 1637. 4 vols.
Lobel, E. *ΣΑΠΦΟΥΣ ΜΕΛΗ*. Oxford, 1925.
Loiseau, J. Abraham Cowley, sa vie, son oeuvre. Paris, 1931. Abraham Cowley's reputation. Paris, 1931.
Lovejoy, A. O. The great chain of being. Cambridge, Mass., 1936.
Lovelace, Richard. Minor poets of the seventeenth century. Everyman library. London and New York, 1953.

Lungo, Isidore del, ed. Poliziano. Prose volgari e poesi latine e greche. . . . Firenze, 1867.
Macrin, Salmon. Carminum libellus. Paris, 1528.
—— Carminum libri IV. Paris, 1530.
—— Carminum liber primus, ad Franciscum Valesium Franciae regem huius nominis primum., n.p., n.d. [Paris, 1531].
—— Epitome vitae domini nostri Jesu Christi . . . varia item poematia. Paris, 1549.
—— Hymnorum libri VI. Paris, 1537.
—— Hymnorum selectorum libri III. Paris, 1540.
—— Lyricorum libri II. Paris, 1531.
—— Odarum libri VI. Lugduni, 1537.
—— Odarum libri III. Also contains the Poemata of Card. Jean du Bellay. Paris, 1546.
—— Psalmi VII et Paeanum libri IV. Pictavii, 1538.
Maddison, Carol Hopkins. The source of du Bellay's "Les Louanges d'Amour." MLN, LXXIII (1958), 594–597.
Magni, G. Il barocco a Roma nell' architettura e nella scultura decorativa. Torino, 1911. 3 vols.
Malherbe, François de. Oeuvres. Paris, 1722. 3 vols. Les Poésies. ed. Philippe Martinon. Paris, n.d.
Mallet, Sir Charles Edward. A history of the University of Oxford. London, 1924–7. 3 vols.
Marino, Gian Battista. La lira e vita. Venezia, 1653.
—— Lettere. Venezia, 1627–8.
—— Rime. Venetia, 1608.
Marlowe, Christopher. Works, ed. F. Cunningham. London, 1874.
Marmitta, Giacomo. Rime. Parma, 1564.
Martin, L. C., ed. The poems English, Latin, and Greek of Richard Crashaw. Oxford, 1927.
—— ed. The Poetical Works of Robert Herrick. Oxford, 1956.
Martinius, Antonius, ed. Carmina latina Torquati Taxi. Romae, 1895.
Marty-Laveaux, Charles, ed. Euvres en rime de Jean Antoine de Baïf. Paris, 1881–90. 5 vols.
—— ed. Oeuvres poètiques de Jean Dorat. Paris, 1875.
—— ed. Oeuvres poètiques de Remy Belleau. Paris, 1878. 2 vols.
Marullus, Michael Tarchaniota. Epigrammata et hymni. Parisiis, 1561.
—— Neniae. ejusdem epigrammata nunquam alias impresa. M. Antonii Flaminii . . . Carminum libellus. Fano, 1515.
—— Carmina. ed. Alessandro Perosa. Zurich, 1951.
Mathews, Frédéric. Anacréon. Paris, 1927.

Mencaraglia, Lucianus, ed. Flametta by Ugolino Verino. Florentiae, 1940.
Menzini, Benedetto. Arte poetica con alcune canzoni et elegie. Roma, 1690.
Meozzi, Antero. Azione e diffusione della letteratura italiana in Europa. Pisa, 1932.
Milton, J. The Poems of John Milton, English, Latin, Greek and Italian, arranged in chronological order, with a preface by H. J. C. Grierson. London, 1925. 2 vols.
Minturno, Sebastiano. De poeta. Venezia, 1559.
—— L'arte poetica. Venezia, 1564.
—— Poemata Tridentina. Venetiis, 1564.
—— Rime et prose . . . ed. Girolamo Ruscelli. Venetia, 1559.
Molza, Francesco Maria. Poesie. Milano, 1808.
Montera, Pierre de. L'humaniste napolitain Girolamo Carbone et ses poésies inédites. Naples, 1935.
Moorman, F. W., ed. The Poems of Robert Herrick. Oxford, 1947.
Mullinger, J. B. The University of Cambridge, Cambridge, 1873–1911. 3 vols.
Murray, J. R. The influence of Italian on English literature of the sixteenth and seventeenth centuries. Cambridge, 1886.
Mutio, Girolamo. Rime e diverse. Vinegia, 1551.
Navagero, Andrea. Carmina 5 illustrium poetarum . . . Venetiis, 1548.
—— Carmina 5 illustrium poetarum . . . Bergomi, 1753.
—— Doctissimorum nostra aetate italorum epigrammata . . . Lutetiae, n.d. [1548].
Nethercot, A. H. Abraham Cowley: the Muse's Hannibal. London, 1931.
Neri, Ferdinando. Il Chiabrera e la Pléiade francese. Torino, 1920.
Nolhac, Paul de. Ronsard et l'humanisme. Paris, 1921.
—— Ronsard et ses contemporains italiens. Paris, n.d. [1921].
Norwood, G. Pindar. Berkeley, Calif., 1945.
Olschki, Leonardo. La poesia volgare del '500. Firenze, 1933.
Palmer, Henrietta R. List of English editions and translations of Greek and Latin classics before 1641. London, 1911.
Paterno, Ludovico. Le nuove fiamme. Lyone, 1568.
Peletier, Jacques. Oeuvres poètiques, ed. Paul Laumonier. Paris, 104.
—— Oeuvres poètiques. Paris, 1547.
—— L'art poètique. Lyon, 1555.
Perosa, Alexander, ed. Christofori Landini carmina omnia. Florentiae, 1939.

Perosa, Alexander, ed. Alexandri Braccii Carmina. Florentiae, 1944.
—— ed. Michaelis Marulli Carmina. Zurich, 1951.
Pesenti, G. Poesie latine del Bembo. GSLI, LXIX (1917), 341–50.
Pico della Mirandola, Giovanni. Hymni. Argentorati, 1511.
—— Opera, Basileae, 1557.
Picot, Emile. Des français qui ont écrit en italien au xvie siècle. Paris, 1902.
—— Les français à l'université de Ferrare au xve et au xvie siècle. Paris, 1902.
—— Les français italianisants au xvie siècle. Paris, 1906–7.
—— Les italiens en France au xvie siècle. Bordeaux, 1901–18.
—— Les professeurs et les étudiants de langue française à l'université de Pavie au xve et au xvie siècle. Paris, 1916.
Pindar, ed. Aldus. Venice, 1513.
—— Ed. Callierges, Rome, 1515.
—— Ed. Cratander, Basel, 1526.
—— Ed. Brubachius. Frankfurt, 1542.
—— Ed. Erasmus Schmidt. n.p., 1616.
—— Ed. Johannis Benedictus. Salmurii, 1620.
—— Ed. A. Boeckh. 2 vols. Gothae et Erefordiae, 1830.
Poliziano, Angelo. Prose volgari inedite e poesie latine e greche, ed. Isidoro del Lungo. Firenze, 1867.
Pontano, Giovanni Gioviani. Carminum quae quidem extant omnium. Basileae, 1556.
Praz, Mario. Crashaw. Brescia, 1945.
—— Secentismo e marinismo in Inghilterra. Firenze, 1925.
—— Studies in seventeenth century imagery. 1939.
Preisendenz, C. ed. Anacreon. Leipzig, 1912.
Raby, F. J. E. A history of Christian latin poetry from the beginnings to the close of the middle ages. Oxford, 1927.
—— A history of secular latin poetry in the middle ages. Oxford, 1934. 2 vols.
Racan, Honoré de. Mémoires pour la vie de M. de Malherbe.
Rand, E. K. Milton's latin verse. SP, XIX (1922).
Raymond, M. L'influence de Ronsard. Paris, 1927. 2 vols.
—— Baroque et renaissance poétique. Paris, 1955.
Regenos, G. W. The influence of Horace upon Robert Herrick. PQ, XXVI (1947), 268–84.
Rémond, François. Carmina. Viennae, 1617.
Ricci, C. Baroque architecture and sculpture in Italy. London, 1912.
—— Vita barocca. Milano, 1904.
Robinson, D. M. Pindar, a poet of eternal ideas. The Johns Hopkins University studies in archeology, 21. Baltimore, 1936.

Rolfe, John Carew and Charles E. Bennett, edd. Horace the complete works. Boston, New York, and Chicago, 1901.

Ronsard, Pierre de. Abbrégé de l'art poètique françois. Paris, 1565.

—— Oeuvres complètes, ed. Prosper Blanchemain. Paris, 1857.

—— Oeuvres complètes, ed. Paul Laumonier. Paris, 1914–19.

—— Oeuvres complètes, édition critique, ed. P. Laumonier. Paris, 1914–

—— Oeuvres complètes, ed. Hugues Vaganay. Librairie Garnier Frères. Paris, n.d.

Rossi, Pietro. Marc Antonio Flaminio. Vittorio Veneto, 1931.

Rossi, Vittorio. Il quattrocento. Milano, 1953.

Rota, Bernardino. Delle poesie. Napoli, 1726.

—— Poemata. Venetiis, 1567.

Ruscelli, Girolamo, ed. I fiori delle rime de' poeti illustri. Venetia, 1558.

Sainati, A. La lirica latina del rinascimento. Pisa, 1919.

Sainct-Gelays, Mellin de. Oeuvres complètes, ed. Prosper Blanchemain. Paris, 1873.

Saintsbury, George. Elizabethan literature. London, 1893.

—— The history of the English lyric. London, 1912.

Sandys, J. E. A History of Classical Scholarship. Cambridge, 1903–8. 3 vols.

Sannazaro, Jacopo. Opera. Parisiis, 1725.

Sappho. Ed. E. Lobel. Oxford, 1925.

Scaliger, Julius Caesar. Poetices libri septem. n.p., 1581.

—— Poemata. n.p., 1574.

—— Poemata sacra. Coloniae, 1600.

Scherer, Margaret. Marvels of ancient Rome. New York and London, 1955.

Scott, G. The architecture of humanism. London, 1914.

Scott, Mary Augusta. Elizabethan translations from the Italian. Boston, 1916.

Sébilet, Thomas. attrib. L'art poètique françoys. Paris, 1555 (1st ed. 1548).

Secundus, Joannis. Opera nunc secundum in lucem edita . . . Parisiis, 1561.

Sells, A. Lytton. The Italian influence in English poetry. Bloomington, Ind., 1955.

—— Animal Poetry. Bloomington, Ind., 1955.

Shafer, Robert. The English ode to 1660. Princeton, 1918.

Sharp, R. L. Donne to Dryden. The revolt against the metaphysicals. Chapel Hill, 1940.

Sherillo, M. Un romantico del rinascimento: Jacopo Sannazaro. Nuova Antologia, CCXXXIX (1925), 337–47.

Shuster, G. N. S. The English ode from Milton to Keats. New York, 1940.

Silver, I. The Pindaric odes of Ronsard. Paris, 1937.

—— Did Du Bellay know Pindar? PMLA, 56 (1941), 1007–19.

—— Ronsard and Du Bellay on their Pindaric collaboration. Romanic Review, 33 (1942), 1–25.

Sinclair, T. A. and F. A. Wright. A history of later Latin literature till the end of the seventeenth century. London, 1931.

Spingarn, J. E. Jacobean and Caroline criticism. CHEL, VII, chapt. 11. Cambridge, 1911.

Spinula, P. F. and M. A. Flaminio. Davidis regis et vatis inclyti psalmi. Basileae, 1558.

Sprat, Bishop Thomas, ed. The works of Mr Abraham Cowley, with "life." London, 1680 (1st ed., 1668).

Stephanus, Henricus, junior. ed. Anacreon. Lutetiae, 1554.

Swain, Barbara. Fools and folly during the middle ages and the Renaissance. New York, 1932.

Tasso, Bernardo. Libro de gli amori . . . hinni et ode . . . Vinegia, 1534.

—— Rime II. Bergamo, 1749.

Tasso, Torquato. Carmina latina, ed. Antonius Martinius. Romae, 1895.

Tillyard, E. M. W. The Elizabethan world picture. London, 1943.

Toffanin, Giuseppe. Il cinquecento. Milano, 1950.

—— La fine dell' umanesimo. Milano, 1920.

Trissino, G. G. La poetica. Vicenza, 1529.

—— Rime. Vinegia, 1529.

—— Sophonisba. Vinegia, 1549.

Upham, Alfred Horatio. The French influence upon English literature from the accession of Elizabeth to the Restoration. New York, 1908.

Vaganay, Hugues, ed. Oeuvres complètes de Ronsard. Librairie Garnier Frères. Paris, n.d.

Verino, Ugolino. Flametta, ed. Lucianus Mencaraglia. Florentiae, 1940.

Vietor, K. Geschichte der deutschen Ode. München, 1923.

Viperanus, I. A. Carminum. Naples, 1606.

—— Poemata. Naples, 1606.

Waller, A. R., ed. The Poems of Abraham Cowley. Cambridge, 1905.

Wallerstein, Ruth. Richard Crashaw, a study in style and poetic development. Madison, Wis., 1935.

Warren, Austin. Richard Crashaw, a study of baroque sensibility. Louisiana State University, 1939.

Wasserman, Earl R. The inherent values of eighteenth century personification. PMLA, LXV (1950), 435–63.
Weibel, W. Jesuitismus und baroksculptur in Rom. Strassburg, 1904.
Wilkinson, L. P. Horace. Cambridge, 1945.
Willey, Basil. The seventeenth century background. London, 1950.
Williamson, Edward. Bernardo Tasso. Storia e letteratura. Raccolta di studi e testi, 39. Roma, 1951.
Williamson, George. The Donne tradition. Cambridge, Mass., 1930.
—— The Senecan style in the seventeenth century. PQ, XV (1936).
Wright, F. A. and T. A. Sinclair. A history of later Latin literature till the end of the seventeenth century. London, 1931.
Zanta, L. La renaissance du stoicisme au xvie siècle. Paris, 1914.

Index